Sharks upon the Land

Historian Seth Archer traces the cultural impact of disease and health problems in the Hawaiian Islands from the arrival of Europeans to 1855. Colonialism in Hawaiʻi began with epidemiological incursions, and Archer argues that health remained the national crisis of the islands for more than a century. Introduced diseases resulted in reduced life spans, rising infertility and infant mortality, and persistent poor health for generations of Islanders, leaving a deep imprint on Hawaiian culture and national consciousness. Scholars have noted the role of epidemics in the depopulation of Hawaiʻi and broader Oceania, yet few have considered the interplay between colonialism, health, and culture – including Native religion, medicine, and gender. This study emphasizes Islanders' own ideas about, and responses to, health challenges on the local level. Ultimately, Hawaiʻi provides a case study for health and culture change among Indigenous populations across the Americas and the Pacific.

Seth Archer is Assistant Professor of History at Utah State University. From 2015 to 2017 he was the Mellon Research Fellow in American History at the University of Cambridge.

Studies in North American Indian History

Editors

Frederick Hoxie, *University of Illinois, Urbana-Champaign*
Neal Salisbury, *Smith College, Massachusetts*
Tiya Miles, *University of Michigan, Ann Arbor*
Ned Blackhawk, *Yale University*

This series is designed to exemplify new approaches to the Native American past. In recent years scholars have begun to appreciate the extent to which Indians, whose cultural roots extended back for thousands of years, shaped the North American landscape as encountered by successive waves of immigrants. In addition, because Native Americans continually adapted their cultural traditions to the realities of the Euro-American presence, their history adds a thread of non-Western experience to the tapestry of American culture. Cambridge Studies in North American Indian History brings outstanding examples of this new scholarship to a broad audience. Books in the series link Native Americans to broad themes in American history and place the Indian experience in the context of social and economic change over time.

Also in the Series:

Allan Greer *Property and Dispossession: Natives, Empires and Land in Early Modern North America*

Kealani Cook *Return to Kahiki: Native Hawaiians in Oceania*

Matthew Babcock *Apache Adaptation to Hispanic Rule*

Kiara Vigil *Indigenous Intellectuals: Sovereignty, Citizenship, and the American Imagination, 1880–1930*

Lucy Murphy *Great Lakes Creoles: A French-Indian Community on the Northern Borderlands, Prairie du Chien, 1750–1860*

Richard White *The Middle Ground: Indians, Empires, and Republics in the Great Lakes Region, 1650–1815*, 2nd ed.

Gary Warrick *A Population History of the Huron-Petun, A.D. 500–1650*

John Bowes *Exiles and Pioneers: Indians in the Trans-Mississippi West*

David J. Silverman *Faith and Boundaries: Colonists, Christianity, and Community among the Wampanoag Indians of Martha's Vineyard, 1600–1871*

Jeffrey Ostler *The Plains Sioux and U.S. Colonialism from Lewis and Clark to Wounded Knee*

Claudio Saunt *A New Order of Things: Property, Power, and the Transformation of the Creek Indians, 1733–1816*

Jean M. O'Brien *Dispossession by Degrees: Indian Land and Identity in Natick, Massachusetts, 1650–1790*

Frederick E. Hoxie *Parading through History: The Making of the Crow Nation in America, 1805–1935*

Colin G. Calloway *The American Revolution in Indian Country: Crisis and Diversity in Native American Communities*

Sidney L. Harring *Crow Dog's Case: American Indian Sovereignty, Tribal Law, and United States Law in the Nineteenth Century*

Sharks upon the Land

Colonialism, Indigenous Health, and Culture in Hawai'i, 1778–1855

SETH ARCHER

Utah State University

CAMBRIDGE
UNIVERSITY PRESS

CAMBRIDGE
UNIVERSITY PRESS

University Printing House, Cambridge CB2 8BS, United Kingdom

One Liberty Plaza, 20th Floor, New York, NY 10006, USA

477 Williamstown Road, Port Melbourne, VIC 3207, Australia

314–321, 3rd Floor, Plot 3, Splendor Forum, Jasola District Centre,
New Delhi – 110025, India

79 Anson Road, #06–04/06, Singapore 079906

Cambridge University Press is part of the University of Cambridge.

It furthers the University's mission by disseminating knowledge in the pursuit of
education, learning, and research at the highest international levels of excellence.

www.cambridge.org
Information on this title: www.cambridge.org/9781107174566
DOI: 10.1017/9781316795934

© Seth Archer 2018

First published 2018

Printed in the United Kingdom by TJ International Ltd. Padstow Cornwall

A catalogue record for this publication is available from the British Library.

Library of Congress Cataloging-in-Publication Data
NAMES: Archer, Seth, 1974– author.
TITLE: Sharks upon the land : colonialism, indigenous health, and culture in Hawai'i,
1778–1855 / Seth Archer, Utah State University.
DESCRIPTION: Cambridge, United Kingdom ; New York, NY : Cambridge University
Press, 2018. | Series: Studies in North American Indian history | Includes bibliographical
references and index.
IDENTIFIERS: LCCN 2017054705 | ISBN 9781107174566 (hardback)
SUBJECTS: LCSH: Hawaiians – Health and hygiene – History – 19th century. | Hawaiians
– Diseases – Social aspects – History – 19th century. | Public health – Hawaii – History –
19th century.
CLASSIFICATION: LCC RA447. H38 A73 2018 | DDC 362.1089/9942–dc23
LC record available at https://lccn.loc.gov/2017054705

ISBN 978-1-107-17456-6 Hardback

For Amber,
up life's hill

Contents

Figures

Tables

Acknowledgments

Thanks are due to many people who helped this book along to completion. Scott Manning Stevens introduced me to Native North America and colonial encounters in a fascinating NEH summer institute he led in 2005. Soon after, Scott generously supported me in a bid for graduate study. Brett Rushforth, Kris Lane, Chris Grasso, Paul Mapp, Cindy Hahamovitch, Chandos Brown, and Doug Fordham made important contributions to my graduate training and early research. Susan Wladaver-Morgan, David A. Johnson, and Carl Abbott shepherded my first peer-reviewed article to publication in the *Pacific Historical Review*. Grateful acknowledgment is made to the University of California Press for allowing me to reproduce brief portions of the article here. At UC–Riverside, Steve Hackel proved a patient, steady, and supportive PhD advisor, granting me the intellectual freedom to follow my passions. Bill Deverell opened his USC graduate seminar to me as a first-year student, exposing me to excellent scholarship and resources in western American history and also introducing me to scholars throughout the region. David Igler offered critical guidance during early and late stages of my dissertation and read chapter drafts meticulously. Cliff Trafzer and the Rupert Costo Fund at UC–Riverside provided crucial resources for Hawaiian-language study. Rebecca "Monte" Kugel, Kendra Field, David Biggs, Randy Head, Steve Hindle, and Dan Lewis all provided vital scholarly and professional support during the dissertation phase.

In Hawai'i, 'Alika McNicoll served as my first *kumu* (teacher) in Hawaiian language, while William H. "Pila" Wilson served as my language examiner and advisor on the recent history of the language. Thanks are due to a number of archivists, librarians, and museum specialists on the islands: Melissa Shimonishi and Luella Kurkjian of the Hawaiʻi State Archives, Barbara Dunn of the Hawaiian Historical Society, Matt Kester of BYU–Hawaiʻi Archives, Tia Reber and Leah Pualahaʻole Caldeira of the Bishop Museum, Viola Yee of the Maui Historical Society/ Bailey House Museum, and Christine Faye of the Kauaʻi Museum.

Special thanks to John Barker of the Hawaiian Mission Houses Archives for going above and beyond the call of duty to locate and digitize documents. One day in the archives, Ronald Williams Jr. helped me to identify a key aspect of my argument. John Charlot shared an unpublished translation of a crucial document from 1825. M. Puakea Nogelmeier offered generous advice on language and translations. Charles (Kale) Langlas and Jeffrey (Kapali) Lyon discussed with me the life and work of Davida Malo and various other matters pertaining to Hawaiian history. Later, they kindly shared with me their forthcoming translation of Malo's *Moʻolelo Hawaiʻi*.

In the world of Hawaiian health and medicine, thanks to Kim Kuʻulei Birnie of Papa Ola Lōkahi, the Native Hawaiian Health Board; Maile Taualii of the Program on Native Hawaiian and Indigenous Health, University of Hawaiʻi at Mānoa Department of Public Health Sciences; and Marlene Oishi and Jeannine Johnson of the Queen's Medical Center Hawaiʻi Medical Library. I am also indebted to Justin Kepoʻo Keliʻipaʻakaua and to Ashlie Duarte-Smith – graduates of the Hawaiʻinuiākea School of Hawaiian Knowledge at UH Mānoa – for assisting with difficult translations. Thanks also to Sasha Watson for French translations and Heather J. VanMouwerik for Russian translations.

Larry Kessler and Gregory Rosenthal were superb fellow travelers in Hawaiian and Pacific history, and both provided essential support and friendship, reading more chapter drafts than I can recall. Steve Aron and Louis Warren offered helpful comments on early versions of these chapters. Peter Atkinson advised me on parasite-borne diseases in the Pacific, and John Ryan Fischer answered queries about Polynesian mammals. Neal Evenhuis shared his expertise on Hawaiian insects.

Institutional support was essential to this project. The UC Pacific Rim Research Group, the UC Humanities Research Institute, and the Huntington Library all supported me during the research and writing of the dissertation. UC PacRim supported me for a summer of research in the Honolulu archives. UCHRI's Andrew Vincent White and Florence Wales White Dissertation Fellowship enabled me to focus exclusively on research and writing during academic year 2013–14. The Huntington's

Molina Fellowship in the History of Medicine and Allied Sciences provided me with two months of library research in 2014.

Warm thanks to Gary Gerstle, Nick Guyatt, Sarah Pearsall, and Andrew Preston for bringing me to Cambridge as the Mellon Research Fellow in American History in 2015. The Mellon Fund provided essential time and space for revising the book and also paid for the illustrations that grace its pages. Thanks to the Cambridge Americanists who welcomed me to England and taught me so much about so many things. In later stages, helpful chapter reviewing was provided by Sarah Pearsall, Nick Guyatt, Sujit Sivasundaram, Gary Gerstle, Tom Smith, Merve Fejzula, Jane Dinwoodie, and my former classmate Nicolette Rohr.

By the time this book appears in print, I will have a new home in the Department of History at Utah State University. Thanks to Dean Joseph P. Ward, Department Head Tammy Proctor, and committee members Victoria Grieve, Susan Cogan, and Clayton Brown for hiring me and to the rest of team for welcoming me aboard.

On research leave at the Huntington Library in 2014, Fred Hoxie generously offered to read the introduction of my unfinished dissertation. Later, he found this book a home at Cambridge University Press. Many thanks to Fred, the anonymous reviewers, and editor Deborah Gershenowitz and her team – Kristina A. Deusch, Ruth Boyes, Rogini Pavithra, and Karin Kipp – for guiding this project from manuscript to completion. Before the book went into production, Josh Garrett-Davis read it all; he deserves a special shout-out for late-stage reviewing and early-stage believing.

Thanks to my parents Dave and Anitra for their unflagging support, basement writing space, occasional proofreading, and making this achievement possible in the first place. Thanks to my brothers Andy and Phil for guidance and inspiration. Thanks to Amber for knowing where the paragraphs should be, and for everything else that matters.

Note on Language and Terminology

In Hawai'i, as in other colonized spaces, language is contested. There is good reason for this. As the Hawaiian proverb says, "In language there is life, in language there is death."[1] Scholarship written for a broad audience must weigh culturally appropriate language against the demands of clarity and understanding. A cursory glance at recent scholarship reveals the elusiveness of a standardized Hawaiian orthography. Some consider further standardization as a colonial imposition; hence, the small island next to Maui appears variously in written form as Lāna'i, Lana'i, and Lanai. This presents obvious difficulties for readers. As a student of the language myself, I adhere to the best practices established by my mentors, striving always for internal consistency. This means including diacritical marks – the 'okina (') and kahakō (ˉ) – except where the original source does not, and correcting spellings that would otherwise cause confusion with brackets. Hawaiian words appear in italics the first time they are used and in regular script thereafter, except where italics appear in the quoted text.

Translation poses its own challenges. Consider the word pō'ino, a contraction of pō (time of, state of) and 'ino (wicked, immoral, spoiled, contaminated). As applied to women in menses, pō'ino in nineteenth-century texts has generated translations ranging from "unlucky" to "dangerous."[2] A lot hangs on these differences. Readers

---

[1] "I ka 'ōlelo no ke ola, i ka 'ōlelo no ka make." Hawaiian scholar Mary Kawena Pukui offered an alternative: "Life is in speech, death is in speech" ('Ōlelo No'eau, 129).

[2] Malo, Hawaiian Antiquities, 29 ("unlucky"); Malo, Mo'olelo Hawai'i, trans. Langlas and Lyon, 218 ("dangerous"). See also Pukui and Elbert, Hawaiian Dictionary, s.v. pō, 'ino,

will not always agree with my translations or with the translations I have chosen, though more often than not the translation that appears is the only one thus far attempted.

The people at the heart of this book are referred to as Hawaiians, as Islanders, or by the town, district, or island from which they hailed (for example, "Kauaʻi Islander," "Kula resident"). Choice of identifier is typically determined by context. Despite the recommendation of some scholars, I avoid Native Hawaiian, *kānaka maoli* ("true/genuine people"), and *kānaka ʻōiwi* ("Indigenous/Native people").[3] Culturally and politically significant today, these terms are mostly anachronistic for the period under study and sometimes muddle important distinctions between people of different or mixed ancestry. When relevant to the discussion, persons of mixed descent are identified in the text as "part Hawaiian" or by the Hawaiian term *hapa haole* ("part foreign").

Regardless of where they were born, people lacking Hawaiian ancestry are never identified in this book as Hawaiian. Before 1820 visitors arrived from the British Isles, France, Spain, New Spain (Mexico), the United States, Canada, Russia, Ukraine, the German and Baltic states, Canton, and the South Pacific. In the latter chapters of this book, foreigners in some numbers began to settle on the islands. Sometimes a shorthand for these diverse newcomers is necessary. To Hawaiians they were all – with the possible exception of Tahitians – *haole* (foreign). That term took on racial connotations later in the nineteenth century. "Western" is a wholly imperfect description for these people, their ideas, and their institutions, but it will have to suffice in certain places where "foreign(er)" fails to convey the type of introduction or intrusion.

Nineteenth-century Hawaiians spelled their names in various ways; name changes were not uncommon. In general I employ the name most commonly used by scholars and by contemporary Hawaiians to refer to their ancestors. For example, the royal governor of Oʻahu appears in the text as Boki rather than Kamāʻuleʻule, his given name, or Poki, which may be a closer pronunciation. An exception is where sources indicate that the individual preferred an alternative to the name commonly used today; for example, *Davida* rather than David Malo. Monarchs are most often

---

pō ʻino. For an alternative translation of the prefix *po-*, see Andrews, *Dictionary*, s.v. *po*, *poino*.

[3] For discussion, see Blaisdell, "'Hawaiian' versus 'Kanaka Maoli' as Metaphors"; Wood, *Displacing Natives*, chap. 1, esp. 12–13; Silva, *Aloha Betrayed*, 12–13; Young, "Interdisciplinary Study of the Term 'Hawaiian'"; Kauanui, *Hawaiian Blood*; Brown, *Facing the Spears of Change*, ix–xiii.

identified by their given name (Kauikeaouli) and sometimes by their title (Kamehameha III). When a person identified by foreigners does not appear elsewhere in the records, I employ the imposed name, however inaccurate, rather than guess at the actual one.

Hawaiian society was divided into two major classes in this period. The overwhelming majority of Islanders were commoners, or *maka'āinana* ("children of the land"), while the *ali'i* (chiefly) class comprised about 1 percent of the population. Both terms are gender-neutral. I follow the convention of using "commoner(s)" for the former and "chief(s)" for the latter, though I frequently make a point of identifying female chiefs as "chiefesses," since chief is gendered in English. A list of important persons appears in Appendix D.

While Hawai'i in this period was known to much of the world as the Sandwich Islands – and to the Chinese as the Sandalwood Mountains[4] – I use Hawai'i or the Hawaiian Islands when discussing the archipelago and its people, regardless of era. I refer to the largest island in the chain as either the Big Island or Hawai'i Island.

---

[4] Thanks to Gregory Rosenthal for this reference.

Introduction

Ku'ua nā 'ōlelo. (Release the words.)

In 1824 the chief minister of Hawai'i wrote a letter to his cousins King Liholiho and Queen Kamāmalu. The royal couple had been away for six months on a diplomatic tour of Britain. "Here is my message to you," Kalanimoku began:

> We have been consumed here by death from sickness . . . Keeaumoku . . . died, and was returned to Kai[l]ua. Pihoo . . . is dead. [Kiliwehi] is dead. Eeka is dead. [Kaumuali'i] is dead, just nine nights ago . . . [Kawelo] is dead . . . By and by, we may all be dead here from sickness; you should come back.[1]

This letter never reached the king and queen, who had already died after contracting measles in London. Both monarchs were in their twenties. These losses were not unexpected. Islanders had begged the royal delegation not to leave Hawai'i, and thousands grieved on the beach when they departed.[2] Some months later, a lunar eclipse on the islands caused a panic, with some interpreting it as an omen that their king and queen would perish abroad. "In tones of deep anxiety and distress," the people observed that "'*the moon is sick, very sick – an evil moon – evil indeed! – the gods are eating up the moon.*'" American missionary Charles S. Stewart learned that an earlier eclipse had anticipated the deaths of several chiefs. While Rev. Stewart could not abide these signs and explanations, he acknowledged that

---

[1] Karaimoku [Kalanimoku] to Rihoriho [Liholiho], June 2, 1824, CWM/LMS box 4, folder 6, SOAS. The translation is mostly by Nogelmeier (Corley and Nogelmeier, "Kalanimoku's Lost Letter," 99), though I have opted for different word choices and order in places; e.g., "consumed" for *pau*, and "By and by" for *Ma muli* (*lit.*, "At later"). Kiliwehi was daughter of Kamehameha and half-sister of Liholiho (Kamehameha II); the third of three wives Kalanimoku lost between 1821 and 1824, she was predeceased by Likelike (d. 1821) and Keōpūolani (d. 1823). 'E'eka was a chief in the service of Ka'ahumanu (Kahananui, *Ka Mooolelo* [sic] *Hawaii*, 217; Kamakau, *Ruling Chiefs*, 224).
[2] W[illia]m Ellis to G[eorge] Burden, Nov. 20, 1823, CWM/LMS box 4, folder 3, SOAS; Ellis to W[illia]m Alers Hankey, Nov. 23, 1823, ibid.; Kamakau, *Ruling Chiefs*, 256.

Hawai'i was in fact a "land of disease and death, and, in many respects, of inconceivable corruption and horror."[3]

It was not the first time these sentiments had been aired on the islands. Chief Minister Kalanimoku's letter of 1824 was, in some ways, old news. In 1819 a French expedition discovered that the death of King Kamehameha just weeks before its arrival had triggered the collapse of Hawaiian religious law. The kingdom had entered a period of cultural and political transformation that would last to midcentury.

In the pages that follow, I argue that health was the national crisis of Hawai'i for more than a century. More chronic than labor strife and land-use disputes, more pressing than self-determination and the struggle for sovereignty, the introduction of new diseases resulted in reduced life spans, rising infertility and infant mortality, and persistent poor health for generations of Islanders.[4] The *ma'i malihini* (introduced diseases) also left a deep imprint on island culture and on the Hawaiian national consciousness. In general, these diseases paid no mind to boundaries of class, age, sex, or region.

Most historians have a grasp of the impact of disease on the people they study. Bubonic plague in Europe, smallpox in North America, and yellow fever in the equatorial zones all factor into narratives of world history. Epidemics not only struck down countless people in the past, they also had social and political consequences that justify their presence in general histories and textbooks. More difficult to access are the personal and cultural dimensions of disease: not only what it felt like to be unable to bring a pregnancy to term or to lose family members in their prime but also how these widely shared experiences were stitched into the cultural fabric. These questions are uniquely pertinent to Indigenous societies. Failing to uncover these experiences, scholars neglect a crucial aspect of the human past – indeed, one of the major connecting threads of Indigenous history.

Hawai'i was home to half a million people in the eighteenth century. By 1850 the population had been reduced by as much as 90 percent.

---

[3] Stewart, *Private Journal*, 253, 295. See also journal of Sybil Moseley Bingham, Feb. 5, 1822, HMCS; Elizabeth Edwards Bishop (Jan. 15, 1824), "A Journal of Early Hawaiian Days," esp. 82. Kamakau narrated this event as a solar rather than a lunar eclipse (*Ruling Chiefs*, 266). For other astronomical portents, see Corney, *Voyages*, 86; Mathison, *Narrative of a Visit*, 473.

[4] Only leprosy (Hansen's disease) has garnered adequate attention by historians, yet morbidity and mortality to leprosy were dwarfed by earlier diseases, which also set the context for Islanders' experience of this ancient scourge. Recent works include Herman, "Out of Sight, Out of Mind, Out of Power"; Moran, *Colonizing Leprosy*; Law, *Kalaupapa*; Inglis, *Ma'i Lepera*.

The trend continued through the end of the century, buffered slightly by a slow-growing part-Hawaiian population. European and American merchants began to remark on the depopulation of Hawai'i just twenty-five years after British navigator James Cook arrived there in 1778. By the time American missionaries showed up in 1820, population decline was noted by virtually every writer – including a few Hawaiian writers – discussing the islands and their people. The problem was not limited to a particular demographic or region, and no respite would occur by century's end. The monarchs who ruled the Kingdom of Hawai'i during its hundred-year existence provide a telling example. Founder Kamehameha had as many as fourteen children. The seven monarchs who followed him produced only one surviving child, who happened to be *hapa haole* (part-Hawaiian).[5]

By illuminating four generations of island life amid colonial incursions, this book endeavors to place the cultural impact of health in its proper place. If the romantic conception of the Hawaiian Islands as a benign tropical paradise is overdue for a corrective historical narrative, so too is the story of colonialism in Hawai'i. Disease, poor health, and population loss were not bit players in a cast of colonial disruptions that tore at the heart of Hawaiian life. Instead they were colonial disruptions of the first order. Their impact endures. Native Hawaiian health disparities today constitute the surest evidence of the legacy of colonialism and Indigenous struggle for the islands. It is for this reason that advocates of Hawaiian sovereignty champion "health decolonization" as a critical step on the path to self-determination.[6] A stable and resilient Native population is a necessary condition for self-rule.

HEALTH AND CULTURE

The Hawaiian people employed a metaphor for their high chiefs who wandered from district to district devouring the fruits of their subjects'

---

[5] Albert Kūnuiākea was the son of Kauikeaouli (Kamehameha III) and Jane Lahilahi Young, who was herself *hapa haole*. There is little scholarship on Hawaiians of mixed descent before 1855.

[6] Marshall, *Potent Mana*, esp. chap. 3; McMullin, *Healthy Ancestor*, chap. 1. See also Mihesuah, "Decolonizing Our Diets"; Else, "Breakdown of the *Kapu* System"; Gracey and King, "Indigenous Health Part 1"; Gracey et al., "Indigenous Health Part 2"; Mailer and Hale, "Decolonizing the Diet." While nutrition plays a role in the following pages, the broader subject awaits its historian. For research into the relationship between Indigenous cultural revitalization and mental health, see Kirmayer et al., "Rethinking Resilience from Indigenous Perspectives"; Gone, "Redressing First Nations Historical Trauma."

labors. They were "sharks who travel on the land."[7] Beginning in 1778 sharks of a far more ravenous variety roamed the islands in the form of new communicable diseases. Islanders met with a series of devastating epidemics that undermined their health, their subsistence, and eventually their sovereignty. Health travails also shaped Hawaiian culture. This book is not about how Hawai'i lost its sovereignty while maintaining its culture – the typical story – but rather how culture was transformed in the midst of Hawaiian self-rule. In the period under study, the islands saw the rupture and collapse of Hawaiian religious law; a rapid transition from orality to widespread literacy; and a substantial refashioning of marriage, family life, and labor, all while maintaining a hereditary monarchy. Health history is one way to organize our understanding of these complex processes: changes in health imposed limits and forced compromises on Hawaiians that subsequent forms of colonialism were able to exploit.

Sharks upon the Land elaborates a new theme in global Indigenous history: the juncture between colonialism, health, and culture. Scholars have only sketched in broad outline the processes of Native health and culture change amid the disruptions of colonialism. For a variety of reasons, including simple geography, these transformations were nowhere more evident than the remote North Pacific. This book proceeds from an understanding of religion, sexuality, gender, and family structure as cultural forms. Indeed, as I will argue, religion and gender were inseparable in the Hawaiian past, as women and men had discrete religious practices, drawing various kinds of understanding from their rituals and cosmologies. Medicine and healing are also cultural forms. Beyond diagnosis and treatment of the body, medicine consists of the attitudes, understandings, behaviors, and beliefs that practitioners and patients bring to treatment. If the cultural dimension of medicine pertains today – consider placebo regimens, faith healing, mindfulness practices, and divergent results of cancer treatment – how much more so in colonial Hawai'i where medicine was everywhere a spiritual matter.

As applied to the Hawaiian past, religion, medicine, and gender are all problematic categories: each blends into the other, and none can be effectively separated for scholarly observation. Translation itself is vexing. In the Hawaiian historical context, religion was medicine was culture, and so on. The whole is what I refer to as the Hawaiian cultural toolbox,

---

[7] In Hawaiian: *he manō holo 'āina ke ali'i*. See *Fornander Collection of Hawaiian Antiquities*, 6:393–94; Pukui, *'Ōlelo No'eau*, 87.

a metaphor I borrow from the scholar of religion Craig Martin.[8] The fact that Hawaiians had no discrete words for "religion," "gender," and "sexuality" in no way indicates that these phenomena did not exist. While religion is an "unstable category" that fails to "translate from one historical moment to the next with fidelity,"[9] historians can hardly dispense with it. Instead of rejecting cultural tools for which the world's languages do not accord, scholars must try to understand and explain social and cultural phenomena in their particular historical context: to grasp the individual tools and comprehend the larger toolbox.

It bears mentioning that the notion of culture itself has its origins in cultivation. The "roots" of culture, that is to say, run deep. For many of the world's people, place and culture were inextricably bound: how people lived on the land *was* culture. Studies of health history only reinforce this conception of a thin line between nature and culture. For the purposes of this book, health is to be understood as a biosocial and biocultural phenomenon, neither simply culturally "constructed" nor merely biological.[10]

Any health history must consider the ways in which health (including nutrition, medicine, and healing practices), overlapped, obscured, and contributed to other social problems, including poverty, land loss, displacement, and political marginalization. Yet however these social phenomena interacted over the long history of European and American colonialism, it is clear that health problems came first for Indigenous people in Hawai'i. And health problems lasted: through all manner of kings, commodities, legal regimes, and land reform. A comprehensive study of colonialism must address disease and its consequences as principal causes and prime movers.

Native Hawaiians today rightly celebrate cultural survival and revitalization as well as their strategic incorporation of foreign peoples, technologies, and practices through the ages. The persistence, against all odds and laws, of the Hawaiian language and hula schools are shining examples of Islander resilience.[11] Yet strategic incorporation and cultural

---

[8] Martin, *Critical Introduction to the Study of Religion*.
[9] Fowles, *Archaeology of Doings*, 4. For the problem of defining religion in non-Western contexts, see also Josephson, *Invention of Religion in Japan*; Nongbri, *Before Religion*.
[10] This point can be pushed too far when scholars imply that human disease is *limited* by social facts; e.g., "Pathogens and diseases are not simply agents or actors whose effects historians can recount; the effects of disease do not exist apart from the way that humans respond to them" (Nash, "Beyond Virgin Soils," 97).
[11] Momiala Kamahele, "'Ilio'ulaokalani: Defending Native Hawaiian Culture," in Fujikane and Okamura, eds., *Asian Settler Colonialism*, 76–98; Sahlins, "Goodbye to *Tristes Tropes*," 8–11.

persistence were not all: the colonial experience in Hawai'i also involved adaptation, accommodation, and outright colonization. The health impact, above all, proved a challenge. Disease, in a word, *colonized* Hawai'i, forcing adaptations on Islanders that resonate down to today.

SOURCES AND HISTORIOGRAPHY

Colonial Hawai'i is uniquely apposite for a study of health and culture change. In epidemiological terms, the islands' small size and isolation limited variables that present challenges for more diffuse or porous regions. Isolation, which hampered Islander immunity to introduced diseases, was also the primary contributing factor to the scale of epidemics in this period. In addition, the relative uniformity of culture across the archipelago in the late eighteenth century permits a coherent assessment of cultural change over time. Despite being politically divided, the islands were socially, culturally, and economically linked before and after the arrival of Cook. Hawai'i's late encounter with colonialism, and the obsessive journalism and correspondence of colonial agents, also resulted in a rich body of documentation, the vast majority of which has survived. Eighteenth-century observers enjoyed considerable advantages over their predecessors in documenting and comparing Native populations, disease morbidity, and cultural change. Cook's third Pacific voyage alone produced eight published accounts of the islands, while nineteenth-century New England missionaries penned perhaps the most voluminous literature (per square mile) on colonialism to date. This body of work is supplemented by rich Hawaiian traditions that track cultural trends and political dynasties back to the sixteenth century.

Literacy in the latter decades of this study presents an enormous advantage. Hawaiian-language documents constitute a unique documentary trove unparalleled by Indigenous peoples perhaps anywhere in the world.[12] These documents offer an unusually rich record of Indigenous health, allowing us to see the effects of colonization from Native perspectives. The abundance of sources addressing health and disease before 1855 is surprising given that these matters were hardly considered newsworthy at the time. When Hawaiian-language newspapers began to circulate in the late 1830s, Islander health was already an old story – part and parcel of Hawaiian life, almost too obvious to comment on. Barring a destructive epidemic or public health crisis, the everyday suffering and health concerns of common

---

[12] Silva, *Aloha Betrayed*; Nogelmeier, *Mai Pa'a i ka Leo.*

Islanders did not attract the attention of politicians or newspaper editors. Personal letters are more revealing but have garnered less scholarly attention than newspapers and government documents. Even so, the everyday suffering of Hawaiians from chronic disease, infertility, and infant mortality can be elusive. This book draws upon a varied archive of letters, travel journals, published works, and other sources to uncover Hawai'i's health past. Wherever possible, Hawaiian voices take center stage.

While mindful of the warnings of poststructuralism and postcolonialism, I am less skeptical than some scholars about the ability of foreign observers and languages to illuminate developments in Native society.[13] In many cases, foreigners provided the sole written record of a particular time and place, shedding light on phenomena that would otherwise be lost. In Hawai'i the historical record is especially rich, textually and visually, enabling us to trace developments in island life and health across many decades. While such accounts must be read against the grain, they are essential to elucidating processes of colonialism, Native health, and cultural change.[14]

The story of Hawaiian health remains to be told. While scholars have noted the role of epidemics in the depopulation of Hawai'i and broader Oceania, few have considered the effects of disease on island society and culture – including religion, medicine and ideas about the body, and gender and sexuality. Equally neglected by scholars have been Islanders' own ideas about – and responses to – disease and other health challenges on the local level. The seminal work on disease and colonialism in Hawai'i, now more than a quarter century old, is marred by blanket statements and crude caricatures of Native life.[15] The broader historical scholarship on health and disease in the Pacific is either too narrow to draw conclusions about the overall impact or too broad to get beyond population figures and rates of decline.[16] Some historians overlook

---

[13] E.g., Wood, *Displacing Natives*; Silva, *Aloha Betrayed*; Lyons, *American Pacificism*.

[14] While "no representation transparently mirrors a fixed past reality," Oceanian encounters were "messy, embodied episode[s] ... involving multifaceted interactions of gendered, classed Indigenous and foreign persons"; the documentation produced by foreigners is "littered with traces of Indigenous agency" (Douglas, *Science, Voyages, and Encounters*, 21, 19, 26).

[15] Bushnell, *Gifts of Civilization*. The author follows nineteenth-century missionaries in blaming Hawaiians for their own mortality (ibid., 264–65, 270).

[16] E.g., work on Hawai'i by Robert C. Schmitt and colleagues (see bibliography); Stannard, *Before the Horror*; Crosby, "Hawaiian Depopulation as a Model"; A. F. Bushnell, "'The Horror' Reconsidered."

Hawai'i because of its poor fit with broader Pacific currents; others lump the islands in without attending to important differences of culture and ecology.

Historical anthropologists have focused intently on island society and culture in the colonial era, adding much to our understanding of sociocultural and political change amid European and American incursions. Yet for all their depth and breadth, these studies rarely address the cultural impact of disease and ongoing health challenges. Anthropologist Marshall Sahlins characterized the unprecedented mortality of the Hawaiian chiefs as an "optical illusion, the effect of a cultural demise."[17] In fact, the Kingdom of Hawai'i struggled to survive for most of the century, and "cultural demise" is a dubious reading at best.

Historians of colonial Hawai'i have focused overwhelmingly on politics and the law.[18] While this scholarship has effectively traced the complex developments leading to the US overthrow of the monarchy in the 1890s, it has tended to underestimate the scale of change to Native life in earlier periods, particularly in areas such as religion, health, and gender and sexuality.[19] Common Hawaiians (*maka'āinana*) are routinely overlooked.[20] Yet introduced diseases, infertility, and chronic poor health affected commoners at least as much as the ruling classes; the experiences of the former – while more difficult to uncover – are therefore essential to this study. Even so, maka'āinana are too often confined to the margins of the pages that follow. Rectifying this shortcoming is a charge to future scholars.

[17] Sahlins, *Anahulu*, 1:135. Elsewhere Sahlins mischaracterized the population of Waialua, O'ahu, in the 1840s as "heroic[ally] ... unwilling ... to reproduce itself" in the face of a "subsumed existence" (ibid., 1:176). See also Sahlins, "Cosmologies of Capitalism," 434–35.

[18] E.g., Daws, *Shoal of Time*; Merry, *Colonizing Hawai'i*; Osorio, *Dismembering Lāhui*; Mykkänen, *Inventing Politics*; Silva, *Aloha Betrayed*; Kashay, "Agents of Imperialism"; Banner, *Possessing the Pacific*, chap. 4. Exceptions include Kame'eleihiwa, *Native Land*; Ralston, "Hawaii 1778–1854" and "Changes in the Lives of Ordinary Women"; Chang, *World and All the Things upon It*, chaps. 1–3.

[19] E.g., the "material effects of colonialism on the Hawaiian Islands occur[ed] only after the illegal overthrow of Lili'uokalani in 1893" (Beamer, *No Mākou ka Mana*, 15).

[20] Important exceptions include Osorio, *Dismembering Lāhui*; Rosenthal, "Hawaiians Who Left Hawai'i." A related problem in the scholarship is a tendency to mystify structures of social inequality or to valorize the ali'i class; e.g., Kame'eleihiwa, *Native Land*, 19–49, 321–27; Young, *Rethinking the Native Hawaiian Past*, xiv, 27–31; Silva, *Aloha Betrayed*, 15–44; Andrade, *Hā'ena*, 71–74; Beamer, *No Mākou ka Mana*, 8–49; Kapā'anaokalāokeola Nākoa Oliveria, *Ancestral Places*, 44–45.

For its teleology and lack of Native perspectives, the Fatal Impact narrative of Pacific Island history was discarded decades ago.[21] However, in two areas Fatal Impact was on point. First, geographic isolation, which varied dramatically across the Pacific, played a critical role in ecological change after contact. Second, introduced diseases were lethal, consequential, and enduring among populations previously unexposed to outsiders. Recent Pacific Islands scholarship, even the work of environmental historians, has tended to minimize both effects of contact.[22] More than twenty years ago, with Fatal Impact already considered outmoded, a scholar at the Pacific History Association's annual meeting observed that "polemics" had prevented Pacific historians from "dealing with disease." The result, he concluded, was that the cultural and social impact of epidemiological incursion "awaits careful analysis."[23] It does still.

CONTRIBUTIONS AND COMPARISONS

Beyond intervening in Pacific history, this study contributes to a new generation of scholarship that is rethinking the boundaries – geographical and chronological – of colonial America and the early Republic.[24] Hawai'i rarely enters the US history narrative before the 1880s, yet the islands bore importantly on American geopolitical concerns from the 1840s and on American evangelicalism from 1810.[25] For New England merchants, Hawai'i was a principal station in the Pacific trade, which was vitally important from the very founding of the nation. For traders and

---

[21] Moorehead, *Fatal Impact*. For criticisms, see, e.g., Dening, *Performances*; Matt K. Matsuda, "*AHR* Forum: The Pacific," *American Historical Review* 111 (2006): 771–72; Newell, *Trading Nature*, 18–19.

[22] E.g., Hau'ofa, "Our Sea of Islands"; D'Arcy, *People of the Sea*; Thomas, *Islanders*; O'Malley, *Meeting Place*; Matsuda, *Pacific Worlds*; Ballantyne, *Entanglements of Empire*; Chang, *World and All the Things upon It*. An important exception is Igler, "Diseased Goods" and *Great Ocean*. For a Pacific archipelago where introduced disease was less destructive due to the islands' proximity to neighbors and earlier contact with Europeans, see Molle and Conte, "Nuancing the Marquesan Post-Contact Demographic Decline," esp. 255–56, 270.

[23] Chappell, "Active Agents versus Passive Victims," 316. See also D'Arcy, *People of the Sea*, 127–28; Karskens, *Colony*, 376–78.

[24] E.g., Taylor, *American Colonies*, esp. xiv–xvii; Hackel, *Children of Coyote*; Igler, *Great Ocean*; Pekka Hämäläinen, "The Shapes of Power: Indians, Europeans, and North American Worlds from the Seventeenth to the Nineteenth Century," in Barr and Countryman, eds., *Contested Spaces of Early America*, 31–68; Samuel Truett, "Borderlands and Lost Worlds of Early America," ibid., 300–24.

[25] By the mid-nineteenth century, US residents of varied backgrounds dreamed of an American Hawai'i (Greenberg, *Manifest Manhood*, 231–61).

administrators in the Pacific Northwest, the islands were not only essential to their business but intimately connected to their communities. The first book copyrighted in the United States was Connecticut native John Ledyard's first-person account of the discovery of Hawai'i and the killing of Cook (1783). It was a best seller. The "Sandwich Islands" were clearly on the American radar. While there is some risk of teleology in couching Hawaiian history in an American frame, the impact of Western nations was immediate, and the eventual US annexation of the islands is best understood when traced back to the eighteenth century.[26] As for American history, historians of all periods now recognize the advantages of gazing beyond the nation's borders to make sense of its past.[27]

Comparative developments across the Pacific are also critical to this study. Similar patterns can be identified in this period across the Society Islands (Tahiti) and New Zealand (Aotearoa, to the Māori); yet comparisons with the Americas and, indeed, with Indigenous societies globally are no less revealing. Forms of colonialism in Hawai'i followed patterns established by Europeans centuries before, and the responses of Islanders were not always unique. Such comparisons hardly suggest that Indigenous peoples are all of a kind or that their histories are interchangeable but rather that Euro-American colonialism and Indigenous responses shared broad features across time and space. For the Americas, in particular, Hawai'i presents a useful comparison to regions where European colonialism was principally trade-based, sporadic, or informal. Given the voluminous and comprehensive nature of the sources, the Hawaiian story may compel us to reconsider certain aspects of colonialism in Indigenous societies.

Both for what happened, and what did not, Hawai'i provides an interesting comparison. Before 1855 the islands did not meet with foreign conquest, enslavement, widespread famine, or forced migration and removals.[28] While Native warfare took its toll – particularly Kamehameha's fifteen-year unification campaign – conflicts of this nature predated European contact by centuries, and the new technologies employed by Hawaiian combatants (ships, firearms, and gunpowder) did not contribute significantly to population decline.[29] In short, while epidemics in the Americas, Island

---

[26] Cf. Arista, "Histories of Unequal Measure," 163; Beamer, *No Mākou ka Mana*.

[27] E.g., Bender, *Nation among Nations*, 3–5; White, *Encountering Revolution*, 9.

[28] Crosby was the first to make this observation ("Hawaiian Depopulation as a Model," 180–83).

[29] Deserving of further study is Stannard's claim that Polynesian warfare mostly took the lives of men and thus had little effect on reproduction rates (*Before the Horror*, 61–62, 137).

Southeast Asia, and elsewhere featured forms of violence as corollary or precipitating factors, introduced disease in Hawai'i exacted its costs largely unaided by famine, warfare, enslavement, or displacement. If Polynesia was exceptional in this respect, this study may contribute to broader scholarship on the wide range of factors associated with Indigenous health in colonialism's wake.[30]

Sharks upon the Land pushes the field of Native health history beyond epidemiology and demography into the realm of Indigenous cultural responses to changing health conditions. For decades, scholars of Indigenous peoples have narrated their histories as if Native actors were of sound body and mind when they traded, negotiated, fought, and otherwise engaged with newcomers.[31] To convey the lived experience of past Indigenous peoples, historians need to illuminate the challenges to health, well-being, and survival that individuals and communities faced on a regular basis. Recent scholars have worked hard to give voice to Native peoples and provide a more accurate portrait of Native agency and resilience in the midst of Western expansion. But eschewing the subject of Native American population decline – and of Native people's actual suffering – risks misunderstanding such basic processes as resistance, ethnogenesis, nationhood, and cultural persistence.[32] Colonialism lives on in the bodies of the colonized.[33]

This study takes as a principal focus the ways that health adversity was inscribed into island culture over time. Recent work on colonialism and

---

[30] The Marquesas, Fiji, and the Northwest Coast all present similar cases, though none was as isolated as Hawai'i (Dening, *Islands and Beaches*, esp. 155, 237–39; Hays, *Burdens of Disease*, 187–90; Boyd, *Coming of the Spirit of Pestilence*, xiii, 4–5). Recent work on the North American "maize revolution" points to iron deficiency and other metabolic and immunological consequences in the centuries before European contact (Mailer and Hale, "Decolonizing the Diet," 12–13).

[31] Thomas A. Foster makes a similar point about Atlantic slavery: the well-nourished bodies with proportional musculature depicted in paintings, books, and films are a far cry from the bodies that slavery created ("Queering Enslaved Men's Experiences: Same-Gender Intimacy and Sexual Vulnerability," paper delivered at Cambridge American History Seminar, Oct. 10, 2016).

[32] Blackhawk, *Violence over the Land*, 1–15, 280–93.

[33] For recent work on epigenetics related to colonial trauma, see National Congress of American Indians, "American Indian and Alaska Native Genetics Research Resource Guide," 2012, genetics.ncai.org/files/NCAI%20genetics%20research%20resource%20guide%20FINAL%20PDF.pdf. Related work includes Gone, "Redressing First Nations Historical Trauma"; Megan Vaughan, "Metabolic Disorders in Africa: Biology, History and Metaphor," paper delivered at Cambridge World History Seminar, Jan. 28, 2016.

Indigenous health has focused on the broad range of disruptions that enabled the spread and exacerbated the impact and duration of epidemics.[34] In this scholarship, colonial incursions are the root causes of Native peoples' health problems and numerical decline. But what if the chain of causation is reversed? What if health is understood as central to colonialism and resulting social inequalities? In such a story, health problems such as infertility and malnutrition would form an essential part of the colonial process.[35]

This book also reflects the central role of women and gender. Women's presence in the documentary record is remarkable given that explorers, merchants, and evangelists tended to focus their efforts on elite men. Like Indigenous women elsewhere in the colonial world, Hawaiian women "forced their way into the sources."[36] Elite and commoner women alike carved out spaces for themselves in the colonial encounter and in ongoing relations with settler society. In addition to women themselves, both women's and men's ideas about biological sex and gender roles, as well as the fraught sexual politics that grew out of colonial incursions, play important roles in the chapters that follow. This book, then, is in no small part an examination of sexual politics and gendered power in island society.

The grim story told in these pages underscores Indigenous peoples' dramatic demographic and cultural recovery in the twentieth century. By 1920 there were fewer than a thousand native speakers of Hawaiian; today, fluency is approaching ten thousand across North America and the Pacific.[37] Meanwhile, the State of Hawai'i now recognizes it as an official language of government and commerce, and colleges have begun to offer degrees in Hawaiian language and culture. Perhaps most importantly, the islands' total population of people of Hawaiian descent has increased every decade since the 1970s. A host of social problems – inequality, environmental degradation, and ongoing health disparities – continue to plague Hawai'i, yet with every passing day the islands grow more Hawaiian.

SCOPE AND OVERVIEW

Every study has limits. Scholars of the Pacific have focused on two important issues that take a back seat in this book: Euro-American discourses

---

[34] E.g., Jones, "Virgin Soils Revisited"; Kelton, *Epidemics and Enslavement*; Cameron et al., *Beyond Germs*; Nash, "Beyond Virgin Soils."
[35] For further discussion, see Archer, "Colonialism and Other Afflictions."
[36] Fur, *Nation of Women*, 140.
[37] William H. (Pila) Wilson, email message to author, March 6, 2012.

about Pacific peoples, and Islanders' own impact on the broader world. This literature has contributed immensely to our understandings of Pacific labor and migration networks, nineteenth-century science and Protestant missions, and global imperialism.[38] If the winds of change blow too consistently in one direction in this book, it is due to my particular interest in Indigenous societies and cultural change. I do not mean to suggest that Islanders were always on the receiving end of global transformations. By focusing on change rather than persistence, however, this study reveals much about how Indigenous people thought about themselves, their bodies, and their society in relation to others. Readers can find a robust historiography on early modern Euro-American notions of national and cultural difference – that is, on race. Yet questions of difference are rarely viewed from the perspective of the colonized. The experience of health, and the important health disparities between Natives and newcomers worldwide, present unique opportunities to access Indigenous notions of difference.

I employ no single theory or method in this book. Instead, I rely upon a broad scholarship in colonial and Indigenous history and the history of health and medicine, as well as my understanding of Hawaiian culture and kinship. To set scientific ways of knowing against folkways and other Indigenous forms of knowledge is a false binary. Both have value and validity, even if Indigenous knowledge does not enjoy the authority of science among the general public (or what used to constitute the general public). While our contemporary language of viruses, bacteria, and immunity was not known to people at the time, that is no reason to believe that microbes were not at work or that people did not powerfully experience their effects. Thus I utilize contemporary medical science at various places in the text to illuminate the health struggles of the book's protagonists.[39] I make no claims to an insider's perspective on the Hawaiian experience, past or present. All scholars bring their particular life experience and understandings to their work, and I believe there is room for voices of

---

[38] E.g., Sivasundaram, *Nature and the Godly Empire*; Thomas, *Islanders*; O'Malley, *Meeting Place*; Ballantyne, *Entanglements of Empire*; Gascoigne, *Encountering the Pacific*; Conroy-Krutz, *Christian Imperialism*; Rosenthal, "Hawaiians Who Left Hawai'i"; Chang, *World and All the Things upon It*. For discursive and ideological aspects of Indigenous depopulation, see, e.g., Berkhofer, *White Man's Indian*; Dippie, *Vanishing American*; Brantlinger, *Dark Vanishings*; O'Brien, *Firsting and Lasting*.

[39] Of course, medical science has a history of its own that should be subjected to historical scrutiny (Nash, "Beyond Virgin Soils," 85–86).

various kinds. Insider or out, there is no "neutral shelter."[40] While I offer no solutions of my own to the ongoing problems of Hawaiian and Indigenous health, this study may provide a useable past for those who would engage in this important work.

The progressive and compounding nature of Hawaiian health struggles in this period calls for a chronological narrative. Chapter 1 traces epidemiological and cultural exchanges between Hawaiians and the Cook expedition. I argue that the introduction of venereal disease was a catastrophe with major repercussions for island authority, the roles of women, and the health of all Islanders. In Chapters 2 and 3, I trace Hawaiian exchanges with the outside world over the course of two generations, including a robust sex trade and the accumulation of ships and arms by the ruling chiefs. Unregulated and uncontrollable by either Hawaiians or foreigners, these exchanges enabled Kamehameha to conquer the islands and resulted in a series of social and cultural adaptations. Tuberculosis assailed Islanders, followed by a cholera-like epidemic that killed thousands. In spite of the harmful forces operating on the islands from the outside, Hawai'i in this period remained firmly Native ground.

By 1825 the ecological and cultural isolation that defined island life was a distant memory. Islanders were routinely in contact with North Americans, Europeans, and other Pacific Islanders. Yet at home health remained a primary concern for many, including the monarchy. Chapter 4 addresses the cultural revolution of 1818–25. I argue that sexual politics and ongoing health concerns – including low fertility – played critical roles in the ruling chiefesses' decision to overthrow the *kapu* system of religious law and seek a new path in alliance with Anglo-American missionaries. Chapter 5 focuses on Hawaiian attitudes toward the dual crises of poor health and population decline amid a concerted program of Protestant evangelism and social engineering. Influenced by missionaries and mindful of evidence from the recent past, Islanders came to view disease and depopulation as inexorable and the Hawaiian people as possibly destined for extinction. Chapter 6 addresses the fertility crisis and three major epidemics. Hawaiian lives and bodies were under siege by new microbes and new laws in the 1840s to control Native labor and sexuality.

---

[40] Cooter, "The End? History-Writing in the Age of Biomedicine," esp. 7. For the ethics of writing Indigenous history, see, e.g., Richter, "Whose Indian History?," esp. 386–88; Edmunds, "Native Americans, New Voices," esp. 737–39; Miller and Riding In, eds., *Native Historians Write Back*.

The depopulation crisis ultimately led the Kingdom to import foreign laborers for a nascent plantation complex, changing Hawai'i forever.

In 2012 the University of Hawai'i Maui College introduced a new degree program in Hawaiian Studies called *Ho'oulu Lāhui* ("increase the nation/ people"). The motto was made famous by King David Kalākaua in the 1870s with the Native Hawaiian population at an all-time low. *Ho'oulu lāhui* was the keystone of Kalākaua's rule, and he meant it quite literally: Hawai'i needed more Hawaiians.[41]

The survival of this motto across Hawaiian society is a reminder of the demographic aspects of cultural persistence and political self-determination.[42] Hawai'i's demographic challenges did not begin with the US-led coup in 1893, or with the importation of plantation labor in the mid-nineteenth century, or even with the whaling and sandalwood booms in the decades before that. The problem began, precisely, with the arrival of British naval captain James Cook in January 1778.

---

[41] *"Ka Hooulu Lahui," Ka Nuhou Hawaii*, April 21, 1874; *"Ma ka la 22o Apr. haiolelo ka Moi ..."* [On April 22 the King said ...], *Ka Nupepa Kuokoa*, May 9, 1874.

[42] See, e.g., Kekaha Solis, *"Ho'oulu Lāhui," Honolulu Star-Bulletin*, Aug. 24, 2008.

PART I

ENCOUNTERS

I

Pox Hawaiiana

[I]t will appear it has been we ourselves that has entailed on these poor, Unhappy people an everlasting and Miserable plague.
> —Edward Riou, HMS *Discovery*, 1778

[N]ot a pig could be purchased, without a girl was permitted to bring it to market.
> —John Rickman, HMS *Discovery*, 1779

It started with sex. "Knowing himself to be injured, with the Vener[e]al disorder," William Bradley solicited sex from Kaua'i Islanders anyway.[1] For this infraction, he received two dozen lashes. It was not the first time Bradley had been disciplined on James Cook's third Pacific voyage of discovery, and it would not be the last. One year later to the day, Bradley had "connextions with women" on Hawai'i Island while again "knowing himself to have the Venereal Disorder on him."[2]

In assisting their illustrious captain in the discovery of new lands and peoples, men like Bradley saddled Pacific Islanders with devastating new diseases. Before their arrival at the Hawaiian Islands, Cook's men had already consorted with Tahitians, Tongans, Sāmoans, and others. Nor did officers abstain from carnal activities, however much they complained about reckless and licentious seamen.[3] Sexual encounters occurred despite Cook's on-again off-again prohibitions – and island chiefs' taboos – on

---

[1] Henry Roberts, in Beaglehole, *Journals*, 3:266n.

[2] William Charlton, ibid., 3:511n. To Cook's lieutenant, Bradley was one of the "most notorious Rascals that ever stept on board a ship" (John Williamson, ibid., 3:240n3).

[3] See David Samwell, ibid., 3:1154; Ledyard, *Journal of Captain Cook's Last Voyage*, 109.

the practice. On his first voyage to the South Pacific in 1769 to record the transit of Venus, Cook grew concerned about Natives' susceptibility to sexually transmitted infections at the Society Islands (Tahiti).[4] He determined nothing could be done except bar his men from disembarking and Natives from boarding the ships, a prohibition regularly ignored on both sides. Seven years later, at Tahiti, Cook's astronomer noted that half the crew was "ill with the fowl disease."[5] Six weeks after that, "there were scarce hands enough able to do duty," with more than thirty men laid up with venereal symptoms.[6] Unfortunately for Hawaiians, newcomers arrived on their shores in roughly this shape in January 1778.

The story of Cook's "discovery" of the Hawaiian Islands has been told many times. The Hawaiian discovery of Europe is, for obvious reasons, less well known. Given the nature of the documentation and of island traditions, there are limits to what can be gleaned from eighteenth-century Hawaiian perspectives. But whatever else can be said about the encounter, disease transmission was a critical aspect. Syphilis and gonorrhea were daily physical reminders and potent symbols of the Hawaiian encounter with Europeans. These unwelcome reminders would persist for decades.

This chapter begins with a survey of precolonial life and ecology as context for the epidemiological encounter. Scant attention has been paid to the spread of diseases that transformed island society and set the stage for more than a century of health challenges. Equally neglected by historians are the dynamic alliances between island women and foreigners that would shortly undermine chiefly authority. Finally, sex and disease offer a new perspective on the much-discussed killing of Cook at Kealakekua Bay. In the end, Cook's introduction of syphilis, gonorrhea, and probably tuberculosis had a disastrous effect on the Hawaiian people, with repercussions rippling through the generations.

Despite their role in spreading pestilence and paving the way for British empire over one-third of the globe, Cook's men left a valuable record of Pacific Island peoples and cultures. Scholars sometimes dismiss these "Cook books" for their cultural bias and imperial role.[7] Yet the son of a

---

[4] See Wharton, ed., *Captain Cook's Journal*, 76–77. Note that Cook's men were not the first Europeans to spread venereal disease at the Society Islands; see Banks, *Endeavor* journal, 1:413–14. SLNSW.

[5] William Bayly, in Beaglehole, *Journals*, 3:233n4.

[6] Rickman, *Journal of Captain Cook's Last Voyage*, 191. See also Ledyard, *Journal of Captain Cook's Last Voyage*, 61–64.

[7] E.g., Obeysekere, *Apotheosis of Captain Cook*; Silva, *Aloha Betrayed*; and most recently, Chang, *World and All the Things upon It*: Cook "could not see the [people] at Kaua'i

Scottish farm worker and his literate crewmen (hailing from such far-flung places as Switzerland, northern Wales, and Connecticut) were hardly of one mind or voice; together they had wider exposure to a broader swath of Pacific Island peoples than anyone in the eighteenth century, including Islanders themselves. This ethnographic record is essential. While none of Cook's men were disinterested observers, some were deeply interested in island cultures and in the immediate consequences of contact. The expedition journals must be read with a critical eye, yet the epidemiological and cultural encounter cannot be understood without them.

"TRUE PARADISE"

In the 1966 Hollywood epic *Hawaii,* an American missionary doctor played by Gene Hackman cradles the body of a Maui prince dying of measles in the surf at Lahaina. In a soliloquy over the noble chief, the doctor expresses in perfect capsule form the beleaguered trope of the "ecological Indian": "When Captain Cook discovered these islands fifty years ago, they were a true paradise. Infectious disease was unknown; they didn't even catch cold."[8] That was far from the case. Yet the perception of Hawai'i as prelapsarian persists, even among some scholars.[9] If the islands were not saddled with smallpox, malaria, venereal disease, or tuberculosis before 1778, they were hardly free from disease.[10] Like other Indigenous populations, Hawaiians lived short lives and contended with a number of challenges to health and well-being.[11]

clearly, as Western fantasies of discovery and superiority obscured his vision"; he "wrote about the people of Hawai'i as yet another group of 'Indians,' one of many such groups he encountered as he intruded upon lands that were unknown to him" (27). For "Cook books," see Clayton, *Islands of Truth,* chap. 4.

[8] "Quarantine," *Hawaii,* DVD, directed by George Roy Hill (Santa Monica, CA, 2005). The film was an adaptation of James A. Michener's 1959 novel of the same title.

[9] E.g., Kame'eleihiwa, *Native Land,* 26, 48–49, 322; Stannard, *Before the Horror,* 42 ("comparatively paradisiacal environment," "exceptionally robust and nearly disease-free people"); Hilgenkamp and Pescaia, "Traditional Hawaiian Healing and Western Influence," esp. 34.

[10] For the possibility of endemic tuberculosis, see Snow, *Early Hawaiians,* 150; Hommon, "Formation of Primitive States," 36; Kirch, *Feathered Gods,* 243; cf. Stannard, *Before the Horror,* 77–78. Whether or not tuberculosis was present in some form, its reintroduction by Europeans proved costly. For the debate on which Europeans (re)introduced tuberculosis, see A. F. Bushnell, "'The Horror' Reconsidered," 129; O. A. Bushnell, *Gifts of Civilization,* 277; Stannard, *Before the Horror,* 70–72; Stannard et al., "Book Review Forum," 292.

[11] Kirch, *Feathered Gods,* 243–44.

Thanks to the late date of contact and the number and diversity of early visitors, precontact Hawai'i is better understood than most Indigenous societies. Hawaiian oral traditions also thrived both before and after contact. *Mo'olelo* (accounts, histories), *mo'okū'auhau* (genealogies), *mele* (songs, poems), and *no'eau* (proverbs) largely agree with contemporary archaeology regarding human settlement of the archipelago.[12] Apparently no one lived on the islands before about 800 CE. Human settlement occurred in two major waves: the first originating in the Marquesas Islands ca. 800–1000 CE, the second from the Society Islands (Tahiti) beginning about 1000 and continuing through the fourteenth century. Hawaiian language is full of references to *kahiki* (Tahiti) as the ancestral homeland, and even contemporary names for Hawaiian geographical and topographical features echo this distant past. The channel separating the islands of Lāna'i and Kaho'olawe is Kealaikahiki ("the way to Tahiti"), and the western tip of Kaho'olawe – the nearest point on the islands *to* Tahiti – is Kealaikahiki Point.

Polynesian settlers made the voyage north in double-hulled canoes with sails of woven tree bark. Veritable Noah's arks, these vessels carried plants and seedlings, animals of both sexes, tools, implements, and much else needed for survival in a new land. Voyagers had planned prudently, as the Hawaiian archipelago had few cultivable or edible species. Most of what came to be grown and cultivated on the islands originated in the South Pacific, including taro, sweet potato, banana, coconut, and the paper mulberry tree (*wauke*), which Hawaiians used for clothing and sleeping mats.[13] Polynesians, of course, also brought their languages, deities, and customs.

About 1400, for reasons as yet unclear, voyages to and from Hawai'i came to an end. This is confirmed again by archaeology and the *mo'olelo*, which after 1400 refer exclusively to "people and places whose frame of geographic reference is limited to" the islands.[14] Isolation was only partly due to geography. Pacific trade winds played an even more important role

---

[12] Kirch, *How Chiefs Became Kings*, esp. 77–87; Kirch, *Shark Going Inland*, 126. See also Kame'eleihiwa, *Native Land*, 19–22; Hommon, *Ancient Hawaiian State*, 214–15. Court-appointed genealogists were responsible for memorizing genealogies that anthropologists have determined stretch back hundreds of years with remarkable accuracy. Ali'i relied on these genealogies to cement their authority.

[13] Kirch, *Feathered Gods*, chap. 9; Bushnell, *Gifts of Civilization*, 7.

[14] Kirch, *How Chiefs Became Kings*, 87. This isolation was highlighted by Tahitian navigator and priest Tupaia's 1769 Pacific Islands map that did not include Hawai'i, Rapa Nui (Easter Island), or New Zealand; see D'Arcy, *People of the Sea*, 123. Maritime technological innovations of the western and southern Pacific, such as the *drua* sailing vessel, did not make their way to Hawai'i (ibid., 142).

by blowing westbound Manila galleons (1565–1815) and other ships well south of the Hawaiian Islands en route to the Philippines and well north on their return to the Americas. Nor have archaeologists found evidence of post-1400 contact with the Line Islands or other Pacific archipelagos.[15] Besides the occasional driftwood from a shipwreck or a bird wildly off course, Hawai'i had few if any foreign visitors.[16]

Isolation had major implications for both the ecology and human society that developed between the fourteenth and eighteenth centuries.[17] In the late fifteenth century, a population boom resulting from agricultural innovations sharpened class distinctions. Human sacrifice began to be practiced at certain *heiau* (temples, altars), tapping criminals and members of a reviled, outcast class known as *kauā* (or *kauwā*).[18] By the late sixteenth century, the *ali'i* (chiefs) dressed, lived, and coupled in distinct fashion from the *maka'āinana* (commoners), who were now required to supply their overlords with tribute from the fruits of their agricultural labors. In an apt illustration of the mystification of power dynamics (and the blurring of the human and divine), the annual tribute was called

[15] Nearby atolls, such as Midway, were uninhabited. The closest island of any size, Kiritimati (Christmas Island), about 1,340 miles south, was uninhabited both when Hernando de Grijalva arrived in 1537 and when Cook landed in 1777.

[16] For the presence of small pieces of iron pried from driftwood, see James Cook, in Beaglehole, *Journals*, 3:285–86. Oral traditions suggest visits by mysterious foreigners before 1778 (e.g., Ellis, *Narrative of a Tour*, 446–50). For a tradition about a navigator (allegedly a Spaniard) who arrived with his sister long before Cook, married a Hawaiian chiefess, and remained on the islands the rest of his life, see Jarves, *Kiana*; Fornander, *Account of the Polynesian Race*, 2:109–10, 166; Mary Kawena Pukui, "Ancient Hulas of Kauai," in Barrère et al., *Hula: Historical Perspectives*, 74–89, esp. 81. The possibility of a Japanese or Spanish ship blowing off course to reach the islands has not been confirmed by archaeology. In a recent study, Chang argues that Islanders' knowledge and interest in exploring the broader world persisted throughout this period (*World and All the Things upon It*, chap. 1).

[17] Kirch, *Shark Going Inland*, 230. For arguments against isolation in Pacific history, see, e.g., Hau'ofa, "Our Sea of Islands"; D'Arcy, *People of the Sea*.

[18] The kauā have been little studied. Malo indicated that kauā status was hereditary but did not mention whether it was also permanent. (A special forehead tattoo suggests that possibly it was.) With the exception of *kauā kuapa'a* ("load-carrying outcasts"), these were not chattels or bound labor but a tainted, "abhorred," and "greatly dreaded" class who "lived apart" from other Hawaiians and were denied what we might call basic human rights (Malo, *Mo'olelo Hawai'i*, 303–10; unless otherwise noted, citations are to Langlas and Lyon's definitive translation, in manuscript; for errors and inconsistencies in earlier translations, see ibid., 5–7). Population size and distribution of kauā (before and after 1778) is also unknown. Kamakau believed that kauā – some of whom were buried alive with their masters – disappeared as a social class after the fall of the kapu system. On O'ahu, meanwhile, they were supposedly "lost in the shuffle" during the wars of the 1780s and '90s (Kamakau, *Ka Po'e Kahiko*, 8–9). See also *Kepelino's Traditions of Hawaii*, 142–46; Pukui and Elbert, *Hawaiian Dictionary*, s.v. "kauā, kauwā."

FIGURE 1.1 First Hawaiian-language map of the islands, drawn by a student at Lahainaluna Seminary, Maui. *"Na Mokupuni o Hawaii Nei."*
S. P. Kalama, 1837. Courtesy of Library of Congress, Geography and Map Division.

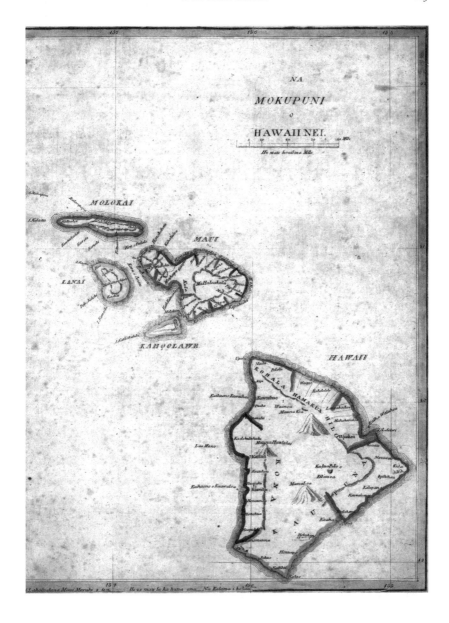

hoʻokupu, "to cause to grow."[19] Shortly, the "entire political economy" of the islands came to depend on this system of taxation.[20] Meanwhile, an etiological tale was developed to explain the existence of commoners who comprised 99 percent of the population.[21] All Hawaiians were once aliʻi, yet long separation caused some to "forget" their genealogies.[22] These were the makaʻāinana, "the people who tend the land."

Early nineteenth-century observers speculated that physical differences between aliʻi and makaʻāinana – in particular, the greater stature and girth of aliʻi – were the result of distinct lines of descent.[23] The obvious candidate for aliʻi ancestry, according to this line of thinking, were the "medieval" Tahitians who subjugated the original Marquesan settlers. Yet oral traditions and genetic studies as yet do not support the theory of distinct descent.[24] Instead, varying labor regimes, lifestyles, nutrition, and endogamous marriage among the aliʻi over many generations provide the best explanation for the body types observed by early visitors.

By the eighteenth century, Hawaiian society had come to be organized around an annual cycle divided between the war deity Kū and the agricultural deity Lono. Lono's season, from fall to spring, was dominated by farming and fertility rituals as well as dance and sporting contests. Lono's months also marked the season for the gathering of tribute. Roving from district to district accompanied by their train of subchiefs, the aliʻi "ate" the land; hence the common title, *aliʻi ʻai moku* (chief who eats the island/district). When the Pleiades disappeared below the horizon in March, Kū's season returned with military exercises, warfare, and the reestablishment of hierarchy.

Cook's men noted few cultural differences between the islands. After interacting with Hawaiians on five or more islands, Welsh surgeon David Samwell opined that Kauaʻi and Niʻihau Islanders "differ[ed] in nothing

---

[19] Kirch, *How Chiefs Became Kings,* 61–63, 73–76; Kirch, *Shark Going Inland,* 175–77, 191–99, 202–3, 207. For a similar Tongan tradition, see Campbell, *Island Kingdom,* 31.

[20] Kirch, *Shark Going Inland,* 232. See also Ralston, "Hawaii 1778–1854," esp. 22–25.

[21] In 1823, makaʻāinana accounted for "at least" 149,000 of the 150,000 "supposed, at present, to be the population of the group" (Stewart, *Private Journal,* 136). See also Kamakau, *Ruling Chiefs,* 222; Linnekin, *Sacred Queens,* 203.

[22] Malo, *Moʻolelo Hawaiʻi,* 285–86. For a similar tradition among the Stó:lō people of present-day British Columbia, see Carlson, *Power of Place, Problem of Time,* 79–86. The tendency of some scholars to naturalize class structures has led to some confusion about change over time; e.g., Dening, *Islands and Beaches,* 53; Kameʻeleihiwa, *Native Land,* chap. 2; Young, *Rethinking the Native Hawaiian Past,* xiv, 27–31.

[23] Freycinet, *Hawaii in 1819,* 53; Stewart, *Private Journal,* 126. For Hawaiian kinship in all its complexity, see Handy and Pukui, *Polynesian Family System;* Linnekin, *Sacred Queens.*

[24] Chiefs and commoners were "a single race" descended from the "same ancestors" (Malo, *Moʻolelo Hawaiʻi,* 268). See also Dibble, *History of the Sandwich Islands,* 87.

material, either in dress, Language or appearance" from those to the east.[25] Other differences were overlooked, yet it was obvious to Britons that these islands constituted a single nation. Hawaiians did not need to "imagine" their nation, as a popular scholarly line has it; they knew it in their bones.[26] If the culture seemed uniform to outsiders, political structures were not. Four major polities were headquartered on the large islands: Hawai'i, Maui, O'ahu, and Kaua'i. The latter three also enjoyed control over their smaller, less populous neighbors, exacting regular tribute and coordinating labor – Maui over Lāna'i and Kaho'olawe, O'ahu over Moloka'i, and Kaua'i over Ni'ihau. Only the Big Island (Hawai'i) featured a divided polity in the late precontact period with roughly eastern and western polities. When the *mō'ī* (king) Kalani'ōpu'u died in 1782, the Big Island was split into three political entities ruled respectively by Kalani'ōpu'u's brother, son, and nephew Pai'ea, who later became the first mō'ī of the unified archipelago, as Kamehameha (Lonely One).[27]

As Cook's ships approached the islands, Kalani'ōpu'u was in the midst of an attempted conquest of eastern Maui. It was not the first time a Big Island or Maui chief had tried to take a neighboring island, and it would not be the last.[28] Scholars and Hawaiians today refer to the islands' historic rulers as chiefs, but archaeologist Patrick Vinton Kirch makes a strong case for divine kingship.[29] More than intermediaries, ali'i were seen as exerting control over the *akua* (gods, deities) through ritual and the maintenance of cults.[30] Even after the introduction of Christianity in the 1820s, Hawaiians chiefs were reported giving orders to their new god rather than making petition.[31]

Hawaiian demography has been studied for more than a century.[32] Most of the important questions, including population size and distribution,

---

[25] Samwell, in Beaglehole, *Journals*, 3:1230. Samwell did identify differences in women's dress and the pronunciation of certain consonants, e.g., "k" for "t" on Ni'ihau, which probably dates back to the fourteenth century (Kirch, *Shark Going Inland*, 14).

[26] Anderson, *Imagined Communities*. For an alternative conceptualization, see Clifford, "Indigenous Articulations," esp. 481–82.

[27] Kuykendall, *Hawaiian Kingdom*, 1:29–38.

[28] Fornander, *Account of the Polynesian Race*, 2:156–57; Kirch, *How Chiefs Became Kings*, 104; Kirch, *Shark Going Inland*, 201.

[29] Kirch, *How Chiefs Became Kings*; Kirch, *Shark Going Inland*, 217–18. See also Kame'eleihiwa, *Native Land*, 26, 38, 40–49.

[30] Mykkänen, *Inventing Politics*, 29. See also Valeri, *Kingship and Sacrifice*, 225–26; Sahlins, *Islands of History*, 93.

[31] Emerson, *Pioneer Days in Hawaii*, 159.

[32] E.g., Alexander, *Brief History of the Hawaiian People*; Roberts, *Population Problems of the Pacific*.

average life expectancy, and infant mortality, are unresolved.[33] After decades of research, Kirch arrived at a serviceable estimate of half a million persons, perhaps more, upon the arrival of Cook.[34] To put this number in perspective, the population was two-thirds greater than the entire Native population of California at contact, a land mass twenty-five times its size.[35] Since much of the islands were locked up in high mountains, the population was also densely packed into valleys and foothills.

Islanders suffered from a range of diseases, including respiratory infections, rheumatic fever, osteomyelitis, arthritis, puerperal (childbed) fever, enteritis, sinusitis, mastoiditis, tooth decay, eye infections, ringworm, and ulcers. Congenital malformations such as spina bifida likely occurred on occasion. Archaeologists believe that Hawaiians also contracted zoonotic diseases by living with pigs (trichinosis), chickens (bird flu?), and dogs over several hundreds of years. Having run their course in the human population, these diseases would likely have enabled immunities to develop.[36] Some Hawaiian lives may have been shortened by excessive consumption of 'awa, or kava (*Piper methysticum*), a mildly narcotic plant consumed as a beverage. Modern studies suggest the possibility of liver damage from heavy kava consumption. Various eighteenth-century ali'i seem to have been wasting away as a result of the habit.[37] European visitors observed irritated eyes, weak or emaciated bodies, tremors, and

[33] Schmitt, "Differential Mortality in Honolulu"; Schmitt, *Historical Statistics of Hawaii*; Schmitt, "New Estimates of the Pre-Censal Population"; Gardner and Schmitt, "Ninety-Seven Years of Mortality"; Stannard, *Before the Horror*, 60–61; Kirch, "'Like Shoals of Fish'," 65–67; Cordy, "Reconstructing Hawaiian Population," 112, 125–27. Paleodemography is a notoriously speculative science; reliable figures for contact-era Hawaiian demography remain elusive.

[34] Kirch, *Shark Going Inland*, 152–70, esp. 168. See also Hommon, *Ancient Hawaiian State*, 11–12. Interestingly, half a million is the original figure arrived at by James King in 1779 before he revised it down to 400,000 (King, in Beaglehole, *Journals*, 3:620).

[35] Despite significant differences, Hawai'i and Alta California experienced roughly the same rate of population decline after European contact: 75 to 80 percent in fifty years. For California, see Cook and Borah, *Essays in Population History*. For a skeptical view of these figures, see Henige, *Numbers from Nowhere*.

[36] Kirch, *Feathered Gods*, 243–44; Leslie B. Marshall, "Disease Ecologies of Australia and Oceania," in Kiple, ed., *Cambridge World History of Human Disease*, 482–96, esp. 483; Bushnell, *Gifts of Civilization*, 30. King also observed a number of disabled individuals. It is difficult to say whether these conditions were the result of birth, disease, injury, lifestyle, or age. See James King, manuscript log on the *Resolution* (March 1779), PRO Admiralty 55/122, TNA.

[37] See, e.g., British descriptions of the high chiefs "Koah," Ke'eaumoku, Kahekili, and Kaumuali'i (King, in Beaglehole, *Journals*, 3:504; journal of Archibald Menzies, March 4, 1792, MS 32641, BL; Vancouver, in Lamb, *Voyage*, 3:857–58; Turnbull, *Voyage round the World*, 34–35).

scaly skin. Lt. James King went further, deeming fatalities to ʻawa consumption second only to venereal disease.[38] The *Resolution*'s captain noted that Kalaniʻōpuʻu himself was "totally debilitated and destroyed" by ʻawa, his eyes "full of Rheum," and his hands "shook to such a degree that it was with the utmost difficulty he could put any thing into his Mouth."[39] The mōʻī was also "intirely covered with a kind of Scaliness," which Lt. James Burney recognized as "Marks of a great Yava drinker."[40]

If precontact Hawaiʻi was not free from disease, neither was island ecology unaffected by humans. Like people the world over, Hawaiians cleared land for their use. They harnessed fire to enrich the soil and carve out farming plots. They encouraged the growth of certain wild plant species and discouraged others. They dug ponds and diverted streams for fish aquaculture. Such changes had obvious impacts on the non-human environment. Studies have found that nearly half of all endemic bird species and as many as a third of insect species went extinct as a result of introduced species and human manipulation of the natural environment.[41]

An agricultural powerhouse with a robust and fecund populace, Hawaiʻi had no metallurgy, pottery, ceramics, wheeled transport, or coal power. No cotton, wool, or hemp. (Textiles and sails were woven from finely shredded tree bark.) No cows, sheep, or goats – and, therefore, no dairy – and none of the cereal crops (rice, wheat, maize, barley, quinoa, amaranth, oats) that supply the bulk of global humanity's diet. Lacking a writing system, Hawaiʻi pulsed with non-written literacies of local practice and knowledge of the land and sea. Islanders were expert fishers, navigators, geologists, astronomers, and remarkably productive farmers, using tools of wood, stone, and bone.[42] Their sciences – particularly astronomy and navigation – evince a deep interest in their island world and what lay beyond it.[43]

Their principal food crop was taro (*kalo*), a starchy corm they mashed with water to form the nutritious pudding *poi*. Like maize in Mesoamerica, taro made and sustained human life; thus, the first humans were understood

[38] King, in Beaglehole, *Journals*, 3:612. See also King, manuscript log on the *Resolution* (March 1779), PRO Admiralty 55/122, TNA. King also believed that Hawaiians consumed ʻawa at rate much higher than other Polynesians.
[39] Charles Clerke, in Beaglehole, *Journals*, 3:597–98.   [40] James Burney, ibid., 3:512n4.
[41] Handy and Pukui, *Polynesian Family System*, 224; Bushnell, *Gifts of Civilization*, 174–75; Krech, *Ecological Indian*, 41; Kirch, *Shark Going Inland*, 110–11.
[42] Unlike Indigenous people across the Americas, Hawaiians did not rely much on the bow and arrow for hunting or warfare (Emerson, "Bow and Arrow in Hawaii," 52–55).
[43] E.g., Kapāʻanaokalāokeola Nākoa Oliveria, *Ancestral Places*; Kirch, *Kuaʻāina Kahiko*, 88–97; Chang, *World and All the Things upon It*, 1–23.

FIGURE 1.2 Waimea, Kaua'i. "An Inland View, in Atooi."
John Webber, 1778. Courtesy of State Library of New South Wales (a1673023).

in some mythological accounts as younger siblings to the taro plant.[44] The importance of taro also helps to explain why Lono, one of the four major akua of the Hawaiian pantheon, was an agricultural and fertility deity. With the exception of occasional drought and rare famine, Hawaiians ate "well enough ... to keep them in good nutritional health."[45] Taro in the form of poi was accompanied, when possible, by pork, fish, chicken (occasionally), sweet potato, yams, sea vegetables, sugarcane, coconut, bananas, and other fruit. However, select foods were off-limits to women and girls, including coconut, most cuts of pork, most varieties of banana, some fish, and delicacies such as green sea turtle.[46] Female and male were generally not permitted to eat or prepare food together.[47] Men had their own eating huts off-limits to women.

Like other societies, Hawai'i had a gender division of labor, which was more pronounced on the smaller western islands than on Hawai'i Island and Maui where agriculture required many hands. In general, men farmed

[44] Handy and Pukui, *Polynesian Family System*, 3–4, 212; Handy et al., *Native Planters in Old Hawaii*, 74–76.

[45] Bushnell, *Gifts of Civilization*, 49. The same was true of Tonga and other Polynesian groups before European contact (Campbell, *Island Kingdom*, 26, 31). For precontact famine, passed down in the mo'olelo, see Kirch, *Shark Going Inland*, 201, 208–9. For other episodes, see Schmitt, "Famine Mortality in Hawaii."

[46] For the kapu on green sea turtle, see Bell, "Log of the *Chatham*," *Honolulu Mercury* 1 (Sept. 1929): 19.

[47] Some meals may have been taken in common by maka'āinana in *hale noa* (free houses) on Maui; see Kirch, *Kua'āina Kahiko*, 126–33.

taro and built canoes and dwellings, women made clothes and mats, raised children, and performed other domestic tasks. Yet gender division of labor does not explain why females were forbidden from eating with men. Some scholars argue that females were considered to have a "polluting" effect in Polynesian culture; the word is *haumia*, "defilement." Menstruating women, in particular, were thought to be dangerous and thus confined to special huts during their period.[48] Other scholars posit that females had too much spiritual power to risk close contact with males in intimate situations like eating.[49] Segregated eating was widespread in Polynesia, with women regularly denied foods offered in sacrifice to the deities. In Hawai'i, this included pork, coconut, banana, and certain fish. Importantly, the *'ai kapu* (literally, "eating taboo") constituted one of the principal religious laws of the islands. It was also among the first laws to be broken in the eighteenth century despite the risk of capital punishment.

Anthropologist Marshall Sahlins noted the "essential ambiguity" of women in Hawaiian society, with female "powers of defiling the god" being necessary for survival of the race.[50] In fact, the gender divide cut deeper than that. The Hawaiian language had no discrete word or phrase for gender roles; kapu is the nearest approximation.[51] In this sense, the 'ai kapu was the social structure that both defined and also controlled gender and sexuality. Gender was fundamental to religious practice and understandings. Not only in Hawai'i but across Polynesia, men and women observed different deities.[52] Cook himself recognized this while touring a heiau on Kaua'i. Cook's guides identified two large *ki'i* (wooden idols) as

---

[48] Malo, *Mo'olelo Hawai'i*, 218; cf. Malo, *Hawaiian Antiquities*, 29. See also Dening, *Islands and Beaches*, 88–90. Regarding the menses kapu, Kamakau explained that the akua were "nauseated by bloody things" (*hoopailua ke akua i na mea koko*); S. M. Kamakau, "*Ka Moolelo Hawaii*," *Ke Au Okoa*, Nov. 10, 1870 (my translation). On the other hand, blood was life ("*he ola ke koko*") and therefore sacred (Handy and Pukui, *Polynesian Family System*, 11).

[49] Kame'eleihiwa, *Native Land*, 33–40; Linnekin, *Sacred Queens*, 5. For more on gender and kapu, see Chapter 4.

[50] Sahlins, "Goodbye to *Tristes Tropes*," 9. For a discussion of these vexing issues, see Linnekin, *Sacred Queens*, 13–35; Kame'eleihiwa, *Native Land*, 33–40.

[51] Chun, *No Nā Mamo*, 289. For the disputed origins of the kapu system, see Malo, *Mo'olelo Hawai'i*, 214–21. For gender and *tapu* among the Māori, see Ballantyne, *Entanglements of Empire*, 11–12.

[52] Banks, *Endeavor* journal, 1:425, 430, SLNSW; Malo, *Mo'olelo Hawai'i*, 331–36, 378; Chamisso, in Barratt, *Russian View of Honolulu*, 213–14; William Richards journal, June 22, 1823, ABCFM Papers. I follow Langlas and Lyon in avoiding the term *worship*; "observe" or "hold services" is closer to the meaning of *ho'omana* (Malo, *Mo'olelo Hawai'i*, 163n7). For differences between ali'i and maka'āinana sacred practices, see Mykkänen, *Inventing Politics*, 28–29.

FIGURE 1.3 Heiau at Waimea. Note the androgynous ki'i, in marked contrast to masculine representations of Kū. "The Inside of the House, in the Morai, in Atooi."
John Webber, 1778. Courtesy of State Library of New South Wales (a1673021).

"Eatua no Veheina" (*he/kele akua no wahine*), which Cook translated as "Godess's" but which could also mean "deities of women," "deities for women," or "women's deities" (Fig. 1.3).[53] Interestingly, Cook "doubted" that the people actually worshipped these particular idols, "as they had no objections to our going to and examining them." In fact, Cook's Hawaiian guides were all male and probably had no use for these particular ki'i. Yet women did, as evidenced by their "offerings": strips of kapa cloth hung from the ki'i as well as a "heap of plant" placed before and between them.[54]

---

[53] Cook, in Beaglehole, *Journals*, 3:271. The versatile Hawaiian word *no* typically functions as a preposition and can mean any of the following: "Of, for, because of, belonging to, in behalf of, honoring, to, ... from, resulting from, concerning, about" (Pukui and Elbert, *Hawaiian Dictionary*, s.v. "no"). For Cook's possible mistranslation, see Beaglehole, *Journals*, 3:271n2; Chun, *No Nā Mamo*, 198–99.

[54] Cook, in Beaglehole, *Journals*, 3:271. Exceptions to this rule include a young royal advisor who served as guardian of the female deity Kihawahine in the 1810s ("John Ii's Speech, Delivered at Rev. H. Bingham's Church," *Polynesian*, May 1, 1841).

Numerous scholars have observed that kinship structures afforded Hawaiian women greater social freedoms and, for elites, more political opportunities than their counterparts across the globe.[55] But in other respects women were rendered second-class subjects by a hierarchical and patriarchal society. They were also hardly insulated from physical violence, as the following pages show.

NEW CANOES

While the initial meeting of Britons and Hawaiians at Kaua'i was cordial, relations took a turn for the worse the following year at the Big Island when Cook and thirty or more Hawaiians were killed in a clash at Kealakekua Bay. While the incident has been examined from many angles, hostility related to introduced diseases has scarcely been considered. Syphilis and gonorrhea do not explain the multifarious nature of the Hawaiian–British encounter, yet they bore importantly on the events of 1779.

On Cook's first visit, the fleet had docked at Waimea Bay on Kaua'i, where they remained about two weeks, enjoying the fruits of the island and establishing good relations with local people whom they immediately recognized as cultural cousins to the "Indians" of the South Pacific.[56] Cook learned that he was to be venerated at Kaua'i as a paramount chief: "The very instant I leapt ashore, they all fell flat on their faces, and remained in that humble posture till I made signs to them to rise."[57] This same deference was shown to Cook repeatedly on Kaua'i, as it was a year later on Hawai'i Island. Other British officers also reported the *kapu moe* (prostration taboo) in their presence at O'ahu and Maui.[58] When they returned from the Northwest Coast in November 1778, Cook and his men were greeted by the largest crowds they had seen in the Pacific: "All the Shore of the bay was covered with people," Cook wrote, and they swarmed the ships "like shoals of fish."[59] Corporal John Ledyard of

---

[55] Linnekin, *Sacred Queens*; Grimshaw, *Paths of Duty*; Kame'eleihiwa, *Native Land*; Thigpen, *Island Queens and Mission Wives*.

[56] Cook, in Beaglehole, *Journals*, 3:263–64.

[57] Ibid., 3:269. See also King, Jan. 20, 1778, manuscript log on the *Resolution*, PRO Admiralty 55/116, HSA.

[58] See, e.g., King, in Beaglehole, *Journals*, 3:586; Samwell, ibid., 3:1221. Note that the kapu moe continued to be observed after Cook's killing. Cook apparently had not witnessed this practice earlier in Polynesia (Thomas, *Discoveries*, 356).

[59] Cook, in Beaglehole, *Journals*, 3:490–91.

Connecticut estimated 15,000 people had congregated as the fleet searched for a safe harbor along the treacherous lava-bed shores of the Big Island: "The beach, the surrounding rocks, the tops of houses, the branches of trees and adjacent hills were all covered" with people. There were "shouts of joy" from the men, "women dancing and clapping their hands."[60]

Lines of communication had clearly been open. Cook had not visited the Big Island and knew nothing of its existence. Big Islanders, by contrast, were eager to engage the "new canoes" that had touched at Kaua'i and Ni'ihau the previous winter.[61] Nor was there any indication that the people resented the Britons' killing of a Kaua'i man (who may have been a chief) back in January, though Big Islanders mentioned it to the crew, as proof that they were aware of the expedition's first visit.[62] Most remarkable to the Britons was the Islanders' charity, which seemed to know no bounds. The mariners were fêted and fed to the gills.

Sahlins characterized this cultural encounter as a "historical metaphor of a mythical reality," meaning that people attended to the Britons' return with complex cultural understandings informed more by their own religious and historical traditions than by the actual days' mundane events.[63] In anthropological terms, structure trumped event. While few of these meanings were grasped by Cook's men, it is plausible, as Sahlins argued and as many Hawaiian writers and historians before him stated flatly, that some Hawai'i Islanders viewed Cook as their returning agricultural and fertility akua Lono.[64] The Lono cult was robust on the Big Island, and a number of circumstances led people to view Cook's return as fulfillment of prophecy.[65] Nor was this phenomenon limited to the Big Island. Nineteenth-century Hawaiian historian Samuel Manaiakalani Kamakau noted that Kaua'i Islanders made references to both Lono and Kū upon

[60] Ledyard, *Journal of Captain Cook's Last Voyage*, 103.
[61] Malo, *Mo'olelo Hawai'i*, 421. For the enthusiastic reception, see Ledyard, *Journal of Captain Cook's Last Voyage*, 103–4.
[62] Rickman, *Journal of Captain Cook's Last Voyage*, 223; King, in Beaglehole, *Journals*, 3:497. For the killing of this man, see Williamson, ibid., 3:1348–49.
[63] Sahlins, *Historical Metaphors*, 11; Sahlins, *Islands of History*, 4.
[64] E.g., Kahananui, *Ka Mooolelo Hawaii*, 167–68, 171–73; Kamakau, *Ka Po'e Kahiko*, 54; Kamakau, *Ruling Chiefs*, 92–104; Pukui, *'Ōlelo No'eau*, 139–40.
[65] Cook's return mirrored some Lono prophecies; notably, his arrival during the *makahiki* (new year/harvest festival) and his clockwise circumnavigation of the Big Island, propelled by white sails that looked like Lono's ritual streamers. Elaborate ceremonies were performed on shore to honor or propitiate "Cook-Lono." For early historical accounts of this event, see Kotzebue, *New Voyage*, 2:179–86; Malo, *Mo'olelo Hawai'i*, 442. See also Sahlins, *Historical Metaphors*, 17–28; Kirch, *Shark Going Inland*, 250–64.

the newcomers' arrival the previous year. These rumors swiftly crossed the islands.[66]

The Cook-as-Lono tradition gathered steam after the dramatic events at Kealakekua Bay, culminating in the killing of the explorer and dozens of Islanders. Eight days after the melee, Samwell recorded that the people had a "Notion that Capt" Cook as being Orono [Lono] will come amongst them again in a short time."[67] Eleven years later, a British sea captain at the Big Island was asked when Cook-Lono would return.[68] A close reading of the expedition journals suggests that before his killing, Cook was viewed by Big Islanders as more or less equal to their own mōʻī Kalaniʻōpuʻu and that both leaders shared in the *mana* (spiritual power) of Lono, whose ritual season it was.[69] The previous year Kauaʻi Islanders also seem to have viewed Cook as equal in rank to their mōʻī.[70] The fact that the mōʻī and other paramount chiefs *(aliʻi nui)* in this period enjoyed a status as divine kings only complicates matters. Suffice it to say that local people brought complex, dynamic cultural traditions to bear on their encounter with newcomers, during and especially after the fact. Principal among these were notions of spiritual power.

Culture myths were not the only potent force in the Hawaiian–British encounter. While Cook's ships were probably no more disease-ridden than any other eighteenth-century expedition, the array of pathogens they carried into the Pacific was considerable.[71] Most of the diseases they carried would not have been fatal to Cook's men. In fact, the *Discovery* and *Resolution* lost only a dozen men between 1776 and 1780, of whom five were killed in the clash at Kealakekua Bay. The toll on the Hawaiian side was much higher and would grow exponentially over the course of a generation. Besides pathogens, Cook's ships were infested with vermin

---

[66] Kamakau, *Ruling Chiefs*, 92–95. For other Polynesians initially viewing newcomers in supernatural terms, see Sahlins, "Cosmologies of Capitalism," esp. 412, 440–41; O'Malley, *Meeting Place*, 19, 25.

[67] Samwell, in Beaglehole, *Journals*, 3:1217.

[68] Colnett, *Journal of Captain James Colnett*, 220. For Big Island makaʻāinana allegedly praying to Cook-Lono five decades later, see Lorenzo Lyons to Rufus Anderson, Sept. 6, 1833, HMCS. A Hawaiian-language newspaper obituary for the wife of James Cook identified her as "Lono wahine" (Lono's wife); see *"No Ka Poe Kahiko," Ke Kumu Hawaii*, May 25, 1836.

[69] For local people associating Cook *and* Kalaniʻōpuʻu (and his family) with Lono, see Samwell, in Beaglehole, *Journals*, 3:1161, 1170, 1184, 1201, 1217.

[70] King, Jan. 24, 1778, manuscript log on the *Resolution*, PRO Admiralty 55/116, HSA. In Thomas's terms, Cook was viewed as "not only sacred but dangerously so" (*Discoveries*, 356).

[71] Igler, *Great Ocean*, 44.

when they arrived at Hawai'i. On the *Resolution* cockroaches ran "so thick you would think the Ship Alive."[72] The *Discovery* was "much pesterd" with rats.[73] If these pests did not step, swim, or fly ashore in 1778 or 1779, they certainly made a comfortable home in Hawai'i by 1790. The Old World rat elbowed out its Polynesian cousin within a matter of years, just as it had done in the Americas a few centuries earlier.[74]

Having witnessed the spread of venereal disease on his first two Pacific voyages, Cook tried to prevent a similar outcome at Kaua'i and Ni'ihau.[75] The odds of success were long:

I gave orders that no Women, on any account whatever were to be admitted on board the Ships, I also forbid all manner of connection with them, and ordered that none [of the sailors] who had the vener[e]al upon them should go out of the ships. But whether these regulations had the desired effect or no[,] time can only discover. ... [T]he oppertunities and inducements to an intercourse between the sex, are ... too many to be guarded against.[76]

Cook's sexual quarantine – not the first during his three voyages – is confirmed by other expedition logs.[77] Ships' surgeons were ultimately responsible for determining who would be given shore leave and who would not. Unfortunately, as Cook rightly surmised, both gonorrhea and syphilis are spread without visible symptoms, so the surgeons' examinations would have caught only a portion of the infected. Regardless, Cook's orders were promptly defied. Not only William Bradley but other sailors were punished for going on shore without leave.[78]

Within hours of their return to Hawaiian waters in November 1778, Cook's ships were approached by Islanders off Maui: "Three of the Natives have apply'd to us, for help in their great distress," wrote King. "[T]hey had a Clap, their Penis was much swell'd, & inflamed."[79] King

[72] Bayly, in Beaglehole, *Journals*, 3:238–39n3. For the "multitude of cockroaches" in Honolulu by 1828, see Boelen, *Merchant's Perspective*, 67.
[73] William Harvey, in Beaglehole, *Journals*, 3:243n1. Kamakau thought the ships brought the first fleas to Kaua'i in 1778, but other scholars have argued for a later introduction (Kamakau, *Ruling Chiefs*, 95; cf. Haas, "Flea in Early Hawaii").
[74] Crosby, *Ecological Imperialism*, 190–93.
[75] For Cook's failure to prevent venereal infection at Tahiti in 1769, see Wharton, ed., *Captain Cook's Journal*, 76–77.
[76] Cook, in Beaglehole, *Journals*, 3:265–66.
[77] E.g., King, Jan. 20, 1778, manuscript log on the *Resolution*, PRO Admiralty 55/116, HSA.
[78] Beaglehole, *Journals*, 3:511n2.
[79] King, ibid., 3:498. Sahlins began his classic essay on the Hawaiian-British encounter with this scene but made little of the impact of venereal disease (*Islands of History*, 1–3).

added that "the manner in which these innocent People complained to us, seem'd to me to shew that they consider'd us as the Original authors." Three days later King noticed a man whose infection was months old: "[S]ome parts seemd heald, but in other places the Morbid matter was issuing out[;] this person had an emaciated countenance, haggard eyes, & it was a pain to him to drag along his body."[80]

Cook's ships had arrived off the windward (eastern) coasts of Maui and Hawai'i, neither of which islands they had visited earlier. Nevertheless, ship surgeon David Samwell wrote that "the Disease" – almost certainly gonorrhea – was "pretty universal among them."[81] *Discovery* midshipman Edward Riou heard that

many of the natives had been complaining ... onboard the Resolution of the Venereal disease – one or two of them were examined by the Surgeon who Confirmed it, – they were asked about it & said a great many men & women were afflicted with it on Shore, and spoke of the Isle Atowi [Kaua'i], as if we had left it at that place the Last year.[82]

Samwell noted that "many" Maui Islanders "were infected with Venereal disease & at their own request they had some medicines given to them, for which purpose it seems they came off to the ship."[83] It is not clear what these medicines consisted of – perhaps mercurials – or how Hawaiians employed them, though King wrote that the infected "readily comprehended the manner they should be us'd."[84] There is no indication that British officers examined Hawaiian women as they did men, though both sexes off the coast of Maui were afflicted. Soon enough, infected Hawaiians were spreading gonorrhea back to Britons: "Many of our people contract[ed] it after being here a little time."[85]

Just days before the killing of Cook in February 1779, the surgeon Samwell recorded Hawai'i Islanders treating venereal infections with an herbal remedy. He doubted it would help. Instead he anticipated their "cleanliness" and "simple Manner of living" would serve as

---

"Clap" for gonorrhea dates back to the sixteenth century, from the French *clapoir*, for venereal bubo (*Shorter Oxford English Dictionary*, 5th ed., s.v. "clap").

[80] King, in Beaglehole, *Journals*, 3:498, 500.

[81] Samwell, ibid., 3:1151. Bushnell, a physician, noted the "unmistakable" signs of acute gonorrhea in King's description, "practically diagnostic to anyone who has seen" it (*Gifts of Civilization*, 142).

[82] Riou, in Beaglehole, *Journals*, 3:474–75n5.   [83] Samwell, ibid., 3:1152.

[84] King, ibid., 3:500.   [85] Samwell, ibid., 3:1151.

antidotes.[86] There is no indication in the British logs or in oral traditions of what these herbal remedies consisted.[87] Samwell was astonished to find that venereal infection had spread across the archipelago in less than ten months. In fact he "found the Disorder much more common" at the Big Island and Maui, despite the fact that Europeans had yet to set foot there.[88] Clerke believed that venereal infections "rage[d] more violently" at the islands than elsewhere in the Pacific and that the "dreadfull Symptoms operate[d] more expeditiously."[89] Clerke attributed this fact to Islanders' salt intake.[90] A better explanation would focus on patterns of disease ecology across the far-flung archipelagos of the eastern Pacific.

For his part, Cook "knew of no other way" that Hawaiians could have been infected than by the actions of his own crew. He was forced to admit that the "evil I meant to prevent ... had already got amongst them."[91] All but one of Cook's officers and crewmembers who left journals agreed with this assessment. Riou determined that "we ourselves [have] entailed on these poor, Unhappy people an everlasting and Miserable plague."[92] Clerke could only heap curses upon his "infernal and dissolute" charges: for the "gratification of [their] present passion" sailors would "entail universal destruction upon the whole of the Human Species."[93]

---

[86] Ibid., 3:1186.

[87] In the nineteenth century, Hawaiians treated syphilis and gonorrhea with dozens of plant and mineral substances, including morning glory, 'ōhi'a, kukui, pandanus, 'awa, sugar cane, and even clay. See "Records of medical work done by Dr. Ohule," Hawaiian Ethnographic Notes 1:1500–81, BM; "A Concoction for Venereal Disease in Men," n.d., HEN Archives 68–69, BM.

[88] Samwell, "Observations, Respecting the Introduction of the Venereal Disease," 31.

[89] Clerke, in Beaglehole, *Journals*, 3:576.

[90] King similarly attributed the prevalence of "boils" to excessive salt intake (manuscript log on the *Resolution* [March 1779], PRO Admiralty 55/122, TNA).

[91] Cook, in Beaglehole, *Journals*, 3:474. When a group of sailors left on shore at Ni'ihau found their way to sexual partners, "the very thing happened that I had above all others wished to prevent" (ibid., 3:276). See also Williamson, ibid., 3:1349–50. For Cook's acknowledgment that his men spread venereal disease at New Zealand and Tonga, see Thomas, *Discoveries*, xxiv–xxvii, 331–32.

[92] Riou, in Beaglehole, *Journals*, 3:474–75. At least eight accounts of Cook's third voyage were published in the 1780s. Of these authors, ironically only the surgeon Samwell, who recorded more sexual liaisons than anyone, questioned whether Cook's men had spread venereal disease to Hawai'i; he did so only after the fact. As surgeon, Samwell was responsible for ensuring only healthy men gained access to Islanders; thus, he was a partisan on this question. See Samwell, "Observations, Respecting the Introduction of the Venereal Disease," 29–34.

[93] Clerke, in Beaglehole, *Journals*, 3:576.

"LEFT A DISORDER"

Relations at Kealakekua Bay soured after Cook's men broke an aliʻi-imposed kapu on their encampment. While commoners seemed to pay no mind to the men slipping out of camp to find sexual partners, the chiefs "thought differently, they knew it was a breach of covenant." Ledyard wrote that this was the "beginning of our subsequent misfortunes, and acknowledged to be so afterwards when it was too late to revert the consequences."[94] Discord, that is to say, began with a breach of kapu imposed to keep Hawaiians and Britons (perhaps officers in particular) apart on shore or, at the very least, to keep the Britons under aliʻi authority. By contrast, with the exception of the intermittent kapu placed on the ships – typically upon the visit of an aliʻi[95] – Islanders were free to enjoy Britons as they pleased aboard the ships. It is therefore unlikely that the venereal outbreak was the *cause* of the aliʻi-imposed kapu on the British encampment, since if the people would not get infected on shore, they obviously could (and did) aboard the ships.

The events that followed are murky. A series of insults and minor thefts prompted local aliʻi to assemble war canoes. A British cutter was apparently stolen, for which Cook tried to seize the mōʻī Kalaniʻōpuʻu as collateral. This infuriated the people. Exasperated and perhaps afraid for his life, Cook more than once discharged his musket, killing a bystander. The people then fell upon the navigator, killing him and four of his men. The Britons responded by torching a Hawaiian village and decapitating a few of the fallen Hawaiians as trophies.[96] Despite this precarious state of affairs, relations between the two sides thawed quickly.[97] During the battle itself, "a few Girls" were "on board both Ships all this day."[98] One of these girls (or women) looked upon the burning village – with

[94] Ledyard, *Journal of Captain Cook's Last Voyage*, 109. This breach was "at first done by the officers"; then "our soldiers and sailors saw it and practised it" (ibid.). Samwell interpreted the situation somewhat differently: "The Gentlemen who sleep on shore are mortified" by the kapu, he wrote, "as no Women will on any account come to them. They [the seamen] have offered a large Bribe to the Priest to let a Girl or two come in [to the encampment] at Night, but he was proof against the Temptation & informed them that if any [females] were seen in the place they would be killed." Nevertheless, he noted in the following sentence that "the Women are permitted to come on board the Ship" (Samwell, in Beaglehole, *Journals*, 3:1161).
[95] Samwell, in Beaglehole, *Journals*, 3:1168, 1171.
[96] Ibid., 3:1194–1201, 1212. Like Thomas I see little evidence of Cook growing more violent or irrational, as some have argued, over the course of the voyage (*Discoveries*, 376–77, 396–97).
[97] King, in Beaglehole, *Journals*, 3:612–13.   [98] Samwell, ibid., 3:1204.

people "flying from their Houses all round the Bay, and carrying their Canoes & household Goods on their backs" – and said "maitai [*maika'i*] or very fine."[99] If it is difficult to imagine a kinswoman approving of the destruction of her village, a number of women expressed a desire for alliances with the newcomers, with some directly opposing their chiefs. Hawaiians also continued to trade with the fleet during and after the violence at Kealakekua Bay.

Eight days after the melee, the fleet headed north, commanded now by Charles Clerke. Sailing by Kaho'olawe, Maui, Lāna'i, Moloka'i, and O'ahu, the fleet approached Kaua'i, their initial landfall the previous January. With the ships approaching, Islanders began to climb aboard. Clerke observed "many" people "miserably afflicted" with venereal infections, "which they accuse us of introducing among them during our last visit. They say it does not go away, that they have no Antidote for it, but that they grow worse and worse ... till it totally destroys them."[100] Ledyard concurred that the venereal disease (that "we had ... spread") made the "most shocking ravages."[101] Nevertheless, a steady stream of women and girls continued to approach the ships. The general mood at Waimea, however, was changed from the previous year.[102] Only eleven days since the violence at the Big Island, "an injured and exasperated people" assembled to meet the Britons. They had "heard of our transactions at Owyhee" and knew "us to be no more than men like themselves" – evidence of how fast news traveled across the archipelago. Relations were so sour that the "only hope" Britons had of watering was by "bestowing great presents on all the chiefs" and by the use of "mere force." Had Kaua'i chiefs not protected the foreigners, Islanders "certainly would have attacked us," wrote Ledyard.[103] Lt. James King observed that the "smallest error on our side might have been fatal to us."[104]

Unprompted, one man told the Britons that they had "left a disorder" among the women, "which had killd several of them as well as Men." The man himself was "infectd with the Venereal disease, & describ'd in feeling terms the havock it had made, & its pains &c."[105] If King's informant was

[99] Ibid., 3:1213.   [100] Clerke, ibid., 3:576.
[101] Ledyard, *Journal of Captain Cook's Last Voyage*, 155.
[102] See Samwell, in Beaglehole, *Journals*, 3:1222–23; James Burney, journal on HMS *Discovery*, March 1–7, 1779, SLNSW.
[103] Ledyard, *Journal of Captain Cook's Last Voyage*, 156.
[104] Cook and King, *Voyage to the Pacific Ocean*, 3:89–95.
[105] King, March 1, 1779, manuscript log on the *Resolution*, PRO Admiralty 55/122, TNA. See also King, in Beaglehole, *Journals*, 3:585–86.

correct about Hawaiian fatalities to venereal infection, this suggests Cook's men had spread not only gonorrhea (rarely fatal) but also syphilis in 1778 – a fact that would be confirmed in 1786.

Summing up the health concerns of Islanders, King remarked that "the Venereal is certainly now, the Worst . . . They did not appear to me to have any name for it, & at last calld it sometimes – – – – (burning)."[106] Where the dashes appear in the previous sentence, King left a blank; perhaps he did not know the Hawaiian term or meant to add it later.[107] Visitors elsewhere in Polynesia heard local terms for venereal disease. The naturalist on Cook's first Pacific voyage gathered that the Tahitian word was something like "rottenness."[108]

Until 1838 Western medicine was sharply divided over whether syphilis and gonorrhea were separate diseases or different manifestations of the same disease. It was not uncommon for sailors to carry both infections. Active tuberculosis, lymphatic filariasis (elephantiasis), pubic lice (crabs), and even scabies could also present with genital symptoms. Interestingly, Hawaiian terms for syphilis and gonorrhea suggest that Native physicians opted for the differential diagnosis (Appendix A). Islanders developed various names for gonorrhea, one of which was *kulu*, "to drip, leak, or trickle." The primary manifestation of the disease is a milky pus discharged from the urethra along with inflammation of the genitals.[109] Genital symptoms are more prevalent in males than in females for two reasons: first, the discharge of matter from the penis tends to cause greater discomfort while also being more visible; second, gonorrheal infection in females tends to congregate in the cervix rather than the vulva. Female cases are, for this reason, frequently asymptomatic. Yet both men and women can be "silent" carriers of the disease, which of course only contributes to its spread. In modern populations the probability of gonorrheal infection in male-to-female transmission is about 50 percent for a

---

[106] King, manuscript log on the *Resolution* (March 1779), PRO Admiralty 55/122, TNA.
[107] The Hawaiian language has a dozen or more words for "burn" and at least a half dozen for "sting" (Pukui and Elbert, *Hawaiian Dictionary*, s.v. "burn," "sting").
[108] Banks, *Endeavor* journal, 1:413, SLNSW. By 1773 some Tahitians called venereal disease "*Apa no Pretane* (English disease)" (Cook, *Three Voyages*, 3:190).
[109] Once the gonococcus bacteria takes root in the bloodstream, other problems may ensue: pharyngitis (from oral sex), proctitis (from anal sex), arthritis, dermatitis, and conjunctivitis (typically by transmission from hands to eyes); see Richard B. Rothenberg, "Gonorrhea," in Kiple, ed., *Cambridge World History of Human Disease*, 756–63.

single sexual encounter; from female to male, the percentage is closer to 22 percent per encounter.[110]

Left untreated, gonorrhea is a particular risk to newborns, who can become infected as they pass through the birth canal. The most common manifestation of this mode of infection is gonococcal ophthalmia, a painful, debilitating eye condition that can lead to scarring or blindness in the infant.[111] American missionary Charles Stewart later witnessed a case in which the infant's "[eye]lids were protruded on the cheeks, and swollen to the bigness of pigeons' eggs, while they throbbed almost to bursting with inflammation."[112] Barring treatment for gonorrhea, women and girls can develop any of several pelvic inflammatory diseases (PID), such as salpingitis, oophoritus, and endometritis.[113] PID consists of inflammation or scarring of the lining of the uterus, fallopian tubes, and/or ovaries, a result of the gonococcus traveling up into the reproductive organs.[114] PID tends to cause abdominal discomfort or pain and can lead to ectopic pregnancy and/or miscarriage. A study in Sweden found that sterility occurred in 12 to 16 percent of patients after a single episode of PID. After three episodes, the percentage rose to 60 percent.[115] Since gonorrhea and syphilis were new diseases, complications were much more severe for Hawaiians than they were for the newcomers who passed the gonococcus from ship to shore.[116]

Venereal syphilis is marked by three distinct stages. The first, occurring about three weeks after infection, consists of a relatively painless chancre at the site of infection, typically in the genital or anal region or on the mouth, with few other symptoms.[117] The three-week latency period is significant for the Hawaiian–British encounter. Assuming the typical latency period, Islanders on Kaua'i and Ni'ihau presumably would not have experienced symptoms until Cook's fleet departed for the Northwest Coast. Second-stage syphilis occurs six to twelve weeks after the first sign of infection. At this point the *Treponema* bacteria enters the bloodstream. Symptoms, which can be mild, include a patterned skin rash, typically on

[110] Ibid., 760.   [111] Ibid., 757.   [112] Stewart, *Private Journal*, 200–1.

[113] The sex trade involved a significant number of girls. For young girls in the Marquesan sex trade, see Dening, *Islands and Beaches*, 127.

[114] Thomas Benedek, "Gonorrhea and Chlamydia," in Byrne, ed., *Encyclopedia of Pestilence, Pandemics, and Plagues*, 1:230–33, esp. 231.

[115] Rothenberg, "Gonorrhea," 757.

[116] See Stannard, "Disease and Infertility," esp. 338–39; Bushnell, *Gifts of Civilization*, 30.

[117] Stefan Wörhrl and Alexandra Geusau, "Syphilis," in Byrne, ed., *Encyclopedia of Pestilence, Pandemics, and Plagues*, 2:688–91.

the chest, back, palms of the hands, and soles of the feet. In a majority of cases, moist sores appear in the genital or anal region.[118] Filled with the *Treponema* bacteria, these sores are highly infectious. Second-stage syphilis can involve any of the body's organs, with possible effects on the central nervous system and in red-blood cell production. A second latent phase follows. In as many as two-thirds of untreated cases, "late latent syphilis" can last for life. The remaining cases enter the gruesome tertiary stage, marked by granulomas (or gummas) of the skin, liver, brain, or testes. Slightly less than 10 percent of untreated victims of tertiary syphilis develop heart disease; 6.5 percent develop diseases of the central nervous system.[119]

It is not clear whether Hawaiians progressed more quickly to tertiary syphilis or whether the primary and secondary stages were more aggressive or debilitating than for populations in which the disease was long resident. The latter possibility is likely.[120] In any case, syphilis was highly infectious and shortly affected the health and fertility of countless Islanders.

Modern medicine identifies three other distinct treponemal diseases: endemic syphilis, yaws, and pinta. None of these diseases were present in Hawai'i, and none of them have (or had) the consequences of their venereal cousin. None are sexually transmitted, and none threaten fertility or can be transmitted during pregnancy or birth.[121] Importantly, each offers a degree of immunity to the others. The presence or absence of yaws, in particular, had profound consequences for Pacific Islanders in the era of Cook that scholars are just beginning to grasp. Endemic to Tonga, Sāmoa, Tahiti and other South Pacific islands, yaws seems to have made few if any inroads into Hawai'i and New Zealand. Hawaiians and Māori were thus highly susceptible to venereal syphilis upon the arrival of Europeans. Endemic yaws undoubtedly saved scores of lives in Oceania after 1778 by conferring a degree of immunity to venereal syphilis. Not only was yaws no threat to fertility or reproduction, it also cannot be passed in utero like venereal syphilis. While archaeologists are divided on

---

[118] Powell and Cook, "Treponematosis," 11; Wörhrl and Geusau, "Syphilis," 2:689.

[119] Wörhrl and Geusau, "Syphilis," 2:689. See also Powell and Cook, "Treponematosis," 11. Syphilitic gummas were often confused with leprosy and lymphatic filariasis (elephantiasis); see Chapter 4.

[120] As late as 1837, physicians chronicled the ravages of tertiary syphilis (Chapin, "Remarks on the Venereal Disease"). By the time Hawai'i's first hospital opened in 1859, 60 percent of the 765 patients to be treated in its first four months of operation were infected with venereal disease (Stannard, "Disease and Infertility," 341).

[121] Powell and Cook, "Treponematosis," 30.

the question of yaws in precontact Hawai'i, it is clear that Islanders' treponemal immunities were insufficient to ward off venereal syphilis.[122] The same is true of tuberculosis, which may have been endemic before contact but, if so, offered little if any resistance to the reintroduced disease.

Perhaps the greatest concern for Hawaiians was the tendency of the *Treponema* to cross the placenta and infect the fetus. Congenital syphilis causes major disabilities and developmental problems in survivors, which is why pregnant women today are routinely tested for syphilis.[123] Later visitors to Hawai'i described children with these afflictions. In many cases – it is hard to know how many – *Treponema* infection would have caused miscarriage, premature birth, stillbirth, or the death of an infant. In probably still more cases, infected Hawaiian adults were simply unable to become pregnant in the first place. The prevalence of childless adults and couples presented unique challenges in nineteenth-century Hawai'i.

Besides the venereal scourge, Cook's men may have introduced tuberculosis. Cook's replacement as captain of the *Resolution*, Charles Clerke, died from the disease on the way back to England.[124] Ship's astronomer William Bayly recorded the meeting of Clerke with a high chief on Kaua'i in January 1778: the two men "Nosed" (that is, touched noses and inhaled each other's breath), and then Clerke shook the chief's hand and slapped him on the back. The people were horrified, as this was no way to treat an ali'i nui.[125] The following January, the ailing Clerke took a Hawai'i Islander aboard the *Discovery* as shipmate. According to Cook, the man "remained on board by choise, nor did he take the first oppertunity to go

---

[122] The discussion of yaws can be followed in Pirie, "Effects of Treponematosis and Gonorrhoea"; Judd, "Depopulation in Polynesia"; Stannard, *Before the Horror*, 75–77; Bushnell, *Gifts of Civilization*, 31, 48.

[123] Wörhrl and Geusau, "Syphilis," 2:690. Developmental problems include anemia, jaundice, deafness, neurological problems, enlargement of the liver, spleen, and lymph nodes, and skeletal and skin lesions. For survivors, childhood poses other challenges: malformation of the skull, swelling of the knees, "saber" shins (a deformity of the anterior tibia), "flaring" shoulder blades, "thickening" of the sternoclavicular joint, malformed and weak teeth, and a distinctive "saddle-shaped" nose in which the bridge is collapsed. These marks of congenital syphilis "usually remain visible throughout life, and may occasion social prejudice, because of their association with sexually transmitted disease" (Powell and Cook, "Treponematosis," 21–31, esp. 27).

[124] Ledyard, *Journal of Captain Cook's Last Voyage*, 143. Clerke was in good company: tuberculosis deaths reached an all-time high in England the following year. Lt. James King died from tuberculosis in 1784.

[125] Bayly, in Beaglehole, *Journals*, 3:281n2.

ashore."[126] But he was soon "so ill," according to Lt. James Burney, that "he scarce [ate] anything," and the men on board "were under great apprehensions of his dying."[127] While this unnamed Hawaiian might be a good a candidate for having developed active tuberculosis, his symptoms probably came on too early for tubercular infection via Clerke. It is likely that he was already sick before climbing aboard. Still, tuberculosis is easily spread. While proof of its presence before 1790 is lacking, the disease would soon gain purchase on the population.

Tuberculosis is transmitted through the air by coughing, sneezing, spitting, talking, or simply breathing. Since *Mycobacterium* grows best in aerobic (oxygenated) environments, it tends to attack the lungs. Once the bacteria find a home in the lungs, they replicate, forming a hard lump known as a tubercle. At this point, the disease can either enter a latent state (with patients experiencing few symptoms) or escalate to "active tuberculosis"; however, a latent case can reactivate at any point over the course of an individual's life, typically doing so when the body's immune system is compromised. Symptoms of the disease are not unlike those of influenza or the common cold: low-grade fever, cough, muscle ache, lethargy and fatigue, loss of appetite, chills, sweating, weight loss, and irregular menses.[128]

Among modern populations, tuberculosis escalates to the "active" state in 5 to 10 percent of cases, at which point the tubercles begin to destroy the lungs and to spread to other organs.[129] At this point, the victim appears to waste away – hence, the popular nineteenth-century term "consumption." The younger a patient is, the more likely he or she is to develop active tuberculosis.[130] In an age before antibiotics, "more than

[126] Cook, ibid., 3:487.   [127] Burney, ibid., 3:487n4.

[128] William D. Johnston, "Tuberculosis," in Kiple, ed., *Cambridge World History of Human Disease*, 1061.

[129] Jeffrey Lewis, "Tuberculosis," in Byrne, ed., *Encyclopedia of Pestilence, Pandemics, and Plagues*, 2:703. Tuberculosis can strike the skin, bones, kidneys, spine, and genitals. What is today called "miliary tuberculosis" refers to the disease attacking all the body's major organs simultaneously, a common scenario for infected infants. The diverse physical manifestations of active tuberculosis garnered a variety of names. "Consumption" was typically used for active tuberculosis in the lungs. "Scrofula" identified the disease in its exterior manifestations, especially swelling in the lymph nodes of the neck and other glands. As its meaning grew fuzzy, scrofula was superseded by the adjectival form "scrofulous," often in combination with other physiological or epidemiological terms. See Roger K. French, "Scrofula (Scrophula)," in Kiple, ed., *Cambridge World History of Human Disease*, 998–1000.

[130] Johnston, "Tuberculosis," 1059–68.

half of active tuberculosis cases resulted in death within five years."[131] Infants and young children were particularly vulnerable.

Unlike gonorrhea and syphilis, where the sex act is both necessary and sufficient for infection, tuberculosis involves a number of variables: age, sex, health and nutrition, living conditions and work environment, and duration of exposure. For reasons as yet little understood, in regions where tuberculosis infection is new or on the rise, a person's sex is also a factor, with fatalities significantly higher for females than males.[132] This may have had a bearing on the lopsided Hawaiian sex ratios noted by nineteenth-century observers.[133] Hygiene and public sanitation affect the spread of tuberculosis. In Europe and North America in this period, outbreaks were a direct result of industrialization and urbanization. Crowded, unsanitary workplaces and living spaces, as well as poor diets, eased transmission. The populous, agricultural communities of Hawai'i, with large families congregated in small living spaces, were no less ripe for the spread of the disease. While early visitors showered praise on local people for their cleanliness and daily swimming regimen, New England missionaries later offered universal condemnation of the same.[134] It is difficult to separate the cultural chauvinism and race pre-judice of New England Calvinists from legitimate concerns about hygiene and sanitation amid disease outbreaks. Not only did the missionaries harbor profound anxieties about sexuality – Indigenous peoples' sexual-ity, in particular – they were also terrified themselves of tuberculosis, which had taken many family members back home. Nonetheless, mis-sionaries after 1820 were concerned about Hawaiian health, and they made countless recommendations to improve Hawaiian living conditions. Of course, these recommendations were of limited utility in an age when "miasmas," "vapours," and "unnatural intercourse" were considered the causes of bacterial diseases.

It is important also to note that bacterial diseases of all kinds, then as now, are exacerbated by poverty. This was especially true of tuberculosis in the nineteenth century, but even venereal syphilis can, in "rare cases," be transmitted "by nonsexual contact in communities living under

---

[131] Lewis, "Tuberculosis," 2:703.   [132] Johnston, "Tuberculosis," 1059–68.
[133] See Chapter 6.
[134] For early descriptions of Hawaiian hygiene, see Samwell, in Beaglehole, *Journals*, 3:1186; Meares, *Voyages*, 210; Beresford, *Voyage round the World*, 127; Townsend, "Extract from the Diary," 26.

conditions of poor personal hygiene."[135] The point is that Hawaiian diets, sexual practices, hygiene, and public sanitation had all developed in the absence of bacterial scourges such as tuberculosis, syphilis, and gonorrhea. The new diseases presented sudden, dire challenges to Hawaiian families and to Hawaiian public health.

Regardless of living conditions, the closer a Pacific Island group was positioned to the continents (or to other island groups), "the weaker the *cordon sanitaire*"; thus, the greater likelihood of infection over the centuries, and the more favorable the disease impact for Islanders when the cord was breached again.[136] The opposite was also true: the further afield, the worse the impact. The Philippines provide a telling comparison with Hawai'i in this respect. Positioned just off East and Southeast Asia, the Philippines' encounter with new infectious diseases in the sixteenth century was much less costly to Indigenous life and health than the contemporaneous Columbian exchange for the Americas.[137] Hawai'i's unique disease ecology was a function of the islands' broader ecology. More than 95 percent of Hawai'i's endemic flowering plants occur naturally nowhere else in the world.[138] The only mammals native to the islands before Polynesian voyagers arrived were the monk seal and a species of bat.[139] As a result of this high degree of endemicity, "[i]n no other place in the world [did] so many species of endemic plants and animals become extinct in so short a time."[140] While the islands' human disease ecology in 1778 presents a more complex picture – and was considerably more varied than in 1400 or 1000 – the populace nonetheless proved highly vulnerable to introduced diseases.

MARRYING UP

The ma'i malihini that began to ravage the islands were spread by human contact. If it is hard to imagine how physical contact could have been avoided, sexual intercourse is a different matter. Despite intractable

---

[135] Wörhrl and Geusau, "Syphilis," 2:689. For tuberculosis and poverty in late nineteenth-century South Africa, see Packard, *White Plague, Black Labor*, esp. 28–30.

[136] Donald Denoon, "Pacific Edens?: Myths and Realities of Primitive Affluence," in Denoon, ed., *Cambridge History of Pacific Islanders*, 115.

[137] See Newson, *Conquest and Pestilence*.

[138] Armstrong and Bier, eds., *Atlas of Hawaii*, 63.

[139] Beaglehole, *Journals*, 3:278n3; Kramer, *Hawaiian Land Mammals*, 17; Fischer, "Cattle in Hawai'i," 357.

[140] Bushnell, *Gifts of Civilization*, 23.

stereotypes of Pacific Islanders as sensuous and exotic, island sexual mores varied a great deal, even across Polynesia. Oral traditions, anthropological research, and extensive documentation paint a complex portrait of sexual encounters between Europeans and Islanders in the late eighteenth century. While the "unfettered sexual freedom" supposedly enjoyed by European men in the Pacific is a damaging "myth" that "trivializ[es]" Polynesian culture and societies, the political economy of sex at Hawai'i bore a significance out of scale with the scholarly attention to it.[141]

By all accounts Polynesians had more carnal exchanges with newcomers than did Islanders in Micronesia and Melanesia. Kamchadals in coastal Siberia, Aleutian Islanders, and Northwest Coast peoples were also reticent to engage in or exchange sex with sailors; many if not most of the Northwest Coast Natives whom Britons engaged in sex were actually enslaved in those societies.[142] At New Zealand, Tahiti, Sāmoa, Tonga, and Hawai'i, by contrast, Islanders widely engaged newcomers in sex, often at the bidding of their kinsmen. Sexual exchange at Hawai'i transpired for a variety of reasons in this period and, like so much else on the islands, evolved rapidly.

Cook's men were unanimous about Hawaiians' eagerness to engage them sexually. This was wishful thinking, but not merely so. Cruising the perimeter of Hawai'i Island, Cook wrote that "no women I ever met with were more ready to bestow their favors" on his men than Hawaiians.[143] The comment indicates a lack of reciprocity, which is absurd, but it hardly nullifies the comparison. Blunter still was surgeon David Samwell: "We found no Denial from any of them, young or old, Maid, Widow or Wife, in which they differ from the [Tahitians], the married Women there being chaste and constant to their Husbands." So long as a piece of iron was on the table, Samwell continued, Hawaiian men would offer their wives, daughters, or sisters in exchange. Likewise, an "elderly woman" was "very importunate to engage some of us to lie with her Daughter who was the wife of a Chief & had a Child by him." In short, Samwell "met

---

[141] O'Brien, *Pacific Muse*, 68, 9. Other work on the subject includes Sahlins, *Islands of History*, chap. 1; Ralston, "Changes in the Lives of Ordinary Women"; Chappell, "Shipboard Relations"; Igler, *Great Ocean*, chap. 2.

[142] Cook, in Beaglehole, *Journals*, 3:311; Samwell, ibid., 3:1095; Bayly, ibid., 3:311n4. An American trader in 1792 deemed the Nuu-chah-nulth women of Vancouver Island "remarkable for their chastity" (John Hoskins, "The Narrative of a Voyage, etc.," in Howay, ed., *Voyages of the "Columbia,"* 260).

[143] Cook, in Beaglehole, *Journals*, 3:486. In a similar vein, perhaps: "These people trade with the least suspicion of any Indians I ever met with" (ibid., 3:483).

with none" who would hesitate to offer their loved ones, though "it would be wrong to conclude from this that they allow the same freedoms to each other as they did to us."[144] Here Samwell makes an oblique reference to social rank; in coming decades the burdens of sexual exchange would fall heaviest on makaʻāinana. Yet it is unlikely that Samwell understood either island marriage or kinship structures. Famously complex, Hawaiian kinship was packaged in a simple language of familial relations; for instance, there were no words for husband or wife among commoners, only man, woman, father, mother, uncle, aunt, and so on.[145] Both polygyny and polyandry were practiced. While the aliʻi engaged in dynastic unions of various sorts to differentiate themselves from the makaʻāinana, sexual partnerships, and sex itself, were a different matter.

As elsewhere in the Pacific, Cook's officers did not hesitate to describe same-sex relations. At Hawaiʻi, this discussion revolved around *aikāne*, the young male attendants who performed sexual and other services for male aliʻi. At the Big Island, Samwell reckoned the "business" of the aikāne as "commit[ting] the Sin of Onan upon the old King" Kalaniʻōpuʻu: "It is an office that is esteemed honourable among them & they have frequently asked us on seeing a handsome young fellow if he was not an Ikany to some of us."[146] Not only Kalaniʻōpuʻu but also Kamehameha enjoyed the company and advice of aikāne. Kamehameha's attachment to an aikāne boy did not surprise Samwell "in the least . . . as we have had opportunities before of being acquainted with [this] detestable part of his Character which he is not in the least anxious to conceal."[147] Kalaniʻōpuʻu had at least five aikāne at

---

[144] Samwell, ibid., 3:1182. For an old "priestess" whose religious function was allegedly "no bar to the Performance of her Devotions at the Temple of Venus," see ibid., 3:1085. For Māori agents and participants in sexual exchange with Britons, see Thomas, *Discoveries*, xxiv–xxvii, 184–85.

[145] Linnekin, *Sacred Queens*, 121–25. Cook's men "saw no traces" of marriage among commoners (Clerke, in Beaglehole, *Journals*, 3:596). For difficulty in generalizing about the nature of marriage among makaʻāinana, see Merry, *Colonizing Hawaiʻi*, 343–44. Note that rank was determined bilaterally, that is, through the mother and father equally.

[146] Samwell, in Beaglehole, *Journals*, 3:1171–72. Shortly before violence broke out at Kealakekua Bay, twenty-eight-year-old James King was invited to remain as aikāne to the chiefs (King, ibid., 3:518–19). Translated literally, the word means coitus (*ai*) with a man (*kāne*). Visitors had no difficulty identifying the carnal aspects of aikāne service (e.g., Beresford, *Voyage round the World*, 102–3). It is also well represented in the ethnographic literature (e.g., Malo, *Moʻolelo Hawaiʻi*, 276, 283, 297, 314, 532, 646–47). More research is needed on whether aikāne may have been considered a third gender and, if so, whether that status outlived their service.

[147] Samwell, in Beaglehole, *Journals*, 3:1190. For a discussion of Kamehameha's aikāne, see Kameʻeleihiwa, "Malama LGBT," pt. 1. For "residual heterosexism" in scholarship on Pacific encounters, see Wallace, *Sexual Encounters*, 20.

his service in 1779, some of whom were important advisors. Palea, a "Man of great Consequence," would remain so through the 1780s.[148] In King's judgment, one unfortunate aspect of the aikāne was to divide the "natural affections" of male aliʻi for their wives. Of course Britons' failure to see "Domestick endearments" is hardly evidence of its absence; yet affection did grow between male aliʻi and their aikāne, and it is important to note that the sex act was probably not viewed as distinct from other forms of service to the chief.[149]

While Cook and his men were hyperbolic about Hawaiian sexual mores, their comparisons to other Pacific peoples should not be dismissed outright, especially given the uneven impact of venereal diseases. At the same time that Islanders off Maui demanded an explanation for the diseases they had contracted, young women were trying to climb aboard Cook's fleet. Many of them made their intentions known by "lascivious Motions & Gestures," according to Samwell. Since Cook had forbidden intercourse, the seamen could "not as yet . . . admit them into the Ships, for which [the women] scolded us very smartly."[150] By mid-January, Cook's ships were "so overcrouded" with women that the crew lacked sufficient "room to do the necessary duty of mooring the Ship"; thus, sailors were "obliged to send them over board to the Number of two or three hundred." Samwell gloated: "As to the Choice & Number of fine women there is hardly one among us that may not vie with the grand Turk himself."[151] Over the course of eight weeks at the Big Island, Samwell referenced no less than fifteen days in which women and girls were aboard, most of them staying overnight and some staying as many as three days.[152] The fleet had female companions for the duration of combat at Kealakekua Bay. When the violence subsided, seven island females accompanied the fleet for a week as it explored Maui and the other islands.[153] For a period of two weeks in March 1779, Samwell recorded that "young Women sleep on board the Ships every night," and "[f]ine Girls come off to us every day in great plenty."[154]

[148] King, in Beaglehole, *Journals*, 3:613. See also ibid., 3:502; Morris, "*Aikāne*," 33–34.
[149] King, in Beaglehole, *Journals*, 3:624. Hawaiian mythology suggested the semen of high chiefs was sacred; hence, the aikāne's responsibility for handling it was exalted. See Morris, "*Aikāne*," esp. 37; Fornander, *Fornander Collection of Hawaiian Antiquities*, 4:8–9. For an origin story of male same-sex relations involving the fifteenth-century high chief Līloa of Waipiʻo, see Malo, *Moʻolelo Hawaiʻi*, 646–47.
[150] Samwell, in Beaglehole, *Journals*, 3:1151. See also King, Jan. 20 and 29, 1778, manuscript log on the *Resolution*, PRO Admiralty 55/116, HSA.
[151] Samwell, in Beaglehole, *Journals*, 3:1159.   [152] Ibid., 3:1151–1217, esp. 1157.
[153] Ibid., 3:1220.   [154] Ibid., 3:1224–25.

Following earlier scholars, Sahlins attributed these developments to an "Aphrodisian" culture of sexual "hospitality" on the islands.[155] American missionaries, who would later try to root out sexual commerce, understood it in similar terms.[156] Scholars have tended to agree that social pressures to "marry up" contributed to the volume of sexual exchange in Polynesia, though few have considered the opportunities for women in engaging visitors beyond the acquisition of trinkets.[157] Commoners and even some aliʻi hoped to attain a higher status by coupling with and eventually bearing children to more elite persons. The newcomers' ships, muskets, clothes, and tools all pointed to their considerable mana. Sexual intercourse, then, was a means of accessing spiritual power in the early encounters. A remarkable illustration of Islanders' conceptions of this power was their depositing of umbilical cords (or stumps) on the ships.[158] Stowing the newborn's *piko* in a sacred or protected location – for example, under a tree or boulder – was a Polynesian custom designed to secure the child good fortune.[159] In 1779 women went to some effort to stow piko in gunwale holes and elsewhere on the ships. In similar fashion, Samwell noted that some Islanders had "cut off a lock of a Child's Hair" that they tossed aboard as the fleet sailed away.[160]

It is unlikely that sexual commerce at Hawaiʻi afforded greater autonomy to women and girls in general; after all, their needs and desires were subject to those of the solicitors and agents of the trade (local pimps and madams). Nevertheless, historians have overlooked the potential

[155] Sahlins, *Islands of History*, 9. See also Fornander, *Account of the Polynesian Race*, 2:163; *Fornander Collection of Hawaiian Antiquities*, 5:63; Elbert, "Chief in Hawaiian Mythology," esp. 345. For a recent challenge to Sahlins's notion of "sexual hospitality" in Sāmoa, see Tcherkézoff, *"First Contacts" in Polynesia*.

[156] Arriving at Kauaʻi in 1820, Rev. Samuel Whitney observed that "as a mark of respect the Husband offers his wife, the Father his daughter, and the Brother his sister" (Samuel Whitney journal, May 27, 1820, ABCFM Papers). Sahlins wrote that missionary "obsessions made sexuality emblematic of Hawaiianness," but he knew better: explorers and merchants were responsible for constructing this emblem decades earlier ("Goodbye to *Tristes Tropes*," 4–5).

[157] See Sahlins, *Islands of History*, 10, 15, 22; Linnekin, *Sacred Queens*, 56, 67, 95, 99, 108; Kameʻeleihiwa, *Native Land*, 40–44. For Tonga, see Campbell, *Island Kingdom*, 28; for the Society Islands, see Salmond, *Aphrodite's Island*, 63–64; for New Zealand, see O'Malley, *Meeting Place*, chap. 6.

[158] Samwell, in Beaglehole, *Journals*, 3:1225.

[159] See Pukui, "Hawaiian Beliefs and Customs during Birth, Infancy, and Childhood," esp. 362–68, 378–81; Handy and Pukui, *Polynesian Family System*, 78; Pukui et al., *Nānā i ke Kumu*, 2:15–18.

[160] Samwell, in Beaglehole, *Journals*, 3:1228. Big Island observers of the volcano deity Pele tossed locks of hair into Kīlauea Crater (Ellis, *Narrative of a Tour*, 352).

opportunities for new alliances women sought through sexual exchange. Like the aikāne, women and girls probably saw sexual service more as a means to an end. It was not clear what that end would be, but the mana of the newcomers was worth investigating. Investigation took time; thus, the days spent aboard the fleet.

Beyond marrying up and potential alliances was the issue of violence. King, who suggested that the aikāne might be a cause for marital strain, also observed outright physical violence. In one case, an aliʻi women who had paid too much attention to a British officer during a boxing match was beaten "unmercifully" by her jealous husband. Another "Girl" received a "terrible beating" aboard the ship for "eating the wrong sort of Plantain."[161] If violence against women does not explain why they engaged newcomers sexually, it suggests a motivation for building alliances with them. That motivation would remain in play through the cultural revolution that brought down the kapu system in 1819.[162]

The Hawaiian-British encounter seeded three new destructive diseases on the islands. Gonorrhea and syphilis resulted in birth defects, increased infant mortality, and reduced fertility overall among Islanders of reproductive age. At the same time, and in spite of these harmful diseases, Hawaiians of all classes experimented with trading, sexual exchange, and other engagements with newcomers. Many women and girls sought to gain advantage or improve their lot by playing chiefs and newcomers off one another and, in some cases, siding outright with the Britons.

Unfortunately for Hawaiians, there was a direct correlation between the volume of sexual exchange with foreigners and the transmission of venereal infections and probably tuberculosis. Were Hawaiian agents of the sex trade aware of the toll venereal disease could take on their "clients," apparently including close kin? Why did the ravages of venereal disease not put a damper on sexual commerce? It is difficult to know. On the one hand, materialist and spiritual perspectives were not mutually exclusive, so people could explain disease as having both physical and metaphysical causes. On the other hand, Hawaiians rarely if ever explained disease in strictly materialist terms. Explanations, as we shall

---

[161] King, in Beaglehole, *Journals*, 3:624. As in many other cultures, gender violence is reflected in island myths and legends (Ellis, *Narrative of a Tour*, 119; Beckwith, *Hawaiian Mythology*, 36–37, 39).

[162] Note that at least two female *kāhuna* (priests, experts) were encountered at Niʻihau; see Burney journal, March 11, 1779, SLNSW; Samwell, in Beaglehole, *Journals*, 3:1085, 1226–27.

see, would come to focus more on the "cosmic disorder" that the maʻi malihini implied rather than on symptoms or vectors.[163]

For some Hawaiians the maʻi malihini were proof of the deities' displeasure, or punishment for transgression, like incurable diseases of the past.[164] What had they done to incur this wrath, and which deities needed to be propitiated? What could explain such a curse coinciding with the arrival of newcomers? Why did newcomers (or their deities) want to destroy Hawaiian bodies and powers of procreation? There would be time to ponder these questions before the next cohort arrived.

[163] Louise Marshall, "Religion and Epidemic Disease," in Byrne, ed., *Encyclopedia of Pestilence, Pandemics, and Plagues*, 2:594.
[164] Kamakau, *Ka Poʻe Kahiko*, 95–98; Malo, *Moʻolelo Hawaiʻi*, 352–53.

2

Sex and Conquest

Above, below; the upland, the lowland; the whale that washes ashore – all belong to the chief.
—Hawaiian proverb

After Cook was killed, the ports went quiet. For seven years no one came. Then, in 1786, two separate fleets arrived within days of each other. Never again would a year pass without visitors from abroad.[1] Shortly the islands became the principal stopover for merchants in a new Pacific fur trade that Cook himself had anticipated. Hailing from Britain, France, Spain, and by 1800 overwhelmingly the new United States, Pacific traders pulled in to any safe Hawaiian harbor that would accept them. Most harbors, most of the time, accepted them. Popular ports such as Kealakekua Bay on the Big Island, Waimea Bay on Kaua'i, and La Pérouse Bay on Maui quickly developed into international transit points, with Hawai'i and its people caught up in global networks of exchange.

Hawai'i's renovation as an international marketplace and way station for ocean-going vessels was hardly a blessing. Besides microbes from three continents, Hawai'i was inundated with liquor and tobacco, cheap and malfunctioning firearms, gunpowder, and other commodities, any of which alone might have caused a public health crisis.[2] Introduced livestock trampled agricultural plots and occasionally mauled

---

[1] Kuykendall, *Hawaiian Kingdom*, 1:20. For traditions pertaining to dynastic and military developments of 1779–85, see Fornander, *Account of the Polynesian Race*, 2:200–29.

[2] For liquor, see, e.g., Turnbull, *Voyage round the World*, 37–38. For defective and malfunctioning firearms, see journal of Archibald Menzies, Feb. 24, 1793, and Feb. 2, 1794, MS 32641, BL; Vancouver, in Lamb, *Voyage*, 1161, 1194–95.

commoners.[3] A growing number of women and girls became involved in the sex trade, which migrated inland from coastal areas. Meanwhile, the high chiefs launched interisland wars of conquest employing scorched-earth tactics that left many districts abandoned or barren. The population of the islands plummeted. In just a generation since Capt. Cook, the population had likely been cut in half. (See Appendix B.)

This chapter narrates the world's arrival on Hawaiian shores, highlighting the social and cultural adaptations made by Islanders in the early stages of European and American "trade colonialism."[4] While Islanders were active participants in this commerce, they did not control the trades in any meaningful way. For one thing, the requisite authority to do so was not vested in anyone until the mōʻī Kamehameha – whose rise is narrated in this chapter – united the archipelago. Nor is it clear that Kamehameha could have controlled the islands' exposure to international trade after unification, as his authority was patchy and his own desire for ships and arms trumped most other considerations.

Kamehameha's conquest was hardly limited to military and political engagements. It was at least as much a function of ecology and trade. The mōʻī's rise was itself contingent on factors that continued to bring foreigners to the islands. These exchanges – including sexual commerce – increased competition among aliʻi and drove a wedge between elite men and women. Yet the burden of a chaotic society fell disproportionately on the makaʻāinana, the "children of the land."

PIGS AND PEOPLE

When George Dixon and Nathaniel Portlock (a veteran of Cook's third voyage) arrived at Kealakekua Bay in late May 1786, their ships were "surrounded by an innumerable quantity of canoes" and "vast numbers of both sexes, in the water." Many people came out to see the visitors "through curiosity," others to trade. In exchange for fishhooks and lines, mats, nails, and "other articles of trifling value," the Britons received pork, sweet potatoes, poi, and fruit.[5] The following week on the southern shore of Oʻahu, a ship's surgeon brought some sick seamen ashore to regain their health, but the people "crowded about them in such numbers" that the

---

[3] Fischer, "Cattle in Hawaiʻi," 358.
[4] "Trade colonialism" comes from Shoemaker, "Typology of Colonialism."
[5] Beresford, *Voyage round the World*, 50. See also Portlock, *Voyage round the World*, 58–65.

sailors were forced back on board.[6] Five days later on the western coast of Ni'ihau, the sick were again taken ashore and here "found great benefit from the land air, as they could walk about at their ease, without being molested by the inhabitants." Supercargo William Beresford wrote that the "principal Chief" at Ni'ihau was very helpful in this regard: having received presents from the Britons, 'Ōpūnui (Big Belly) was "wholly attached to us; so that our sick were much better accommodated on his account."[7]

These interactions were hardly a Typhoid Mary moment, but opportunities for infection existed nonetheless. Yet the officers did not indicate the nature of the seamen's ailments. Officers also failed to mention sexual encounters; perhaps the subject had become a sore spot for the Royal Navy after Cook. Seamen were more forthcoming: "Almost every man on board took a native woman for a wife while the vessel remained" at Kealakekua Bay. Hawaiian men considered it either "an honor" for their women to be so employed, according to Scottish sailor John Nicol, or at least to their advantage, "as they got many presents of iron, beads, or buttons." Hawai'i Island chiefesses may have participated in the trysts. "The fattest woman I ever saw in my life our gunner chose for a wife," Nicol wrote.[8] The woman's size is no guarantee of her rank, which Nicol was not observant enough to indicate, but she may well have been ali'i.[9]

Three days after Dixon and Portlock's arrival at the Big Island, an ambitious French expedition modeled after Cook's arrived at Maui. Despite staying less then forty-eight hours, Jean-François de Galaup, comte de la Pérouse, and his Paris-educated surgeon Claude-Nicolas Rollin recorded critical information about Hawaiian health. Following explicit instructions by the Société Royale de Médecine to chronicle both endemic and epidemic diseases among Pacific populations, the Frenchmen noted the obvious effects of venereal disease.[10] The scant dress of Maui women revealed "traces of the ravages," according to La Pérouse, "among much the greater number."[11]

---

[6] Beresford, *Voyage round the World*, 53. See also Portlock, *Voyage round the World*, 73–74.

[7] Beresford, *Voyage round the World*, 54. See also Portlock, *Voyage round the World*, 83–90.

[8] Nicol, *Life and Adventures*, 73–74.

[9] Cf. Linnekin, *Sacred Queens*, 56–57. Linnekin argues that ali'i women consorted only with European men of rank.

[10] For the Société Royale de Médecine's instructions, see La Pérouse, *Voyage*, 1:249–67.

[11] La Pérouse, *Voyage*, 2:50–51. If Hawaiians considered Europeans the cause of disease, La Pérouse "perceived that this remembrance ... had not left on their minds any kind of resentment" (ibid.). La Pérouse's only reference to sexual exchange was that "the women

Despite knowing that the Britons had admitted to infecting Islanders, La Pérouse and Rollin were convinced that the venereal conditions they saw at Hawai'i could not possibly have been spread in 1778–79, as they were too abundant and advanced. An ardent admirer of Cook, La Pérouse blamed the Spanish, who had never been to Hawai'i. Rollin had better reasons for doubting that Cook's men were the agents of infection; he had simply never seen venereal disease spread at such a rate. Rollin visited "several" infected individuals on Maui, observing symptoms that "would have required twelve or fifteen years in Europe." Since gonorrhea does not display progressive symptomatology, Rollin's comment strongly suggests syphilis. According to La Pérouse, Rollin also saw children "of seven or eight years old ... who could only have been infected while yet in their mothers wombs."[12] In fact, children of this age were right on target for birth with congenital syphilis shortly after the arrival of Cook.

The Islanders were "generally and violently affected with lues venerea and leprosy," wrote Rollin. Their symptoms comprised a long list: "buboes, ... warts, spreading ulcers with caries of the bones, ... tumours of the lachrymal and salivary ducts, scrofulous swellings, inveterate ophthalmiae, ... wasting of the eyes, blindness, inflamed itching herpetic eruptions, and indolent swellings of the extremities."[13] Children also suffered from ringworm, low body weight and/or undernourishment, and rickets.

Leprosy was a misdiagnosis, but the extent of health conditions compiled by Rollin in two days is noteworthy. Medical historian O. A. Bushnell shrugged off most of these conditions as the work of scabies mites, describing the coastal residents of southern Maui as "a dirty, unwashed, unkempt, undernourished, and brutish set of miserable people who showed in their bodies the perpetual squalor in which they lived."[14] Yet the eye ailments alone render Bushnell's diagnosis

---

testified to us, by the most expressive gestures, that there was not any mark of kindness which they were not disposed to confer upon us." He did not indicate whether that "kindness" was in fact shown.

[12] Ibid., 2:51.

[13] Rollin, "Dissertation on the Inhabitants of Easter Island and Mowée," in La Pérouse, *Voyage*, 3:179–80.

[14] Bushnell, *Gifts of Civilization*, 46, 53. Rollin explicitly stated that venereal conditions had "combined with" scabies ("Dissertation on the Inhabitants of Easter Island and Mowée," in La Pérouse, *Voyage*, 3:180). A distinct list of health conditions complied by Rollin in California indicates that he knew the difference between scabies and syphilis; see Rudkin, ed., *First French Expedition to California*, 97–120.

insufficient.[15] Even if unrepresentative of the broader archipelago – and, contrary to Bushnell, there is no historical or archaeological evidence of privation among La Pérouse Bay residents before 1790 – Rollin's sample provides a stark contrast with the observations of Cook and his men seven years earlier.[16] Moreover, it is difficult to see what could be gained by exaggerating the health problems of these distant Islanders. There were no plans in 1786 to establish a French colony, let alone a hospital, on the islands and no desire by expedition leaders and funders to sully the reputation of their hero Cook.

Many of the conditions described by Rollin ("buboes," scars, fistula, and "herpetic eruptions") were symptoms of gonorrhea and syphilis. Beyond malnutrition, the children's conditions indicated congenital syphilis to Rollin. "Scrofulous swellings," meanwhile, *might* suggest tuberculosis.[17] If so, it would be the first record of the disease on the islands and proof that Cook's men spread it. The well-trained Rollin did not indicate which parts of the body were swollen. In an age before the cause of tuberculosis was known, the terms "scrofula" and "scrofulous" were bandied about without discrimination.[18]

Anticipating all this and curious about fundamental differences between the "races" of humanity, the Société had asked Rollin to treat Islanders with mercurial remedies to see how their bodies would respond. French scientists were also curious about any plants with "anti-venereal virtue."[19] Yet it is not clear whether Rollin administered remedies of any kind over the course of two days on Maui. Rollin also regretted that the short stay had prevented him from learning anything about the Islanders' own modes of treatment for these conditions. In the end, he supposed they were as yet "ignorant of any means of alleviating their miserable situation."[20]

Rollin did more than check the boxes at Maui. His observations of Hawaiian health were not limited to standard medical questions. Understanding that pork was a mainstay of the Hawaiian diet and noting

[15] For similar eye conditions afflicting Northwest Coast Indians in this period, see Boyd, *Coming of the Spirit of Pestilence*, 287.
[16] For oral traditions about human settlements and agriculture on western Maui, see Handy, *Hawaiian Planter*, 159–61; Handy et al., *Native Planters*, 489–511.
[17] See Hempel, *Dr. Franz Hartmann's Diseases*, 387–92; Roger K. French, "Scrofula (Scrophula)," in Kiple, ed., *Cambridge World History of Human Disease*, 998–1000.
[18] French, "Scrofula," 1000.
[19] La Pérouse, *Voyage*, 1:262–63. "*Lobelia syphillitica*" (great blue lobelia) and "*celastrus inermis*" (staff vine) were suggested by the Société.
[20] Rollin, "Dissertation on the Inhabitants of Easter Island and Mowée," in La Pérouse, *Voyage*, 3: 180.

TABLE 2.1 *Infectious diseases introduced to Hawai'i*

	Disease	Introduced at	Fatalities to 1855
1778	gonorrhea	Kaua'i, Ni'ihau	N/A
1778	syphilis	Kaua'i, Ni'ihau	Kahapai'opio (1818), William Beale? (1824), Hezekiah Kawailepolepo (1838)
1779–1819	tuberculosis	Big Island?	Kahekili II and wife? (1794), John Toohane (1834)
1818–25	influenza[21]	?	Keahiamoe? (1821), George Prince Humehume (1825), Kekāuluohi (1845)
1826	whooping cough	O'ahu	Pauahi, Wahinepio, Kahalai'a Luanu'u and son
1835–40	Hansen's disease (leprosy)	Kaua'i? O'ahu?	Ahia (before 1849?), Kamuli (1848), George Na'ea (1854), Honolulu (1854)
1836	mumps	O'ahu	Kīna'u, Kaikio'ewa
1848	measles	Big Island	William Pitt Leleiohoku I, Keaweamahi, Moses Kekūāiwa, Ka'imina'au'ao, Ka-nuha, Ka'iwi, Kaihe'ekai? (all 1848–49), James Kaliokalani (1852)
1853	smallpox	O'ahu	John (Huanu) Coffin Jones III, Kamahi'ai, hundreds of unnamed victims[22]

that local swine herds were "very measly," he dissected a few pigs to see what could be learned of their condition. (It is not clear whether he understood that some of the worst human diseases began in livestock or whether he knew that the herds predated Cook.) Cutting into the pigs Rollin found their intestines "sprinkled with tubercles, and the viscera

[21] Influenza may have been introduced before 1818, but solid evidence is lacking. Cf. Stannard, *Before the Horror*, 70–71; Stannard et al., "Book Review Forum," 293–94.
[22] See letters by W. Hillebrand, E. Hoffman, E. Bond, J. Wight, W. Humphreys, L. Lyons, R. H. Smyth, G. A. Lathrop, S. P. Ford, W. Newcomb, J. R. Dow, P. H. Treadway, J. D. Paris, P. Cummings, and B. F. Hardy to Royal Health Commission (1853), Boxes 1–3, Series 334, HSA; Greer, "In the Shadow of Death."

TABLE 2.2 *Major disease outbreaks*

	Disease	Islands affected	Notes
1778–79	syphilis, gonorrhea	all	
1804	'ōku'u (typhoid fever, cholera, or dysentery)	Oʻahu	5,000–15,000 dead
1818	(unidentified respiratory)	Oʻahu	60 dead (Marín)
1824–25	(unidentified respiratory)– influenza?	Oʻahu	"many deaths" (Marín); an "epidemic" with "great mortality" (Kotzebue)
1826	whooping cough	Maui, Oʻahu	
1834	(unidentified respiratory)	Maui, Oʻahu	
1844–45	influenza	Oʻahu	
1848–49	measles, influenza, whooping cough	Big Island, Kauaʻi, Maui, Niʻihau, Oʻahu	as many as 10,000 dead
1853	smallpox	Big Island, Kauaʻi, Maui, Oʻahu	as many as 6,000 dead

covered with them."[23] Had the pigs contracted new diseases of their own? It is not clear, yet Rollin suspected a connection between sick people and sick livestock. "Measly" pigs did not bode well for Hawaiian public health.

AUTHORITY AND ALLIANCE

In early August 1787, a British fur trading ship hove in sight of Hawaiʻi Island. For more than seven months, the *Nootka* had been devastated by scurvy while trading at the Northwest Coast. Yet ten days after its arrival at the Big Island, "every complaint had disappeared," and one month later, all the men were recovered. A jubilant Capt. John Meares observed that the island's "zephyrs may be said to have borne health on their

---

[23] Rollin, "Dissertation on the Inhabitants of Easter Island and Mowée," in La Pérouse, *Voyage*, 3:179–80. Bushnell suggested tapeworm or some other bacteria; if tuberculosis, it was not a strain infectious to humans (*Gifts of Civilization*, 46).

wings."[24] Actually, fruit and vegetables were sufficient cures for scurvy. But Meares' crew was the first of many who would discover in Hawai'i a place of healthful refuge.[25] The islands' bounty, recorded in journals and advertised abroad, would draw ever more visitors as the century drew to a close.

Most of the fur traders who stopped en route stayed long enough only to gather provisions, replenish their vitamin C, and make repairs to the ships. British trader James Colnett suggested an alternative by wintering over. Colnett and his third mate Andrew Bracey Taylor, both Royal Navy veterans, kept remarkable journals of their observations of Hawaiian life during a ten-week stay at the islands in 1788. Visiting each of the six largest islands, Colnett and Taylor learned a great deal about Hawaiian politics, culture, commerce, and health at a critical juncture in the islands' history. The day after Colnett and Taylor's arrival, "every Sailor had a Lady in his burth." In fact, few days elapsed that winter without women and girls aboard the ships. A number of these women were actually identified by the Britons.[26] While Colnett and Taylor provided some evidence of coercion by Hawaiian agents in the sex trade, many of the women who boarded the British fleet in 1788 seemed to approach voluntarily. At Moloka'i, Colnett wrote that "many women slept onboard . . . & I believe a good deal out of curiosity."[27]

Sex was not everything they observed. Off Waikīkī, Taylor saw children whose bones were "coming through their skin." They "constantly" requested food – "any article which cou'd be ate[,] stinking fish not excepted." Taylor and Colnett did not stay long enough at O'ahu to ascertain what had caused the malnourishment. Despite the misery of Islanders on southern O'ahu (or because of it?), the traders were "visited by ye Women as usual."[28] Taylor noted that male Islanders who ferried females back to shore seemed to have "plunder[ed] from the Girls such presents as they had received" – evidence of their "wild unthinking brutish Disposition."[29] More likely, it suggests the general exploitation of women

---

[24] John Meares, "Introductory Voyage of the *Nootka*," in Meares, *Voyages*, xvii–xxxix, esp. xxxix.

[25] E.g., Beresford, *Voyage round the World*, 89; Townsend, "Extract from the Diary," 4; Iselin, *Journal*.

[26] Scottish surgeon Archibald Menzies took up with an ali'i named "Nahoupaio," whom the Britons identified as "Sister to Matua" (Taylor, in Galois, *Voyage to the North West*, 61). Other women spending time on the ships included "Naravaron" (also spelled "Narahowe" and "Naraharow") and "Katoomatta" (ibid., 369n74).

[27] Colnett, ibid., 177.   [28] Taylor, ibid., 181.   [29] Ibid., 182.

and girls in the developing sex trade. The "proceeds" of sexual exchange on southern Maui frequently ended up in the hands of pimps or local chiefs.

After three weeks collecting provisions along the coasts of the Big Island, Maui, Molokaʻi, and Oʻahu, the traders arrived at Kauaʻi and Niʻihau, where they stayed for the next two months. The two western-most islands had developed a reputation in the wake of Cook for being the most hospitable in the northeastern Pacific. Colnett was pleased to find the reputation deserved. At Kauaʻi, the "Ship was soon crowded with ... men, women, & Children ... more civiliz'd and friendly" than the Hawaiians to the east.[30] Ten days later, there was "not a man in the Ship [who had not] been onshore & all pleas'd with their reception." The traders' hosts at Kauaʻi were the mōʻī Kāʻeo (Strong) and ʻŌpūnui, the chief who had sheltered Dixon and Portlock's ill seamen in 1786. Over the next two months, Kāʻeo and ʻŌpūnui tried to control Islanders' traffic with Colnett and his men, yet women and girls continued to board the ships unhindered all winter. "Our situation," wrote Colnett, "was as comfortable as could be expected."[31]

If Kāʻeo and ʻŌpūnui were officially in charge at Kauaʻi, the traders' primary ally was a man they identified as "Tholalo," who may have been deaf and apparently lacked the power of speech. Tholalo "constantly attended" the traders, and "with out fee or reward chastis'd his country men guilty of any irregularity." The Britons quickly learned from Tholalo, and from their own female partners, that leadership on Kauaʻi was con-tested. They also learned of a plot to sack the fleet and a successful attempt to steal a ship's anchor: In light of these violations, Tholalo apparently "requested we would revenge ourselves on his Countrymen & he would assist us." At the sight of British muskets, Tholalo was "seizd with an extacy of Joy, cutting many antic capers, endeavoring to explain it was the very thing he thought him[self] in want of."[32] Island men, no less than women, sought advantage with the newcomers.

In the second week of February, Tholalo informed Taylor that the seamen had infected Kauaʻi Islanders with venereal disease. Taylor's journal entry reads simply: "The Seamen catching the Venereal fast, and [Tholalo] gave us to understand we had injurd several Girls residing to windward."[33] The unfortunate "Girls" seem to have lived in eastern

---

[30] Colnett, ibid., 182.   [31] Ibid., 184.

[32] Ibid., 191; Taylor, ibid., 370. Polynesians' interest in acquiring European firearms and ships was widespread; see, e.g., Bligh, *Voyage to the South Sea*, 76.

[33] Colnett, in Galois, *Voyage to the North West*, 191.

Kaua'i, which was also Tholalo's home. Surprisingly, Tholalo's information about the Kaua'i females was the first mention of venereal disease by
Colnett or Taylor at Hawai'i. Now, suddenly, there were "many [seamen]
in a most frightful state with the Dry Pox." Other Britons were
"Discharging from all Parts of ye Body," according to Taylor.[34] In the
medical terminology of the day, "dry" or "latent pox" referred to the flu-
like symptoms of prodromal (early onset) syphilis.[35] For both gonorrhea
and syphilis, prodrome is marked by internal aches and pains without
visible manifestations of the disease. Taylor's reference to the "Dry Pox"
in 1788 is a reminder that European men carried and could spread
venereal diseases even when asymptomatic. Many British seamen would
have been treated for the symptoms of dry pox by a surgeon or by their
own hand. Remedies would have included mercury taken internally,
a regimented diet, and a course of purging and vomiting. Infected
Hawaiians would themselves have been suffering the internal symptoms
of prodromal syphilis and gonorrhea by 1788, though it is unclear
whether they treated internal symptoms. Of the "several Girls residing
to windward" who had been infected by Colnett's men, nothing more is
known. Their kinsman Tholalo was also never heard from again.

In mid-February 'Ōpūnui placed a kapu on women and girls that was
in effect for a single day. According to Taylor, the announcement of the
kapu "caused an immediate stir" on board the ships: "The Girls said they
must go on Shore or their Fathers wou'd be Kill'd." Most of the females
"jumped over board instantly," but then "others came on board ...
careless of ye Taboo. & many of those who went over board[,] seeing
themselves likely to be rival'd came [on] board again."[36] 'Ōpūnui's
authority over local women seemed to be dissolving right in front of
the Britons' eyes. Taylor deemed the traders to have "suffer'd little"
from 'Ōpūnui's kapu on Hawaiian females.[37] The seamen were well
supplied with companions for the duration of their stay at Kaua'i.
By February 19, Taylor observed "Women [in] abundance endeavoring
to get husbands &c."[38] Even when the "prayer kapu" (*kapu pule*) went
into effect at Kaua'i later that week, Taylor happily noted that the "Girls
were not to be prohibited on this account." Three days after that,

[34] Taylor, ibid., 186.
[35] A standard medical manual for British fleets included a section on the treatment of
venereal diseases, including the dry pox; see Falck, *Seamen's Medical Instructor*, 156.
[36] Taylor, in Galois, *Voyage to the North West*, 186.   [37] Ibid.   [38] Ibid., 188.

'Ōpūnui tried once again to call the women off the ships, but "few obey'd him," according to Colnett.[39]

The Kaua'i women's defiance of the ruling ali'i in 1788 was not limited to breaking curfew. Some Kaua'i women actually conspired with the British traders – as Big Island women had done in 1779 – against local ali'i. Was a pattern emerging? Women's actions in 1788 reveal divided, contested, and shifting allegiances. As in 1779, some women sided with their new British allies against their own ruling chiefs. The question is how women (much less girls) perceived of these alliances; how far the alliances could be stretched in the face of conflict; and what, if anything, sexual relations between Hawaiian women and British men had to do with these commitments.

It is clear that chiefly authority in 1788 was contested or divided on more than one island. Oral tradition provides little if any support for the hypothesis that ali'i authority over female commerce and sexual exchange – and even over women generally – had been weak before Cook. Instead, the chiefs' were reputed to have the power of life and death over their people. More likely is that political factions and competing ali'i had been the norm in Hawai'i before Cook and that the arrival of newcomers and their commodities simply exacerbated these divisions. The women and girls who aligned with European traders and other visitors were thus expressing their partisan views, which may or may not have been firm and may or may not have stemmed from the men's status as Europeans or newcomers. Hawaiians initially conceived of the newcomers as wielding considerable spiritual power. Did they still? Perhaps some did, but the effect was wearing off. Islanders increasingly understood the foreigners as men like themselves, with common needs and desires. Colnett, who emphasized Islanders' curiosity and hard bargaining rather than any lingering sense of wonder, also noted that his men were "held very cheap" by locals at O'ahu, "almost to a degree of contempt."[40] What about sexual relations? If sex played any role in the development and maintenance of allegiances, there is scarcely any record of it.[41]

Whatever the broader causes of Hawaiian women's alliances with British seamen, it is clear that Kaua'i females in 1788 were relaying important information about ali'i intentions to British fur traders and even urging the Britons to avenge certain chiefs. On February 23, a "Girl

---

[39] Colnett, ibid., 189.   [40] Ibid., 179.
[41] See Ralston, "Hawaii 1778–1854" and "Changes in the Lives of Ordinary Women";
Linnekin, Sacred Queens; Chappell, "Shipboard Relations."

[who] was always first in her Solicitations" boarded the *Prince of Wales* to inform the crew of a plot to sack the fleet. Colnett wrote that the girl (or woman) was "greatly attach'd to us" and "on first coming onboard flew to her [seaman] husband, bursting into a flood of tears," telling him that the British "were all to be kill'd on tomorrow." When the seaman refused to believe her, she turned to the surgeon Archibald Menzies – who had the best grasp of the Hawaiian language among the visitors – and pleaded with *him*. The next day some Islanders attempted to cut the ship's cable; in response, the seamen fired their muskets at approaching canoes. Despite the rising tensions, Colnett noted that "many women were onboard both Vessels for the night, & not at all alarm'd at what pass'd."[42] The scene is reminiscent of the battle at Kealakekua Bay when island females remained aboard Cook's ships.

Colnett's men left Hawai'i in 1788 "in perfect health," except for "those who had been so unfortunate to catch the disease left by the first discoverers," that is, the Cook expedition. Fortunately, the "constitution & method of diet" of the men had "almost eradicated" the venereal woes of the seamen on the *Prince of Wales* by mid-March when they shipped out.[43] The *Princess Royal* was perhaps somewhat worse off, with "several of [the] people being ill of a disorder contracted from the Women."[44]

THE ODDS

Did Hawaiians fare any better away from their disease-stricken islands? Before sailing on to Canton, Colnett and Taylor took a few volunteers aboard. One was a Moloka'i boy of about twelve whose "parents" had apparently consented to his leaving with the fleet. After crossing the Pacific, Kualelo made his way to Plymouth, England, where he was inoculated for smallpox and "sent to a public school in the neighbour-hood" of his overseer.[45] In March 1792, the teenaged Kualelo returned to Hawai'i on the expedition of George Vancouver. The other Hawaiian recruit, "John Matatuaray" of Ni'ihau, was an ali'i son. Matatuaray sailed with Colnett to Macao and then back across the North Pacific to the Northwest Coast where the fleet was seized by Spaniards and comman-deered to San Blas, Mexico. The young Matatuaray somehow made his way to Mexico City and then sailed north again to Vancouver Island

---

[42] Colnett, in Galois, *Voyage to the North West*, 191. [43] Ibid., 200. [44] Ibid., 204.
[45] Menzies journal, March 3, 1792, MS 32641, BL.

where he died in December 1790 of unknown causes.[46] "Prior to his Death," Colnett wrote, Matauturay "desired to be remembered to his father, Mother, and family, Captain [Charles] Duncan, and Mr. [Capt. John] Etches; and in the Night died without a Groan."[47] It is unclear whether anyone managed to "remember" Matauturay to his family.

At the same time that Colnett and Taylor were making their way across the Hawaiian Islands, Capt. John Meares set off from Macao for the Northwest Coast of North America. (Meares had been at Hawai'i five months earlier with his crew at death's door from scurvy.) At Macao, Meares had on board four Hawaiians eager to return home. All four voyagers had boarded earlier fur trading ships: a chief of "Herculenian Stature" named Ka'iana, probably from the Big Island and possibly a relation of the mō'ī Kalani'ōpu'u; a young woman of indeterminate class and origin whom the Britons called Winee (their attempt at *wahine*, "woman"); and "a stout man and boy from the island of Mowee," both also of indeterminate class.[48] The plan had been to return the Hawaiians home en route to the Northwest Coast, but the *Iphigenia* took a long detour to secure additional furs in the North Pacific. In the process, Ka'iana became the second Hawaiian to visit the Northwest Coast of North America (Winee had been there the year before). Ka'iana finally returned home in December 1788, full of fascinating stories of new places and peoples; he became chief of Puna district on the Big Island and a close advisor (or *kuhina*) to Kamehameha, later clashing with the mō'ī and falling to him at the Battle of Nu'uanu in 1795.[49]

Winee met a different fate. Shortly after Meares's fleet left Macao in January 1788, Winee succumbed to an illness off the Philippines and died aboard the *Iphigenia*. The fleet had encountered some rough weather with "piercing cold" in the South China Sea, but upon reaching the Philippines, "the opposite extreme" was felt. "Such a change," noted Meares, along "with the heavy dews which fell morning and evening,

[46] Barman and Watson, *Leaving Paradise*, 347. See also Etches, *Authentic Statement of all the Facts*.

[47] Colnett, *Journal of Captain James Colnett*, 198.　[48] Meares, *Voyages*, 10.

[49] Menzies, Feb. 10, 1794, MS 32641, BL. Menzies attributed Ka'iana's rise to his knowledge of firearms. For Ka'iana's origin, appearance, and possible relation to Kalani'ōpu'u, see Lamb, *Voyage*, 447n1; Manby, "Journal of Vancouver's Voyage," *Honolulu Mercury* 1 (June 1929): 16; Menzies, March 3, 1792, MS 32641, BL; Lisiansky, *Voyage round the World*, 130–33. See also Barman and Watson, *Leaving Paradise*, 18–22, 271–71, 432–33. For a recent consideration of Ka'iana's rank, expertise, and possible motivations, see Chang, *World and All the Things upon It*, 38–77.

was a very unhealthy circumstance."[50] Still, the fleet was well stocked with provisions, including plenty of fruits and vegetables, and Meares seems to have been a thorough and conscientious captain. It is impossible to say to what extent the voyage itself contributed to Winee's demise, but it probably did not help. While Winee's "spectr[al]" appearance may suggest pneumonia or tuberculosis, the cause of her death ultimately cannot be determined.[51] Kaʻiana was apparently distraught at the loss of his countrywoman. Meares reported that he was "so sensibly affected by the death of Winee, as to produce a considerable alteration in the state of his health: – his fever continued, and baffled all our attentions to relieve him."[52] Eventually, the Herculean Aliʻi did recover and returned home safely on the *Iphigenia*.

The death at sea of Winee and the safe return of Kaʻiana – like the contemporaneous death abroad of Makakule and safe return of Kualelo – can represent the few thousand Hawaiians who shipped out of the North Pacific between 1788 and 1855.[53] The odds for Native Hawaiians surviving abroad in this period were probably no higher than 50 percent. While many of these deaths are recorded – particularly individuals attached to fur trading posts in the Pacific Northwest – the majority of Hawaiian travelers, like the "stout man and boy" from Maui and a second boy who boarded the *Prince of Wales* with Kualelo, simply disappear from the historical record.[54] New scholarship on Pacific Island networks and voyagers has tended to overlook the profound risk to Islanders in undertaking such journeys.[55] While travelers faced unique risks abroad, dozens succumbed to the same diseases as their kinsmen at home. In a few cases – measles in the 1840s and smallpox in the '50s – the same epidemic felled Hawaiians at home, in Canton, and in western North America.

Few European or American reports speak to what must have been a keen Hawaiian awareness of the risks of travel abroad. In 1801, Boston sea captain Amasa Delano met a son of Kamehameha at Oʻahu. Impressed by the boy's physical size and royal bearing, Delano asked whether he might

---

[50] Meares, *Voyages*, 23.   [51] Ibid., 27.   [52] Ibid., 36.
[53] For an estimate of Hawaiian voyagers in this period, see Rosenthal, "Hawaiians Who Left Hawaiʻi," 456–59.
[54] See Chappell, *Double Ghosts*; Barman and Watson, *Leaving Paradise*, 219–433. For other Polynesians dying abroad from infectious disease, see, O'Malley, *Meeting Place*, 29, 31, 57, 68, 75.
[55] E.g., Barman and Watson, *Leaving Paradise*; Okihiro, *Island World*; Thomas, *Islanders*; Matsuda, *Pacific Worlds*; Chang, *World and All the Things upon It*. An important exception is Igler, "Diseased Goods" and *Great Ocean*, chap. 2.

FIGURE 2.1 Rifle petroglyph, Kaloko Honokōhau National Historical Park.
Courtesy of Ed Fornataro, www.bigislandhikes.com.

enlist the boy on his commercial voyage to Canton. The boy's mother was
upset at the prospect, going so far as to mount a protest aboard the
Massachusetts. Delano was sympathetic with her plight but unaware that
the distress likely had as much to do with the possibility of never seeing her
son again than it did mere motherly affection.[56] Eventually the Kingdom of
Hawai'i would establish firm limits on travel and require sea captains to
post bonds for the safe return of Hawaiians. If the kingdom was aware of
the problem, how much more so those who lost loved ones without even the
consolation of burying their bones.[57] Oral tradition – and, later, letters
home – reflects these concerns to some extent. Yet it is important to keep
such losses in perspective: for all the anguish of losing a friend or family
member abroad, the survival rate for Hawaiians at home in this period was
perhaps little better than for those who boarded a foreign ship.

When British fur trader James Colnett returned to the Big Island in
1791, he found the chiefs on a war footing with neighboring Maui
and Moloka'i and the ali'i Kamehameha outfitted with a British sloop.

---

[56] Delano, *Narrative of Voyages*, 392.
[57] For the sacred nature of human bones and for the kapu regarding corpses, see Malo,
     Moʻolelo Hawaiʻi, 355–61.

Colnett was more concerned about the Spanish ships he saw in port. By 1791, Britons, French, Americans, and Spaniards were all calling at the islands, and commercial competition was rapidly growing. Enterprising Hawaiian chiefs now requested weapons and gunpowder above all from the traders. Colnett, for one, was more than happy to supply both commodities in exchange for fresh food at the Big Island.[58]

According to Colnett, the Big Island had seen continual warfare since Cook, accompanied with "a great deal of Sickness which never before his time afflicted them which they allege to having kill'd him."[59] The awkwardly phrased remark, typical of Colnett, requires a moment's explanation. By one reading Colnett was saying that Big Islanders believed that the ma'i malihini had killed Cook (which Colnett himself knew not to be the case). Another reading assumes Colnett's phrasing to be even less precise: Hawaiians claimed to have killed Cook *because of* the ma'i malihini: to wit, they *"have a great deal of Sickness which never before [Cook's] time afflicted them [and] which they allege to having"* been the reason he was killed. If the first reading is the more plausible of the two, either one indicates a cultural iteration of the Hawaiian experience with introduced infectious disease. Twelve years after the return of Cook-Lono, some Hawaiians had fused the religious-political phenomenon of his return with the devastation of the ma'i malihini.

Big Islanders "made strict enquiry" as to whether Cook-Lono would ever return and "when I saw him last." Colnett "could not tell" whether Cook would return, but he knew one thing: "[T]he Spaniards were coming to take their Country from them and make them Slaves." No doubt unsettled by this news, local people then "enquired if Captain Cook had sent" the Spaniards, "how long he would be angry with them [the Hawaiians], and what they should do to get Captain Cook to entreat his [ali'i] to send and assist them against the Spaniards."[60] If Colnett had any advice on this matter, he did not record it.

Colnett's account ends with a retrospective comment about the 1790 explosion of Kilauea crater on Hawai'i Island, "which they say Captain Cook has caus'd."[61] Colnett did not elaborate on who exactly believed that Cook-Lono had caused the eruption, but it is no surprise that the Britons were hearing stories about the event. As many as 400 Hawaiians may have perished, including dozens of warriors (with women and children in tow) on their way home to Hilo after battling Kamehameha's

---

[58] Colnett, *Journal of Captain James Colnett*, 220.   [59] Ibid.   [60] Ibid.   [61] Ibid.

forces in Hamakua district.[62] While it is fair to wonder whether Colnett exaggerated Big Islanders' fixation on the man (or divine king) who happened to be his mentor, the larger context of Colnett's journals does not support such a view. It had been twenty years since Colnett first set out with Cook. Now a thirty-eight-year-old captain and merchant, Colnett had other concerns besides heaping praise on a man already widely considered the greatest British navigator of all time. Given the nature of his accounts throughout the Pacific, it is likely that Colnett recorded the Islanders' comments about Cook simply as he understood them.

BROKEN TEETH

Between 1792 and 1794 a British expedition under George Vancouver made three separate visits to the islands. Modeled on the Cook voyages of which Vancouver was a veteran, the expedition had various goals including making the Hawaiian Islands a British protectorate. Aboard the fleet were the Hawaiian teenager and world traveler Kualelo and a crew of 150 British seamen. The Vancouver accounts paint a harrowing portrait of makaʻāinana life in 1792–94, with chronic warfare, food shortages, and ongoing disease transmission. Among the aliʻi, meanwhile, Vancouver's men noted rising discord and fraught sexual politics.

In marked contrast to Cook, Vancouver hardly noticed the impact of introduced infectious disease. He believed the evident population decline was due solely to internecine warfare. By contrast, the expedition's surgeon and naturalist deemed Hawaiian warfare to be "not of any long continuance or very bloody," though very destructive of property and agricultural productions.[63] While Vancouver's observations of Hawaiian elites, warfare, agriculture, and infrastructure were generally astute, he had little interest in Hawaiian culture and social class. His only concern with common people was that they might attack him, a concern that bordered on paranoia.[64] Fortunately his men were more curious and observant.

Despite the commander's order prohibiting trade "with the Indians," the usual exchange of food, sex, and small trade goods occurred during the

---

[62] Kuykendall, *Hawaiian Kingdom*, 1:36.

[63] Menzies, March 18, 1793, MS 32641, BL: "After the heat of battle ... all animosities were soon forgot, and the vanquishd were admitted to live amongst them [the victors] as friends." As with eighteenth-century military engagements elsewhere, disease took more lives than combat.

[64] Bell, "Log of the *Chatham*," *Honolulu Mercury* 1 (Sept. 1929): 19–20.

expedition's two-and-a-half-week visit in March 1792.[65] At Kealakekua Bay, the fleet's initial harborage, master's mate Thomas Manby and clerk Edward Bell both reported on seamen's encounters with island women, whom Bell described as "the cheapest articles of Traffic" in the island economy.[66] These offshore couplings – which Vancouver failed to mention – apparently took place before any official business. According to Manby, "a slight beckon" by the seamen was "sufficient invitation" for island females to dive "like Sea Nymphs from their Canoes." While Manby deemed the prelapsarian women somewhat less attractive than Society Islanders, he was shortly "reconcile[d]" to their close-cropped hair and missing front teeth. Remarkably, Manby reported that "every woman" they met with at Kealakekua Bay was "deprived ... of her foreteeth."[67] Removal of front teeth was a mourning ritual. Most Big Islanders, it would seem, had lost someone close to them, or perhaps a local chief had perished. On their second visit the following year, Manby reported that Kamehameha himself had knocked out "all his foreteeth," though Manby and the others did not know the reason.[68] The fact that Colnett and other visitors in the late 1780s had failed to mention missing teeth might suggest that mortality was rising on the Big Island by 1792.[69]

Though weapons and gunpowder were in great demand, Vancouver forbid his men from supplying Big Islanders with additional firepower – a humanitarian posture to prevent further warfare, Vancouver claimed, though this was just as much a strategy to block anyone from interfering with his own plans for Hawai'i. On their first afternoon at Kealakekua Bay, Vancouver's men were met by the imposing chief and world traveler Ka'iana, who requested first wine – tea, according to Bell – and then firearms.[70] Manby was surprised that Ka'iana seemed to have forgotten most of his English since returning from the Northwest Coast. Vancouver considered this chief "extremeley disappointed and chagrined" at failing "to procure any fire arms or ammunition." Not only Ka'iana but "all his

---

[65] Vancouver, in Lamb, *Voyage*, 445.
[66] Bell, "Log of the *Chatham*," *Honolulu Mercury* 1 (Sept. 1929): 8.
[67] Manby, "Journal of Vancouver's Voyage," *Honolulu Mercury* 1 (June 1929): 15.
[68] Manby, "Journal of Vancouver's Voyage," *Honolulu Mercury* 1 (July 1929): 40. Kamehameha was mourning his sister Kalola, widow of Kalani'ōpu'u, who died on Moloka'i in 1790. See Kamakau, *Ruling Chiefs*, 149; Fornander, *Account of the Polynesian Race*, 2:238; cf. Lisiansky, *Voyage round the World*, 130.
[69] Mortality rates on the Big Island, as elsewhere, would only be calculated after 1820.
[70] Manby, "Journal of Vancouver's Voyage," *Honolulu Mercury* 1 (June 1929): 15–16; Bell, "Log of the *Chatham*," *Honolulu Mercury* 1 (Sept. 1929): 10. See also Manby, in Lamb, *Voyage*, 447n6.

countrymen ... anxiously solicited" firearms from the Britons and
were "as uniformly refused" by Vancouver.[71] According to the surgeon
Archibald Menzies (who had been at the islands in 1788 with Colnett),
"nothing was now held in greater estimation or more eagerly sought after
than fire arms & powder by those very people who[,] but a few years back[,]
shuddered at the report of a musquet." Now they could handle European
weapons "with a degree of ease & dexterity that equalld the most expert
veteran."[72]

Once it became clear that firearms were not obtainable, Big Islanders
seemed "very indifferent about trading, or having any other communication with" Vancouver and his men.[73] Bell, who had never been to Hawai'i,
was "greatly disappointed" by the scene in general: "We had been lead to
emagine that we should find everything in ... as great plenty here as at

FIGURE 2.2 Hawai'i Island village. Note the absence of firearms. The seated
woman, bottom right, gazes into a European-made mirror. "Village of
Macacoupah, Owhyee."[74]
Thomas Heddington, 1794. Courtesy of Bishop Museum (SXC101636).

---

[71] Vancouver, in Lamb, *Voyage*, 449.   [72] Menzies, March 3, 1792, MS 32641, BL.
[73] Vancouver, in Lamb, *Voyage*, 446.
[74] Perhaps Maka'ula or Mākaha (Pukui et al., *Place Names of Hawaii*, s.v. "Maka'ula";
    Chun, *No Nā Mamo*, 198–99).

[Tahiti] – but comparison between the two places . . . will not bear it." Yet Bell had "reason to suppose that the seeming scarcity" of food and other provisions "was nothing more than" a bargaining strategy "to endeavor to force us, to offer . . . articals [in] a larger & better supply."[75]

One exception to Islanders' indifference was the enterprising aliʻi Kaʻiana, who tried to learn everything he could about the newcomers from Kualelo and encouraged the traveler to remain with him at the Big Island as chief. This was not a bad option for young Kualelo, who had apparently just had his heart broken in Tahiti and now learned that his "friends & relations" at Molokai had been killed in a "destructive war" that "desolated" the island.[76] That desolation became apparent to Vancouver and his men as the expedition sailed north. En route to Oʻahu the fleet was approached by "some few of the natives" off the southern coast of Lānaʻi with little to offer in the way of trade goods. Vancouver deemed the "dreary and desolate appearance of their island . . . a sufficient apology for their coming empty-handed." In contrast to the coastal regions of the Big Island, Maui, and Oʻahu, Lānaʻi seemed to the commander "very thinly inhabited, and incapable of affording any of its productions to strangers." Through his telescope Vancouver could see a "few scattered miserable habitations" set upon a landscape that otherwise appeared barren.[77] Menzies had much the same impression of Lānaʻi and also of its arid neighbor Kahoʻolawe. The western (low-lying) regions of Molokaʻi seemed to Menzies a "naked dreary barren waste without either habitation or cultivation."[78]

Despite these observations, it is unclear whether human populations on western Molokaʻi, Lānaʻi, and Kahoʻolawe had declined since 1779 and, if so, what exactly was the cause.[79] In the first place, and despite Vancouver's claim that Lānaʻi and Kahoʻolawe "had formerly been considered fruitful and populous islands," none of these regions sustained large populations at any point in the eighteenth or early nineteenth century.[80] It was also common for Hawaiians threatened by drought,

[75] Bell, "Log of the *Chatham*," *Honolulu Mercury* 1 (Sept. 1929): 9.
[76] Menzies, March 4, 1792, MS 32641, BL. See also Manby, "Journal of Vancouver's Voyage," *Honolulu Mercury* 1 (June 1929): 13, 16.
[77] Vancouver, in Lamb, *Voyage*, 452.
[78] Menzies, March 6, 1792, MS 32641, BL. The description is representative of Britons' opinions of the drier, agriculturally marginal regions of the islands.
[79] Cf. Stannard, *Before the Horror*, 71, 134–35. For skepticism regarding Stannard's suggested rate of population decline for this period, see Eleanor C. Nordyke, "Comment," ibid., 111–12.
[80] Vancouver, in Lamb, *Voyage*, 856.

famine, warfare, or political commotion to abandon their villages for another island or another region on their home island. Vancouver's view through the telescope does not suffice as evidence of depopulation. Indeed, the Britons proved only that marginal and agriculturally poor regions in 1779 remained so in 1792 and that Islanders continued to be mobile throughout this period. Even the alleged loss of Kualelo's family and friends at Moloka'i, tempting as it is, does not prove population loss from warfare or disease: the source of this information, the upstart chief Ka'iana, was a schemer considered untrustworthy by Europeans and Hawaiians alike.[81] (He also had political designs on Kualelo as a potential ally.) Bell's account of these events differs markedly from that of Menzies. Bell did not mention *any* losses to Kualelo's Moloka'i kin and in fact wrote that "several of his family were [re]settled on the [Big] Island."[82]

While it is possible that warfare on western Moloka'i, Lāna'i, and Kaho'olawe had been costly in terms of lives and agricultural productions, it is just as likely that Islanders such as Kualelo's family fled to the hills or paddled to a neighboring island when war broke out – as Hawaiians had done for centuries before them. Vancouver and Menzies typically assumed the worst when they saw abandoned huts or thinly populated villages; historians have too often followed their lead.[83] Yet if tracking refugees in this period is a daunting task, determining the extent to which losses to warfare (or the occasional famine) had lasting effects on populations in the marginal regions of the archipelago is still more difficult.[84]

Overseeing the collection of fresh water near Waikīkī, Vancouver witnessed a highly cultivated landscape with ingenious irrigation and canal systems. Yet the commander was once again disappointed by the nature of the reception. Like Big Islanders, people at southern O'ahu seemed generally cold or indifferent to the Britons. This was in contrast to Tahiti, where the crew enjoyed "effusions of friendship and hospitality" from local people the previous month. Waikīkī people regarded Vancouver with "an unwelcome austerity" and treated his desires "with a negligent

---

[81] See, e.g., Bell, "Log of the *Chatham*," *Honolulu Mercury* 1 (Sept. 1929): 11, 17–18; Vancouver, in Lamb, *Voyage*, 1152.

[82] Bell, "Log of the *Chatham*," *Honolulu Mercury* 1 (Sept. 1929): 11. For the Hawaiian word *'ohana* (family) possibly having a postcontact origin, see Sahlins, *Islands of History*, 22–26, esp. 25n; Linnekin, *Sacred Queens*, 114–15.

[83] On this point I acknowledge a debt to A. F. Bushnell, "'The Horror' Reconsidered," 137–43.

[84] For Islanders fleeing drought-induced famine, see Menzies, March 29, 1793, MS 32641, BL. For alleged depopulation on western Moloka'i following Kamehameha's conquest, see ibid., March 19, 1793.

indifference."[85] Which is not to say they weren't interested in trade. "Large groups" of women and girls rowed out to the ships to exchange sex for trade goods.[86]

A few days later, at Waimea Bay, Kaua'i, Vancouver was greeted with "distant civility." This was partly a function of the kapu in place, which also prevented some men from gaining access to island women on shore.[87] Yet even after the kapu was lifted, people seemed less eager to host Britons on Kaua'i. Had Hawaiians become jaded about visitors? Vancouver wondered whether the cold reception stemmed from his being recognized (from 1779) by some older residents. Either way, it is clear that the peoples' generosity and enthusiasm were diminished.

While Vancouver's men enjoyed access to island women, the commander himself was scornful of the commerce:

> The eagerness, nay even avidity, with which the men here assisted in the prostitution of the women; and the readiness of the whole sex, without any exception, to surrender their persons without the least importunity, could not fail ... to incur our censure and dislike; and, on reflection, our disgust and aversion. I have read much, and seen something in my several visits to this ocean, of the obscenity attributed to the inhabitants of [Tahiti] and the Society islands; but no indecency that ever came under my observation, could be compared with the excessive wantonness presented in this excursion.[88]

Again the unfavorable comparison with Tahiti. Yet Vancouver was not simply partial to the South Pacific. His indictment of the sex trade on leeward Kaua'i came just after a discussion of Hawaiian agricultural plots and earthworks that had left him with a "very favorable opinion of the industry and ingenuity" of Kaua'i Islanders. Furthermore, the Waimea people provided the crew with everything they needed, and Vancouver himself "had the comfort of finding all things in perfectly good order." It would be a mistake to dismiss Vancouver's comments on the sex trade as mere ethnocentrism, misogyny, or class bias. (Most Hawaiians involved in the trade were maka'āinana.) The sex trade had evolved. On a hike inland from Waimea Bay, Vancouver and his men were "pestered and disgusted" by the "obscene importunities" of local

---

[85] Vancouver, in Lamb, *Voyage*, 456.   [86] Menzies, March 8, 1792, MS 32641, BL.
[87] Vancouver, in Lamb, *Voyage*, 460; Menzies, March 10, 1792, MS 32641, BL.
[88] Vancouver, in Lamb, *Voyage*, 462. See also Vancouver, *Voyage of Discovery to the North Pacific Ocean*, 171. While critical of Hawaiians' tendency to steal (as he saw it), clerk Edward Bell did not complain of their sexual advances or the sex trade in general ("Log of the *Chatham*," *Honolulu Mercury* 1 [Sept. 1929]: 25–26).

women – the earliest evidence of the sex trade having migrated inland.[89] Islanders were no longer simply congregating in port to exchange sex for desirable European trade goods; they were now seeking exchanges in their home villages, perhaps even from the convenience of their own *hale* (sleeping and eating huts). For Vancouver, these developments were to be regretted. In the end, he "consider[ed] this licentiousness as a perfectly new acquirement, taught, perhaps, by the different civilized voluptuaries, who, for some years past, have been their constant visitors." This was a potshot at the fur traders from various nations who had been calling at the islands since 1786.[90]

Common seamen once again held different views from their commander. On March 9, twenty-one-year-old master's mate Thomas Manby "slept warm and comfortable" in between four "pretty females" in a "snug little hut" erected by a Waimea chief for such liaisons.[91] On March 13, Manby spent two hours "rev[elling] in extatic enjoyment" with an unnamed "Royal female" provided by the chief Inamoʻo, regent to the young king Kaumualiʻi. Back on the *Discovery* later that afternoon, Manby heard someone alongside the ship calling for "Mappee." He "instantly knew the voice" to be that of the woman he had "pass'd some happy moments with in the early part of the day." Paddling out in a canoe, she was calling for Manby himself.[92]

Like chiefs on the eastern islands, the Kauaʻi regent Inamoʻo implored Vancouver for firearms. When weapons were refused, Inamoʻo "immediately" requested gunpowder and musket balls instead. Meanwhile, in a pattern common throughout the Pacific Islands – as it had been earlier in the Americas – the young mōʻī Kaumualiʻi adopted the name of King George, "not suffering his [servants] to address him by any other name, and being much displeased with us, as well as his countrymen, if we called him *Tamooere*" [Kaumualiʻi].[93] Various Hawaiian aliʻi, both young and old, would follow Kaumualiʻi's lead over the next few decades while

---

[89] Vancouver, in Lamb, *Voyage*, 462.

[90] Ralston notes that commodities that could be consumed before seizure by the chiefs, such as liquor and tobacco, were especially popular among makaʻāinana ("Hawaii 1778–1854," 28). For Ralston's sources, see ibid., 28n32.

[91] Manby, "Journal of Vancouver's Voyage," *Honolulu Mercury* 1 (June 1929): 20.

[92] Ibid., 23. See also Manby, in Lamb, *Voyage*, 469n2. Earlier in the month Bell noted that the *Chatham* had "no small number" of women aboard at Maui ("Log of the *Chatham*," *Honolulu Mercury* 1 [Sept. 1929]: 14).

[93] Vancouver, in Lamb, *Voyage*, 474; Bell, "Log of the *Chatham*," *Honolulu Mercury* 1 (Sept. 1929): 21; cf. Kamakau, *Ruling Chiefs*, 162. Other Kauaʻi aliʻi also adopted new names; see journal of Archibald Menzies, March 9, 1794, MS 155, NLA.

relations with the Britons remained friendly. Nor were the names adopted by Hawaiians limited to British monarchs and naval commanders. The young adventurer Kalehua took the name of second mate Joseph Ingraham on a fur-trading voyage to the Northwest Coast in 1791; the following year, a Society Islander seems to have taken the name of master's mate Manby.[94] Unlike Indigenous leaders elsewhere in this period, Hawaiians seem to have taken British names without any expectation of mutual exchange.[95]

HULA DIPLOMACY

When the expedition returned to Hawai'i Island in February 1793, Vancouver was alarmed to learn that the mō'ī Kamehameha had forbidden Islanders ("under penalty of death") to supply newcomers with provisions unless he received "*arms and ammunition*" in exchange. Fortunately for the Britons, numerous Islanders were willing to take this risk to obtain metals (scissors, knives, and nails), looking glasses, and textiles.[96] During the previous year Kamehameha had consolidated power on the Big Island and begun a conquest of neighboring Maui, Moloka'i, and Lāna'i. With Vancouver and his men now docked on his home island, Kamehameha's objective was to present his authority as singular and lacking serious challengers, neither of which was true. The Big Island mō'ī oversaw even the most trivial of trades when Vancouver was present and staged the most impressive scenes of statecraft Britons had seen in the Pacific. If it wasn't clear to him in 1792, Kamehameha now understood Vancouver to be an emissary of the British sovereign.[97]

---

[94] Menzies, March 4–5, 1792, MS 32641, BL; Manby, "Journal of Vancouver's Voyage," *Honolulu Mercury* 1 (June 1929): 13. For the adoption of foreigners' names in the Marquesas, see Dening, *Islands and Beaches*, 84, 209–10.

[95] By contrast Ka'ahumanu insisted on a mission wife taking her name in 1828 (Judd, *Honolulu: Sketches of Life*, 15). For a Haida chief's exchange of names with a British fur trade captain, see Robinson, *Sea Otter Chiefs*, chap. 2. For an O'ahu man calling himself "General Washington" in 1798, see Townsend, "Extract from the Diary," 20.

[96] Bell, "Log of the *Chatham*," *Honolulu Mercury* 1 (Oct. 1929): 63.

[97] See Menzies, Feb. 22, 1793, MS 32641, BL; Manby, "Journal of Vancouver's Voyage," *Honolulu Mercury* 1 (July 1929): 40. For their part, Britons viewed Kamehameha as a born leader, combining the enlightened virtues of "an open, cheerful, and sensible mind[,] . . . great generosity, and goodness of disposition" with the imposing physical presence and charisma of a Native chief – these latter traits being necessary for the ruler of an as-yet "savage" people (Vancouver, in Lamb, *Voyage*, 807). Later, American traders had much the same perspective; see Shaler, "Journal of a Voyage."

Among Kamehameha's principal advisors were two British seamen who had been captured in a skirmish off Maui in 1790. Englishman John Young and Welshman Isaac Davis had both married ali'i women and acquired significant landholdings. It appears both foreigners were also due the respect of native-born chiefs.[98] For example, their food and lodgings were governed by strict kapu. Although their physical appearance would have attracted attention early on, there is no record of Hawaiians conceiving of Young and Davis as fundamentally different from their Native chiefs.[99] (Hawaiian society was not hamstrung by racialist notions that ascribed ability or demeanor to ethnicity.) Kamehameha shrewdly estimated the value of the seamen's skills and knowledge as critical to his own goals. Despite being in the service of "his Owhyhean majesty," both Young and Davis served as important informants on island affairs to Vancouver.[100]

Common seamen once again enjoyed the charms of local women. On Maui, Manby luxuriated in the arms of two young women in a "neat[,] well built" hut nestled beside a coconut grove. Amazed at his good fortune, Manby tried to capture something of the experience in his journal, including the women's names as he understood them: "Phiavotos the eldest had scarcely reached her nineteenth year: Movinoo hardly her eighteenth ... Ten thousand execrations did I vent, on the dawning day, that compelled me to break from the arms of these bewitching Girls so lovely and endearing."[101] But what of the young women's experiences? Were they aware of the health risks of sleeping with foreign seamen? It is unlikely that Phiavotos and Movinoo had any say in the matter of spending the night with Manby and with each other, as their sexual favors were provided by the Maui ali'i nui Ke'eaumoku Pāpa'iahiahi. In exchange for his night's enjoyment, Manby presented each woman with "a pair of scissors and small looking glasses." Later, when the fleet readied

---

[98] Menzies, Feb. 25 and March 7, 1793, MS 32641, BL; Vancouver, in Lamb, *Voyage*, 1191. See also Bell, "Log of the *Chatham*," *Honolulu Mercury* 1 (Oct. 1929): 67; Bell, in Lamb, *Voyage*, 1144n2.

[99] In a cryptic passage, Kamakau hinted that the authority of haole ali'i, such as Davis and Young, may have been distinct from that of Hawaiians: "For young stranger chiefs [Kamehameha] made three classes: the Okaka, the 'Ai-'ohi'a, and the Uoio" (*Ruling Chiefs*, 176). Pukui and Elbert define 'Okaka as "a particular company of soldiers belonging to Ka-mehameha" without reference to race or nationality (*Hawaiian Dictionary*, s.v. "'Okaka"). I have been unable to find other references to "'Ai-'ohi'a" ("eater of mountain apple"?) or "Uoio."

[100] Vancouver, in Lamb, *Voyage*, 811, 825.

[101] Manby, "Journal of Vancouver's Voyage," *Honolulu Mercury* 1 (Aug. 1929): 49.

to embark for Oʻahu, they "came down to the Boats" and gave Manby "two small pieces of Cloth folded up very curiously like a Ball." When Manby unfolded the cloth, he discovered "six pearls in each."[102] To Manby, the gift was evidence of fondness or even of mutuality. The reality is more opaque. Had Keʻeaumoku Pāpaʻiahiahi deputized the women once again, as an investment in the growing sex trade? Or were the pearls gifts of their own choosing? It is not clear.

The first news about Hawaiian health and demography came from Maui. Vancouver was under the impression that the island had been continuously at war from 1779 to 1790, with a respite from fighting only during the preceding two years. Given this recent violence, the commander was not surprised to discover destitute locals. The people brought "only a few small packages of salt" to trade, and the condition of their canoes and habitations revealed their impoverishment.[103] Vancouver had nothing more to say about coastal Maui people. Unlike Rollin he did not make a record of Islander health; thus, little more is known of how the people might have weathered the seven-year interval between La Pérouse and Vancouver.[104]

There was, however, every indication that broader Maui had been hit hard over the past decade. King Kahekili II was still seething from the depredations of Kamehameha's forces, including the loss of hundreds if not thousands of lives.[105] "The present reduced condition of the island" (and of Kahekili's wealth) was the work of Kamehameha's soldiers. They had "laid waste the lands on all sides, broken the fences of the plantations, [and] thrown down the banks of the little canals made for watering the crops." Moreover, all the "hogs, dogs, and fowls, that could not be carried away, were killed, or dispersed over the country." Kahekili's "deplorable account" of Maui was also true of the "neighbouring islands" over which he was sovereign at this time. As Vancouver understood it, the attempted conquest by Kamehameha had "humbled and broken the spirit of the people" who were "at that time under the necessity of collecting provisions" from Oʻahu and Kauaʻi for the "maintenance of their numerous army" on windward Maui, Kamehameha's favorite place of attack.[106]

---

[102] Ibid.   [103] Vancouver, in Lamb, *Voyage*, 851.

[104] Sahlins believed that apparent food shortages on Maui could be explained by the regular diversion of resources to Kahekili's standing army in 1791–94 (*Anahulu*, 1:40).

[105] For an early twentieth-century account – informed by oral traditions – of Kamehameha's depredations on Maui, see Fornander, *Account of the Polynesian Race*, 2:226–27.

[106] Vancouver, in Lamb, *Voyage*, 860–61.

The mōʻī Kahekili (Thunder) and his thirty-three-year-old son Kalanikūpule, the crown prince of Maui, elicited Vancouver's only comments about Hawaiian health at Maui and Oʻahu. For more than a decade, Kalanikūpule and his father had been resisting Kamehameha's imperial ambitions for Maui and its neighbors. When Vancouver arrived at Oʻahu, where Kalanikūpule was staying, the prince was so sick that he was unable to meet with the British dignitaries. Kalanikūpule's delegates explained that the prince was too ill "to walk or sit upright" without pain.[107] Two days later, the prince agreed to be raised to the deck of the ship in a chair and then "laid on a sofa in the cabin" for the surgeon Menzies to examine him. Kalanikūpule was "very weak & emaciated from a pulmonary complaint" accompanied by fever. Menzies gave the chief "some medicines" and directions on "how to manage his complaint."[108] While Western medicine in this period could neither explain the cause of tuberculosis nor differentiate its various manifestations, a seasoned British surgeon like Menzies would have had extensive experience (if little success) treating it.

A diagnosis cannot be known, but tuberculosis is a good guess for Kalanikūpule. He would soon have company in his immediate family. Meanwhile, Kalanikūpule's father Kahekili would shortly die of unknown causes, leaving an ailing son in charge of three islands that Kamehameha had already proven he would spare no expense to seize.

The death of Kahekili, the most powerful chief on the islands, deserves a closer look. Vancouver speculated – and Menzies concurred – that Kahekili's "intemperat[e]" use of ʻawa, "which he took in great quantities," had combined with "the toils of long and fatiguing wars" by 1793 "to bring upon him a premature old age."[109] This is curious, since earlier visitors failed to mention the mōʻī's health problems. British merchant Nathaniel Portlock had met with Kahekili on three separate occasions in 1786 (for days at a time) without the least indication that Kahekili's health was anything but robust. Indeed Portlock described him as "an

---

[107] Ibid., 875.   [108] Menzies, March 22, 1793, MS 32641, BL.
[109] Vancouver, in Lamb, *Voyage*, 862. See also Menzies, March 12, 1793, MS 32641, BL. Kauaʻi regent Inamoʻo had also experienced a decline: "His limbs[,] no longer able to support his aged and venerable person, seemed not only deserted by their former muscular strength, but their substance was also entirely wasted away, and the skin, now inclosing the bones only, hung loose and uncontracted from the joints, whilst a dry white scurf, or rather scales which overspread the whole surface of his body from head to foot, tended greatly to increase the miserable and deplorable appearance of his condition" (Vancouver, in Lamb, *Voyage*, 890). The skin condition is diagnostic of ʻawa abuse.

exceedingly stout well-made man about fifty years old," who, unlike the local kāhuna, would not "touch either wine or spirits, nor did he ever use the yava ['awa], but always drank water."[110] William Beresford, Portlock's supercargo, similarly noted that Kahekili was "tall, straight, and well-made" but added that "his eyes seem rather weak, and affected with a kind of rheum [watery or crusty discharge]; but whether this is owing to disease, or to a temporary cold, I cannot say."[111] Kahekili's rheumy eyes in December 1786 suggest that Portlock was probably wrong about the king's abstention from 'awa, yet Portlock and Beresford agreed that Kahekili's body was sound and showed none of the physical signs of heavy 'awa use with which both Britons had become familiar.[112] Two years later, in 1788, Colnett and Taylor met with Kahekili and failed to report any problems with his health.[113] (In 1792, Vancouver had been unable to meet with Kahekili because the king was at battle, defending his possessions against Kamehameha.[114]) Kahekili's physical condition in 1793 – including his heavy consumption of 'awa – thus presents a problem: Why would a robust, "well-made," fifty-five-year-old king suddenly look so frail and be consuming 'awa so aggressively?

One explanation is that Vancouver was right. Long years of warfare, coupled with heavy 'awa consumption, had worn down the formerly hale mōʻī, aging him prematurely. But so quickly? A more intriguing possibility is that Kahekili was aggressively consuming 'awa to treat some disease. One of the principal medicinal herbs in Hawaiian *materia medica*, 'awa was prescribed for innumerable health conditions, including gonorrhea.[115] As mōʻī, there would have been no limits on the amount of 'awa that Kahekili could consume, which would explain the signs of toxicity that Vancouver and Menzies observed in 1793. Given that Menzies had already diagnosed Kahekili's son Kalanikūpule with a "pulmonary complaint" and would soon diagnose one of Kahekili's wives with consumption, it is not unlikely that Kahekili himself was sick with tuberculosis in 1793. Previous historians have suggested old age or

---

[110] Portlock, *Voyage round the World*, 155–58.

[111] Beresford, *Voyage round the World*, 97–98.

[112] Portlock, *Voyage round the World*, 156–57. Portlock had first seen the physical effects of 'awa abuse with Cook in 1778–79. In 1786, he described 'awa use among various kāhuna, including "an old priest" in Kahekili's party, whose skin was marred by the telltale "leprous scurf" (ibid., 157).

[113] See Colnett, in Galois, *Voyage to the North West*, 178; Taylor, ibid., 266.

[114] Vancouver, in Lamb, *Voyage*, 453.

[115] Judd, Hawaiian-language medical book, n.p., HMCS.

'awa abuse as the cause of Kahekili's death, but tuberculosis seems at least as likely.[116]

Scholars have failed to note the double opportunity presented to Kamehameha by the frail health and early death of the mōʻī Kahekili coinciding with the debilitating illness of Kahekili's son, the novice mōʻī Kalanikūpule. More favorable circumstances for conquest can hardly be imagined. Kamehameha shortly triumphed over Kalanikūpule at the Battle of Nuʻuanu. It is unclear to what extent Kalanikūpule had regained his strength by the time of this defeat. The long-term health of the Maui mōʻī proved inconsequential: Kamehameha had him sacrificed to the war god Kū shortly after his capture. And with that, the Kingdom of Maui came to a sudden and inglorious end, less than a year after Vancouver's third and final visit.

The first news Vancouver received upon his return to the Big Island in January 1794 was that Kamehameha had been "cuckolded" by his favorite (and second-highest-ranking) wife, the chiefess Kaʻahumanu (Bird-Feather Cloak). Born on Maui around 1768 to Namahana (the wife of an earlier king of Maui) and Keʻeaumoku (a Big Island chief in exile on Maui and soon-to-be royal governor of that island), Kaʻahumanu was third cousin to Kamehameha through her father. Their marriage had been arranged when Kamehameha was a boy and Kaʻahumanu still a toddler. Importantly, Kaʻahumanu outranked Kamehameha, and thus officially required his deference, though it should be noted that rank and "rights" as a woman were not one and the same in Hawaiian society.[117]

Kamehameha explained to Vancouver that his own high rank "was a sort of licence" for carnal "indulgences" and that this behavior in turn "pleaded [an] excuse for [Kaʻahumanu's] infidelity." Vancouver was

---

[116] Kamakau wrote that Kahekili lived to the age of eighty-seven, an error carried forward by later historians (Kamakau, *Ruling Chiefs*, 166; Fornander, *Account of the Polynesian Race*, 2:260). It is not clear whether Kahekili's premature aging contributed to this miscalculation. Historian A. F. Bushnell described a meeting between Menzies and one of Kahekili's wives whom, the author claims, the former had met in 1788; in the scene, Menzies observes the young woman to be "wonderfully altered" from her previous state, "far gone in a consumption" and with "the appearance of a woman advanced in years" ("'The Horror' Reconsidered," 144). Despite extensive research into the relevant primary sources, I have not been able to verify this meeting, which the author miscited. If Bushnell was correct, Kahekili's wife (one of three) would be the second member of the Maui royal family to be identified as potentially tubercular.

[117] Kaʻahumanu was probably *aliʻi naha*, third-highest rank; Kamehameha was *aliʻi wohi*, fourth-highest (Kirch, *How Chiefs Became Kings*, 36). Nineteenth-century authorities differ as to both the number and classification of aliʻi groupings (Brown, *Facing the Spears of Change*, x).

FIGURE 2.3 An older Ka'ahumanu, with attendant ("*Reine Cahoumanou*"); inset, Ka'ahumanu ("*Femme des Iles Sandwich*"). Louis Choris, 1816. Courtesy of Honolulu Museum of Art (#10867, #12158).

happy to help bring about a speedy resolution to the tiff so that no "adverse party" could take advantage of the situation to unseat Kamehameha; Ka'ahumanu's father Ke'eaumoku was of particular concern to the commander.[118] Together Kamehameha and Vancouver plotted a scheme to reunite the king and queen aboard the *Discovery*. Kamehameha took two sheets of paper and "made certain marks with a pencil on each of them": one sheet indicated that the situation on the *Discovery* was auspicious and Kamehameha could come aboard and reconcile with his wife; the other sheet indicated that all was not well and that a different plan would need to be hatched. Depending on how Vancouver found Ka'ahumanu, he would send one or the other sheet of paper to Kamehameha on shore to indicate the course of action to be

[118] Vancouver, in Lamb, *Voyage*, 1157–59. Vancouver was under the impression that Ka'ahumanu's affair had been conducted with the upstart chief Ka'iana, discussed earlier (ibid., 1142). Other sources identify the attractive young chief Kanihonui as the object of Ka'ahumanu's affection. Kamakau claimed that Ka'ahumanu was "under the influence of liquor" when she "first gave way to her desire ... and slept with Ka-niho-nui" (*Ruling Chiefs*, 194).

taken.[119] As it turned out, Ka'ahumanu was amenable to reconciliation, and the plan worked.

Yet all was not settled. "Surprized" by Ka'ahumanu's final request, Vancouver at first took it "as a matter of jest." The queen asked him to secure a "solemn promise" from Kamehameha that upon her return to his hale "he would not beat her." The mō'ī offered every assurance that "nothing of the kind should take place," yet according to Vancouver, Ka'ahumanu "would not be satisfied without my accompanying them home to the royal residence."[120] If Ka'ahumanu's concern about physical violence were exceptional, it might deserve little comment. However, another female ali'i bore signs of physical abuse, according to the surgeon Menzies. Indeed, the beating of "Tipoke-avee" by Keli'imaika'i (Good Chief) may have inspired Ka'ahumanu's own request for protection. (Keli'imaika'i was Kamehameha's full brother and, thus, brother-in-law to Ka'ahumanu.) Tipoke-avee's alleged misdemeanor, like Ka'ahumanu's, was sexual intimacy with a chief not her husband.[121] In light of later developments, Ka'ahumanu's demand of protection against physical harm (and of her proper restoration as queen) is of greater importance than the couple's sexual dalliances and brief estrangement in 1794, yet historians have largely failed to make note of the former.[122] Ali'i gender relations would continue to be fraught well into the nineteenth century.

Vancouver was not the first or last agent of empire to believe that he had obtained the Sandwich Islands for himself or his monarch.[123] With his chiefs assembled aboard the *Discovery*, Kamehameha "explained the reasons ... that had induced him to offer the island to the protection of Great Britain." First, he identified the various nations that had been represented at the islands since the arrival of Cook. Each of these was "too powerful" to be "resist[ed]." Secondly, as visitors were now arriving more

---

[119] Vancouver, in Lamb, *Voyage*, 1157–1159. For an analogous scene among the Tupinamba of Brazil, see Lévi-Strauss, *Tristes Tropiques*, chap. 28.

[120] Vancouver, in Lamb, *Voyage*, 1160.

[121] Menzies, Feb. 24, 1794, MS 155, NLA. It is unclear what relation Tipoke-avee bore to the ruling chiefs or whether she was formally Keli'imaika'i's wife. A Boston trader contrasted the commercial roles of Northwest Coast Native women with the "unfortunate ladies of the Sandwich Islands" under the "despotic government" of Kamehameha (Jackman, *Journal of William Sturgis*, 34). For the "beating" of Tahitian women for violations of chastity in 1769, see Banks, *Endeavor* journal, 1:345, SLNSW.

[122] An exception is Silverman, *Kaahumanu*, 27–38.

[123] British trader William Brown apparently gained a cession of the major islands (except Kaua'i and Ni'ihau) from Kahekili in 1793. According to Menzies, Brown's "contract" was signed by Kahekili and four Hawaiian advisors, plus Brown and four of his own men (Lamb, *Voyage*, 1196n3).

frequently, Islanders would be "liable to more ill treatment, and still greater impositions … unless they could be protected" by one of the "civilized powers with whose people they had become acquainted."[124]

Did Vancouver put words in Kamehameha's mouth? Later visitors from other nations – notably, Russian naval officers – believed he had.[125] Yet it is not difficult to imagine the Big Island mō'ī seeing matters this way. European and American firepower dwarfed Kamehameha's defenses in 1794, and he and his fellow chiefs had been in desperate pursuit of European arms for half a decade. Kamehameha had eleven *haole* (foreigners) in his inner circle at this point, two-thirds of them Britons. Their advice may well have been along the lines of Kamehameha's statement.[126] Moreover, Vancouver's men had just constructed Kamehameha's first warship, unthinkable without foreign tools and technology. The *Britanee* and other warships would become Kamehameha's principal obsession in the years to come, enabling his conquest of the archipelago.[127] Finally, it should be noted that Kamehameha's power was neither absolute nor uncontested in 1794 and that the volume of foreign traffic would have seemed, to him as to other Islanders, unrelenting and uncontrollable. Only an alliance with an imperial power could ensure the mō'ī's continued rule over the politically volatile Big Island, and only foreign ships and weapons could allow him to extend his rule to the other island polities. It is therefore difficult to maintain that the presence of Europeans "provided no more than contexts and opportunities for the working out of indigenous motivations and tendencies" in the building of a Polynesian kingdom such as Kamehameha's or that his was a "regime built on indigenous foundations and beliefs."[128] As in Tahiti where a similar kingdom was slowly evolving, European influence was central and critical to the process. Later, in the 1810s, Kamehameha wielded sufficient power to banish all foreigners; yet he never chose that path.

---

[124] Vancouver, in Lamb, *Voyage*, 1180.   [125] E.g., Golovnin, *Around the World*, 196–97.
[126] Some of the assembled chiefs dissented; see Menzies, Feb. 25, 1794, MS 155, NLA. For haole advisors to Kamehameha and the Big Island ali'i, including "one Portuguese, one Chinese, and one Genoese," see Vancouver, in Lamb, *Voyage*, 1191–94. Bell listed "eleven white Men who intended remaining in the Island … English, Irish, Portuguese, Genoaese[,] Americans and Chinese" (Bell, ibid., 1194n).
[127] For Kamehameha's "obsession" with warship construction, see, e.g., Langsdorff, *Voyages and Travels*, 166. For an argument against the importance of military technology in Kamehameha's consolidation of power, see D'Arcy, "Warfare and State Formation."
[128] Douglas, "Pre-European Societies," 20 ("provided no more"); Gascoigne, *Encountering the Pacific*, 329 ("regime built").

Probably the "cession" of the Big Island was, for Kamehameha, more of an alliance whereby Britain would offer military protection in exchange for continued hospitality. Of course Hawaiian conceptions of alliance (much less contracts) differed considerably from those of Britons. Until and unless George III boarded a ship and sailed across the Pacific to make good Vancouver's claim, all agreements could be considered tentative at best – even Kamehameha's alleged consent to Vancouver's pronouncement that the mō'ī and his fellow Islanders "were no longer *Tanata no Owhyhee*" (people of Hawai'i) "but *Tanata no Britanee*" (people of Britain).[129] Yet Kamehameha seems to have acknowledged the *realpolitik* of island life amid constant incursions by foreign powers and regular challenges by competing chiefs. Cession or alliance: either made sense in the circumstances.

As Vancouver's fleet readied to leave the Sandwich Islands for the last time in March 1794, they shared a harborage at Ni'ihau with two American ships.[130] It was a sign of things to come. In fact, Vancouver's three visits would mark the high point of British influence in Hawai'i. By 1800, the British had virtually disappeared from Hawaiian ports, replaced wholesale (and then some) by Americans.[131] As early as 1802, a British merchant at Hawai'i was ready to cede the entire Pacific to the United States, since it appeared there was "scarcely an inlet in these most unknown seas" that American commerce had "not penetrated."[132]

Sailing west from Kaua'i and Ni'ihau, Vancouver's fleet passed the "orphan" island of Nihoa. Vancouver was aware of the uninhabited rocky atoll from the reports of Colnett, Duncan, and other British merchants. Menzies was curious what Hawaiians themselves knew of this island 137 miles west of Kaua'i and Ni'ihau. Before leaving Kaua'i, Menzies had "questioned several of the Natives" about Nihoa, but "all of them declared that they knew nothing of it, & naturally enquired of us the

---

[129] Vancouver, in Lamb, *Voyage*, 1182.

[130] Ibid., 1202. On Kaua'i Vancouver and his men attended a massive hula. Some six hundred dancers, mostly women, performed in honor of the unnamed pregnant wife of Kaua'i regent Inamo'o. The ceremony would be "frequently" repeated until she was "brought to bed" to deliver. It is not clear whether fertility on Kaua'i had already been affected by the ma'i malihini, but the scale of the hula and the repeat performances suggest that the stakes for royal procreation in 1794 were high. See Vancouver, in Lamb, *Voyage*, 1199–1200. See also Menzies, March 11–12, 1794, MS 155, NLA. For a discussion of this type of hula, see Malo, *Mo'olelo Hawai'i*, 424–26.

[131] Bradley, *American Frontier in Hawaii*, 17.

[132] Turnbull, *Voyage round the World*, 14.

size of it – the distance it was from them & whether it was inhabited?"[133] In fact, legends and songs survived among Islanders about Nihoa, which has a rich archaeological record; yet apparently no contact had been made with the island for generations.[134] If all the world seemed to be arriving at Hawai'i in the 1790s, Hawaiians themselves had not reached their closest neighboring island.

How and when did sexual exchanges at Hawai'i evolve from a cultural imperative to "marry up" to a proper market? For many Islanders, "market" forces were already at play in 1779. Iron, for instance, was clearly a valuable commodity. By 1786 chiefs and agents regularly took a cut of the proceeds, and the sex trade itself grafted easily onto traditional forms of tribute. But the fact that sexual exchange persisted without interruption late into the nineteenth century makes any argument about the development of new forms of exploitation and commodification – say, in the 1840s – difficult to sustain.[135] Nor is it clear that women's sexuality was "dramatically altered" from an earlier "positive" status in Indigenous society.[136] Other trades came and went over the course of the nineteenth century; the sex trade never abated.

The greater Hawaiian market of the late eighteenth century was a commercial free-for-all, unregulated and without precedent on the islands or in the broader Pacific. From 1786 to 1795 the islands were beset by chronic, costly warfare; the continued spread of introduced infectious diseases; and a rapidly changing social and political scene. Relations between maka'āinana and visiting seamen were dynamic and unpredictable, with island women in particular undermining chiefly authority. Within their own ranks, contentious sexual politics threatened ali'i unity. For enterprising Islanders, the decade was a mad scramble for new knowledge, technology, and diplomatic relations that could protect them against a vast, foreign world beyond their control. Introduced diseases were just one of many foreign commodities people would have to learn to control or, short of that, to endure.

---

[133] Menzies, March 15, 1794, MS 155, NLA.
[134] The steep slopes of Nihoa had at one time been "intensive[ly] cultivat[ed]"; religious structures also dot the island (Emory, *Archaeology of Nihoa*, 3, 7–50). In 1822 Ka'ahumanu sailed with a British captain to claim Nihoa for her kingdom (Kamakau, *Ruling Chiefs*, 153).
[135] Cf. Linnekin, *Sacred Queens*, 185–86.   [136] O'Brien, *Pacific Muse*, 90.

PART II

REVOLUTIONS

3

The Dark Ocean

[T]rying to persuade them the world was so made, they could not believe
a word of it; they said, putting a finger under the globe, if they were there
they should drop off.

—Ebenezer Townsend, *Neptune,* 1798

To explain the multifarious and unpredictable threats to his people in the
1830s, a Hawaiian writer employed metaphor: "If a big wave comes in,
large fishes will come from the dark Ocean which you never saw before,
and when they see the small fishes they will eat them up."[1] In terms of
population loss, the metaphor was apt. In fact, depopulation was the
defining feature of colonialism in this period. If Hawai'i shared this fate
with other Indigenous societies in the wake of European contact, the
causes were distinct. Unlike North America there was no foreign military
conquest and no removal of the Native population. Before 1820 there was
no encroachment on land or large-scale settlement by non-Natives, as in
Australia and southern Africa; no exploitation of aboriginal labor and
natural resources, as in British India; and no program of cultural imperialism. Many of these developments would come to pass but not before
profound changes in island society and culture had already transpired.
Nor was population loss a function of outmigration despite claims to that
effect then and since.[2] Depopulation was instead the work of a steady

---

[1] Davida Malo to Kīna'u and Mataio Kekūanāo'a, qtd. in Kuykendall, *Hawaiian Kingdom,*
1:153.
[2] E.g., Malo, "On the Decrease of Population," 127–28; Schmitt, *Demographic Statistics of
Hawaii,* 38–41, 182. Hawaiian voyagers were mostly male and too few in this period to
have a significant effect on island demography.

stream of visitors from around the globe, the germs and commodities they left in their wake, and rising antagonism among Hawaiian elites in a new world born of contact with the West.

The colonial process in Hawaiʻi was vicious, lethal, and inexorable. But no one was at the helm. Typical models and metaphors of colonialism obscure more than they illuminate. Conquest and domination are difficult to sustain until later in the nineteenth century and then must be qualified by the roles played by Native monarchs and elites of mixed descent. There was no frontier against which a colonial vanguard could be enlisted to push and nothing in the way of a borderlands region separating cultural groups.[3] Nor was Hawaiʻi a bicultural or hybrid society before 1820: there were Hawaiians, there were foreigners, and eventually there were people of mixed descent.[4] But no one eluded chiefly authority; and empires could hardly be pitted against each other when their agents sought little more than food, water, and sex. There was no "mutual need" between Islanders and newcomers, and thus Hawaiʻi was not a "middle ground."[5] No one's stay on the islands was "premised on the elimination" of the Natives.[6]

What, then, was Hawaiʻi? A commercial colony, a "maritime enclave," an imperial way station?[7] From the vantage of western Europe and the United States, perhaps; yet no one beyond the eight seas controlled the islands.[8] Power remained firmly in the hands of a chiefly class comprising about 1 percent of the population.[9] The scholarship on settler colonialism is enamored with Hawaiʻi, but the paradigm is a poor fit in this period.[10] Foreigners were neither permanent nor sufficient in number to *settle*

---

[3] The islands' small size and pie-shaped land divisions (*ahupuaʻa*), spreading outward from the coast to the mountains, resulted in political authority extending far into the interior and uplands.

[4] For New Zealand as a "hybrid world," see O'Malley, *Meeting Place*, 9, 226; for the "bicultural society" of the Mississippi and Missouri basins, see Hyde, *Empires, Nations, and Families*, chap. 1.

[5] For the preponderance of "middle grounds," after Richard White's eponymous work, see Shoemaker, ed., *Clearing a Path*, ix; Richard White, "Preface to the Twentieth Anniversary Edition," in *Middle Ground*, xi–xxiv.

[6] Wolfe, *Settler Colonialism*, 2.   [7] Osterhammel, *Colonialism*, 10–12.

[8] For similar observations about broader Oceania, see Douglas, *Science, Voyages, and Encounters*, 18–22. The eight seas (*nā kai ʻewalu*) refer to the channels separating the major islands.

[9] For the proportion of chiefs to commoners, see Stewart, *Private Journal*, 136.

[10] Settler colonial scholarship on Hawaiʻi includes Banner, *Possessing the Pacific*, chap. 4; Kauanui, *Hawaiian Blood*; Hixson, *American Settler Colonialism*, chap. 7; Conroy-Krutz, *Christian Imperialism*, chap. 4; Rohrer, *Staking Claim*.

anything, and their authority (if not their influence) was sharply limited. As late as 1810 only sixty foreigners resided on Oʻahu, the islands' hub of international commerce.[11] Most, moreover, were temporary residents. Foreigners in Hawaiʻi were captives, deserters, beachcombers, and dreamers. The few who became chiefs became *Hawaiian* chiefs – speaking the Hawaiian language, marrying local women, enforcing (and themselves adhering to) the kapu, and serving at the pleasure of the mōʻī and his ministers. To the extent that anyone brought a "settler ideology" to the remote North Pacific in this period, it was of no consequence.[12] The islands were not for the taking. From the Big Island to Niʻihau, Hawaiʻi was still Native ground.[13]

Imperial agents in Europe and the US could fantasize all they liked of an entrepot, plantation system, or other gold mine in the North Pacific. For now they were just traders. The colonial disruptions that cut at the heart of Hawaiian life and society in this period were thus neither directed by foreigners nor a function of foreign presence in any significant numbers. Most of the colonial disruptions were invisible to the outside world.

By 1800 foreign trade incursions had "broke[n] the subsistence nexus" of traditional Hawaiian society, with the chiefs monopolizing the trades and demanding new forms of labor from the makaʻāinana in order to pay.[14] In the 1810s Hawaiʻi became a single kingdom ruled by the mōʻī Kamehameha. For the aliʻi, these decades proved a struggle to maintain authority in a world where the akua seemed unable or unwilling to help. Since the high chiefs were intermediaries between the deities and the people, chiefly sway among the people was undermined by disease and poor health. Some chiefs and chiefesses began to question the new world that Kamehameha had built. Was it healthy? Could it be sustained? Was it, in a word, *pono* (righteous, proper, effective, balanced)?

This chapter explores the challenges faced by the Hawaiian ruling classes and Native physicians by the twin forces of trade colonialism and poor health. Chiefs and physicians made up distinct groups, yet

---

[11] Jarves, *History of the Hawaiian or Sandwich Islands*, 198. As late as 1836 there were only 600 foreign residents on the entire archipelago – one half of 1 percent of the total population – three-quarters of them in bustling Honolulu and the rest confined to coastal areas (Schmitt, *Demographic Statistics of Hawaii*, 43).

[12] For "settler ideology," see, e.g., Hixson, *American Settler Colonialism*, vii–viii, chap. 1. New Zealand offers a useful comparison with Hawaiʻi in this period; see O'Malley, *Gathering Place*; Ballantyne, *Entanglements of Empire*.

[13] DuVal, *Native Ground*; Ballantyne, *Entanglements of Empire*, 10.

[14] Ralston, "Hawaii 1778–1854," 25.

both were affected by dramatic changes in the peoples' health. A single epidemic – the *'ōku'u* ("squatting disease") of 1804 – posed the single greatest challenge to the Hawaiian medical order while also delaying Kamehameha's conquest of Kaua'i and Ni'ihau for a decade. By the 1810s, foreign physicians (and others posing as such) gained considerable political influence over the high chiefs.

HEAPED-UP BODIES

In January 1796 a former captain of the Vancouver expedition met with Kamehameha on newly conquered O'ahu. Wearing "European clothes" under a "beautiful" bird-feather cloak large enough almost to cover his nearly seven-foot frame, the mō'ī offered William Robert Broughton himself a cloak, along with "twenty hogs, and some cocoa-nuts."[15] Yet little more was to be had at Waikīkī: no fresh water, no taro, no vegetables. The "situation of the natives," wrote Broughton, was "miserable, as they were nearly starving: and, as an additional grievance, universally infected with the itch."[16] Earlier reports of scabies had only come from Maui, and it is unlikely that Broughton confused it with venereal disease, as he identified each condition on the Big Island. Thus, scabies may have been a new affliction at O'ahu.[17] The hunger at Waikīkī was the result of Kamehameha's recent conquest of the island. The mō'ī's attentions seemed to be "entirely engrossed" by a warship that English carpenters were building for him. The plan was to conquer Kaua'i and thereby reign supreme across the archipelago. Broughton "dissuaded" Kamehameha from this course of action, arguing that only "famine and disease" would result from further conquests; but with "so large a supply of muskets and ammunition, together with some 3 and 4 pounders [cannons] for his boats," the mō'ī would not be stopped. By this point Kamehameha enjoyed the service of some sixteen Europeans.[18]

Six months later Broughton found conditions at Waikīkī worse than in February, with "all the hogs" having been destroyed by Kamehameha's men when they left to conquer Kaua'i and most of the crops having "perished through neglect of cultivation." It is doubtful that these conditions extended very far inland, yet like other visitors, Broughton generalized

[15] Broughton, *Voyage of Discovery*, 38–39.   [16] Ibid., 40.
[17] Six months later, scabies was observed on the Big Island (ibid., 70).
[18] Ibid., 41–42. By December 1802 Kamehameha had "upwards of twenty vessels, of different sizes, from twenty-five to fifty tons" (Turnbull, *Voyage round the World*, 60).

from conditions on shore. The "scarcity" of food had caused the "destruction of many of the unfortunate natives, who, through absolute want, had been induced to steal" and were therefore executed. Meanwhile Broughton wrote that Kamehameha had lost "six thousand of his people" in the conquest of Oʻahu.[19] Like Vancouver, Broughton chalked all these losses up to war. Yet Broughton's own men had been "infected with the venereal disease, contracted at the Sandwich Islands."[20] Like others, Broughton failed to make the connection.

No one could make that mistake with the ʻōkuʻu. It is ironic but probably not unusual that the worst epidemic in living memory gave birth to a rich body of medical lore. By the end, thousands had perished, and Kamehameha's conquest was ground to a halt. The principal observers were eastern Europeans sailing for Tsar Alexander I of Russia. The tsar's officers were highly educated scientists and naturalists, physicians, and ethnographers for whom Cook and Vancouver set the standard. Their observations of Hawaiian life and health in 1804 have been largely ignored by historians.

One day after the arrival of the tsar's fleet, six canoes with a dozen Hawaiian men approached off the eastern coast of the Big Island. The men climbed aboard, "shook hands with every one they saw," and greeted the newcomers with what sounded to the captain like "how do you do[?]"[21] The greeting suggested the extent of Anglo-American influence by 1804. Tsar Alexander's "Russian" delegation to Hawaiʻi would communicate exclusively in English for the duration of their stay. On the Big Island, the naturalist determined that most Islanders "of any rank or distinction" could now speak English.[22]

[19] Broughton, *Voyage of Discovery*, 71. Estimated mortality in the Battle of Nuʻuanu alone ranges from 300 to 10,000 (Schmitt, "Catastrophic Mortality in Hawaii," 67).
[20] Broughton, *Voyage of Discovery*, 48. Likewise, a Connecticut fur trader wrote that his men had contracted "Sandwich Island girl disease" during a weeklong stay at the Big Island in 1798 (John Hurlbut, log of the *Neptune*, qtd. in Eiseman, "On the Neptune, Three Years under Sail").
[21] Lisiansky, *Voyage round the World*, 98. See also the earlier edition of Lisiansky's journal (1812), in Barratt, *Russian Discovery*, 29–54. Lisiansky, who had spent seven years in Britain and the US, apparently penned both the Russian and English versions of his *Voyage* (Lisiansky, *Voyage round the World*, xvi–xxi; Barratt, *Russian Discovery*, 185).
[22] Langsdorff, *Voyages and Travels*, 164. Langsdorff and other journalists observed that Big Islanders understood English better than Marquesan, a related Polynesian tongue. One of the expedition's crewmen, apparently fluent in North Marquesan, tried to communicate with Hawaiians but could not be understood (Langsdorff, *Voyages and Travels*, 162; F. I. Shemelin journal, in Barratt, *Russian Discovery*, 97; N. P. Rezanov journal, ibid., 85).

After the greeting committee had departed, an old man paddled up to the *Nadezhda* (Hope) with "quite a young girl" whose "awkward behaviour" indicated to the commander Adam Johann von Krusenstern that she was a virgin.[23] Krusenstern declined the offer. The following day another girl who spoke some English and was "very immodest" was again refused by the seamen.[24] Russian refusal of the girls probably had less to do with their age or behavior than with their skin conditions. According to Krusenstern, there was hardly an Islander "whose skin was not scarred, either in consequence of the venereal disease or of the use of the ['awa]; though among the lower or poorer classes, these marks could not arise from the latter." Here Krusenstern revealed more than he realized. Scholars are divided on the question of when 'awa consumption among the maka'āinana rose to the level of toxicity marked by the characteristic scaly "scurf skin," yet by the 1810s Hawaiians of all social classes were treating venereal and other maladies with regular doses of 'awa.[25] They would continue to do so for a century. Krusenstern unwittingly diagnosed two conditions in one. Some Islanders' skin conditions were being exacerbated by heavy consumption of 'awa.

As many as ten Islanders spent two full days aboard the *Nadezhda* in June 1804, enabling a ship clerk to observe them up close: "Their bodies were covered with some kind of sore which excreted morbid matter of a reddish-white color." Following Krusenstern's lead, Fedor Ivanovich Shemelin proposed 'awa consumption, venereal disease, and the "torrid climate" as possible explanations but ultimately rejected all three after consulting with a young Hawaiian informant. According to Shemelin, "Kenokhoia" believed that seawater was the main cause of the people's

---

[23] Krusenstern, *Voyage round the World*, 1:193. Barratt translated "awkward behaviour" as "bashfulness and modesty" (I. F. Krusenstern journal, in Barratt, *Russian Discovery*, 87). The scene made an impression on various members of the expedition, e.g., Shemelin, ibid., 91. For young girls in the Māori sex trade, some of whom were enslaved, see O'Malley, *Meeting Place*, 154.

[24] Krusenstern, *Voyage round the World*, 194–96. Shemelin was more impressed: "With amazing agility [she] leapt . . . onto the ship by way of the side-ropes and, at the first step on deck, said in English, 'Good morning!' Looking at all with merry eyes full of animation, she held out her hand to everyone approaching her, or else went up to individuals and did the same . . . Her vivacity was matchless" (Shemelin, in Barratt, *Russian Discovery*, 92).

[25] Corney, *Voyages*, 104–5. For 'awa use among commoners, see Handy, *Hawaiian Planter*, 201–5; Titcomb, "Kava in Hawaii," 136–38; Whistler, *Polynesian Herbal Medicine*, 185–86. On 'awa as treatment for "incurable" diseases, see Chun, *Hawaiian Medicine Book*, 64–65. 'Awa was used for venereal disease into the twentieth century; see Mouritz, "Path of the Destroyer," 115.

skin eruptions. "As proof," Kenokhoia noted that the Islanders who lived inland and bathed with fresh water were "quite free of the sores."[26] It is not hard to imagine people living far from the coast with its constant stream of foreigners were less afflicted by diseases of the skin, but Shemelin was apparently satisfied with Kenokhoia's seawater explanation. In any case, what seemed obvious signs of venereal disease in Krusenstern's account now appear less so. The distribution of skin eruptions across the body sounds more like 'awa overuse, scabies, or perhaps tuberculosis than gonorrhea or syphilis. While none of the Russians mentioned "the itch" in 1804, scabies should not be eliminated as a possible contributing factor, especially given that Broughton had reported people on the Big Island "generally affected by it" in 1796.[27] The cartographer wrote that the people were also "all lousy."[28] While louse-spread typhus was never reported in nineteenth-century Hawai'i, lice and scabies together constituted a general plague among the islands' poor by the 1820s.[29]

Shemelin's counterpart aboard the *Neva*, the clerk Nikolai Ivanovich Korobitsyn, was not sure whether the peoples' abundant scarring was the result of venereal disease or something else: a "scorbutic disease," for instance. This is an odd conjecture. If any disease was unlikely to afflict Hawaiians on their home islands, it was scurvy. Taro and sweet potatoes are loaded with ascorbic acid (vitamin C), which renders scurvy a near impossibility, even on famine rations. Russia, on the other hand, had long experience with endemic scurvy, while expeditions in the North Pacific had to be hypervigilant to prevent the disease below decks.[30] Already at the Big Island one sailor had apparently come down with scurvy from the long voyage, while another crew member may have been on the verge

---

[26] Shemelin, in Barratt, *Russian Discovery*, 96–97. See also N. I. Korobitsyn journal, ibid., 79; Langsdorff, *Voyages and Travels*, 162; Lisiansky, *Voyage round the World*, 103. On "Kenokhoia," who traveled to St. Petersburg with the expedition, acquiring the name "Vasilii Moller," see Barratt, *Russian Discovery*, 102. Later American observers also attributed skin conditions to bathing in seawater (Stewart, *Journal of a Residence*, 155).

[27] See Broughton, *Voyage of Discovery*, 70.

[28] E. E. Levenshtern (Löwenstern) journal, in Barratt, *Russian Discovery*, 108. Another translation reads "scabby" for "lousy" (Moessner, *First Russian Voyage*, 110). Abundant body lice were observed on the Society Islands in 1769; see Banks, *Endeavor* journal, 1:339, SLNSW. Boyd argues that Northwest Coast Indians were afflicted by body lice in this period, yet the evidence he cites could (again) refer to scabies (*Coming of the Spirit of Pestilence*, 285–87).

[29] See Chapter 5.

[30] Roger K. French, "Scurvy," in Kiple, ed., *Cambridge World History of Human Disease*, 1001.

of it.[31] Korobitsyn likely used his own experience to understand the Hawaiians' skin conditions. Yet early nineteenth-century European medical terminology did not help matters: while "scurvy" and "scurf" have entirely distinct etymologies, they tended to be mixed up in the medical literature, particularly since one of the clinical manifestations of scurvy is dry, rough skin and lumps on the scalp.[32] It is also important to consider the possibility that poor diet or even malnutrition among the maka'āinana on the Kona coast may have resulted in something that looked like scurvy. At least five expedition journalists described Islanders as "lean" or unimpressive of build compared to the Marquesans they had just visited.[33] The cartographer meanwhile was so concerned about the poor rations at the Big Island that he was reduced to prayer: "May God grant us health since salt meat, peas, grits, and hardtack are our [only] food."[34] No one in 1804 reported on the actual diet of Big Islanders.

   Korobitsyn was the first foreigner (and the only member of the expedition) to record Hawaiian treatments for skin afflictions. The people on the Big Island, wrote Korobitsyn, "consider aienia root an effective preventative against the disease in question, and for the same reason will drink sea water which, they suppose in their ignorance, is also quite efficacious."[35] Despite the slur, Korobitsyn here provided better information about Hawaiian herbal medicine than any previous observer. Oral history and the documentary record provide countless references to 'aiea

---

[31] Löwenstern, in Moessner, *First Russian Voyage*, 115.

[32] French, "Scurvy," 1001. References to both "dry scurf" and "dry scurvy" no doubt led to considerable confusion among practitioners and laypeople. See, e.g., Linden, *Treatise on the Three Medicinal Mineral Waters*, 229–30; Spilsbury, *Treatise on the Method of Curing the Gout*, 33, 117, 120. Scottish seaman Alexander Campbell noted "dry scurvy" in 1809, as did British trader Peter Corney in 1815 (Campbell, *Voyage*, 131; Corney, *Voyages*, 104–5).

[33] Korobitsyn, in Barratt, *Russian Discovery*, 79; Krusenstern, ibid., 88; Shemelin, ibid., 97; Rezanov, ibid., 84; Langsdorff, *Voyages and Travels*, 162. See also Langsdorff, *Remarks and Observations on a Voyage*, 134: "The islanders we had an opportunity to observe were naked, unclean, not well built, of middle stature, and with dark, dirty, brown skin covered with rashes and sores, probably the result of drinking cava or of venereal disease."

[34] Löwenstern, in Moessner, *First Russian Voyage*, 112.

[35] Korobitsyn, in Barratt, *Russian Discovery*, 79. See also Andreev, *Russkie otkrytiia*, 171. (Thanks to Heather VanMouwerik for reviewing Korobitsyn's original Russian.) '*Aieana* seems to have been an older form of the word 'aiea (Pukui and Elbert, *Hawaiian Dictionary*, s.v. "'aieana"). Of course Korobitsyn may have been mistaken in claiming that the people drank seawater; perhaps the saltwater was mixed with herbs or filtered and treated in some way that has not been recorded.

(*Nothocestrum*) in the islands' medical arsenal.[36] Korobitsyn thought they were using the "root" of the tree, which may be true, though the common preparation was by mashing, cooking, cooling, and applying the plant material (leaves and bark) to the skin with kapa cloth.

But what was the skin condition (or conditions) for which ʻaiea was being used? Korobitsyn offered his opinion that the "incontinent" (promiscuous) Islanders were continuing "to infect one another."[37] This suggests that the disease was venereal, yet scabies, tuberculosis, and other infectious diseases could also be passed through intimate contact. Ultimately, it cannot be determined whether the Russians were observing the work of ʻawa consumption, scabies, syphilis, tuberculosis, or some combination of these. In any case, the Russian reports show that skin conditions were onerous, aggressive, and widespread at the Big Island.

Russian refusal of girls off the Kona coast did not dissuade other Hawaiians from approaching the fleet. Three days after the second girl was turned away, "about a hundred young women" approached the fleet at dusk, "exhibiting ... the most unequivocal token of pleasure, not doubting of admittance." Capt. Yuri Lisiansky forbade his men on the *Neva* from all "licentious intercourse" with the natives.[38] The following night, the women came again at dusk, "resolved" this time on gaining access to the ships. Forced to seek the assistance of a local chief to place the ship under kapu, Lisiansky proposed the ban in order to prevent his men from catching venereal disease, of which "several of the inhabitants of both sexes ... bore evident marks."[39]

Scheduled to rendezvous at Kodiak Island in Russian America, Lisiansky wanted first to meet the king, Kamehameha, at his new stronghold of Honolulu. Heading north in the *Neva*, Lisiansky got word that "a species of epidemic disease was raging" there, so he beat a course to Kauaʻi instead, where he met with the mōʻī Kaumualiʻi. Like Broughton and other visiting sea captains, Lisiansky was sympathetic with the Kauaʻi

---

[36] E.g., Kaaiakamanu and Akina, *Hawaiian Herbs of Medicinal Value*, 4; Hawaiian Ethnobotany Online Database, s.v. "ʻaiea, hālena," http://data.bishopmuseum.org/eth nobotanydb/. See also Mann, *Enumeration of Hawaiian Plants*, 191; Hillebrand, *Flora of the Hawaiian Islands*, 307–9; Rock, *Indigenous Trees of the Hawaiian Islands*, 417–21. Four species are found on the islands today, at least two of which – smallflower ʻaiea tree (*Nothocestrum breviflorum*) and longleaf ʻaiea shrub (*Nothocestrum longifolium*) – are endemic to the Big Island. Smallflower ʻaiea, which grows in drier, low-lying forests, particularly on the western half of the island, is probably the plant that was being used by coastal people.
[37] Korobitsyn, in Barratt, *Russian Discovery*, 79.
[38] Lisiansky, *Voyage round the World*, 101. [39] Ibid., 103.

chiefs' desire to remain (with Ni'ihau) independent of Kamehameha's rule. Lisiansky informed Kaumuali'i about the epidemic that had recently halted Kamehameha's forces in their planned conquest of his island. This news was "extremely gratifying" to Kaumuali'i, who was "determined to defend himself to the last." The Kaua'i mō'ī had good reason to believe he could do so, equipped as he was with three six-pounder cannons, forty swivels guns, "a number of muskets, and plenty of powder and ball." Kaumuali'i, Lisiansky learned, also had five Europeans in his service.[40]

It is not clear whether Kaumuali'i understood the scale of Kamehameha's military force in 1804, but Lisiansky did. On the Big Island the captain had learned from the haole chief John Young that Kamehameha commanded some seven thousand Hawaiian soldiers and fifty foreigners, twenty-one schooners and hundreds of war canoes, six hundred muskets, dozens of swivel guns, cannons of various sizes, and "a sufficiency of powder, shot, and ball" – in other words, more than ten times the firepower of Kaumuali'i. These forces had all been removed to Honolulu in 1803 to prepare for the invasion of Kaua'i. Lisiansky was convinced that barring the outbreak of disease at southern O'ahu, Kamehameha would have easily conquered Kaua'i and Ni'ihau. In his words, Kamehameha "certainly would have reduced [conquered] Otooway [Kaua'i] last spring, if a disease ... had not spread amongst his troops, and destroyed the flower of his army."[41] Some new disease delayed Kamehameha's conquest of the archipelago.

Events surrounding the epidemic and the terminology used to describe it are revealing. The outbreak was first reported among Kamehameha's army encamped at Honolulu. Warriors were struck dead within days, even hours.[42] People on errands "would die before [they] could reach home," according to Kamakau, who also noted that those who "managed to hold out for a [full] day had a fair chance" of survival but that such survivors "generally lost their hair." Hence, one name for the disease was *po'okole* ("head stripped bare").[43] More common was *ma'i 'ōku'u*

---

[40] Ibid., 111–13. For Kaumuali'i's facility with spoken English by 1804, see V. N. Berkh journal, in Barratt, *Russian Discovery*, 104.

[41] Lisiansky, *Voyage round the World*, 115–16, 133. By 1810 Kamehameha's arsenal had forty-two warships (Kuykendall, *Hawaiian Kingdom*, 1:49–50). His first attempt to conquer Kaua'i, in 1796, was apparently halted by bad weather that some interpreted as an omen (Kamakau, *Ruling Chiefs*, 172–73; see also 'Ī'ī, *Fragments*, 15–16). For introduced infectious disease among the Māori preventing military conquest in 1835, see Evison, *Te Wai Pounamu*, 84–85.

[42] Kamakau, *Ruling Chiefs*, 189; 'Ī'ī, *Fragments*, 33. See also Berkh, in Barratt, *Russian Discovery*, 105.

[43] Kamakau, *Ruling Chiefs*, 189.

("squatting sickness"). It was highly contagious: "One would go to bury someone [and] bec[o]me ill and die"; thus, corpses were left to rot.[44] A chronicle published in the Hawaiian-language press in 1863 indicated that the epidemic lasted "almost three months or more with many deaths occuring from day to day ... The death toll was greater where there were more people."[45]

Three candidates have been suggested for the disease: cholera, typhoid fever, and bacillary or amoebic dysentery. Each of these diseases is caused by ingesting food or water tainted with human or animal fecal matter, and each presents with acute diarrhea, causing loss of water and electro-lytes, which can lead quickly to death.[46] (Typhoid fever is additionally known for its characteristic fever and headache.) 'Ōku'u itself translates as "squatting" or "crouching," indicating a classic diarrheal infection – in this case, spread by the crowded, unsanitary conditions in camp. The 'ōku'u was also the first disease characterized in later Hawaiian-language documents as an *ahulau*, typically translated as "pestilence" or "epidemic" but meaning literally "heaped up," as of dead bodies.[47] The word *ahulau* is suggestive of the scale of devastation at Honolulu.

Based on the available evidence, microbiologist O. A. Bushnell favored typhoid fever to cholera or dysentery.[48] Yet earlier scholars, including Hawaiians, made the case for cholera. In *Ka Nupepa Kuokoa*, Kamakau mentioned that the bodies of victims turned black. (Darkening of the skin is characteristic of cholera-induced dehydration.) An anonymous writer for the same newspaper explicitly identified the 'ōku'u as "*kolera o Asia*"

[44] Kahananui, *Ka Mooolelo Hawaii*, 232.
[45] W. Kahala, "No ka Mai Ahulau," *Ka Nupepa Kuokoa*, Feb. 28, 1863. See also Schmitt, "Okuu," 361; Mouritz, *Our Western Outpost*, 20–21, 34–35. Historians have dated the 'ōku'u anywhere from 1802 to 1807; the Hawaiian-language press invariably dated it to 1804 (W. H. Kaaukaukini, letter to the editor, *Ka Hae Hawaii*, April 7, 1858; *Ka Hae Hawaii*, Sept. 19, 1860). Lisiansky indicates that it began no later than spring 1803.
[46] K. David Patterson, "Amebic Dysentery" and "Bacillary Dysentery," in Kiple, ed., *Cambridge World History of Human Disease*, 568–71, 604–6; Reinhard S. Speck, "Cholera," ibid., 642–49; Herbert L. DuPont, "Diarrheal Diseases (Acute)," ibid., 676–80; Charles W. LeBaron and David W. Taylor, "Typhoid Fever," ibid., 1071–76.
[47] Pukui and Elbert, *Hawaiian Dictionary*, s.v. "ahulau." For the 'ōku'u as a "*ma'i ahu-lau*," see W. H. Kaaukaukini, letter to the editor, *Ka Hae Hawaii*, April 7, 1858; Davida Malo, qtd. in "Honolulu, Nov. 29, 1862," *Ka Nupepa Kuokoa*, Nov. 29, 1862; W. Kahala, "No ka Mai Ahulau," *Ka Nupepa Kuokoa*, Feb. 28, 1863.
[48] Bushnell, *Gifts of Civilization*, 103, 281–82. See also Francis L. Black, in Stannard et al., "Book Review Forum," 269–79, esp. 275. I am not aware of accounts that identify fever or headache with the 'ōku'u. Malo wrote that the prominent medical kahuna Kama believed the 'ōku'u was the same illness as the *ikipuahola*, a legendary epidemic of the time of Waia (*Mo'olelo Hawai'i*, 622).

(Asiatic cholera).[49] Of course, there was no way in 1804 to distinguish the causative microbial agents of digestive infections, and the existing evidence simply does not allow for definitive identification of the epidemic. Hair loss, for instance, does not match any of the proposed diseases. Yet the microbiology of the disease is less important than the source of infection and the human toll. Hawaiian scholar Davida Malo was about ten years old when the ʻōkuʻu struck. He later wrote that it had killed the majority of the people "from Hawaiʻi to Niʻihau."[50] That is doubtful. Many others believed the epidemic to be confined to Oʻahu. In 1970 Hawaiʻi's state demographer argued that the loss of life had been exaggerated, with fatalities rising in documentary records and oral tradition over the course of the nineteenth century.[51] In fact, a number of observers at Oʻahu in 1803–6 failed to mention the epidemic at all.[52] Medical historian Robert C. Schmitt guessed that fatalities were probably confined to Oʻahu, falling somewhere in the range of five to fifteen thousand. Kamehameha had some seven thousand warriors encamped at Honolulu; if Schmitt is correct, half or more may have died. While casualties were worst along Honolulu's shores, it is not possible to determine the extent of the epidemic. Still, Schmitt was correct to judge the ʻōkuʻu among the top three worst epidemics in island history.[53]

A number of factors contributed to the outbreak and spread. The bustling port town of Honolulu was central. If Honolulu was not yet the "cesspit of the Pacific," it was well on its way thanks to foreign merchants, the Islanders they drew to town, and Kamehameha's new military installation.[54] While the king himself preferred to stay at nearby Waikīkī, foreign merchants had been enjoying Honolulu ("sheltered bay") ever since British merchant William Brown coasted into the harbor in 1794. The calm conditions and lack of treacherous lava rock made Honolulu a preferred port of call. In 1803, Kamehameha's army was encamped along the beach near present-day Kakaʻako Waterfront Park downtown. The king's shipbuilders meanwhile were busy constructing large war canoes and ships in the harbor. It is unlikely that ancient kapu

[49] Kamakau, *Ruling Chiefs*, 189; "Honolulu, Nov. 29, 1862," *Ka Nupepa Kuokoa*, Nov. 29, 1862. Schmitt also favored cholera ("Okuu," 362).
[50] Malo, "On the Decrease of Population," 125.
[51] Schmitt, "Okuu," 362. Stannard largely ignored this warning in *Before the Horror*, 54–58.
[52] This includes Turnbull, Langsdorff, and Shaler; the last was on Oʻahu in 1803 and again in 1805 (Shaler, "Journal of a Voyage"; Schmitt, "Okuu," 360).
[53] Schmitt, "Okuu," 363.   [54] Bushnell, *Gifts of Civilization*, 182.

regarding hygiene and sanitation were being observed by Kamehameha's massive army.[55] The kapu system had evolved for rural life with low population density. Honolulu harbor in 1803 was the opposite. Like most armies before the twentieth century, Kamehameha's troops were probably ill-fed and living in some degree of filth for the duration of their time at Honolulu.[56] Given that cholera, typhoid fever, and the major dysenteries had not struck Hawai'i – at least not in living memory – sewage disposal was as yet a low priority on the islands. Contaminated drinking water in Honolulu harbor may have been the rule rather than the exception in 1803.[57] Meanwhile, flies and (apparently abundant) cockroaches easily passed fecal bacteria from excrement to food and water sources. Finally, regardless of how well Kamehameha fed his own men, the poor nutrition of local people exacerbated the effects of the 'ōku'u, decreasing the odds of survival.

While local people at O'ahu may have observed traditional kapu for burial of the dead, including various cleaning rituals after handling a corpse, it is unlikely that the heaped-up bodies were treated with anything so hygienic or that the area around Kamehameha's encampment was subject to any useful sanitation before or during the 'ōku'u.[58] On the Big Island, Lisiansky had learned from a "chief priest" at Kealakekua Bay that, epidemic or not, the island poor were simply buried "any where along the beach."[59] Burial practices, like all Hawaiian ritual forms, varied according to rank. Most of Kamehameha's warriors were owed nothing in terms of burial, so their corpses would have been disposed by whatever means – and in whatever manner – was most convenient.

Finally, a number of observers remarked on the uncleanliness of Hawaiian dwellings, temples, and even bodies.[60] Physician and naturalist

---

[55] Ibid., 190.

[56] For "shortage of food" in Kamehameha's army, see Berkh, in Barratt, *Russian Discovery*, 105. Islanders had various treatments for diarrhea and dysentery, including Polynesian arrowroot combined with clay.

[57] Bushnell, *Gifts of Civilization*, 183, 191. For tainted water on the Kona Coast in 1807, see Iselin, *Journal*, 70. Drinking water in 1830s Honolulu had to be drawn from "shallow wells dug through the coral to tide level"; it was "slightly brackish," "distasteful," and "[p]robably ... rather insanitary" (Bishop, *Reminiscences of Old Hawaii*, 35).

[58] For burial customs, see Malo, *Mo'olelo Hawai'i*, 355–61; Green and Beckwith, "Hawaiian Customs and Beliefs Relating to Sickness and Death," 151–53.

[59] Lisiansky did not name the kahuna with whom he conversed; John Young served as interpreter (Lisiansky, *Voyage round the World*, 121–22).

[60] E.g., Lisiansky, *Voyage round the World*, 105–7; Langsdorff, *Voyages and Travels*, 162; Korobitsyn, in Barratt, *Russian Discovery*, 79; Shemelin, ibid., 96–97; Lisiansky journal (1812 edition), ibid., 33–34. See also Langsdorff, *Remarks and Observations*, 134.

Georg Heinrich von Langsdorff described the people at Kona as "naked, unclean, ... and with dark, dirty, brown skin covered with rashes and sores." Of course Europeans tended to see all Pacific peoples as more or less dirty. Yet few observers had been critical of *Hawaiian* hygiene or sanitation before 1804; in fact, the opposite was typically observed, particularly in reference to their frequent bathing. Now, however, Lisiansky was surprised at the "uncommonly filthy" condition of Kamehameha's royal residence at Kona. The adjoining heiau were "so neglected and filthy [that] they might be taken rather for hog-sties than places of worship."[61] Lisiansky was not ignorant of a possible reason for the untidiness: Kamehameha had temporarily relocated his government to Oʻahu.[62] Yet the catalog of filth on the Kona coast continued. In the huts of the common people, "dirtiness and slovenliness were everywhere apparent," wrote Lisiansky. The clerk Shemelin, otherwise sympathetic toward Hawaiians, observed "filth and a disgusting lack of cleanliness" on their bodies.[63]

To be sure, none of the Russians set foot on Oʻahu where the ʻōkuʻu was raging; and their unfavorable comparison of Hawaiian hygiene with the Marquesans whom they had just visited is proof of nothing in particular.[64] Yet it is possible that the Hawaiian kapu regarding sanitation and hygiene, like those regarding eating and the mixing of the sexes, had been regularly violated, ignored, or set aside by 1804. If so, the people were even more vulnerable to new bacterial infections.[65]

BONE, FLESH, BLOOD

Though devastating, the ʻōkuʻu offered Islanders an opportunity to think about medicine and how to improve it. Yet this would not be so simple as changing therapeutics or tracking down new herbs. Medicine and healing were essentially religious matters. On this point, the sources are unambiguous: the "foundation" of medical practice was the akua, who determined

[61] Lisiansky, *Voyage round the World*, 105–107. See also Lisiansky journal (1812 edition), in Barratt, *Russian Discovery*, 43.

[62] Lisiansky, *Voyage round the World*, 107.

[63] Lisiansky, in Barratt, *Russian Discovery*, 33–34; Shemelin, ibid., 96–97. For "a want of cleanliness" among Natives at Hilo in 1832, see the Sarah Joiner Lyman journal, in Martin, *Lymans of Hilo*, 45.

[64] E.g., Korobitsyn, in Barratt, *Russian Discovery*, 79; Rezanov, ibid., 84; Shemelin, ibid., 97; Langsdorff, *Remarks and Observations*, 134.

[65] An American missionary in 1823 wrote that servants ate from the "same dishes and calabashes with their master" (Stewart, *Private Journal*, 132).

whether the patient would survive and heal or sicken and die. Prayers and offerings to whichever akua guided the practice of a *kahuna* (priest, expert) were essential. Prayer, wrote Kamakau, was the "guide to knowledge and skill whereby [the kahuna] learned to heal and to recognize the mysterious things inside" the body. For aspiring physicians, prayer superseded knowledge about specific diseases and their treatment.[66] In a basic way, medicine was religion, and vice versa.

In common with Polynesian medical practice elsewhere, Hawaiian kāhuna admitted no distinction between spiritual and physical medicine.[67] All branches of the medical profession implored the deity or ancestral spirit to direct their practice and to intervene on their behalf. One way of illustrating the connection of the medical profession to the divine is to recognize that both physicians and priests in Hawai'i were known as kāhuna and that all kāhuna, whether temple priests or surgeons or obstetricians, were specialists in divine power, serving as intermediaries between the people and the gods.[68] Thus, the whole panoply of supernatural understandings and aspects of Hawaiian religion applied in the realm of medicine.

Religion did not proscribe specialization. Eight or more groups practiced the healing arts, including fertility specialists, obstetricians, and pediatricians; surgeons who lanced tumors and infections; diagnosticians who palpated the body; and those who practiced by "critical observation" and "insight." There were also sorcerers who employed black magic to cause illness or death and specialists who used counteracting sorcery, like an exorcist, to *thwart* sorcerers. Finally, there were specialists who "treated the spirits of illness," about whom little is known.[69] Other practitioners included bonesetters, massage therapists, and midwives.[70] There was apparently no specialty dedicated to the treatment of infectious diseases.

---

[66] Kamakau, *Ka Po'e Kahiko*, 107. For the original essay, see S. M. Kamakau, "*Ka Moolelo Hawaii: No Na Kahuna Lapaau*," *Ke Au Okoa*, Aug. 25, 1870. See also Malo, *Mo'olelo Hawai'i*, 376–81.

[67] Chun, *Hawaiian Medicine Book*, 23–26; Dening, *Islands and Beaches*, 62–63; Campbell, *Island Kingdom*, 43–44; Salmond, *Between Worlds*, 402, 503–5; Salmond, *Aphrodite's Island*, 253.

[68] Gutmanis, *Kahuna La'au Lapa'au*, 14. It was for this reason that Polynesians often viewed ships' surgeons as priests; e.g., Salmond, *Aphrodite's Island*, 207. Kāhuna were drawn from both ali'i and maka'āinana classes; see Kepelino, *Kepelino's Traditions of Hawaii*, 60–61.

[69] Kamakau, *Ka Po'e Kahiko*, 98. [70] Gutmanis, *Kahuna La'au Lapa'au*, 14.

Among the two classes of obstetricians were those responsible for fertility, whether by potions, diet, or prayer; and those charged with delivering babies. The stock of these specialists appreciated as people struggled to bear viable and healthy offspring. Yet kāhuna did not act alone. Aliʻi and perhaps some makaʻāinana performed religious ceremonies to encourage conception.[71]

The Hawaiian surgeon (*kahuna ʻō ʻō*) used sharpened bamboo or bone to make incisions. In addition to lancing boils and removing tumors and ulcers, the surgeon also performed circumcision or subincision on prepubescent boys and abortions for women.[72] The hands-on diagnosticians (*kāhuna hāhā*) were known for their visual charts in the shape of the human body to illustrate a patient's illness. Pebbles were arranged on the ground or on a stone table. The kahuna would kneel over the "body" and move the pebbles in the region of the malady to demonstrate his diagnosis and intended practice. The *papa ʻili ʻili* (table of pebbles) also served as a teaching tool for apprentices. According to Kamakau, the kāhuna hāhā were of the order of Lono, said to be the first kahuna hāhā and who then became their *ʻaumakua* (ancestral spirit).[73] The principal role of this group was to diagnose and treat internal ailments. Along with kāhuna who relied on critical observation and insight, Kamakau considered the kāhuna hāhā to be the most skilled and knowledgeable of physicians.[74]

As was true of folk medicine elsewhere, physicians relied upon proximity, suggestion, and metaphor. An ominous dream, unexpected weather, even stubbing one's toe could be interpreted as an omen. If the patient's ailment was internal, the *kahuna lapa ʻau* (general term for physician) might

---

[71] The aliʻi ceremony is *ho ʻomau keiki*; see Pukui and Elbert, *Hawaiian Dictionary*, s.v. "mau," def. 3.

[72] While circumcision was common, it is unclear how frequently subincision was practiced; the latter procedure might have affected venereal disease transmission and even male fertility. For both procedures, see Malo, *Mo ʻolelo Hawaiʻi*, 348–51; Pukui et al., *Nānā i ke Kumu*, 39–40. Surgeons were also responsible for preventing premature closure of the anterior fontanel on infants. Kamakau's term for this practice is "*ho[ʻ]opa[ʻ]a manawa*," literally, "to hold back the fontanel" (Kamakau, "*Ka Moolelo Hawaii: No Na Kahuna Lapaau*," *Ke Au Okoa*, Aug. 25, 1870). Barrére misinterpreted this procedure as keeping the fontanel "closed" (Kamakau, *Ka Poʻe Kahiko*, 98). The fontanel had spiritual significance throughout Asia and the Pacific. The highest of the body's three *piko* (organs of power and procreation), the fontanel was associated with "feelings, affections, sympathy" and could also "refer to the spirit of a human being" (Handy and Pukui, *Polynesian Family System*, 86).

[73] Kamakau, *Ka Poʻe Kahiko*, 106. See also Larsen, "Medical Art in Ancient Hawaii," 34.

[74] Kamakau, *Ka Poʻe Kahiko*, 112.

FIGURE 3.1 Kapu wand acquired by John Ledyard in 1778–79. A kahuna lapaʻau might have wielded such a wand made of *koa* wood, red and yellow bird feathers, and human hair.
Courtesy of Mark and Carolyn Blackburn Collection of Polynesian Art/ Bridgeman Images (BPA399521).

choose a red fish for an offering because of its shared color with human blood and organs. Foods with names that had negative connotations would be removed from the patient's diet; for example, *heʻe* (octopus), since *heʻe* also means "to flee," and the kahuna did not want the illness to flee from the medicine or treatment.[75] Food, in fact, was fundamental to medical practice, since the digestive system was understood as the seat of many disorders

[75] Gutmanis, *Kahuna Laʻau Lapaʻau*, 23–24.

(as it was of emotions, intellect, and character).[76] "Opening" foods were administered at the commencement of treatment and "closing" foods at completion. Many kāhuna lapaʻau also had favorite remedies employed as universal cures.[77]

Training for kāhuna lapaʻau began as early as five years of age. Traditionally, the medical profession was entirely male with the exception of midwives and nurses, about whose training and selection little is known. While female kāhuna have been common since the early twentieth century, the profession was officially off-limits to them under the kapu system.[78] This did not stop them from practicing. Yet male dominance of the medical profession raises questions about women's roles in society. Malo suggested that women practiced their own medicine, which makes sense given the gender divide in sacred matters. For instance, when a person took ill, local women observed the "female healing god," while the kāhuna lapaʻau performed their own tasks to make the person well.[79] It is worth noting that women were also forbidden from touching or looking upon certain male kiʻi, which may have driven a deeper gender wedge into Native medicine.[80] Wholly obscure to foreign visitors, women's medicine was hardly clearer to Malo, Kamakau, and other nineteenth-century male writers.

When a chief took sick, the first duty of the kahuna was to make an offering to the deity. Depending on the patient and ailment, any of the four major akua could be invoked, though Lono (patron deity of herbal medicine) and Kāne were more popular than Kanaloa and Kū.[81] Numerous other healing deities are identified in the sources and in oral tradition. Malo named Maʻiola as a healing deity. The literal translation of *maʻi ola* ("to cure sickness") has led scholars to question whether this was an actual deity or an incantation to the gods. A further complication is a deity named Mauli Ola (Breath of Life).[82] Given the size of the Hawaiian

[76] Ibid., 14.
[77] E.g., a Native physician in the 1870s used the moa plant (*Psilotum* spp.) as a universal purgative ("Records of medical work done by Dr. Ohule," Hawaiian Ethnographic Notes 1:1500–81, BM).
[78] Gutmanis, *Kahuna Laʻau Lapaʻau*, 20. For Tahiti, see Banks, *Endeavor* journal, 1:425, SLNSW.
[79] Malo, *Moʻolelo Hawaiʻi*, 378. Malo also indicated that medical practices for aliʻi were different from those for makaʻāinana. These differences included incantations. The presiding kahuna "prayed each time" an aliʻi took medicine (ibid., 380).
[80] Journal of William Richards, June 22, 1823, ABCFM Papers.
[81] Malo, *Hawaiian Antiquities*, 96, 111.
[82] Ibid., 107, 109–10n1; see also Malo, *Moʻolelo Hawaiʻi*, 378. It is not clear why Chun left out Maʻiola in his translation (*Ka Moʻolelo Hawaiʻi*, 58, 207). Medical lore seems to have

pantheon and the diversity of medical practice, it is no wonder that uncertainty and confusion surround many of these traditions. Yet it is clear that the various classes of medical practitioner invoked distinct deities. There was likewise considerable regional variation to kahuna observance in this period, as there was elsewhere in Polynesia.[83] Finally, it remains unclear whether physicians were drawn primarily from the ali'i or maka'āinana class.[84] Yet those who served the ruling chiefs certainly enjoyed an elevated status.

And what of sorcery? Historian of medicine Richard Kekuni Blaisdell objected to characterizations of 'anā'anā as sorcery or "black magic." He described their methods instead as "psychospiritual": 'anā'anā was a way of "influencing, or explaining, events that might be unfavorable to some while favorable to others."[85] That may be true, yet nineteenth-century authorities would hardly recognize Blaisdell's defanged psychospiritualists. For one thing, Kamakau wrote that the people of old recognized two principal types of disease: that which came from within the body and that from without, with the latter originating in nonphysical causes.[86] Kāhuna 'anā'anā clearly traded in the latter. They were not psychologists or prophets (*kāula*). Their spiritual power was threatening. This explains the pervasive fear of being prayed to death and the exorcist order that protected against or reversed the spell of sorcerers. Speculation about 'anā'anā surrounded chiefs who died prematurely and even some, like Kamehameha, who died elderly.[87] Beyond spiritual medicine, there were also *kuni* priests who could harm an individual – as in Vodou – by burning some object that came from them. Hair was commonly used in this manner and for that reason was guarded closely by its owner.[88] In sum, while the dark arts were not always employed for harm, Blaisdell's rebranding of 'anā'anā obscures more than it illuminates.

grown up around this deity; see Gutmanis, *Kahuna La'au Lapa'au*, 93–94; Rodman, *Kahuna Sorcerers*, 179.

[83] For Hawai'i, see Ellis, *Polynesian Researches*, 4:89–92; Malo, *Mo'olelo Hawai'i*, 331–40. For Tonga, see Campbell, *Island Kingdom*, 29.

[84] Larsen, "Medical Art in Ancient Hawaii," 27; Abbott, *Lā'au Hawai'i*, 98; Bushnell, *Gifts of Civilization*, 62.

[85] Blaisdell, "Historical and Philosophical Aspects of Lapa'au."

[86] Abbott, *Lā'au Hawai'i*, 98. See also Kamakau, *Ka Po'e Kahiko*, 95–115.

[87] Ellis, *Polynesian Researches*, 4:292–95; Kahananui, *Ka Mooolelo Hawaii*, 210; Malo, *Mo'olelo Hawai'i*, 362–75.

[88] See Theodore Kelsey, "Hawaiian Kuehu Treatment," in Gutmanis, *Kahuna La'au Lapa'au*, 89–92. For sorcery elsewhere in Polynesia, see Dening, *Islands and Beaches*, 62, 249–50.

One might expect blame for new diseases to have fallen on the sorcerer kāhuna. Yet there is no evidence of a specific class of kāhuna being blamed for a disease outbreak, much less a witch craze.[89] If kāhuna 'anā'anā were a source of speculation whenever a high chief died, this suspicion apparently did not carry over to disease outbreaks generally. It is also surprising – perhaps revealing – that Hawaiian sources make scant mention of the medical profession's dealings with epidemics after 1778. Nineteenth-century authorities had a good deal to say about introduced infectious diseases and the toll they took on Islanders, but rarely are kāhuna mentioned in connection with the ma'i malihini. This fact supports the popularly held notion that the ma'i malihini, being of foreign origin, required treatment by foreigners.[90] All the same, introduced diseases posed a threat to the Native medical order.

In 1823 English missionary William Ellis was under the impression that Islanders "accustomed to associat[ing] with foreigners" in Honolulu had a "decided preference" for their medicine.[91] Yet nowhere was Native medicine eliminated or wholly discredited; and in the backcountry especially, lapa'au continued (and continues) to thrive.[92] While the services of European and American physicians were typically welcome, introduced medical practices and understandings tended to merge with local medicine, as was true in other colonial spaces.[93] Nevertheless, by the late nineteenth century, Western medicine was dominant and the kahuna orders mostly relegated to local service.

Medical historian O. A. Bushnell characterized the Hawaiian medical order as ignorant, hapless, fearful, and unable or unwilling to innovate. The problem, Bushnell determined, was Hawaiian culture itself. Before the arrival of Christian missionaries, Hawaiians lacked the "cultural and psychological preparations for coping with infectious diseases." Epidemic diseases were "new and mystifying – and terrifying."[94] It is true that the

---

[89] Consider, by comparison, responses to epidemics among Northwest Coast Indians (Boyd, *Coming of the Spirit of Pestilence*, 50, 81, 166, 169).

[90] Pukui et al., *Nānā i ke Kumu*, 2:95, 158; Bushnell, *Gifts of Civilization*, 97, 104–6, 114; Gutmanis, *Kahuna La'au Lapa'au*, 54, 78, 86–87.

[91] Ellis, *Polynesian Researches*, 4:335.

[92] Little is known about regional variation in medical practice and healing. Kahuna medicine was everywhere proprietary, as it remains today. Competing kāhuna also employed different remedies and therapeutics. It is difficult to know how well oral traditions represent medicine before 1804, yet lapa'au in many places was little affected by foreign medicine, including the folk medicine practiced by Westerners who were not physicians.

[93] Osterhammel, *Transformation of the World*, 184.

[94] Bushnell, *Gifts of Civilization*, 37.

ma'i malihini were initially baffling. But there is no evidence that people gave up in despair – as Bushnell claimed – or failed to seek treatment and innovate with new remedies. Hawaiians placed a high value on *kokua*, or helping the sick and infirm, but it is absurd to characterize this cultural value as ignorance. Few people on earth knew their local botany as well as Hawaiian kāhuna. This extended to the use of cathartics and enemas, both of which "sometimes exhibited with success," according to an American observer in 1804, as well as bloodletting and scores of other non-herbal remedies.[95]

Beyond bits and pieces in oral tradition and by outside observers, the eighteenth-century practice of lapa'au remains hazy. Much more is known about how the ali'i responded to introduced diseases.

SURFING, LAMENTING, AND MORE SURFING

The 'ōku'u was the first epidemic for which the identity of victims is known. In addition to the hundreds or thousands of Kamehameha's warriors, four prominent ali'i perished: O'ahu high chief Keaweaheulu Kalua'apana, one of Kamehameha's principal war leaders and great-grandfather of two future Hawaiian monarchs (Kalākaua and Lili'uokalani); twenty-four-year-old O'ahu chiefess and wife of John Young, Namokuelua; chiefess and wife of Isaac Davis, Nakai Nalima'alu'alu, probably in her late twenties or early thirties; and Ka'ahumanu's father Ke'eaumoku Pāpa'iahiahi, who had been largely responsible for Kamehameha's rise over the previous two decades.[96] If the differential effects of the ma'i malihini were not yet clear to Hawaiians, the deaths of the young wives of two prominent foreigners – Young and Davis, neither of whom took ill – was ample demonstration. Kamehameha himself contracted the 'ōku'u, according to Kamakau, but survived. The king's advisors (*kuhina*) "all died."[97]

Other chroniclers had a different take on these events. Royal advisor John Papa 'Ī'ī, who lost relatives in the 'ōku'u, believed the epidemic motivated the ruling chiefs to train "promising members" of court in medicine.[98] It is unclear whether this involved a reorganization of the

---

[95] Shaler, "Journal of a Voyage," 168.   [96] Spencer, ed., *Buke 'Oihana Lapa'au*, 101.
[97] Kamakau, *Ruling Chiefs*, 189–90.
[98] 'Ī'ī, *Fragments*, 46. See also Brown, *Facing the Spears of Change*, 40. According to 'Ī'ī, Kamehameha was taken ill in late 1803 or early 1804 while staying with his chiefs in Waipi'o. Kamehameha's medical kahuna Papa ('Ī'ī's namesake) nursed the king back to health, at which point Kamehameha returned to Honolulu. 'Ī'ī added that Keōpūolani, the king's highest-ranking wife and the mother of the future Kamehamehas II and III, also

medical profession, the establishment of more formal training, or a recruitment effort. Foreigners apparently played little if any role in the reorganization. The Spanish jack-of-all-trades Francisco de Paula Marín, for instance, makes no mention in his diary of the recruitment effort or the training of additional kāhuna lapaʻau. Marín, who had been living on Oʻahu for a decade, served as interpreter and sometime physician to Kamehameha, in both of which roles he was just one of many such servants. Marín enjoyed a small family of two or more Hawaiian wives and at least three children by 1805.[99] Britons John Young and Isaac Davis also had children. Lacking Western physicians to treat them, foreign residents may well have supported the training and recruitment of additional medical kāhuna. On the other hand, some foreign residents remained prejudiced against the kāhuna and when sick may have relied on their own wits or on the folk medicine practiced by their Hawaiian wives and family members.

For all the information on individual fatalities, it is difficult to establish the physical and psychic toll of the ʻōkuʻu. An 1863 letter published in a Hawaiian-language newspaper suggested that there was "no other sickness like this one spoken of" in Kamehameha's generation.[100] More information survives about specific kāhuna lapaʻau. Papa was personal physician to Kamehameha and, according to ʻĪʻī, "owner" of the houses of healing. Another kahuna named Kūʻauʻau – whose father (or grandfather) Kama was a kahuna before him – treated commoners. Kūʻauʻau was said to have prepared medicines and treated patients in an "entirely different" way from Kama.[101] It is not clear what these differences consisted of, yet Kama himself was expert in at least four types of kahuna practice, including obstetrics, pediatrics, diagnostics, and palpation; he had also developed a reputation for treating the "hidden" or "evanescent" illnesses of childhood. According to Kamakau, if children took the medicines prescribed by Kama at the proper time, "they would not get

became ill with the ʻōkuʻu, narrowly avoiding going the "way of all earth" (*Fragments*, 33–35, 53). In response to the ʻōkuʻu, Kamehameha had three kapu breakers sacrificed at a heiau (ibid., 35).

[99] Gast and Conrad, *Don Francisco de Paula Marin*, 137. Marín recorded beating his wives (he did not supply their names); more than one woman tried to run away, but it is not clear whether any succeeded (ibid., 210, 214).

[100] W. Kahala, "*No ka Mai Ahulau*," *Ka Nupepa Kuokoa*, Feb. 28, 1863: "*Aole no he mai e ae e like me keia mai i oleloia.*" Kahala was quoting an "old man from the time of Kamehameha I" (my translation).

[101] ʻĪʻī, *Fragments*, 46. See also Malo, *Moʻolelo Hawaiʻi*, 622–23.

a sudden illness ... or an introduced disease."[102] Yet Kamakau did not provide evidence or elaborate on this claim. It is one of the rare instances of kahuna practice being identified as efficacious against the maʻi malihini.

After the epidemic, Kamehameha and his fellow chiefs turned their attention to farming and "care" of the people.[103] Again, it is difficult to know the reason. Yet a return to traditional practice makes sense given the king's long exposure to foreigners and his ceaseless stockpiling of foreign commodities, all culminating in the worst disease outbreak in living memory. It is not difficult to imagine Kamehameha and fellow chiefs interpreting the devastation of the ʻōkuʻu as a warning. Perhaps it was best to return to the soil, observe the akua, and nurture the *lāhui* (people/ nation).

After the ʻōkuʻu, foreign visitors observed Islanders smoking tobacco, drinking distilled liquor, missing front teeth, and lacking agricultural surplus. American supercargo Isaac Iselin noted another development on the Big Island: a "great want of hands to improve it"; that is, to make the island more fruitful. Depopulation along the Kona coast had been the result of "a kind of epidemic or yellow fever, said to have been brought to these Islands a few years ago, and which makes havoc amongst the natives."[104] Iselin referred to the ʻōkuʻu, yet like William Shaler before him, he also understood that the absence of the king and his retinue had contributed to the decrease in local population.[105] If food and good water were in short supply on the Kona coast, women were not: "A great many females come swimming to the ship," wrote Iselin. During his five weeks at Kealakekua Bay in 1807, Iselin's ship was "more or less encumbered" by Hawaiian women, men, and some children. In fact, for the duration of Iselin's two months at the islands, the ship was "almost incessantly surrounded and crowded by the natives."[106]

If the presence of women had not changed, there was now evidence of chiefs taking a cut. Kamehameha himself had stored up some $10,000 in

---

[102] Kamakau, *Ka Poʻe Kahiko*, 103–4. Some aliʻi themselves gained a reputation as medical practitioners. Boki, first cousin of Kaʻahumanu, was apparently skilled at administering the poisonous gourd enema (*waikī*), which seems to have been a universal remedy, treating fever, headache, chills, constipation and cramping, respiration, sores, and ulcers (ʻĪʻī, *Fragments*, 47).

[103] Kamakau, *Ruling Chiefs*, 190.   [104] Iselin, *Journal*, 68.

[105] Shaler "Journal of a Voyage," 163. For a possible famine following drought on Maui in 1806–7, see Whitman, *Account of the Sandwich Islands*, 65.

[106] Iselin, *Journal*, 70, 71, 80.

American coin, part of which had been earned "as a kind of tribute from the belles [who] visit the ship."[107] It is consistent with traditional tribute relations that the "chief who ate the district" would take a cut of the people's "harvest." Yet Iselin was certain that many people evaded paying tribute by stealth; if so, the pimps and madams who rowed sex workers out to the ships may well have been beneficiaries of such evasion.[108] It is difficult to know how commoners felt about the chiefs taxing sex work. Foreigners, for their part, were happy to complain on behalf of maka'āinana they saw as exploited.[109]

Two years after Iselin's visit, Scottish sailor Archibald Campbell learned that Kamehameha had ordered the execution of his nephew (and foster son) for allegedly sleeping with Ka'ahumanu.[110] 'Ī'ī later explained that the execution of court favorite Kanihonui had "aroused" the queen's "wrath" to such a degree that she "considered taking the kingdom by force and giving it to the young chief, Liholiho," Kamehameha's son (and the future Kamehameha II).[111] Fifteen years after Ka'ahumanu's request of physical protection against Kamehameha (after an alleged sexual liaison), Ka'ahumanu was again unwilling to concede to her husband's impulses or his absolute rule. For his part Kamehameha would not dare to punish a wife who outranked him – at least not publicly – for a violation that was, in any case, minor. But he could hurt her just the same; and hurt her he did, by executing her lover. Elite sexual politics seemed to be at something of a wrangle. While she mourned the death of Kanihonui, Ka'ahumanu's advisors put the question to her nephew, the teenager Liholiho, about replacing the king. Liholiho's matter-of-fact response, according to 'Ī'ī: "I do not want my father to die." After a day of "surfing, lamenting, and more surfing" on the Kona coast, Ka'ahumanu's advisors decided against the risky move, and the queen's wishes were again rendered moot.[112]

[107] Ibid., 78–79. For the king's offer of island women ("excepting the chiefs' wives") to American sailors in late 1805, see Patterson, *Narrative of Adventures*, 68. Kamehameha also continued to stockpile arms and ammunition; see Thomas W. Walker, supercargo's log for the brig *Lydia* (Sept. 26, 1806), Beinecke Library, Yale University.

[108] For pimps and madams, see Cox, *Adventures on the Columbia River*, 38.

[109] E.g., L. A. Gagemeister, in Barratt, *Russian View of Honolulu*, 169; Golovnin, *Around the World*, 208.

[110] Campbell, *Voyage*, 153. A reprise occurred in March 1812, with the guilty parties identified as Kamehameha's "favourite queen" and "one of the king's body-guard"; the latter was executed by strangulation (Cox, *Adventures on the Columbia River*, 37).

[111] 'Ī'ī, *Fragments*, 50–51. See also Golovnin, *Around the World*, 195.

[112] 'Ī'ī, *Fragments*, 50–51. For the beating of the chiefess Kuwahine for alleged infidelity to Kalanimoku, see ibid., 29.

So long as it could be done "in secret," ali'i women "seldom scruple[d] to break" kapu, according to Campbell.[113] One chiefess at O'ahu, whom Campbell believed to be a wife of Kamehameha but was more likely simply a woman at court, invited Campbell to sit and eat with her, but he declined out of respect for island law.[114] As Kamehameha's star was rising (en route to exclusive control over the archipelago), ali'i women were simultaneously defying the laws that ensured his rule. Commoners were less likely to take these risks. Virtually all traders reported numerous days in which Hawaiian women and girls were barred from entering the water or visiting ships. Yet Islander health apparently had no bearing on the application of the kapu to commoners and their activities. There is no evidence of new kapu put in place specifically to protect Islanders from the ma'i malihini before 1810.[115] Nor can this be attributed to timeless dictates of religion. By 1790, if not earlier, kapu were often applied at the desire of the ali'i (as well as various foreigners) without regard to particular deities or tradition. When Vancouver introduced a cattle herd in 1794, Kamehameha immediately imposed a kapu on the animals. Weapons, ships, and various other commodities were likewise protected by kapu.

Alcohol was now a concern. Campbell believed that non-medicinal consumption of 'awa had largely given way to distilled liquors, in particular 'ōkolehao ("iron bottom"), a spirit made from ti leaves (*Cordyline fruticosa*) and distilled in cast-iron pots.[116] Some women at court had taken to drinking with two Aleutian Islanders temporarily in residence. Campbell wrote that Ka'ahumanu herself enjoyed getting the Alutiiq women drunk, and "by the end of the entertainment, her majesty was generally in the same situation."[117] 'Ī'ī concurred about the quantity of liquor flowing through O'ahu. Stills in "great" number were found in

---

[113] Campbell, *Voyage*, 134. In 1815 a British trader enjoyed wine below decks with a woman he identified as "step-sister" of Prince Liholiho. It is unlikely that this "Maroo" was Kamāmalu (Liholiho's full sister), who was only thirteen years old in 1815; but if she was ali'i, Maroo was taking liberties: she "pressed me very much to remain" at the Big Island (Corney, *Voyages*, 47).

[114] Campbell, *Voyage*, 90. It is not clear whether this woman, "Tamena," had any official connection to Kamehameha. She may have offered Campbell the seat due to his lack of feet; he lost both feet to frostbite on the Northwest Coast.

[115] See, e.g., Bushnell, "Hygiene and Sanitation," 16–27, 34–35; Gast and Conrad, *Don Francisco de Paula Marin*, 259–62, 284–92; Gutmanis, *Kahuna La'au Lapa'au*, 78; Bushnell, *Gifts of Civilization*, 190–91.

[116] For 'ōkolehao in 1805, see Patterson, *Narrative of Adventures*, 67.

[117] Campbell, *Voyage*, 153–54.

several districts.[118] It may be true that most chiefs had their "own still" by 1809; but if so, this luxury did not extend to makaʻāinana.[119] Foreigners rarely described makaʻāinana as "debauched" or "dissolute," terms they frequently applied to aliʻi. Not only sober, Hawaiian commoners were, according to Campbell, the "most industrious people I ever saw."[120]

Kamehameha's bid for control of the islands had been costly for Oʻahu. Campbell's captain Leonty Andrianovich (Ludwig August von) Gagemeister characterized the mōʻī as a despot who ruled by intimidation and kept the makaʻāinana in a state of dependency and poverty: "[T]he position of the common farmer ... is a wretched one and very hard, for the king will sometimes ... take as much as two-thirds of all the taro and sweet potatoes he has grown ... There are many who have not had the chance to eat their own meat, or even sample it, despite their possessing a sufficient number of pigs and dogs." Gagemeister also mentioned that Kamehameha had begun to import workers from various parts of the islands to aid in the construction of ships, barns, and the like. Food and wages were not part of the deal. Gagemeister believed that hunger had caused many fatalities, yet he was also aware that commoners secretly cultivated small plots to avoid forfeiting all in tribute (an age-old strategy to defend against the "sharks who travel on land"). Migrant laborers would have no such opportunity. Yet there are no reports of Kamehameha's laborers starving to death or even suffering from malnutrition. Nevertheless, Gagemeister believed that the king's despotism had decreased the islands' population to "barely 100,000."[121]

About this time, the Spanish horticulturalist, architect, chiefly advisor, and physician to the king Francisco de Paula Marín began to keep

[118] ʻĪʻī, *Fragments*, 85.

[119] Campbell, *Voyage*, 133. See, e.g., Cox, *Adventures on the Columbia River*, 44.

[120] Campbell, *Voyage*, 115. See also Cox, *Adventures on the Columbia River*, 48–49.

[121] Gagemeister, in Barratt, *Russian View of Honolulu*, 169. For Gagemeister's facility with English; see ibid., 13. The population of the islands was probably closer to 150,000 in 1809; see Appendix B. Kamehameha moved his government back to the Kona coast in 1812. This allowed the mōʻī to spend more time fishing and farming, yet it was hardly retirement. He continued to stockpile weapons, gunpowder, and ammunition and to trade for iron and ship's stores to build new sloops and warships. He also forced makaʻāinana to harvest and prepare sandalwood for the lucrative new trade. See Chamisso, *Voyage around the World*, 115, 182–83. Kamehameha's move was not well timed as the Big Island was emerging from a three-year drought (Sahlins, *Anahulu*, 1:33–34). But later reports of famine have not been confirmed (Schmitt, "Famine Mortality in Hawaii," 113; cf. Cottrell, "Splinters of Sandalwood," 10, 35–36).

a journal. Though complicated by its transmission through a second party (the original document was lost), Marín's journal documents periodic, nonfatal illnesses and other health issues of the people. The level of detail is surprising. For instance, Marín recorded the menstrual cycles of Ka'ahumanu and other women at court. It is not so strange as it sounds. How Marín knew about women's cycles explains his reason for recording it. Chiefly women retreated to special huts during their period.[122] For an advisor to know that Ka'ahumanu, say, would be separated from the king for a few days each month could be useful information indeed.

The first entry of Marín's diary reads, "Kings brother dies November 1809. His bones thrown away." The decedent was Kamehameha's forty-four-year-old brother Keli'imaika'i. The cause of his death is unknown. Two months later, Marín recorded his treatment of the Maui high chief Boki for an unknown illness. Boki's older brother was apparently convinced by Marín's skills and ordered him to "cure" their mother.[123] It is not known what ailed Boki and his mother (or what Marín prescribed as a cure), yet it is clear from the journal that the chiefs were frequently sick with chronic illnesses in the 1810s. Ka'ahumanu was sick in January 1810, August 1811, August 1819, March 1821, and December 1821, when she was "at deaths door."[124] Her cousin, Kamehameha's chief minister "William Pitt" Kalanimoku, was sick in November 1811, July 1812, and March 1818. Kalanimoku's uncle Ka'uhiwawae'ono was sick from February 1812 until his death in April. In December of that year, Kamehameha lost a three-year-old daughter (possibly Nanaulu), who died "swoln."[125]

Marín provided the first named fatality to syphilis: "The day 10 Jan[uar]y [1819] died Cajabay-o-pio of the venereal."[126] It is unclear whether Marín treated this person, but archaeological evidence suggests that the Spaniard was familiar with the disease. Of fifteen skeletons buried at his compound between 1815 and about 1850, two individuals bore

---

[122] Malo, *Mo'olelo Hawai'i*, 216. See also Handy and Pukui, *Polynesian Family System*, 10–11.

[123] Gast and Conrad, *Don Francisco de Paula Marin*, 200. Boki's brother was "William Pitt" Kalanimoku; he adopted the British prime minister's name in the 1790s.

[124] Gast and Conrad, *Don Francisco de Paula Marin*, 259. See also ibid., 200; Freycinet, *Hawaii in 1819*, 19; Karl Gillesem, in Barratt, *Russian View of Honolulu*, 163, 182–83; Bingham, *Residence*, 148.

[125] Gast and Conrad, *Don Francisco de Paula Marin*, 202. The child's mother was not recorded.

[126] Gast and Conrad, *Don Francisco de Paula Marin*, 225. I have been unable to locate Cajabay-o-pio [Kahapai'ōpi'o?] elsewhere in the written record.

signs of treponemal infections, both presumably wives of Marín and also likely sisters to one another.[127] It is possible that Cajabay-o-pio – *ʻōpiʻo* is "child of" or "junior" – was Marín's own child with one of these wives. Within a decade of Cajabay-o-pio's death, other victims of syphilis would be identified in foreigners' journals and letters.

DOCILE BOXERS

In 1816 a German physician with the Russian-American (Alaska) Company went rogue and built a fort on Kauaʻi. Georg Anton Schäffer had been sent to the islands to gain a monopoly on the lucrative sandalwood trade for the Russian-American Company. To achieve this, Schäffer would need to ingratiate himself with the ruling chiefs who controlled the trade. He did so by attending to their health. Quickly raising suspicions among Americans on Oʻahu, the "Russian spy" shortly fell out of favor with the ruling chiefs and fled to Kauaʻi where he offered protection to the mōʻī Kaumualiʻi against Kamehameha's long-planned conquest. Schäffer had a large stone fort erected at Waimea Bay and began to fancy himself coruler of Kauaʻi with Kaumualiʻi. Growing wise to Schäffer's ambitions, Kaumualiʻi commandeered the fort and sent the physician packing.[128]

After dismissing Schäffer in 1815, Kamehameha elicited the services of English-Portuguese adventurer John Elliot de Castro as physician. In his role as king's physician, Castro met the Russian tsar's expedition at Oʻahu in November 1816 and arranged a meeting between the officers and the king. Both Schäffer and Castro, like the Spaniard Francisco de Paula Marín and the Frenchman Jean Baptiste Rives before them, gained the trust and confidence of the ruling chiefs by ministering to their health.

Historians have overlooked the important role played by foreign medical men (and those posing as such) on the islands. Foreign physicians saw bright prospects due to the chronic health problems of the nobility. Schäffer was perhaps the first foreign physician to plan his strategy ahead of time, and he may have been instructed by the Russian-American

---

[127] Michael Pietrusewsky et al., "The Search for Don Francisco de Paula Marin: Servant, Friend, and Advisor to King Kamehameha I, Kingdom of Hawaiʻi" (January 2016), p. 9, www.researchgate.net/publication/303363729. Both women were apparently buried in the 1810s. For Marín's sister wives in 1812, see Cox, *Adventures on the Columbia River*, 39.

[128] Chamisso, *Voyage around the World*, 116; Kotzebue, *Voyage of Discovery*, 1:303–5. Schäffer built his Russian Fort Elizabeth in Waimea Bay overlooking the site where Cook made landfall in 1778. The ruins of the fort can be visited today.

Company to use his medical skills to earn the king's favor. Schäffer claimed to have treated Kamehameha for a "heart illness" and Ka'ahumanu for a "severe fever" before his dismissal in 1815. These "treatments" enabled the physician, as he put it in a letter to the Company, to "win over the friendship and trust" of the king.[129] Castro, Rives, and Marín managed to do the same thing, if with less scheming ahead of time.[130]

A total of seven Russian ships visited the islands on eleven occasions between 1809 and 1826, staying an average of eighteen days.[131] The tsar's German and eastern European officers were, according to one scholar, "better read, more literate, [and] more intellectually curious than any whaling captain of the day."[132] They also spoke excellent English. While not without biases, the tsar's officers left astute observations of Hawaiian life and health during a tumultuous time. These observations deepen our understanding of the sex trade, the kapu system, ali'i consumption patterns, and population decline.[133]

The sex trade was thriving at O'ahu. While anchored off Honolulu, Capt. Otto von Kotzebue wrote that the ship was "from morning to evening ... surrounded by the fair sex."[134] According to naturalist Adelbert von Chamisso, "propositions" were "shouted at us by all the women round about and by all the men in the name of the women."[135] Tobacco use had become so common among Islanders that "young children smoke before they learn to walk." Adults smoked so much that some "f[ell] down senseless, and often died in consequence." That is unlikely, though Kotzebue himself sampled "extremely strong" tobacco on the Big Island. Smoking had become "one of the principal pleasures here," with a tobacco pipe in every hut.[136] Ali'i women had taken to hanging German-made wooden and brass tobacco pipes from their clothing (Fig. 3.2).[137]

---

[129] Bolkhovitinov, "Adventures of Doctor Schäffer," 59. See also ibid., 75n22, for an earlier mistranslation of Ka'ahumanu's illness as "yellow fever."
[130] For Rives' work as physician to the ali'i, see Arago, *Narrative of a Voyage*, 98.
[131] Barratt, *Russian View of Honolulu*, 41, 45.   [132] Ibid., vii.
[133] Loss of life was not limited to the islands. When sixteen Hawaiians eager to return home boarded a British fur trade ship at Canton in 1815, "several" of them died "shortly after" setting off from the Asian mainland (Corney, *Voyages*, 38, 41).
[134] Kotzebue, in Barratt, *Russian View of Honolulu*, 145. Two years later Golovnin observed that "only commoners indulge in this appalling practice; the chiefs and people of rank will not trade their daughters or wives for any sum" (Golovnin, ibid., 239).
[135] Chamisso, *Voyage around the World*, 119.
[136] Kotzebue, in Barratt, *Russian View of Honolulu*, 231.
[137] Corney, *Voyages*, 110; Kotzebue, *Voyage of Discovery*, 1:306–7. Chiefesses also hung small mirrors from their garments (Campbell, *Voyage*, 137; Freycinet, *Hawaii in 1819*, 7).

FIGURE 3.2 Women smoking. *"Une femme d'Owhyhée"* (left); *"Irini, Femme des Iles Sandwich"* (right).
Jacques Arago, 1819. Courtesy of Honolulu Museum of Art (#25829, #25826).

Kotzebue was the first foreigner to provide extended comments about Liholiho, the heir apparent and son of Kamehameha and Keōpūolani, the highest-ranking chiefess on the islands. The officers met the twenty-year-old prince in a "neat and small" dwelling house where he was "stretched out on his stomach." From this position Liholiho "indolently raised his head to look at" his guests and then went back to his business, which seemed to the Russians to consist of nothing but relaxation. As an ambassador for the tsar, Kotzebue was aghast at this indifferent reception, describing Liholiho as a corpulent "monster" with a "stupid vacant countenance," whose name – which Kotzebue believed translated as "dog of all dogs" – suited him perfectly.[138]

That Liholiho's father elicited such a different reaction from the officers suggests their opinions of the prince were not mere chauvinism. Kamehameha struck them as strong, competent, judicious, even wise.

---

[138] Kotzebue, *Voyage of Discovery*, 1:308–9. The Russians confused the prince's name with the Hawaiian word for dog, *'ilio*. Chamisso described Liholiho as "weak and soulless" (Barratt, *Russian View of Honolulu*, 175).

On a tour of his personal heiau, Kamehameha grasped a ki'i and proclaimed, "'These are our gods, whom I worship; whether I do right or wrong, I do not know; but I follow my faith, which cannot be wicked, as it commands me never to do wrong.'" For a "savage" who had "raised himself by his own native strength of mind to this degree of civilization," this avowal of Native religion "indicated much sound sense" to Kotzebue. Such a king "deserves to have a monument erected to him" or, at the very least, a more suitable heir than Liholiho. Kotzebue also wrote that while Kamehameha was "fond of wine" and graciously supplied it to guests, he himself did "not indulge in it to excess," as Liholiho seemed to do.[139]

In an early discussion of depopulation, the naturalist Chamisso considered the consequences. For one thing, he feared the trend would not be reversed. He also expressed regret that the culture would disappear with the people. Hoping to document island life before it was too late, Chamisso asked Kotzebue to let him stay. The request was denied. Still bitter twenty years later about being thwarted in this heroic effort Chamisso sounded a chord from the budding European discipline of anthropology: "No one appears to have thought of investigating and thus saving from oblivion" the island culture of Hawai'i. That was a shame, since shedding light on their history could "perhaps" illuminate the broader "history of mankind."[140]

When Vasily Mikhailovich Golovnin arrived at Honolulu on a supply mission to Kamchatka the following year, there was little sign that a cultural revolution was imminent. A Big Island chief who wanted to drink to the health of the *Lūkini* (Russians) observed kapu by stepping outside to toast. Other chiefs were governed by kapu that seemed arbitrary to Golovnin. One male chief was forbidden from eating pork, another jumped from the Russian ship when chicken was served at dinner, and a third would not share the Russians' fire in order to light his cigar. At Kamehameha's "state house" Golovnin noticed that Liholiho was not permitted to enter the house since he outranked the king through his mother's line.[141] Like Chamisso and Corney before him, Golovnin

[139] Kotzebue, *Voyage of Discovery*, 1:312, 308–9, 311. On Kamehameha's "temperate" consumption of food and drink, see also Golovnin, *Around the World*, 192; but cf. Cox, *Adventures on the Columbia River*, 37, 45. Critics of Liholiho's drinking were legion; see Chapter 4. For chiefly consumption of liquor in 1816, see Kotzebue, in Barratt, *Russian View of Honolulu*, 199, 202.
[140] Chamisso, *Voyage around the World*, 125. See also Golovnin, *Around the World*, 190, 212.
[141] Golovnin, *Around the World*, 178–83, 208.

observed heavy liquor consumption among the ali'i, notably among the chiefesses. In at least one instance, the intoxication of a Kona coast chiefess resulted in blows being exchanged between her and other chiefs, including her "second husband."[142] Liquor did not come cheap. The going rate for a bottle of rum in 1818 was a goat kid; a large goat fetched two bottles.[143]

Like many ships' officers and traders before him, Golovnin was entertained by military practices ("sham battles") and boxing matches. In the latter entertainment, "only two pairs fought and not very well at that." The problem, thought Golovnin, was that "though many came forward they could not agree to fight, each one considering himself weaker than his opponent." The Americans in attendance explained to Golovnin that Hawaiians "had completely lost their former warlike spirit, courage, and skill with hand arms." Finding Euro-American weapons "much more convenient," the American commentators continued, the people "took to guns and cannon, which they never learned to handle properly, and abandoned their own methods."[144]

Accounts of drunken chiefesses and docile boxers shortly led observers to invoke societal "fatigue" or "ennui" among the Hawaiian ruling classes or even a general "cultural decline." Similar characterizations of Native North Americans, Aboriginal Australians, and other Pacific Islanders prepared foreigners to see Hawaiians in this light. Too often these characterizations – loaded glosses of change over time – have found their way into the scholarship.[145] Besides the obvious demographic decline, the most important factor contributing to such allegations was the chiefs' consumption, to which foreigners paid careful attention.[146] Scenes of ali'i extravagance and luxury, in foreigners' accounts, were typically set beside observations of maka'āinana labor in the sandalwood and sex trades. Living and working conditions for the maka'āinana were grim, and

---

[142] Ibid., 180–84.
[143] Golovnin, in Barratt, *Russian View of Honolulu*, 221. Note, however, that goats had multiplied "prodigiously" on O'ahu in 1796; see Broughton, *Voyage of Discovery*, 34–35.
[144] Golovnin, *Around the World*, 187.
[145] E.g., Dening, *Islands and Beaches*, 127–28, 197, 226–31; Crosby, "Virgin Soil Epidemics," 296–297; Stannard, "Disease and Infertility"; Diamond, *Guns, Germs, and Steel*, 214; Newell, *Trading Nature*, 133–36. For an early scholarly reference to cultural "fatigue" in the context of 1810s Hawai'i, see Kroeber, *Anthropology*, 403.
[146] Foreigners also alleged increased liquor and tobacco use, infanticide and abortion, "covetousness," and the abandonment of various island customs; e.g., Mathison, *Narrative of a Visit*, 469–78.

the ruling chiefs were racking up huge debts leveraged by makaʻāinana labor in sandalwood; yet these phenomena were no departure from past practice, much less signs of sociocultural fatigue.[147] Hewing closely to Euro-American sources, anthropologist Marshall Sahlins characterized the chiefs' "conspicuous and invidious" consumption of the 1810s as a "political economy of grandeur."[148] These terms are of questionable usefulness in the Hawaiian context. Prestige mattered to aliʻi who were in regular competition with each other for position. But, again, it is not clear that this behavior was fundamentally different from the 1770s (or '90s), much less that of hereditary monarchies worldwide in this period. Nor is this any excuse for aliʻi treatment of the makaʻāinana, which some historians naturalize in the guise of cultural norms.[149]

Traders commented on aliʻi consumption patterns because their business counted on it and because they had concerns about Hawaiian debts being paid back. Scholars' attention to consumption is another issue. Naturally, there is a tendency to scan the 1810s for a cause of the cultural revolution. But as with the names they adopted and the clothes they wore, aliʻi consumption may augur less than scholars imagine. Consumption mirrored earlier patterns but with different commodities being consumed (liquor, tobacco) and accumulated (clothing, accessories, weapons, iron). Claims of sociocultural fatigue or decline are also gendered. This is obvious in Golovnin's boxers, who had lost their warlike spirit. Many such comments – by observers and scholars – serve to feminize Hawaiians.[150] Observers criticized aliʻi extravagance in collecting silks, clothing, and other luxuries, which was made possible by makaʻāinana selling their bodies in port and harvesting sandalwood in the uplands.[151]

---

[147] On debt, Kamehameha was the exception to the rule, but his wealth and power were also exceptional. For aliʻi debts and makaʻāinana labor in the sandalwood trade, see, e.g., Malo, "On the Decrease of Population," 126–27. Arista argues that the social effects of aliʻi indebtedness have been exaggerated by historians and that the debt narrative itself is ethnocentric, with scholars leaning too heavily on Anglo-American sources that privilege thrift and "self-control" ("Histories of Unequal Measure," chap. 2). See also Rifkin, "Debt and the Transnationalization of Hawaiʻi."

[148] Sahlins, *Anahulu*, 1:3, 54, 57, 64, 70. See also Sahlins, "Cosmologies of Capitalism," 432–34.

[149] Kameʻeleihiwa, *Native Land*, 19, 21–22, 26, 36; Kapāʻanaokalāokeola Nākoa Oliveira, *Ancestral Places*, 44–45.

[150] E.g. Bushnell, *Gifts of Civilization*, 193–96, 292–94; Sahlins, *Anahulu*, 1:76–81; Sahlins, "Cosmologies of Capitalism," 432–34. Infantilizing of Pacific Islanders, meanwhile, was nearly universal in this period (e.g., Golovnin, *Around the World*, 190–96).

[151] E.g., Golovnin, *Around the World*, 211–12. Golovnin believed that "young women" in 1818 were still the "most important article of trade" at the islands.

Yet Euro-American observers never compared sex work at Hawai'i with prostitution in their home countries. Nor did foreigners recall that George Washington had been inaugurated in diamond-studded shoes or that King George III and Tsar Alexander could outfit an army in their personal evening gowns. A more accurate view of consumption is that ali'i continued to acquire prestige goods in a pattern consistent with earlier behavior and that some boxing contestants had grown tired of fighting on demand for the entertainment of foreign ships' captains.

Alcohol and tobacco consumption are another matter. If ali'i consumption of liquor was perhaps consistent with their earlier use of 'awa, the short- and long-term health effects of heavy tobacco and liquor consumption were not. By 1805 the chiefs had many options to choose from: imported rum, brandy, gin, and vodka as well as 'ōkolehao (ti-leaf liquor). Chiefly women also seemed to consume a high volume of liquor and tobacco, while their earlier consumption of 'awa was much lower than that of their male counterparts. By 1818 even maka'āinana had begun to consume liquor regularly and to trade for it.[152] Even so, none of this points to societal "fatigue" or "cultural decline." Like people throughout human history, Hawaiians drank and got drunk for various reasons. As in Native North America, consumption of intoxicants also had social and ritual functions. Inevitably, social problems arose from liquor and tobacco, but island society was hardly coming apart at the seams.

During the first two decades of the nineteenth century, Kamehameha continued his campaign for hegemony. Only the 'ōku'u epidemic of 1804 could stop the mō'ī from achieving his destiny of archipelago-wide supremacy. While nothing so lethal would strike Hawai'i for a generation, the years following the 'ōku'u offered little reprieve. Commoners were reported to be living in squalor, afflicted by venereal diseases, tuberculosis, and scabies. Consumption of new intoxicants such as liquor and tobacco began to take a toll. In the 1810s, the chiefs leveraged the labor of commoners in the sandalwood and sex trades to purchase foreign luxuries.

Kamehameha's new world was, in a word, unhealthy. While dissent was seldom heard, alternative visions for a Hawaiian future would surface shortly after his death.

---

[152] Ibid., 210–11.

4

Throwing Away the Gods

At sea is an omen, in the wide sea.[1]

In May 1819 the mōʻī Kamehameha died at his home in Kailua-Kona. Six months later the ruling chiefs nullified the kapu system of religious law that had governed island life for centuries. This revolution, as much cultural as political, set society reeling into the unknown. Scholars in search of an explanation have focused on intermittent meddling by foreigners, Kamehameha's death, and the everyday kapu violations by commoners; yet none of these accounts for the "cataclysmic overturning . . . of ancestral wisdom" that Hawaiʻi witnessed from 1819.[2] Several factors – internal and external, long term and short – contributed to the collapse of state religion. Three have received scant attention: Hawaiian health, the Tahitian precedent, and the role of elite women.

A number of aliʻi, especially women, came to believe that the traditional laws had failed to keep Islanders alive and healthy.[3] Not everyone agreed, but Kamehameha's widows Keōpūolani and Kaʻahumanu found support among kin, especially close relatives. Some chiefs decided that the akua had betrayed them or had themselves succumbed to foreign incursions. Others said the gods had lied.[4] Ultimately, Kaʻahumanu and

---

[1] "Ma kai 'ouli, ma kai akea" (ʻĪʻī, Fragments, 38). From a chant associated with the kapu loulu ceremony for the "prevention of epidemics, famine, destruction" (Pukui and Elbert, Hawaiian Dictionary, s.v. "loulu," def. 4).

[2] Kameʻeleihiwa, Native Land, 79.

[3] Credit is due to Kameʻeleihiwa, who was the first to suggest this possibility (Native Land, 80–82). This chapter is, in part, an effort to elaborate on her observation.

[4] Corney, Voyages, 102. The term is "wahaheʻe" (lit., "slippery mouth"); see Pukui and Elbert, Hawaiian Dictionary, s.v. "wahaheʻe." For the "failure" of the gods

Keōpūolani decided that a new course would be required to bring "new life" to the nation.[5] In the short term, that course would be guided strictly by Hawaiian elites, absent imperial agents or missionaries. The second-class status of chiefesses also bore on their decision.[6] Nullification, they hoped, would give them greater control over their own lives while also sanctioning their authority in the sacred and political realms. In this sense, the health crisis provided a political opportunity for Ka'ahumanu and Keōpūolani. Yet gender and health were also related problems. By overturning the religious laws that marginalized them, the ruling chiefesses aimed to improve the health of their people in general and to reverse declining fertility of the ali'i in particular. The latter goal was, by every indication, the more important to them. Among the many Hawaiians unable to bear children was the leader of the cultural revolution herself, Ka'ahumanu.

The presence of Tahitians at court on O'ahu and the Big Island persuaded some chiefs that dispensing with the kapu system would not bring their kingdom tumbling down. Society Islanders had a few years earlier nullified their own religious laws, a move that coincided with the first Tahitian teachers and emissaries settling in Hawai'i. In the long run, Tahitian influence was at least as great among chiefesses as chiefs, and probably more so.

For maka'āinana, Polynesian diplomacy and elite sexual politics had little bearing on their lives. Nor was the overthrow of the kapu system necessarily a shock to their worldview, religious or otherwise. Maka'āinana and ali'i religious practice and ideology were distinct, as we have seen. The cultural revolution of 1819–25 was state-ordered, unevenly administered, and met with indifference by a broad swath of the population. Yet the long-term consequences were profound, not least in the political alliance forged between reformer chiefs and Anglo-American missionaries who arrived in 1820.

Meanwhile, introduced diseases continued to take a toll. Chronic infections that had plagued Hawaiians since 1778 now found company

---

elsewhere in Polynesia in this era, see Salmond, *Between Worlds*, 512; Newell, *Trading Nature*, 113.

[5] Elisabeta Kaahumanu (Dec 20, 1825), in *Ka Manao o na Alii* [Thoughts of the Chiefs], 5.

[6] Comparative work on elite women and the dismantling of Polynesian religious law remains to be done; Hawaiian chiefesses may have been unique in this respect. See, e.g., Gilson, *Cook Islands*, 8–9, 35–36; Dening, *Islands and Beaches*, 125–28, 188, 213; Campbell, *Island Kingdom*, 53–63; Evison, *Te Wai Pounamu*, 17; Salmond, *Between Worlds*, 442, 508–17; O'Malley, *Meeting Place*, chap. 7; Ballantyne, *Entanglements of Empire*, chap. 1.

with acute infections that sometimes reached epidemic levels. The disparity between Islander and foreigner health grew stark. Foreigners were few in number – perhaps 150 permanent residents in 1819 – but their families grew quickly.[7] Hawaiians of all classes struggled to bear children at all. Mixed marriages and a thriving sex trade added only a handful of mixed-descent individuals to Hawaiian society. The population continued to slide.

This chapter addresses the abolition of *'ai kapu* (segregated eating), state-ordered iconoclasm, and the consequential decisions of chiefesses and their close kin that steered island society on a new course. These decisions culminated in the settling of an American Protestant mission that would exert a powerful influence for decades to come.

RITES AND STRATEGIES

Little is known of Kamehameha's health in the years before his death. German filibuster and physician Georg Anton Schäffer claimed to have treated him for a "heart illness" in 1815, but Schäffer is hardly a reliable source, as we have seen. The first record of Kamehameha's final illness comes from Francisco de Paula Marín, who was recalled from Honolulu to attend to him on April 15, three weeks before his death. Marín, assisted by Kamehameha's chief minister "William Pitt" Kalanimoku, royal physician John Elliot de Castro, and the Native physicians Kū'au'au and Kuakamauna, treated the king until his death on May 8.[8] An enema was administered on April 27, and Marín recorded that the king was suffering from diarrhea on May 1. Apparently no other documentation of Kamehameha's final illness is extant.

It is unlikely that the mō'ī succumbed to the flu-like outbreak that struck southern O'ahu in late 1818. (Marín recorded sixty deaths, most if not all along the southern coast.) Kamehameha was residing on the Big Island at this time, and later descriptions of his demise do not indicate respiratory illness. Yet the king's younger sister Pi'ipi'i Kalanikaulihiwakama may

---

[7] See Appendix B.
[8] Kamakau, *Ruling Chiefs*, 210. A key figure in what follows, William Pitt Kalanimoku held the office of *kālaimoku* (*lit.*, "island carver"), which may have been coined for him; but see Malo, *Mo'olelo Hawai'i*, 32–33, 289–90, 514–46, esp. 544n18. Kalanimoku attended to secular affairs, including warfare. To avoid confusion I refer to him as Chief Minister, as Island Carver, or simply by his name.

FIGURE 4.1 Kamehameha holding a *pāhi'uhi'u* for tabletop games. The bottle
contains rum or brandy. "Tamehameha – *Roi* of Sandwich Islands."
Mikhail Tikhanov, 1818. Courtesy of Scientific–Research Museum of the Russian
Academy of Arts (P–2109).

have been a victim.[9] In the weeks before Kamehameha's death, Marín
recorded that the king's wife Ka'ahumanu and son Liholiho were also
sick. Perhaps a bug was going around court. While there is no record of
the king having caught this supposed infection, an already compromised
immune system would have impeded his recovery. Portraits by ships' artists
also suggest that the king had lost weight. By autumn 1818 he looked gaunt,
his eyes hollow (Fig. 4.1).[10]

---

[9] Golovnin, *Around the World*, 206; Barratt, *Russian View of Honolulu*, 332–33. Marín's
reference to the death of the king's "sister" on Sep. 13, 1815, could not have been Pi'ipi'i; it
is unclear who this chiefess was (Gast and Conrad, *Don Francisco de Paula Marín*, 217).

[10] Kamakau wrote that the king was "a long time ill" (*Ruling Chiefs*, 210), yet he seemed
well to a French trader in January (Birkett, "Hawai'i in 1819," 75). Students at
Lahainaluna Seminary later described him as refusing food and "very weak" in his last

Influenza, no less than syphilis and tuberculosis, was a serious risk to a population with little or no previous exposure to it.[11] Adult mortality tended to be high in early epidemics across Oceania.[12] Yet little is known about either the morbidity or mortality rates for these and earlier proposed outbreaks. It is possible that some of the sixty victims identified by Marín had succumbed to bacterial pneumonia, one of the more common consequences of the flu, particularly among populations with less than optimal care; yet this, too, cannot be ascertained. A later flu outbreak in 1848–49, part of a global pandemic originating in Europe, would be better documented.

The death of the mō'ī traditionally meant a holiday from the kapu system. In this respect, Kamehameha's death was little different from earlier suspensions of kapu, though in this case a particularly raucous period of "free eating" and other liberties ensued. Yet by the time a French scientific expedition arrived at the Big Island in August 1819, the kapu system had been reinstated. Capt. Louis Freycinet wrote that the "strict laws of tabou forbid women to eat with men, except when in a canoe at sea, where it would be impossible to do otherwise." He also learned that "a man who had eaten with women … would no longer have the right to eat with other men," lest the men be polluted.[13] The captain's wife Rose Freycinet noted that high chiefess Likelike was forbidden to board the ship to dine with her husband William Pitt Kalanimoku.[14] Kapu observance is noteworthy given that Liholiho's rule was as yet uncertain.[15] Greater chaos might be expected after the death of the kingdom's long-ruling

days (Kahananui, *Ka Mooolelo Hawaii*, 207–8). In January 1820 Marín again recorded a flu-like outbreak on O'ahu. On January 11: "All the people ill of coughs." On January 13: "There are many people ill of coughs and fevers." On January 19: "The people very sick." The seasonality and symptoms described by Marín suggest both outbreaks were influenza or another respiratory infection. High chiefs Boki and Liliha both took ill in the 1820 outbreak. See Gast and Conrad, *Don Francisco de Paula Marin*, 236–37. An ali'i named Kaihi might have succumbed in this outbreak, but the cause of his death is unknown (ibid., 237).

[11] Alfred W. Crosby, "Influenza," in Kiple, ed., *Cambridge World History of Human Disease*, 807–11.

[12] Leslie B. Marshall, "Disease Ecologies of Australia and Oceania," in Kiple, ed., *Cambridge World History of Human Disease*, 482–96, esp. 486.

[13] Freycinet, *Hawaii in 1819*, 68. For nonbinary genders in the Marquesas, see Dening, *Islands and Beaches*, 88–89.

[14] Rose Freycinet journal, in Bassett, *Realms and Islands*, 158. See also Freycinet, *Hawaii in 1819*, 23.

[15] Freycinet, *Hawaii in 1819*, 19.

founder. Yet in the event, order had largely been restored.[16] While French observers would not see the cataclysm occur, within three months of their departure, the centuries-old system of religious law system crumbled. Journals kept by various crew members illustrate the early phases of this cultural revolution while at the same time providing the most extensive observations of Hawaiian health since 1804.

Most scholars argue that the kapu system had deteriorated over time.[17] Contemporaries' observations temper this view somewhat. In December 1816 Adelbert von Chamisso explained that despite many changes to the islands, "[a]ll the restrictive laws of the *tabu* ... are preserved in their full, inviolable strength .... Intercourse with Europeans has thus far had very little influence on the outward social order, way of life, or customs of these people."[18] Two years later Golvnin wrote that the kapu were "strictly observed" by women, commoners, and even foreign advisors to the chiefs.[19] While French observers noted that Kamehameha's heiau was in disrepair – a result of the weeks-long holiday following his death – heiau destruction was standard practice after the mōʻī's death, not a sign of social upheaval or cultural change.[20] To mourn the king's passing, chiefs shaved their heads, knocked out their front teeth, tattooed his name on their arms, and burned circles into their skin.[21] Other developments eluded French understanding altogether; for example, Kaʻahumanu's creation of a new office for herself as *kuhina nui* (roughly, Great Counselor).[22] It was clear to all that Kaʻahumanu

[16] See ibid., 22–23, 72–73, 78.
[17] E.g., Jarves, *History of the Hawaiian or Sandwich Islands*, 201–12; Hopkins, *Hawaii*, 172–93; Kalākaua, *Legends and Myths of Hawaii*, 431–38; Kuykendall, *Hawaiian Kingdom*, 1:66–68; Bradley, *American Frontier in Hawaii*, 125; Webb, "Abolition of the Taboo System"; Levin, "Overthrow of the *Kapu* System"; Daws, *Shoal of Time*, 56–60; Davenport, "Hawaiian Cultural Revolution"; Seaton, "Hawaiian *Kapu* Abolition"; Sahlins, *Historical Metaphors*, 55–56; Bushnell, *Gifts of Civilization*, 195–97.
[18] Chamisso, in Barratt, *Russian View of Honolulu*, 213–14.
[19] Golovnin, *Around the World*, 209; "Golovnin's Visit to Hawaii in 1818," trans. Joseph Barth, *The Friend* (July 1894): 50.
[20] Freycinet, *Hawaii in 1819*, 74.
[21] Other chiefs scorned such behavior. When the *Uranie*'s surgeon asked Kamehameha's chief minister why he had neglected to knock out his front teeth, Kalanimoku allegedly replied, "The number of madmen is already large, I did not want to increase it" (ibid., 77). For the physicality of Māori mourning rituals for high-ranked decedents, see Ballantyne, *Entanglements of Empire*, 194–99.
[22] *Kuhina nui* is not be confused with *kahuna nui* (high priest). Kameʻeleihiwa suggests in one place that Kaʻahumanu subsumed the role of kālaimoku; later, she affirms that William Pitt Kalanimoku (Kaʻahumanu's first cousin) kept the office (*Native Land*, 74,

intended to rule alongside her twenty-one-year-old nephew and foster son Liholiho.[23]

Kamehameha and Ka'ahumanu are familiar names to Pacific scholars; Ka'ahumanu's first cousin, Chief Minister William Pitt Kalanimoku, whose letter opens this book, is less well known. He was a critical player at a critical moment in Hawaiian history. With the French anchored off Maui, Kalanimoku boarded the *Uranie* and asked the ship's priest to baptize him. According to Louis Freycinet, Kalanimoku told the priest that his mother had been baptized on her deathbed and that he himself had "for a long time wished to become a Christian."[24] Freycinet requested that the baptism be delayed until he could return from a visit with the king on shore. When Liholiho heard about the impending ceremony, he donned his military jacket and notified his five wives, his younger brother Kauikeaouli, and the co-regent Ka'ahumanu. Dozens of courtiers and the Frenchman Jean Rives also rowed out to attend the ceremony.[25] Ka'ahumanu and Liholiho's favorite wife Kamāmalu were provided with front-row seats on deck. Rose Freycinet wrote that Kalanimoku "appeared strongly moved" throughout the ceremony.[26] The "Island Carver" was christened "Louis" after the ship captain who served as godfather.[27]

During the baptism, Louis Freycinet claimed that the new king Liholiho "had word passed to me" that he too would like to be baptized but that "political considerations" prevented him.[28] Liholiho never was baptized, but Kalanimoku's brother, the high chief Boki, requested and received baptism aboard the *Uranie* a few days later. Freycinet believed that Boki's motivation derived solely from his brother receiving the rite.[29] Perhaps so, yet Boki's wife Liliha attended the ceremony, as well as three foreign ship

---

154–55). While sources are murky, kuhina nui and kālaimoku seem to have been distinct positions. See, e.g., Mykkänen, *Inventing Politics*, 115, 142, 166–67.

[23] Kamehameha himself ordered the infant Liholiho to be given to Ka'ahumanu as guardian (*kahu hānai*); see 'Ī'ī, *Fragments*, 15; Kamakau, *Ruling Chiefs*, 220.

[24] Freycinet, *Hawaii in 1819*, 24. The details of Kamakahukilani's baptism are unknown, if in fact she was baptized.

[25] Rives arrived on the islands as a youth and by 1815 had at least one Hawaiian wife and twin daughters. He served as interpreter, secretary, advisor, and physician, obtaining lands on four islands before leaving for Mexico in the '30s.

[26] Freycinet, *Hawaii in 1819*, 24–28; Rose Freycinet journal, in Bassett, *Realms and Islands*, 159.

[27] Rivière, *Woman of Courage*, 103.   [28] Freycinet, *Hawaii in 1819*, 28.

[29] Ibid., 35. See also Rose Freycinet journal, in Bassett, *Realms and Islands*, 169. Arago, for one, was skeptical about the motives of both chiefs (*Narrative of a Voyage*, 106–9).

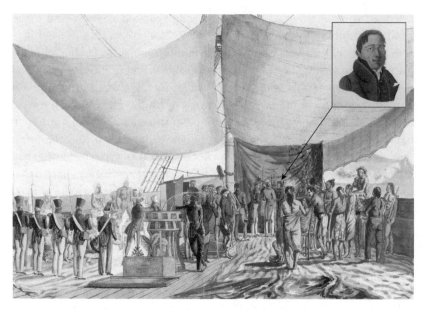

FIGURE 4.2 Baptism of Kalanimoku (*"Baptéme du premier ministre du Roi des Sandwich"*); inset, Kalanimoku (*"Kraïmokou, Surnommé Pitt, 1ᵉʳ Ministre du Roi"*).
Jacques Arago, 1819, courtesy of Honolulu Museum of Art (#21487); inset, Alphonse Pellion, 1819, courtesy of British Library.

captains who served as witnesses. In this way, two Hawaiian high chiefs were baptized into the Catholic Church.

What prompted the brothers' interest in baptism, and what were they trying to accomplish? Writing four decades later, Kamakau claimed that Kalanimoku had been confused: the Island Carver had boarded the *Uranie* along with the septuagenarian haole ali'i John Young; when Freycinet and the Abbé de Quélen asked Young "what Kalani-moku's rank was," they learned he was chief minister to the king and a "wise, kind, and careful man," so they baptized him without Kalanimoku "knowing whether what he was doing was right or wrong."[30] This could be whitewashing, since the chiefs banned the Catholic Church in 1827. Yet it is also unlikely that

[30] Kamakau, *Ruling Chiefs*, 325–26. Kamakau, confusingly, used kuhina nui (Ka'ahumanu's office) here for Kalanimoku, rather than kālaimoku; he did not report on Boki's baptism. John Papa 'Ī'ī took issue with Kamakau's account, arguing that Jean Rives rather than John Young had convinced Kalanimoku to be baptized; but 'Ī'ī was strongly anti-Catholic and mistaken about various aspects of this event (Brown, *Facing the Spears of Change*, 142–43).

a powerful ruling chief would permit an important diplomatic and religious ceremony to take place literally behind his back. It is also unlikely that Freycinet and the Abbé de Quélen conspired to baptize a powerful chief they barely knew and whose wrath they could scarcely afford to incur, anchored as they were in the Island Carver's kingdom.

One of the first foreigners to interview Kalanimoku learned that the chief minister had simply "yield[ed] to an inclination he had long entertained ... to declare himself publicly a convert to Christianity."[31] The key word here is "publicly." Whatever his personal feelings, beliefs, or understanding of Christianity (much less Roman Catholicism), Kalanimoku had determined that certain advantages could be gained by displaying his connection with the French, and especially with their kāhuna.[32] Of course being sprinkled by a foreign priest was not the same as becoming a Christian or even expressing an interest in Christianity. Ship captain Otto von Kotzebue was probably correct that the Island Carver had little if any sense in 1819 of the doctrinal differences between Catholicism and the Protestantism he would embrace a few years later.[33] The Maui chiefs' dealings with Tahitian teachers on the islands from as early as 1818 suggest that Kalanimoku knew about iconoclasm and Christian conversion in the South Pacific, but evidence is spotty.[34] Whatever else it may have been, Kalanimoku's baptism was a shrewd move by a ruling chief interested in securing the favor of powerful foreigners in an uncertain time. Boki immediately understood as much and followed his brother's lead.

The strategic choices by Kalanimoku and Boki fit a pattern across Polynesia. A high-ranking chief repudiated the gods – sometimes to win the support of foreigners and missionaries – more often as a move against a rival chief who controlled the Native priestly order. The provocation was followed by the rogue chief winning over a critical mass of the ruling chiefs and then the official overturning of the taboo system, which resulted in war. The high-ranking Tongan chief Ulakai, for example, said he had "given up his gods" out of preference for British and Tahitian missionaries in 1826. One year later the Tongan king Alemotuʻa officially broke the

[31] Kotzebue, *New Voyage*, 2:201.
[32] As early as 1816 Kalanimoku greeted visiting ship captains with "God bless you" (Kotzebue, in Barratt, *Russian View of Honolulu*, 143).
[33] Kotzebue, *New Voyage*, 2:203.
[34] Ellis claimed that Liholiho had "heard what Pomare and the Tahitian chiefs had done in the Society Islands" (*Narrative of a Tour*, 112.)

tapu and himself publicly defied the gods.[35] Though this particular rupture proved temporary, the Tongan ruling class proceeded to incorporate Christianity and its representatives over the next few years, following the Hawaiian pattern, which had in turn followed a Tahitian pattern. The sequence of events across Polynesia bears more than a passing resemblance.[36] Yet there is little evidence that Hawaiian chiefs realized (as they soon would) that a broader Polynesian reform movement was under way. It is also important to note that public rejection of the deities did not always coincide with conversion to Christianity. Hawai'i, for one, had yet to be visited by missionaries. Instead, ali'i such as Kalanimoku, Boki, and Ka'ahumanu acted and reacted according to present circumstances. Their judgment suggested that the akua were growing unpopular and that state religion (the kapu system) as a whole was in trouble.

AILMENTS, ENIGMAS

Writing some years after his return to France, Louis Freycinet was under the "general impression" that the islands' population had been "singularly reduced" in recent years. In fact, Hawai'i lost as much as one-third of its population between 1805 and 1823. Enumerating the various causes that foreign writers had attributed to this trend, Freycinet identified Kamehameha's wars of conquest, alcohol, earthquakes, introduced diseases, "fatigue among the lower classes" from labor in the sandalwood trade, and "debauchery and infanticide" stemming from "poverty and privation." (Debauchery probably indicated alcohol or 'awa abuse.) According to Freycinet's informants on the islands, a number of densely populated villages had been "abandoned in recent years and are now reduced to ruin." Freycinet himself noted that sandalwood, the islands' principal industry, had been depleted, with no substantial replanting.[37]

While earthquakes and "infanticide" had taken few lives, each of the remaining factors on Freycinet's list bore some responsibility for Hawaiian mortality in the generation since Cook. Nineteenth-century writers and more recent scholars tend to agree that forced labor in the sandalwood trade exacerbated the effects of population decline among the

---

[35] Campbell, *Island Kingdom*, 52–54.
[36] See Douglas, "Religion"; Gascoigne, *Encountering the Pacific*, 370; Sissons, *Polynesian Iconoclasm*.
[37] Freycinet, *Hawaii in 1819*, 65, 88.

maka'āinana.[38] Adding insult to injury, processed sandalwood (*'iliahi*) had been a major remedy for venereal diseases.[39] Presumably, infected persons were forced to find alternatives. As for infanticide, Freycinet provided an ethnocentric and misinformed view of what was in fact a major cause of depopulation: sharply decreased fertility.

Ka'ahumanu personified the trend. The second-most powerful woman in the kingdom next to Keōpūolani (her fellow widow), Ka'ahumanu was herself childless. Had she borne any children, they would have been kings. Not only childless, Ka'ahumanu was also ill in 1819. At Freycinet's arrival, she was "complaining of feeling generally unwell" and "sighing and complaining in such a way as to make me believe that she was about to die." While the queen's "plump appearance" and "air of prosperity" led Freycinet to question whether she was in fact ill, he nonetheless prescribed medicine that royal advisor Jean Rives administered.[40] It may seem surprising that the queen would accept medicine from an unknown foreigner, but Rives, who now enjoyed considerable influence, seems to have sanctioned it. Freycinet failed to identify the medicine or how Ka'ahumanu fared afterward.

Other observers noted an imbalance in Hawaiian sex ratios. "On the basis of ... observations" – not described – midshipman Nicolas François Guérin "concluded that there were fewer old men than old women in the Islands." If so, this phenomenon was probably limited to southern O'ahu and the Kona coast of the Big Island. Yet Guérin's observation, if accurate, is difficult to explain. There is no direct evidence that syphilis or other infectious diseases had taken a disparate toll on the sexes. 'Awa, liquor, and tobacco consumption, on the other hand, may have shortened men's lives enough to create an apparent imbalance in the elderly population. Guérin seems to suggest as much by attributing the gender imbalance to the "prolonged habits of debauchery among men." Yet within a decade, observers would note exactly the opposite trend; that is, fewer women than men. In fact, Freycinet's men believed that Hawaiians were targeting female births for infanticide. Tuberculosis may be a likelier explanation. Epidemiologists have found that in societies newly exposed to the tuberculosis bacillae, there is a tendency toward differential susceptibility and mortality in women – young women in particular. (The reverse is also

[38] Malo, "On the Decrease of Population," 126–27; Sahlins, *Anahulu*, 1:57; Cottrell, "Splinters of Sandalwood."
[39] Krauss, *Ethnobotany of Hawaii*, 199.   [40] Freycinet, *Hawaii in 1819*, 19.

true: higher male mortality in populations where the disease is on the wane.[41]) In any case, skewed sex ratios among Hawaiians would persist.

The etiology of tuberculosis would not be understood until 1882, but ships' physicians saw plenty of it. In their medical notes, surgeon-naturalists Jean René Constant Quoy and Joseph Paul Gaimard categorized Hawaiians' tubercular conditions under the category "Catarrhs," typically infections of the mucous membrane, congestion of the lungs, and coughs of various kinds. Catarrh was just one of the dozens of descriptive terms applied to tubercular symptoms in the era before microbiology. Quoy wrote that catarrhal infections "appeared to be very frequent" at the islands. These infections "caused frequent coughing, and developed into tuberculosis of the lungs resulting in death." Quoy witnessed "a young girl, stretched on some mats under a shed, dying from this terrible disease." Collectively, the two French surgeons "saw several tall, strong, vigorous men afflicted with a persistent coughing that would surely become fatal."[42] Gaimard attributed the widespread nature of the disease to the islands' variable and quickly shifting climatic conditions, coupled with the peoples' lack of proper attire and (ironically) their tendency to sleep out in the open.

Two other diseases were of concern to Quoy and Gaimard: scabies and syphilis. Quoy was struck that Islanders were "more or less covered with large scabies-like pimples, some of which were festering." These sores were "particularly noticeable in the joints and on the hands." Hawaiians of all ages showed signs of scabies, as did "several" foreigners who had "liv[ed] here for a long time." Contagion seemed to require long exposure, and Quoy was pleased that none of his men caught it during the *Uranie*'s three-week visit.[43]

Freycinet's "strict prohibition" on women boarding the ship also seems to have kept venereal infections at bay. When the expedition departed, there were "only a small number of infected individuals," according to Quoy. Gaimard, for his part, heard that syphilis was "much more prevalent" on Oʻahu than on the Big Island where he failed to see any "definite cases." On the other hand, he noted, "ophthalmia, ... tumors,

[41] Armus, *Ailing City*, 251–52.
[42] Freycinet, *Hawaii in 1819*, 58. Like earlier expeditions, the French took precise measurements of Hawaiian bodies, recording everything from the angle of the lower jaw to the width of the foot. Hardening racial ideas and increasing interest in craniometry encouraged particular attention to skull shape and size. Quoy, for one, adopted a highly racialist perspective later in his career (Douglas, *Science, Voyages, and Encounters*, 224–25).
[43] Freycinet, *Hawaii in 1819*, 57.

and lachrymal and salivary fistulas could very well have been manifestations of the disease."[44] Gaimard also deemed it "possible" that "certain skin eruptions and ichorous ulceration of the conjunctiva" (discharge from infected eyes) were signs of syphilis. Gaimard learned from a European resident of Maui that venereal disease there "manifested itself frequently by the presence of pimples in the groin and in the armpits and by cankers," which squared with the observations of an earlier French surgeon in Polynesia.[45] Artist Jacques Arago described the "large-jowled" king as himself "eat[en] up with I know not how many horrible diseases."[46] Yet he did not specify, and no one else recorded Liholiho's supposed illnesses.

Gaimard learned that island women "sometimes" died in childbirth and that they "invariably" did so when vaginal birth was not possible.[47] In fact, Hawaiians, like people the world over, had procedures for caesarean delivery. Maternal fatality was always high in such procedures, but death was by no means inevitable.[48] Gaimard practically acknowledged as much when he noted that island midwives "make it their occupation to attend to those who are in labor."[49]

Like surgeons before him, Gaimard also identified what he thought was leprosy, probably incorrectly. Yet the reasons for his error deserve comment. Gaimard recorded two cases: "a man suffering from elephantiasis whose leg was covered with consuming ulcers, and a woman whose nose bones no longer existed and who was making a kind of whistling noise," which the surgeon took as a "true symptom" of leprosy.[50] The woman without a nose (*ihu 'ole*) was probably suffering from tertiary syphilis rather than leprosy, which was otherwise unrecorded on the islands until the '30s. (Syphilitic saddlenose is diagnostic of advanced syphilis.) Still, leprosy should not be ruled out given that the disease attacks the face and nose. The man with the badly ulcerated leg presents a more interesting problem for the history of Hawaiian health. *Elephantiasis graecorum* was the scientific term for leprosy (Hansen's disease), which was often

[44] Ibid. Congenital lacrimal fistula refers to an abnormal opening from the face into the eye or tear duct. Salivary fistula is an abnormal channel running from the salivary duct, oral cavity, pharynx, or esophagus to the surface of the face or neck.
[45] Freycinet, *Hawaii in 1819*, 57–58. For the earlier surgeon, see Fleurieu, *Voyage round the World*, 1:168–71.
[46] Arago, *Narrative of a Voyage*, 90.   [47] Freycinet, *Hawaii in 1819*, 58.
[48] Jane Elliott Sewell, "*Cesarean Section: A Brief History*," exhibition brochure, National Library of Medicine (1993), www.nlm.nih.gov/exhibition/cesarean/.
[49] Freycinet, *Hawaii in 1819*, 59.
[50] Ibid., 58. See also Freycinet, *Voyage Autour du Monde*, 575.

confused with the unrelated parasite-borne infection lymphatic filariasis (*Elephantiasis arabum*) common throughout the tropics. To prevent confusion, medical practitioners distinguished "true leprosy" (Hansen's disease) from filariasis or "false leprosy." No doubt this is what Gaimard had in mind when he identified the Hawaiian woman's lack of nose as a "true symptom" of leprosy. But if he was incorrect about the woman's condition, Gaimard's misdiagnosis of the man presents more intriguing possibilities.

Swelling and thickening of the skin of the legs, buttocks, and genitals are characteristic of lymphatic filariasis but *not* of leprosy, which tends to affect the face, hands, feet, and joints.[51] Hawaiians themselves reflected these differences in their language, using their reading of the Old Testament to distinguish leprosy, *ma'i Hebera* ("Hebrew disease"), from filariasis, *ma'i elepani* ("elephant sickness"). Despite the distinct symptomatology of these two disfiguring diseases, medical historian O. A. Bushnell deemed the man with the ulcerated leg as possibly an early case of leprosy, though he was quick to add that the condition might have been "advanced syphilis, tuberculosis, scabies, or several other kinds of mutilating diseases" – but not filariasis.[52] The reason Bushnell made an exception for filariasis is that the microscopic worm that causes the infection is transmitted by mosquitoes, which were unrecorded until 1826 when a visiting ship famously dumped mosquito larvae in the harbor at Lahaina, Maui.[53]

Perhaps the man had traveled elsewhere in the tropics and contracted filariasis abroad. Elephantiasis was so common at the Society Islands in 1822 that one to four in one hundred Tahitians were affected by it, according to missionaries.[54] Given Gaimard's brief description of the man, we cannot even be sure that he was a native of Hawai'i. (Travel to and from the South Pacific had recently resumed after a long pause.) Another possibility is that mosquitoes had already arrived by 1819. Hawaiians on the moist leeward side of the islands – and in mountains across the archipelago – could not yet record the presence of mosquitoes in writing. The fact that Euro-Americans spotted mosquitoes in the bustling

[51] Todd L. Savitt, "Filariasis," in Kiple, ed., *Cambridge World History of Human Disease*, 726.
[52] Bushnell, *Gifts of Civilization*, 288.
[53] Black flies (*Simuliidae* family), which also carry and transmit the parasitic nematode worm, do not live on the islands (Neal L. Evenhuis, email to the author, 23 Sept. 2014).
[54] Montgomery, ed., *Journals of Voyages and Travels*, 1:250. For filariasis at Tonga, see Campbell, *Island Kingdom*, 32.

port city of Lahaina in 1826 does not rule out the possibility that the pests had already made a home at the islands and begun to spread disease. In fact, other reports of elephantiasis predate the supposed introduction of mosquitoes in 1826.[55]

Nothing more is known of the man with the ulcerated leg, yet French observers identified another Islander with this ailment. Freycinet described the high chief Boki as "tall and of enormous girth, with horribly ulcerated legs." He was "like an inert mass hardly able to move about." During his baptism, when his legs were concealed by pants, Boki appeared to Freycinet "unhealthy" and "sunk in a sort of lethargy."[56] An earlier Russian delegation made no mention of Boki's "girth" or difficulty moving about. Mikhail Tikhanov's portrait of 1816 reveals a medium-sized, lithe-limbed man bearing no extra weight (Fig. 5.1). Could Boki have grown "enormous" in two and a half years by diet alone? Or was his "girth" and difficulty moving about a function of his "horribly ulcerated legs," that is, a result of lymphatic filariasis or some other disfiguring disease? If disease seems more likely than diet, filariasis cannot be settled upon given that mosquitoes were as yet unrecorded. Syphilis, tuberculosis, and even 'awa consumption are all possibilities for Boki and the man with the ulcerated leg.

Labor exhaustion, poverty, substance abuse, decreased fertility, and, of course, infectious disease plagued Islanders on the eve of a cultural revolution. The people's struggles were not lost on the revolutionaries.

QUEEN AND ICONOCLASTS

In November 1819 Ka'ahumanu persuaded her nephew and foster son Liholiho, now Kamehameha II, to sit with her and eat. Some weeks earlier the high-ranking chiefess Keōpūolani (Liholiho's birth mother) had done the same with her young son Kauikeaouli, the future Kamehameha III.

---

[55] E.g., Stewart, *Private Journal*, 201. For the introduction of mosquitoes, see Culliney, *Islands in a Far Sea*, 271–72; Stannard et al., "Book Review Forum," esp. 293; Bushnell, *Gifts of Civilization*, 50–51. For filariasis at the Marquesas, see Dening, *Islands and Beaches*, 146, 240. Bushnell erred by claiming that filariasis did not strike the islands in the nineteenth century (*Gifts of Civilization*, 50, 178); a US Navy surgeon stationed in the Pacific reported both diseases afflicting Honolulu patients in the early 1880s (Heffinger, "Elephantiasis Arabum").

[56] Freycinet, *Hawaii in 1819*, 34. For 'awa consumption allegedly leading to "ulcers," see Kotzebue, in Barratt, *Russian View of Honolulu*, 217–18. For 'awa abuse leading to paralysis, see "Records of medical work done by Dr. Ohule," Aug. 25, 1870, Hawaiian Ethnographic Notes 1:1518, BM. French impressionist Paul Gauguin, in the Marquesas, was afflicted by an ulcerated leg before his 1903 death to syphilis.

Without repercussion from the gods or people, the ruling chiefs had nullified the 'ai kapu. Word went out to all the islands that the sexes could now eat together "of all things prohibited equally"; on O'ahu, heiau were set ablaze.[57] The fall of the kapu system was a cultural revolution without parallel in Hawaiian history. Scholars have identified a number of causes ranging from cultural "fatigue" to problems of succession to economic and political turmoil – even the oscillation of the Pleiades.[58] Yet scarce attention has been paid to Hawaiian health or to the chiefesses who themselves orchestrated the revolution.

Most scholars present nullification as the work of Liholiho or of the ruling chiefs as a whole.[59] In fact Liholiho was mostly an accomplice, and the chiefs were far from united. Two factions vied for control of the islands after Kamehameha's death. On one side were Ka'ahumanu and her relations, to whom I will refer for the sake of convenience as the "Maui chiefs." Descended from the ruling family of Maui, the group included the highest-ranking chiefess of her time (and widow of Kamehameha), Keōpūolani; Chief Minister William Pitt Kalanimoku; Ka'ahumanu's siblings John Adams Kuakini, George Cox Ke'eaumoku, Kalākua Kaheiheimālie, and Lydia Nāmāhāna Pi'ia; and Kamehameha's heir Liholiho and his five wives (three of whom were also his half sisters).[60]

---

[57] Marín journal, Nov. 6–7, 1819, in Gast and Conrad, *Don Francisco de Paula Marin*, 234. The Hawaiian term for nullification is *ho 'onoa* (*lit.*, "to free from taboo"). Retrospective accounts include Samuel and Nancy Ruggles journal, March 30–31, 1820, HMCS; Sybil Moseley Bingham journal, Aug. 9, 1822, HMCS; Kotzebue, *New Voyage*, 2:199; "Letter from Mr. Bishop to the Corresponding Secretary, Dated Kairua [Kailua], Nov. 30th," *Missionary Herald* 23 (Aug. 1827): 246–47; Ellis, *Narrative of a Tour*, 111–12, 193; Kahananui, *Ka Mooolelo Hawaii*, 216–18, 231; Dibble, *History of the Sandwich Islands*, 142–43; Jarves, *History of the Hawaiian or Sandwich Islands*, 248; John Papa 'Ī'ī, "Na Hunahuna no ka Moolelo Hawaii," *Ka Nupepa Kuokoa*, April 3, 1869; Bingham, *Residence*, 162; Kamakau, *Ruling Chiefs*, 219–28.

[58] For "cultural fatigue," see Kroeber, *Anthropology*, 403. For political turmoil, see Davenport, "'Hawaiian Cultural Revolution.'" For the Pleiades, see Sissons, *Polynesian Iconoclasm*. Sissons views the Polynesian religious revolutions as "connected episodes of a single regional event" (ibid., 79), yet there is scant evidence that Hawaiians in 1819 viewed it that way. Despite his prejudices and mistaken chronology, Dibble – an early commentator – insisted that a "train of circumstances and the concurrence of many and various influences" were at play (*History of the Sandwich Islands*, 144).

[59] F g, Kuykendall, *Hawaiian Kingdom*, 1:65–68; Daws, *Shoal of Time*, 56–57; Mykkänen, *Inventing Politics*, 35–41, but cf. 45; Chun, *No Nā Mamo*, 310. Previous scholarship also failed to distinguish between state religion and that of commoners.

[60] Liholiho's five wives by order of marriage were Kamāmalu (his half sister), Kīna'u (half sister), Kekāuluohi (half sister), Pauahi/Kalanipauahi (niece), and Kekau'ōnohi (niece). All five marriages were childless. In sharing Kamehameha as husband, Keōpūolani and Ka'ahumanu were *punalua* (literally, "two springs") to each other (Handy and Pukui,

A powerful kahuna and healer by the name of Hewahewa also supported the Maui chiefs' reforms. A rebel faction hoping to preserve the kapu system was led by the Big Island chief Kekuaokalani. While Kamehameha had designated Liholiho as heir, he entrusted his war god statue (Kūkā'ilimoku) to Big Island comrade Kekuaokalani, planting the seeds for an uncertain succession.[61]

Eventually a battle would decide the matter. Island Carver Kalanimouku's forces defeated the rebels on the Kona coast, and Kekuaokalani paid with his life.[62] But before all this was the singular act of breaking the 'ai kapu. What was the nature of the chiefesses' authority, and how did the mō'ī's death influence their decision? While Kamehameha's maintenance of the kapu system had kept it vital, detractors and some outright defectors surfaced in the 1810s. Many, perhaps most, of these chiefs were influenced by Tahitian advisors who had recently taken places at court. Yet it is also the case that the founder of the kingdom was outranked by at least two of his wives. Those two wives were, in turn, dual mothers to the new king Liholiho – Keōpūolani by birth, Ka'ahumanu through *hānai* (adoption). Liholiho himself outranked his father, who apparently referred to the boy as "my chief" and "my god," among other names.[63] The popular conception today of Kamehameha's rule as unified and durable is not supported by the historical record. Events immediately following his death reveal a contingent and exceptional rule.[64] Like an intestate aristocrat, the mō'ī left his relations in a bind.

If one purpose of the kapu was to protect the sacred from the profane, in practice this meant keeping men and women separate for religious and ritual functions.[65] Maka'āinana women, as we have seen, were quick to

Polynesian Family System, 56–65). In addition to Kamehameha, Keōpūolani was also married to Kalanimoku, according to Malo; see Langlas and Lyon, "Davida Malo's Unpublished Account of Keōpūolani," 40. Kamakau described Keōpūolani as a "good student of human nature" (*Ruling Chiefs*, 227).

[61] For the makeup of the two political factions, see, e.g., Mathison, *Narrative of a Visit*, 361–478; Kamakau, *Ruling Chiefs*, 227–28. Beamer argues that nullification was in large part an effort by Ka'ahumanu to "marginalize" Kekuaokalani (*No Mākou ka Mana*, 83).

[62] Mathison, *Narrative of a Visit*, 447–48. Kamakau described the conflict as the "war for free eating" (*Ruling Chiefs*, 261). For more on these conflicts, see Kuykendall, *Hawaiian Kingdom*, 1:67–70; Kame'eleihiwa, *Native Land*, 137–67.

[63] Kamakau, *Ruling Chiefs*, 220.

[64] Sahlins, *Anahulu*, 1:60. Memorialization of Kamehameha is especially visible today on O'ahu and the Big Island; see Wharton, *Painted King*; Kamehiro, *Arts of Kingship*.

[65] "John Ii's Speech, Delivered at Rev. H. Bingham's Church," *Polynesian*, May 1, 1841; Kamakau, *Ruling Chiefs*, 222–23. See also Kame'eleihiwa, *Native Land*, 33–40; Valeri, *Kingship and Sacrifice*; cf. Linnekin, *Sacred Queens*, 34.

defy their chiefs and in some cases to broker alliances with foreigners and elicit violence against aliʻi. But those were commoners. Nullification was the act of chiefesses and their close male kin. In spite of their high rank, Kaʻahumanu and Keōpūolani were constrained by their husbands and by the state religion. Constraints included dietary restrictions, segregation, involuntary marriage, and, for Kaʻahumanu at least, physical violence inflicted by her husband. While there was some risk of diminishing their own status by nullifying kapu, it is unlikely that either Keōpūolani or Kaʻahumanu viewed the action as "repudiating" their "divine rank" or "declaring an end to the entire concept of sacred rank," as one scholar has argued.[66] Instead, nullification enhanced the power of the Maui chiefs, among whom the two women enjoyed exalted status and influence, while also aligning them with the Tahitian chiefs who had taken the same leap of faith a few years earlier.

Inherent distinctions also mattered. Virtually everyone agreed that Kaʻahumanu had more natural gifts for leadership than her ward Liholiho.[67] Such judgments are compelling in light of the male chauvinism that marked both Western and Polynesian societies. For Hawaiians, aliʻi had to earn the right to continue to rule, and Liholiho had done little to prove his mettle while Kaʻahumanu had been serving effectively for decades.[68] Nevertheless, it is difficult to see how chiefly women could have been considered "equal" to men in terms of "personal authority" before 1819.[69] The ʻai kapu was a potent symbol of women's second-class status and exclusion from the sacred realm. In Malo's words, the ʻai kapu was the "basic foundation" of men's religious observation of "male gods."[70] Beyond women's ritual exclusion, male chiefs could give away their wives to cement political alliances; chiefesses apparently had no say

---

[66] Davenport, "Hawaiian Cultural Revolution," 16.

[67] Birkett, "Hawaiʻi in 1819," 83–84.

[68] Liholiho's drinking diminished him in the eyes of foreigners and probably did not help his reputation among Hawaiians. Hawaiian students at Lahainaluna Seminary later wrote that rum had become his "daily bath water" by 1819 (Kahananui, *Ka Mooolelo Hawaii*, 213–15). See also journal of Sybil Moseley Bingham, Jan. 1 and Feb. 18, 1822; Feb. 8, 1823, HMCS; journal of Levi Chamberlain, April 28 and July 6, 1823, HMCS; Gast and Conrad, *Don Francisco de Paula Marin*, 247–83; Kotzebue, *New Voyage*, 2:196–97; and Stewart, *Private Journal*, 91–92. For a Marquesan ruler whose authority was "diminished" in part by his drinking – and who, like Liholiho, was childless – see Dening, *Islands and Beaches*, 218. Bingham believed that the chiefs' desire to consume alcohol freely influenced them to accept nullification (*Residence*, 78–79).

[69] Linnekin, *Sacred Queens*, 5–6. Neither is it clear that male aliʻi "lost their *mana*, their efficacy and directedness" after 1819 (ibid., 72–73).

[70] Malo, *Moʻolelo Hawaiʻi*, 26.

in the matter.[71] High-ranking chiefesses were also taken as spoils of war and in power plays. Apparently feuding with his half brother around 1800, Kamehameha simply "took" his wife.[72] But against whom – and for whom – did the chiefesses revolt? It may be that neither Ka'ahumanu nor Keōpūolani viewed nullification as binding on the people. At the coronation ceremony for Liholiho, Ka'ahumanu gave a speech defending her decision to break kapu. Filtered through a missionary lens and only recorded decades after the fact, the speech must be used with caution. Yet according to longtime foreign resident John Parker Palmer (informant to chronicler and missionary William D. Alexander), Ka'ahumanu addressed the people as follows:

> If you wish to continue to observe my father's laws, it is well and we will not molest you. But as for me and my people, we intend to be free from the tabus. We intend that the husband's food is the wife's food and shall be cooked in the same oven, and that they shall be permitted to eat out of the same calabash. We intend to eat pork and bananas and cocoanuts [*sic*], and to live as the white people do. If you think differently, you are at liberty to do so; but as for me and my people we are resolved to be free.[73]

Big Island rebels, to be sure, would not be granted "liberty" to stage an uprising against the kingdom. But observance or nonobservance of the kapu would be left to the people to decide. It is tempting, if risky, to read a class distinction into Ka'ahumanu's recorded statement. Ka'ahumanu's "people" included her immediate kin, the Maui chiefs, but who else? Maka'āinana were not explicitly invited to enjoy the new rights snatched by the self-appointed Great Counselor, and it is difficult to know whether the peoples' "rights" registered for Ka'ahumanu at all.[74]

In the short term, the impact of nullification on religious and legal practice depended on a host of factors, including distance from the centers of chiefly power (southern O'ahu, the leeward Big Island) and which chiefs "ate" (oversaw) the district. Historian Lilikalā Kame'eleihiwa suggested that ongoing depopulation had caused people "to question the

---

[71] E.g., Liholiho gave his wife Kekāuluohi to the Kaua'i *kaukau ali'i* (low-ranking chief) Charles Kana'ina in 1821 (Kamakau, *Ruling Chiefs*, 253). In 1823 Liholiho apparently "took" Boki's wife; see Gast and Conrad, *Don Francisco de Paula Marin*, 272. See also Bingham, *Residence*, 128.

[72] 'Ī'ī, *Fragments*, 49–50. The woman mentioned was Ka'ahumanu's sister, Kalākua Kaheiheimālie (later known as Hoapiliwahine).

[73] Alexander, "Overthrow of the Ancient Tabu System," 83.

[74] Kamakau wrote that, upon nullification, the "chiefs and people mingled on an equality" (*Ruling Chiefs*, 261). If so, the fraternization was brief.

power of their own Gods" and to undermine "their belief in the state religion."[75] But it is difficult to know what maka'āinana thought about these developments. There is little evidence that commoners considered the state religion "utterly worthless," as American missionaries later wrote; nor is it clear that commoners "ardently desired" its downfall.[76] For either to be the case, state religion would have to be relevant; for most maka'āinana, it was not.[77] As for their own religion, commoners spirited devotional objects into the mountains or hid them in caves.[78] Healing rituals, observance of the 'aumakua, and sorcery continued to be practiced in private. By every indication, sacred objects and practices retained their mana.

But state religion was shattered. In June 1822, Ka'ahumanu and her brother Big Island governor John Adams Kuakini ordered the public burning of more than one hundred ki'i and *akua lā 'au* ("wooden gods"), including a favorite image observed by Ka'ahumanu's late husband Kamehameha.[79] Whether Ka'ahumanu had decided to "live as the white people do," or to *live* – in Kame'eleihiwa's reading – as the white people were living and Hawaiians were not, she and Keōpūolani were embarking on a new path. Foreign goods and ideas, gender restrictions, and the "categorical ambivalence" about women's roles in society all probably played a role in this momentous decision.[80] Yet disease, population loss, and the conspicuous health disparities between Islanders and foreigners were at least as

---

[75] Kame'eleihiwa, "Synopsis of Traditional Hawaiian Culture," 4. See also Kame'eleihiwa, *Native Land*, 140.

[76] Jarves, *History of the Hawaiian or Sandwich Islands*, 210–11.

[77] See, e.g., Corney, *Voyages*, 101.

[78] Geo[rge] Bennet to W[illia]m A[lers] Hankey, 1 Aug. 1822, CWM/LMS box 3B, folder 10, SOAS.

[79] "Extracts from Auna's Jounal," in Montgomery, *Journal of Voyages and Travels*, 2: 93–94; Bingham, *Residence*, 162. This instance of iconoclasm – the most significant in Hawai'i – does not match the seasonality Sissons identifies as central to Polynesian religious revolutions (*Polynesian Iconoclasm*, 1, 149–50). With the exception of Marín on O'ahu, other sources fail to indicate when desecration of heiau and sacred images began and how widespread the practice was, though there is clear evidence of it by summer 1820 ("Sandwich Mission: Copy of a letter from the King and Queen of Atooi" [broadside], 1821, HMCS; Dan[ie]l Tyerman to [William Alers Hankey], Aug 9, 1822, CWM/LMS box 3B, folder 10, SOAS; Tamehameha [Liholiho] to "*Ka poe* American Board" [ABCFM], March 18, 1823, ABCFM Papers; Dibble, *History and General Views*, 66–67). For distinctions between sacred images and the deities they represented, see Ellis, *Journal of a Tour*, 194; Malo, *Mo'olelo Hawai'i*, 163n3, 337–39; Dibble, *History of the Sandwich Islands*, 98; Kamakau, *Ka Po'e Kahiko*, 12, 54, 87.

[80] For "categorical ambivalence," see Sahlins, *Historical Metaphors*, 47; Linnekin, *Sacred Queens*, 22.

important. In an early sign of aliʻi distancing themselves from Native medicine, Gov. Kuakini rejected his physicians' promises of a cure for his edema and terminated their financial support.[81] Perhaps most important of all was the fertility of the aliʻi. While Keōpūolani had borne three surviving children, Kaʻuhumanu and Liholiho – despite eight marriages between them – were both childless.[82] If the chiefly class could not be sustained by new births and surviving children, the kingdom was finished.

THE LONG NECKS

On March 30, 1820, the New England ship *Thaddeus* came in sight of the Big Island. Having left Boston six months earlier, the Congregationalist and Presbyterian missionaries on board had no idea either that Kamehameha was dead or that state religion had collapsed. Unarmed and accompanied by women and children (twenty-two persons total), the newcomers seemed to pose little threat. To the chiefesses, they may have posed an opportunity. Before the delegation had been granted permission to dock at Kailua Bay, Liholiho and his wives boarded the *Thaddeus* to share dinner with the "long necks." Mission wife Nancy Ruggles was pleasantly surprised when the wives declared "they wish[ed] to learn to read."[83] In consultation with his advisors, Liholiho gave the missionaries leave to stay for one year, provided their physician settle at Kailua-Kona and serve him exclusively.[84]

To understand why Keōpūolani, Kaʻahumanu, and other chiefs were attracted to missionaries and their program, we must return to 1807, when two young men boarded an American merchant ship off the coast of Kaʻū on the Big Island. Sailing first to the Pacific Northwest and then to China, "Henry" ʻŌpūkahaʻia and "Thomas" Hopu arrived in New York in 1809. They were shortly shuttled to Connecticut for Christian education at

---

[81] Bingham, *Residence*, 79.

[82] Only three of Keōpūolani's eleven children survived to adulthood, all of whom happened to be Kamehameha's children. A high rate of close endogamous marriage (inbreeding) as a possible cause for decreased fertility among aliʻi men and women deserves further study. For the possibility of Queen Pōmare of Tahiti divorcing a spouse who could not provide her with offspring, see O'Brien, "Think of Me as a Woman," 112.

[83] Nancy Ruggles journal, April 6, 1820, HMCS; see also ibid., April 1, 1820. The ABCFM did not allow women to be missionaries; hence, their identification here as "mission wives." For "long necks," see Dibble, *History of the Sandwich Islands*, 161; Kamakau, *Ruling Chiefs*, 247.

[84] Bingham, *Residence*, 90–91. In this way, Liholiho followed a pattern set by his father; see Chapter 3. For chiefly discussion about mission wives and the delegation's lack of weapons, see Bingham, *Residence*, 107.

the Foreign Mission School in Cornwall. Their classmates included five other Hawaiians (Kaua'i prince Humehume among them), Marquesans, South Asians, Chinese, and American Indians. 'Ōpūkaha'ia, Hopu, and Humehume fought in the War of 1812 aboard American ships. Humehume was injured in the English Channel and given a medical discharge. Hopu's ship was captured by the British, and the young Hawaiian was imprisoned for several months on St. Kitts where he witnessed Africans in chains and "had a great desire to return to America."[85] (Both Humehume and Hopu later returned home.) 'Ōpūkaha'ia, who had survived the war unscathed, converted to Christianity and began a New England tour to promote the Foreign Mission School. In 1818 he succumbed to typhus and died at Cornwall. 'Ōpūkaha'ia's death and the publication of his heavily edited "memoir" inspired a broad fund-raising effort for a Sandwich Islands Mission.[86]

Probably no one in Hawai'i knew the extent of this new interest in their islands. Yet various changes were afoot that would make island rulers more receptive to the missionaries when they finally arrived. A few months after the death of 'Ōpūkaha'ia, British sandalwood trader Peter Corney had a revealing discussion with Maui governor "George Cox" Ke'eaumoku. Corney, a chief officer on the schooner *Columbia*, had made several visits to the islands between 1815 and 1818; he also employed Hawaiian seamen on his ship. Corney wrote that Ke'eaumoku "sets the wooden gods and priests at defiance; he says, that they are all liars, and that the white men's God is the true and only God."[87] The governor's motivations are difficult to divine, yet the general thrust of his comments cannot be dismissed outright. During mourning ceremonies for Kamehameha in 1819, Ke'eaumoku reportedly became intoxicated and "broke up" the kāhuna's efforts to determine whether the mō'ī had fallen prey to sorcery, implying that Ke'eaumoku held the kāhuna in contempt.[88] Another possibility is that he had heard about the recent iconoclasm and conversions at Tahiti and wanted to import the movement.[89] On the other hand, despite

---

[85] Hopoo, "Memoirs of Thomas Hopoo," 46.

[86] Dwight, *Memoirs of Henry Obookiah*; see also *Narrative of Five Youth*. For an important revision of the 'Ōpūkaha'ia story, see Chang, *World and All the Things upon It*, 82–92. For a Māori convert with a similar trajectory and influence on British evangelism, see Ballantyne, *Entanglements of Empire*, 223–25.

[87] Corney, *Voyages*, 102.

[88] Kamakau, *Ruling Chiefs*, 214. See also Kahananui, *Ka Mooolelo Hawaii*, 210.

[89] Sissons argues that Hawaiian iconoclasm was "carried out in at least partial emulation" of earlier events at Tahiti (*Polynesian Iconoclasm*, 64); but cf. Ellis, *Narrative of Tour*, 112; Dibble, *History of the Sandwich Islands*, 142–43.

later pleading by his sisters Kaʻahumanu and Lydia Nāmāhāna Piʻia, Keʻeaumoku was never baptized. Nor did he renounce his multiple wives or the kāhuna he continued to consult about spiritual matters. He was also deeply concerned about ʻanāʻanā and employed the exorcist kāhuna for protection against the sorcerer kāhuna.[90] He did all this after his supposed confession to Corney about the "true and only" God.

No doubt a formal alliance with Britons in 1818 would have been helpful to the aliʻi; that may be explanation enough for Keʻeaumoku's comments. Yet Kamehameha's conquests had also created a division in island politics. Keʻeaumoku, as we have seen, was apparently ready to overthrow the mōʻī and replace him with Liholiho in 1809.[91] Kamehameha had also recently executed Kanihonui, the lover of Keʻeaumoku's sister (Kaʻahumanu) and a favorite at court. Perhaps Keʻeaumoku's resentment was still running hot in 1818. The kāhuna acted at the behest of the mōʻī. If Keʻeaumoku was unhappy with Kamehameha, it would hardly be surprising if his feelings toward the kāhuna were also negative. Keʻeaumoku, then, had plenty of reasons for doubting the intentions and legitimacy of island priests: very likely his grievance was not with Hawaiian religion per se but with the state religion that Kamehameha and his priests controlled.

When Corney questioned other chiefs about religious practice, they told him they went to the heiau "more to feast than to pray, which I believe to be really the case."[92] Here Corney made a category mistake by imagining that religion could be divided from politics, law, and elite social life. Going to the heiau "to feast" can hardly be taken as the stirrings of revolution or even indifference to state religion. (Indeed, the fact that aliʻi continued to show up at the heiau might suggest the opposite.) Despite rogue chiefs and everyday violations of kapu by commoners, the broader system of religious observation and social control was largely uncompromised in 1818. While foreigners were quick to comment on chiefs applying kapu rules to their own advantage, there was probably as much continuity as innovation in this behavior.[93] The same can be said of reports of male aliʻi freely breaking kapu in public, while chiefesses could only do so in private.[94]

[90] Sahlins, *Anahulu*, 1:84–87.
[91] As late as 1816 a foreign observer believed that Keʻeaumoku and Chief Minister William Pitt Kalanimoku were conspiring to retake Maui from Kamehameha (Chamisso, in Barratt, *Russian View of Honolulu*, 175).
[92] Corney, *Voyages*, 101–2.   [93] See, e.g., Cox, *Adventures on the Columbia River*, 45.
[94] Golovnin, *Around the World*, 209. More research is needed on the payment of fines by kapu breakers to avoid capital punishment. For two cases in the 1810s, see Gast and Conrad, *Don Francisco de Paula Marin*, 205; Freycinet, *Hawaii in 1819*, 89.

In spring 1820 the young travelers Hopu and Humehume returned to Hawai'i with the charter delegation of New England missionaries. It is hard to overestimate the importance of Hopu and Humehume as emissaries. Their literacy, their English-language skills, and the social capital they had gained with Americans piqued the Maui chiefs' interest. Despite the questionable parentage of both young men, their experience and travels abroad could not be gainsaid.[95] Already by summer 1820, the Kaua'i mō'ī Kaumuali'i (father of Humehume) had ordered a church built on the site of a Waimea heiau.[96] The symbolism was apparent to all. In July Humehume wrote to Boston to say that "my father is much pleased" at the presence of the newcomers: "[H]e is willing to do all he can for them, give them as much land as they wish to have & furnish them with such … provi[s]ions as they may … need. He says all he wants is to have them teach his people and not behave" like other "white men." Such generosity came at a price. Humehume asked the ABCFM to send "several mecanacks" [mechanics], house and ship carpenters, cabinet makers, brick makers, a farmer, and a sawmill. "[T]hese my father is very anxious to have." Also, "a good physition. one that is capable of doing his duty."[97]

Kaumuali'i and his wife Deborah Kapule Kekaiha'akūlou (who was not Humehume's mother) also took the opportunity to dictate a letter to the ABCFM. Later reproduced as a broadside to shore up support for the mission, Kaumuali'i's letter begins by thanking commissioner Samuel Worcester for sending a Bible:

I think it is a good book … I hope my people will soon read this and all other good books. I believe that my idols are good for nothing; and that your God is the only true God, the one that made all things. My gods I have hove away; they are no good; they fool me; they do me no good … Now I throw them all away. I have none now.[98]

---

[95] Humehume's mother was maka'āinana, as were both of Hopu's parents.

[96] Missionaries Samuel Ruggles and Samuel Whitney first visited an enthusiastic Kaumuali'i on Kaua'i in early May 1820, before proceeding to Honolulu. They returned to Waimea in late July 1820 to set up a mission station (Joesting, *Kauai*, 122–23). Both Humehume and another Foreign Mission School student, William Kanui, eventually apostatized; see [Hopu] to [Worcester], 3 May 1821, ABCFM Papers.

[97] [Humehume] to Worcester, 27 July 1820, ABCFM Papers. For similar dynamics among the Māori and British missionaries, see Ballantyne, *Entanglements of Empire*, 59–64, 76–77.

[98] "Sandwich Mission: Copy of a letter from the King and Queen of Atooi" (broadside), 1821, HMCS. Deborah Kapule added a short note to mission wife Nancy Ruggles's mother: "I am glad your daughter comes here. I shall be her mother now, and she be my daughter." Kapule added that once Ruggles had learned Hawaiian, she would "learn me how to read, and write, and sew; and talk of that great Akooah, which the good people in America love" (ibid.). For more on the broadside, see Forbes, *Hawaiian National Bibliography*, 1:367–68.

The Rev. Samuel Ruggles recorded a similar sentiment. "The God of America is good," a commoner at Waimea allegedly stated, "but the Gods of Atooi [Kaua'i] are good for nothing; we throw them all away; by and by the American God will be the God of Atooi."⁹⁹ A letter from Hopu, in his own hand, was equally explicit: "Truely Owhyhee [Hawaiian] idols are no more seen. They are all burn [*sic*] up in the fire."¹⁰⁰

Jehovah and *palapala* (reading and writing) were not the only reasons for Kaumuali'i to ally with the newcomers. The mō'ī had run up enormous debts in the sandalwood trade and may have seen the mission as an escape valve.¹⁰¹ Another possibility is that he and Deborah Kapule were happy to discard a kapu system enforced by the Maui chiefs – and perhaps happy to abandon some of the akua – but had no intention of abandoning their own deities. Otto von Kotzebue later learned that the Kaua'i ali'i could hardly wait for Kamehameha to die so they could reclaim their independence.¹⁰² Nevertheless, Kaumuali'i and Deborah Kapule's joint letter, as well as comments by Kaua'i Islanders, indicates their approval of the mission and its god, such as they understood them.

The Maui chiefs would not be such an easy catch. For two years they were watchful, testing the *kāhuna pule* ("prayer experts") for possible advantages they could offer. Apparently pleased with the medical services of Dr. Thomas Holman, Liholiho expressed an interest in the missionaries building him a palace; the third floor, he assured them, would be dedicated to the "worship of Jehovah."¹⁰³ Ka'ahumanu apparently warmed to the missionaries after an illness she suffered in 1821. With severe "paroxysms" afflicting her in December, mission leader Hiram Bingham thought the queen was on her deathbed. He later wrote that when she had improved, Ka'ahumanu "and her friends set a higher value on the religion which we were endeavoring to inculcate."¹⁰⁴

---

⁹⁹ Samuel Ruggles journal, June 17, 1820, HMCS. For a Big Island chief who "threw ... away" his ki'i, see Ellis, *Narrative of a Tour*, 48. There are numerous Hawaiian translations for the verb "to throw (away)"; Ka'ahumanu and others used *kiola*, i.e., "*Ua kiolaia ia*" (Elisabeta Kaahumanu [Dec. 20, 1825], *Ka Manao o na Alii*, 6).

¹⁰⁰ [Hopu] to [Worcester], May 3, 1821, ABCFM Papers.

¹⁰¹ Other chiefs joined the Mission for precisely this reason. For Kaumuali'i's debts, see Joesting, *Kauai*, 87–94. The sandalwood trade reached its peak in 1821–22 with more than 26,000 piculs – one picul equals 135 pounds – exported to China (ibid., 91).

¹⁰² Kotzebue, *New Voyage*, 2:196.

¹⁰³ Bingham, *Residence*, 132. For Holman's "successful" medical efforts, see ibid., 104.

¹⁰⁴ Ibid., 148–49. For an ill Marquesan chief who claimed that "he would believe in Jehova ... if he would cure him[,] and so would all the people," see Richard Armstrong journal, Dec. 3, 1833, HMCS.

Through autumn 1823 mission labors were confined to Oʻahu, Kauaʻi, and the leeward Big Island. Yet even in these locales, makaʻāinana had practically no exposure to Christianity.[105] Missionary writings shed some light on those who did. When Bingham prompted people in upland Kauaʻi to reflect on the Creator and the beauties of nature, their response suggested to Bingham that they knew no such creator. What about "Jehovah, the God of heaven?" Bingham asked. "ʻIt is your god, is it not?' 'Yes, and is he not *yours* also?' 'No,' they replied, 'our gods are all dead.'"[106] Perhaps, but this had little bearing on local religion and rituals. By 1823 missionaries estimated that two-thirds of commoners observed their akua and ʻaumakua in private.[107] Evangelicals had difficulty understanding how religion could survive the death of the gods; they were equally confused about distinctions between local and state religion.

Hawaiians, for their part, were largely unfamiliar with the contours of American Protestantism. Island religion was "instrumental" and active, marked by ritual and activity rather than theology or belief per se.[108] A great deal was lost in translation. When Hopu first introduced the missionaries to the Maui chiefs, he explained that the newcomers would teach them about "the One who made heaven and earth" and about the imminent day of judgment: "ʻHereafter will come the great day [*la*] when all will be judged before God.'" The chiefs responded, "ʻIs the sun [*la*] going to grow bigger?' . . . and they said among themselves, 'This traveler is telling tall tales!' and called him a romancer."[109] Yet Protestant theology was of little concern to chiefs whose primary interest was building an alliance with powerful foreigners. With a seemingly benign program of palapala and clean living, the newcomers had the added advantage of not exploiting island labor, the chiefs' hereditary spoils. Nonetheless, the mission would eventually draw critics among chiefs and foreign merchants alike who preferred their "kanakas" at work.[110]

Kamakau believed that the aliʻi immediately saw the advantages of palapala. Chiefesses, in particular, became "proficient" in writing out

[105] W[illia]m Ellis to G[eorge] Burden, June 18, 1823, and Oct. 5, 1823, CWM/LMS box 4, folder 3, SOAS.
[106] Bingham, *Residence*, 143.
[107] William Richards journal, June 22, 1823, ABCFM Papers; Asa Thurston and Artemas Bishop to ABCFM, Aug. 5, 1824, qtd. in Sahlins, *Anahulu*, 1:73.
[108] Mykkänen, *Inventing Politics*, 44. For the Māori, see O'Malley, *Meeting Place*, 181–82; Ballantyne, *Entanglements of Empire*.
[109] Kamakau, *Ruling Chiefs*, 247.   [110] Kotzebue, *New Voyage*, 2:254–62.

Bible verses translated by the kāhuna pule.[111] A short condolence letter from Liholiho to the queen regent of Tahiti suggests how the chiefs understood the role of palapala in relation to the broader missionary agenda. Liholiho's letter – if authentic – also hints at how he may have been thinking about the role of the new religious system in international diplomacy.[112] The occasion was the death of Tahitian king Pōmare II, apparently from alcohol-related causes. "I have compassion towards you on account of your son's dying," Liholiho wrote in Hawaiian. "Love to you and the *alii,* chiefs of your islands. I now serve the God of you and us. We are now learning the palapala. When I become skilful in learning I will then go and visit you. May you be saved by Jesus Christ."[113]

Liholiho's diplomatic correspondence presented him as a devoted Christian determined to spread literacy among his people. Daily life offered another view. The following spring Liholiho could be heard arguing with his mother Keōpūolani about mission rules. According to the Rev. Charles S. Stewart, Liholiho complained that the missionaries "'do not permit us *to drink rum,* or do any thing we formerly did. Their teachings are false and evil – their prayers are not good.'" Other male chiefs – those "fond of dissipation," according to Stewart – agreed with the king, but they distinguished between missionaries' educational and religious programs:

Part of their teachings are *true* and *good.* It is well to attend to the "palapala" ... but, there is no good in the "pule" ... the preaching, and the Sabbaths. In India, we are told, they have the *palapala*; and are so rich, that all the people in England and America go there for property: but they keep their stone and wooden gods still. It will be well for us, then, to secure the palapala – for it will make us rich – but let us cast off the pule – it is of no use![114]

By 1823 ali'i and maka'āinana alike had misgivings about the Sandwich Islands Mission. British missionary William Ellis reported that Big Islanders generally approved of the missionaries, although some "had heard that in several countries where foreigners had intermingled with the original natives, the latter had soon disappeared, and should missionaries come to live at Waiakea, perhaps the land would ultimately become theirs,

[111] Kamakau, *Ruling Chiefs,* 248–49.
[112] The letter was published in Bingham's 1847 memoir: By mid-1822 Liholiho "had become able to write a letter of business or of friendship ... The following is a translation, with the exception of the signature, which, as to name, title, and orthography is strictly his own" (Bingham, *Residence,* 171–72).
[113] Ibid.   [114] Stewart, *Private Journal,* 196–97.

and the … natives cease to be its occupiers." Ellis assured the people (probably maka'āinana) that the mission had been "especially designed, and eminently calculated, to prevent a consequence so melancholy." The Americans had come, he explained, to save Hawaiians from themselves. Their own "sanguinary wars … their extensive and cruel practice of infanticide, their frequent intoxication, and their numerous diseases, partly [en]gendered by vicious habits" threatened to dispossess them of life and limb. Indeed, "there was every reason to fear the Hawaiian people would soon be annihilated, unless some antidote was found."[115]

VERY STRONG MEDICINE

With the kapu system dismantled and the gods discarded, American missionaries had reason to be hopeful. But securing the chiefs' cooperation in a "civilizing" mission and converting them to Christianity were hardly faits accomplis. State religion had been abolished, but Hawaiian religious cosmology and lifeways obviously had not. As in many Indigenous societies, Islanders were typically willing to add new religious ideas and practices to their repertoire, yet they rarely rejected old ones.[116] Among other factors that precluded the adoption of conventional Protestant theological notions in this period was non-literacy. Yet American evangelicals would not be deterred. "Describe the character of man as it is," the ABCFM instructed its recruits back in Boston: "depraved, unholy, and enslaved to sin; and you need not fear but its likeness will be recognized."[117]

That was wishful thinking. But other means of securing ali'i favor would shortly be discovered; namely, Tahitians. Scholars have been slow to recognize that a handful of British missionaries and their Tahitian converts played a central role – perhaps *the* central role – in securing the chiefs' acceptance of the missionary program.[118] The public and private writings of this small, multicultural delegation also comprises one of the richest records of Hawaiian life in the early nineteenth century.

---

[115] Ellis, *Journal of a Tour*, 181–82.   [116] Cf. Kuykendall, *Hawaiian Kingdom*, 1:66–67.

[117] ABCFM, *Instructions of the Prudential Committee*, 44. ABCFM leaders in Boston contemplated the possibility of "radiating … religion" outward from Hawai'i as early as 1822 ("Mission to the Sandwich Islands," *Religious Intelligencer* 7 [1822], 415; *Boston Recorder* 7 [1822], 190).

[118] E.g., Matsuda, *Pacific Worlds*, 153–57. Relying too heavily on American sources, scholars also tend to read a US imperial posture back onto the 1820s. An important exception is Douglas, "Religion."

With a Pacific base in the Society Islands, the London Missionary Society (LMS) sent delegations to not only Hawai'i but Tonga, Samoa, and the Cook Islands.[119] In this way, a network of evangelical efforts eventually secured a foothold not only for Protestantism but also for Anglo-American commercial and political influence among all the major Polynesian groups.

After six years in Tahiti, twenty-eight-year-old British missionary William Ellis sailed for Hawai'i with two fellow LMS missionaries and four Tahitian converts – Tau'ā, Auna ("a chief of some rank"), and their unidentified wives – along with five other Tahitians, all apparently from the island of Huahine.[120] Arriving at the Big Island, the delegation learned that other Tahitians had found their way to the chiefs. On the Kona coast, a Borabora man named Toketa (or Toteta) served as personal teacher to Gov. John Adams Kuakini; and in Honolulu, Kahikona served as teacher to Aarona Keali'iahonui, son of Kaua'i mō'ī Kaumuali'i.[121] American missionaries in Honolulu also enjoyed the service of Tahitians as assistants and nannies.[122]

Dialogue between Hawaiian and Tahitian chiefs, conducted via foreign ships, had been opened by Kamehameha and Pōmare I years before. A plan to intermarry their princes was foiled by the Tahitian king's death.[123] At some point – it is not clear when – the Maui chiefs learned of the baptism of Pōmare I's son, Pōmare II, who had earlier forsaken his gods and ordered the destruction of temples and images.[124] When the LMS delegation arrived at O'ahu, Ka'ahumanu and her retinue were "remarkably inquisitive" about developments at the Society Islands. Scholars have argued that traditions about Kahiki (the land of origin to the south) contributed to the chiefs' warm embrace of the Tahitian

---

[119] Gilson, *Cook Islands*, 20–24; Campbell, *Island Kingdom*, 52–54. Hawaiians, along with other Pacific Islanders, were themselves later "potent catalysts of change" in the Marquesas (Dening, *Islands and Beaches*, 103).

[120] Ellis, *Polynesian Researches*, 4:34. See also journal of Sybil Moseley Bingham, Aug. 9, 1822, HMCS; Barff, ed., "Memoir of Auna," Hamilton Library, Univ. of Hawai'i at Mānoa.

[121] Barrère and Sahlins, "Tahitians in the Early History." Missionaries reported that Toketa was the brother of Auna's wife and had not been heard of for "nearly 30 years" (Geo[rge] Bennet and Daniel Tyerman to George Burden, Aug. 10, 1822, CWM/LMS box 3B, folder 10, SOAS). For Toketa's home island, see Ellis to Burden, Oct. 5, 1823, CWM/LMS. Kahikona seems to have remained with Keali'iahonui and his third wife, former queen consort Kekau'ōnohi, into the '30s.

[122] Mission leader Hiram Bingham had at least one Tahitian missionary assistant, while Bingham's wife Sibyl employed a Tahitian nanny.

[123] Ellis, *Journal of a Tour*, 50.

[124] Ibid., 112; see also Dibble, *History of the Sandwich Islands*, 142–43.

missionaries: more "culturally amenable" to Hawaiians than Anglo-American Protestants, the Tahitian kāhuna seemed a natural choice to replace the discarded priests of the kapu religion.[125] Yet the earlier dialogue opened by Kamehameha and the more recent iconoclasm by Pōmare II were probably at least as important.

Ellis believed that by answering various of Liholiho's questions, the Tahitians removed some of his "prejudices against Christianity."[126] In fact, by summer 1822 some Maui chiefs had made up their minds about the Anglo-American-Tahitian missionary program. Maui Island governor George Cox Ke'eaumoku "came publicly forth and declared his intention of having himself and his people become regular pupils" of the missionaries. The next day Ke'eaumoku tried to persuade his sister Ka'ahumanu to do the same, but she was not prepared to take that step. Meanwhile Liholiho declared himself ready for "regular instruction," though some missionaries were skeptical of his intentions.[127] Still, the Tahitians kept up daily prayer with the royal family during their stay.[128] Ka'ahumanu, Kalanimoku, and other Hawaiian chiefs also began to correspond with the Tahitian chiefs by letter.[129] On the Big Island, Gov. John Adams Kuakini declared new prohibitions (kapu) on murder, theft, infanticide, distilling spirits, and violating the Sabbath.[130]

On his second visit the following spring, Ellis was joined once again by Tau'ā, this time with his "family" and a woman named Taamotu who

[125] Barrère and Sahlins, "Tahitians in the Early History," 23–24. See also Kame'eleihiwa, *Native Land*, 143–44; Chang, *World and All the Things upon It*, 92–96. Sissons, by contrast, argues that Tahitians proactively exported their movement to Hawai'i and elsewhere (*Polynesian Iconoclasm*).

[126] W[illia]m Ellis to G[eorge] Burden, July 9, 1822, CWM/LMS box 3B, folder 10, SOAS. Ellis's Tahitian was excellent; with the help of a language instructor appointed by Liholiho, he was soon able to preach in Hawaiian in a "plain and intelligible manner" (ibid.).

[127] Sybil Moseley Bingham journal, Aug. 9, 1822, HMCS.

[128] Ellis to Burden, July 9, 1822, CWM/LMS. The royal family "expressed their pleasure at our friends [the Tahitians] remaining with them, and not going on to the Marquesas" as originally planned (ibid.). See also Montgomery, *Journal of Voyages and Travels*, 2:18, 32–33. Auna and his wife lived more than a year with Ka'ahumanu and her new husband (the deposed Kaua'i mō'ī) Kaumuali'i in Honolulu before returning to Tahiti in 1824 (Bennet and Tyerman to Burden, Aug. 10, 1822, CWM/LMS). Toketa seems to have arrived in 1818 and remained until 1825 (Barrère and Sahlins, "Tahitians in the Early History," 25–32).

[129] W[illia]m Ellis to [George] Bennet and [Daniel] Tyerman, Feb. 18, 1823, CWM/LMS box 4, folder 3, SOAS.

[130] Ellis to Burden, Oct. 5, 1823, CWM/LMS.

served as a companion to Ellis's wife Mary.[131] The delegation stayed almost two years, living together for a good part of it.[132] Despite Ellis's reference to Tau'ā's family, there is no record of any of the four Tahitian women – Taamotu, Auna's wife, Tau'ā's wife, and Sybil Bingham's nanny – having children in tow (though missionaries could have failed to mention them). While little can be said about particular women's interactions in this encounter, the mere presence of Polynesian women seems to have played a critical role in winning over the chiefesses.[133] Indeed Ellis credited the Tahitians with convincing the queen to "put away" her husbands and to live, as they did, in Christian monogamy.[134] In private correspondence, Ellis identified Tau'ā as a "constant spiritual companion" to Keōpūolani, contributing to the "clear and scriptural views" which afforded her comfort in her "last hours."[135]

Yet it may be that Tahitians proved the efficacy of Christianity simply by arriving and surviving. This small group of Polynesians had discarded their akua, learned to read and write, and sailed the Pacific, not as bondspeople or servants – at least, not Tau'ā and Auna – but as missionary helpers to foreigners who seemed to treat them with respect. For embattled Hawaiian chiefs feeling the squeeze of merchants and other foreigners, these were no small matters. Finally, for those chiefs committed to Kamehameha's legacy, comfort could be found in the mō'ī's earlier sanctioning of diplomacy and intermarriage between the two groups.

This is not to say that the British-Tahitian missionary delegation was always well received, particularly by maka'āinana. When Ellis preached at Hilo in 1823, an old woman interrupted him to declare her devotion to the akua: "'Great is Pele, the goddess of Hawaii [Island]; she shall save Maaro.'" (Maaro was a local chief, present for the sermon, who happened

---

[131] Ellis, *Polynesian Researches*, 4:282–85, 295–97. It is not clear whether Taamotu, whom Kamakau identified as "Ka-'au-a-moku," had been along for the first visit (*Ruling Chiefs*, 254).

[132] Ellis to Burden, Oct. 30, 1823, CWM/LMS box 4, folder 3, SOAS.

[133] Few sources shed light on Polynesian women's conversations and exchanges in this period; Toketa's journal grants no more access than his fellow Anglo-American missionaries (Barrère and Sahlins, "Tahitians in the Early History").

[134] Ellis to Burden, June 18, 1823, CWM/LMS. Deposing a husband had potentially serious consequences for kinship networks, which reinforces the gravity of the chiefesses' decision. For renunciation of plural spouses in Fiji, see Luker, "Mothers of the Taukei," 77–82.

[135] Ellis to Burden, Oct. 5, 1823, CWM/LMS. For the influence of Tau'ā's wife ("Kauawahine") on Keōpūolani, see Green, *Notices of the Life of … Puaaiki*, 12. Kamakau later wrote that Tahitians taught Keōpūolani "the word of God and the road to heaven" (*Ruling Chiefs*, 254).

FIGURE 4.3 *Left,* William Ellis; *right,* Makoa (the facial tattoos represent goats, a popular style).
Charles Taylor, 1826, courtesy of British Library; William Ellis, 1823, courtesy of British Library.

to be ill.) Another congregant then began to sing a song "in praise of Pele, to which the people generally listened, though some began to laugh." Someone suggested that Pele herself was present for the sermon, which led Ellis to inquire of the old woman, "Oani," whether she had listened to his sermon and understood its message. She said she had. Ellis then asked her whether "she thought Jehovah was good, and those [people] happy, who made him their God. She answered, 'He is your good God (or best God), and it is right that you should worship him; but Pele is my god, and the great god of Hawaii.'" Oani then proceeded with her song in praise of Pele. As a clarification for readers, Ellis explained that Oani "did not dispute that Jehovah was a God" but rather the proposition that he was "the only God." Pele, too, was a god and "dwelt in her, and through her would heal the sick chief then present. She wished [Maaro] restored [to health], and therefore came to visit him."[136]

---

[136] Ellis, *Journal of a Tour,* 176–77. For a kahuna who inquired about "Jehovah" being able to understand prayers in Hawaiian, see Bennet and Tyerman to Burden, Aug. 10, 1822, CWM/LMS. For a Marquesan's observation that Jehovah was a "true God, but not the only true God," see Richard Armstrong journal, Dec. 8, 1833, HMCS; see also Gascoigne, *Encountering the Pacific,* 373. For more on Oani, see Stewart, *Visit to the*

Ellis had a notion that Oani's challenge stemmed from his own violation of Pele at Kīlauea Crater earlier that month. To the great consternation of local people, the British missionary partook of wild 'ōhelo berries without praying or making an offering to the volcano goddess. When villagers in nearby Kealokomo heard of this infraction, they told Ellis that the missionaries had escaped "only because we were *haore* [haole], foreigners. No Hawaiian, they added, would have done so with impunity, for Pele was a dreadful being."[137] Some Big Islanders thus clearly conceived of the akua's powers as constrained when it came to foreigners.

Back in Hilo Ellis rebuked his congregants for believing in an "imaginary deity" (Pele), noting that Jehovah was "the only true Physician, who could save both body and soul." But this only inflamed Oani, who "assum[ed] a haughty air," exclaiming "'I am Pele. I shall never die. And those who follow me, when they die, if part of their bones be taken to Kirauea [Kīlauea], will live with me in the bright fires there.'" Ellis' Hawaiian guide Makoa then intervened, arguing that Pele's party had "'destroyed the king's land, devoured his people, and spoiled the fishing grounds. Ever since you came to the island,'" Makoa continued, "'you have been busied in mischief.'" Oani responded by naming a number of chiefs who had recently perished. "'Who destroyed these?'" she asked. "'Not Pele, but the rum of the foreigners, whose God you are so fond of. Their diseases and their rum have destroyed more of the king's men, than all the volcanoes of the island.'" Ellis regretted that foreign contact had spread disease but noted that "intoxication was wholly forbidden by Jehovah." Finally, he warned Oani of the "fearful doom" that awaited her should she refuse the true god. Again, Oani responded, "'I shall not die, ... but *ora no*,'" that is, live on.[138]

While it is difficult to measure Oani's local support, Ellis indicated that the Hilo people were "not indifferent to the discussion." Congregants apparently "continued in very earnest conversation for some time." Others preferred to change the subject. When Ellis visited the ill chief Maaro a few days later, Maaro told him that "native doctors" had been administering medicines to him "which he trusted would give relief." Ellis had no problem with that, so long as the priests did not employ

---

South Seas, 2:105–11. For a later fictionalization, see "The Last Priestess of Pele," *Harper's New Monthly Magazine* (Aug. 1851): 354–59.

[137] Ellis, *Journal of a Tour*, 151.

[138] Ellis, *Journal of a Tour*, 178–79. Makoa had apparently served for "many years" as Kamehameha's messenger (ibid., 63).

"incantations" or make "offerings to their former gods." To this, Maaro "made no reply" but turned the conversation, saying he "regretted that he was not able to furnish us with a canoe, and that his sickness had not allowed him to be more with us."[139] Ellis got the hint, but it is not clear that he understood there was no such thing as Native medicine without "incantations" – that island medicine could not be separated from its religious context. As for Oani's earlier challenge, both Maaro and Ellis were diplomatic enough not to raise the subject.

Some Hawaiians by 1823 were drawing explicit comparisons between Natives' and foreigners' bodies. Waipiʻo village chief Haʻa inquired of Makoa, the missionaries' guide, about some medicine he saw being prepared. Makoa told Haʻa that it was "very strong medicine," so strong that "if a native only smelt it, his breath would be taken away." (Makoa may have been thinking of medicinal hartshorn, a bottle of which missionaries had once "handed him to smell of.") Makoa went on to observe to Haʻa that "'they are strange people, very unlike us; for frequently, after being sick all night, they get up in the morning, take medicine which would send us all to sleep, and then walk on all day, as if nothing were the matter with them.'"[140] While it is not clear whether Makoa was referring to the missionaries or foreigners in general, his comparison would find company in years to come.

A few months later, Ellis and his Tahitian assistants visited Keōpūolani, Kaʻahumanu, and other high chiefs at Lahaina, Maui. Here another priestess of Pele with "thousands" of followers arrived. The unnamed priestess wore "prophetic robes" with edges burned in honor of the volcano goddess, and she carried "a short staff or spear." When the Maui chiefs asked her business, the priestess responded that she had been with Pele in a "trance or vision" and wished to complain about the sacrilegious behavior of foreigners at Kīlauea Crater on the Big Island. If the chiefs did not banish these foreigners, the priestess threatened, Pele would "take vengeance by inundating the country with lava, and destroying the people."[141] According to Ellis, Kaʻahumanu responded to this provocation by declaring the priestess a liar, burning her priestly accoutrements, and sending her away. While missionaries supported this move,

[139] Ibid., 179, 185.
[140] Ibid., 201. See also Ellis, *Narrative of a Tour*, 360–61. Missionaries wrote that Ellis had a "useful proficiency" in medicine and the ability to "ingratiate himself" with Islanders (Tyerman and Bennet to ABCFM, Aug. 9, 1822, CWM/LMS box 3B, folder 10, SOAS).
[141] Ellis, *Narrative of a Tour*, 258. Research on the Pele cult and other '20s resistance movements would be a welcome addition to the scholarship.

the kuhina nui acted without their prompting. Indeed, despite their having her ear for a decade, missionaries would never be able to command Kaʻahumanu.

On Oʻahu, meanwhile, some chiefesses sensed the urgency of the missionary message. At the same time that Ellis and Makoa were touring her native island, the Big Island chiefess Kapiʻolani sat down to tea with the mission wives at Kailua on windward Oʻahu. According to Elizabeth Edwards Bishop, the chiefess "inquired how long before the missionaries would give her a Bible in the Hawaiian tongue, adding 'We want it soon, because by and by we shall die.'"[142] Kapiʻolani was about forty years old and apparently in good health.[143] Kapiʻolani's concerns can be explained by a number of recent deaths. In March 1821 William Pitt Kalanimoku's favorite wife Likelike had died at the age of twenty-one from complications of childbirth; the infant also perished.[144] Two years later Keōpūolani, queen consort and the highest-ranking chief, died at the age of forty-five from a tumor or abscess.[145] The period of the queen's final illness was two weeks, during which time she was in and out of "stupor" and occasionally too weak to speak. She was seen by two foreign physicians, both well trained and able practitioners, who determined that they could be of "no f[u]rther use to her."[146] Her condition was incurable.

Hawaiʻi was again plunged into mourning at the death of Keōpūolani, the highest-ranking chief on the islands and a symbol of the monarchy. The "entire district" of Lahaina "sent forth one uninterrupted sound of lamentation." The wailing was "so overwhelming" that guns fired in

---

[142] Elizabeth Edwards Bishop, "A Journal of Early Hawaiian Days," *The Friend* (Sept. 1900): 72.

[143] Kapiʻolani died in 1841, about sixty years old, from complications of a lumpectomy performed by missionary physician Gerrit Judd.

[144] Likelike died March 4, 1821. See journal of John Young (compiled by Dorothy Barrère), March 10, 1821, HSA; Gast and Conrad, *Don Francisco de Paula Marin*, 247; Bingham, *Residence*, 127; Kamakau, *Ruling Chiefs*, 250. Bingham claimed that Kalanimoku asked missionaries whether Likelike "had gone to *heaven*" (*Residence*, 128).

[145] Marín recorded the cause of death as an "ulcer on the back-bone" (Gast and Conrad, *Don Francisco de Paula Marin*, 281). Stewart described the condition as an "abscess between the shoulders" (*Private Journal*, 211). A spinal tumor or peritoneal (abdominal) abscess might have caused the symptoms described in Stewart's account; the latter condition could have terminated in sepsis or organ failure.

[146] Stewart, *Private Journal*, 211. The physicians were Abraham Blatchley, an American missionary, and Liholiho's personal physician Dr. Law of Scotland. For the latter, see ibid., 155. Levi Chamberlain noted in his diary that word had come from Blatchley that "a mortification had taken place & that there is very little room to hope she will recover" (Chamberlain journal, Sept. 15, 1823, HMCS).

Keōpūolani's honor "could scarce be heard through the din."[147] Two
months after Keōpūolani's burial, a royal delegation sailed for Europe to
secure an alliance with Great Britain.[148] King Liholiho, his principal wife
Kamāmalu, the high chief Boki and his wife Liliha were joined by four aliʻi
advisors, the Frenchman Jean Rives, and a number of attendants.[149]
In London the four high chiefs caught measles, and the king and queen
both died.[150] Back in Hawaiʻi, Kaʻahumanu's brother and principal advisor George Cox Keʻeaumoku died of an unknown disease at the age of
thirty-nine. Two months after that, Kaʻahumanu's new husband, the
deposed Kauaʻi mōʻī Kaumualiʻi, died of unknown causes at the age of
forty-six.

The Maui chiefs' receptiveness to the mission must be understood in
the context of these losses.[151] With the royal delegation yet to return from
London, the kuhina nui (now regent) Kaʻahumanu announced the
Sabbath as an official day of rest across the archipelago. Whether she
had accepted the missionary program, co-opted and taken control of it,
or made herself – in the words of one scholar – the "mediative role to

[147] Stewart, *Private Journal*, 224. See also Ellis to Burden, Oct. 5, 1823, CWM/LMS.
Baptized shortly before her death, Keōpūolani was considered by missionaries
a wholehearted convert (Bingham, *Residence*, 190–97; Stewart, *Private Journal*,
207–13); Kamakau later described her as having become "meek," in the Christian
sense (*Ruling Chiefs*, 261). Yet as with the Tahitians Tauʻā, Auna, and their wives, the
reality was probably less clear: "conversion" poorly reflects the dynamic social maneu-
vering and cultural borrowing at work in such situations. Eventually island Christians
would generate their own accounts; see Chapter 5.

[148] Liholiho was partial to Britain. In private correspondence a British missionary noted that
the king "frequently mentioned" Hawaiʻi as "belong[ing] to King George" (Bennet to
Hankey, Aug. 1, 1822, CWM/LMS). Ellis was under the impression that "discerning"
chiefs were concerned that Liholiho would squander the $25,000 he appropriated from
government coffers, or return to the islands "deeply ... in debt" (W[illia]m Ellis to
G[eorge] Burden, Nov. 20, 1823, CWM/LMS box 4, folder 3, SOAS). Ellis also noted
that Liholiho had been drinking heavily for days before *L'Aigle* departed.

[149] The British captain refused passage to either British or American missionaries; the
delegation instead carried letters of introduction (Ellis to Burden, Nov. 20, 1823, and
W[illia]m Ellis to W[illia]m Alers Hankey, Nov. 23, 1823, CWM/LMS box 4, folder 3,
SOAS; H[iram] Bingham to Geo[rge] Burden, Nov. 24, 1823, CWM/LMS box 4, folder
6, SOAS).

[150] [George Hill and George Burden] to Madam and Gentleman [Hawaiian chiefs], Sept. 6,
1824, CWM/LMS box 4, folder 6, SOAS. In April 1821, a nineteen-year-old Kamāmalu
suffered an unidentified illness that Russian surgeons deemed "dangerous" enough to
postpone their departure (Gillesem, in Barratt, *Russian View of Honolulu*, 182–83n2).
See also Gast and Conrad, *Don Francisco de Paula Marin*, 249. Liholiho was so sick
in January 1822 that the "alarm was given, that the king was dying at Waikiki"; he
recovered in "about two weeks" (Bingham, *Residence*, 158–59).

[151] Kameʻeleihiwa, *Native Land*, 152–57.

divinity," Ka'ahumanu had set a new course for the islands.[152] She was
not alone. Kalanimoku, Ulumāheihei Hoapili, and other ali'i followed her
lead, making public declarations of their desire for the people to live as
Christians. In Kalanimoku's case, he attributed his success in putting
down a rebellion on Kaua'i to his new god Jehovah.[153] As a sign of his
allegiance, he erected a new, stone house for himself adjacent to Rev.
William Ellis's grass hale.[154]

Other Hawaiians, however, decided that missionaries themselves were
to blame for the carnage. In May 1824, following the mō'ī Kaumuali'i's
funeral at Honolulu, American missionary Charles Stewart was
approached by a "small party of natives" who accused him of *"praying
their chiefs to death* – that [Kaumuali'i] was dead by my prayers – that
I was killing [Kalanimoku], and soon there would not be a chief left on
Oahu." Stewart dispelled these "superstitious" notions, explaining that
no person could pray another to death; but the people responded that "my
words were *'falsehood only.'"*[155] A few months later, the Big Island
chiefess Kapi'olani committed an act that secured her place in the annals
of Anglo-American missiology. Peering over Kīlauea Crater, Kapi'olani
challenged Pele to strike her dead. Surviving this provocation, Kapi'olani
had proven the gods ineffectual against her and, implicitly, against
Christianity. It is not clear whether Kapi'olani knew that she was reprising
Ellis's performance at Mauna Kea the year before, though she certainly
would have been aware of the 'ōhelo berry incident and his censure by the
Pele partisans. In any case, Kapi'olani had publicly declared her support
of the missionary faction and her disavowal of the akua.

Some scholars have viewed Kapi'olani's defiance of Pele as yet another
case of ali'i women using their personal and political authority to overcome

[152] Mykkänen, *Inventing Politics*, 48. The suggestion that Ka'ahumanu saw herself as
mediator between the Christian god and her people may derive from a letter published
by the Mission Press. The Hawaiian phrasing is fairly obscure: "My entrails [heart/mind]
have much aloha for you [people]; it is my desire that all of us shall turn towards the face
of Jehovah, our Father . . . The entrails [heart/mind] receive the word of God from above;
together with that, a part of your entrails [heart/mind] carries the love that my own
entrails [heart/mind] feel for you" (Elisabeta Kaahumanu [Dec. 20, 1825], *Ka Manao
o na Alii*, trans. Lōkahi Antonio).
[153] Kala[n]imoku (Dec. 16, 1825), in *Ka Manao o na Alii*, 2–4. In private correspondence
Ellis characterized Kalanimoku as a "steady friend" to the mission by 1823 (Ellis to
Burden, Oct. 30, 1823, CWM/LMS). It is unclear whether missionaries were aware of
Kalanimoku's and Boki's earlier baptism as Catholics.
[154] Ellis to Burden, May 26, 1823, CWM/LMS box 4, folder 3, SOAS.
[155] Stewart, *Private Journal*, 292–93.

a second-class ritual status.[156] Yet Kapiʻolani had other reasons to defy the akua. She had lost four fellow chiefs, including three cousins, in the past year. Like her fellow survivor Kaʻahumanu, Kapiʻolani was childless. A year later Kapiʻolani was baptized into the Congregational Church. The ceremony coincided with a flu-like outbreak on Oʻahu that carried off untold numbers. Whether missionaries were to blame for these deaths or held up as Hawaiians' only hope of survival, the stakes were high.

The return of the royal bodies in 1825 was a watershed moment for the Sandwich Islands Mission. Five of the eleven Hawaiians who sailed for Britain did not survive. The state funeral reportedly made a "deep impression" on Islanders.[157] With a twelve-year-old Kamehameha III (Kauikeaouli) guided by the "Protestant" Maui chiefs, the path was clear for the missionary program. "Let our hearts be holy before Jehovah our God," the boy-king declared in a speech composed for him by missionaries: "[G]o forth in His ways and keep all His commandments in order that our souls may live in the world to come." It is difficult to know what Kauikeaouli or his audience would have made of this rhetoric. Yet with venereal disease and tuberculosis still raging and with infertility on the rise, another line from the speech probably resonated: "Let us ... forsake those sins which will contaminate our bodies."[158]

Never before had so many ruling chiefs died in peacetime. Perhaps Hawaiʻi was at war. If so, the enemy remained invisible. Like Kapiʻolani, Kaʻahumanu had lost most of her closest advisors and kinsmen, and she had no children. She was faced with of restoring the akua and returning to the old ways or accepting the missionaries' promise of a new life.[159] On the model provided by her Tahitian advisors, Kaʻahumanu threw in her lot with the missionaries. A new path would be required to bring "new life" (*ke ola hou*) to the nation.[160] Yet a new path did not entail the rejection of old practices or ideas, particularly for makaʻāinana. Nor did it entail blind faith. Indeed, for many Hawaiians the missionary program was only as good as its results. The presence of

[156] Linnekin, *Sacred Queens*, 7?–73.
[157] Levi Chamberlain to William Ellis, Nov. 3, 1825, CWM/LMS box 5A, folder 4, SOAS.
[158] Kamakau, *Ruling Chiefs*, 319. See also Kauikeaouli (Nov. 20, 1825), in *Ka Manao o na Alii*, 1–2.
[159] For thoughtful reflections on another aliʻi faced with this choice, see Brown, *Facing the Spears of Change*, 57.
[160] Elisabeta Kaahumanu (Dec. 20, 1825), in *Ka Manao o na Alii*, 5.

missionary families, moreover, was contingent on the beneficence of the ruling chiefs. If the mission failed to improve Hawaiian life by reversing depopulation and improving the peoples' health – if Christianity itself proved a poor fit for Hawai'i – the chiefs would not hesitate, as one chiefess noted in 1825, to discard it for another creed.[161]

[161] The chiefess Lydia Nāmāhāna Pi'ia was quoted by Kotzebue, *New Voyage*, 2:208–9. Similarly: "[D]uring the last war between England and the United States, an American jokingly told [Kamehameha] that the United States had a right to make war on him and take the islands from under the English flag. The King understood the significance of a flag, and told the American that he was not a fool, that he had many flags of different nations, and that if one would not do, he could easily change it for another" ("Golovnin's Visit to Hawai'i in 1818," trans. Joseph Barth, *The Friend* [July 1894]: 52).

PART III

ACCOMMODATIONS

5

Great Fatalism

The axe is laid at the base of my tree.
—Ka'ahumanu, O'ahu, 1825

I think we are a dying people.
—Davida Malo, Maui, 1837

Late one night in 1826, Rev. William Richards received the royal governor
of O'ahu at his mission post on Maui. According to Richards, Boki had
called to ask "various questions" about Christianity. A number of chiefs
had formed an alliance with missionaries by this point, attending church,
reading the Bible in Hawaiian, and encouraging their people to follow
suit. Boki was on the fence, weighing the missionary program against
other options presented by merchants and the small resident foreigner
community. Boki's considerable influence in island life and his reluctance
as yet to join the mission made Richards eager to entertain his queries, no
matter the hour. After simple questions about the Ten Commandments
and keeping the Sabbath, Boki asked Richards about the Israelites' "great
crime" earning God's wrath in a plague that killed 24,000.[1] What had
piqued Boki's interest in this Hebrew Bible story, Richards did not say,
though missionaries were fond of quoting it for the tangible consequences
of idolatry and sexual immorality.[2] Richards also failed to mention that

---

[1] William Richards journal, June 23, 1826, ABCFM Papers.
[2] E.g., L[orrin] Andrews, in Malo, "On the Decrease of Population," 128–29n2.
(The Biblical passage is *Numbers* 25.) A few months earlier, missionaries gained assur-
ances from Ka'ahumanu and Kalanimoku that Honolulu-area women would no longer

24,000 dead was not far afield from Hawai'i's own losses during Boki's short lifetime. Perhaps closer to home were the recent deaths of his sister, brother-in-law, and nephew to an outbreak of whooping cough.

Unlike his brother and cousins, Boki would never be won over to the missionary cause. Yet his query suggests he may have seen Hawai'i's future along the same lines as his brethren, the Protestant chiefs. Indeed, many Hawaiians by the mid-'20s had come to view disease and population loss as inevitable and inexorable. Others thought they were cursed, like the plagued Israelites. As early as 1823 a high chiefess in the prime of life implored the missionaries for a Bible in the Hawaiian language: "'We want it soon, because by and by we shall die.'"[3]

Surprisingly, there has been no research on how Islanders' attitudes about their long-term prospects may have influenced the thinking of foreigners, as opposed to vice versa. Scholars tend to view gloomy sentiments expressed by Islanders and other Indigenous people along a continuum from missionary brainwashing to Natives parroting "vanishing race" discourse or Protestant jeremiad. The documentary evidence – private correspondence and public writings by Hawaiians – suggests otherwise. From the moment they gained literacy, Islanders employed deterministic metaphors about foreigners pushing them out, just as invader species had been pushing out Native plants and animals since 1778. Hawaiians in some numbers identified island populations – human and nonhuman – as under siege by newcomers and facing a gradual decline in numbers and in vigor. While evangelicals' humanitarian postures had some influence, Hawaiian fatalism was largely sui generis. Physical evidence was proof enough for many of what lay ahead. Many Hawaiians began to conceive of the *akua* (deities) and *'aumakua* (ancestral spirits) as themselves weakening against the onslaught.[4] Since the people and gods were one with nature, it followed that both were declining with the rest of island life. By 1839 Davida Malo observed that Hawaiians were "small fish" destined to be eaten by larger ones.[5] Ten years after that,

---

visit the ships for "unlawful intercourse" (H[iram] Bingham to Geo[rge] Burden, Sept. 13, 1825, CWM/LMS Papers, box 5A, folder 4).

[3] Elizabeth Edwards Bishop, "A Journal of Early Hawaiian Days" (July 3, 1823), *The Friend* (Sept. 1900): 72–74. The chiefess quoted is Kapi'olani.

[4] Kame'eleihiwa, *Native Land*, 78. Island life of all kinds was under attack. Introduced species tended to grow vigorously and unchecked; e.g., Vancouver's small cattle herd from Alta California had gone feral, stripped the landscape, and mauled a number of Islanders (Fischer, "Cattle in Hawai'i").

[5] Davida Malo to Kīna'u and Mataio Kekūanāo'a, Aug. 18, 1837, qtd. in Kuykendall, *Hawaiian Kingdom*, 1:153. For analogous notions among the Māori, see Lange, *May the*

FIGURE 5.1 Boki with unidentified chiefesses. "The Eldermen from Voagu [O'ahu] Island aboard the *Kamchatka.*" Mikhail Tikhanov, 1818. Courtesy of Scientific–Research Museum of the Russian Academy of Arts (P–2111).

People Live, chap. 4; Ballantyne reads Māori crises of the '30s from the perspective of British humanitarian rhetoric (*Entanglements of Empire*, chap. 6). For fatalism among Christian Indians in 1780s Oneida country, see Silverman, *Red Brethren*, 137–46.

a visitor noted a "general impression" among Islanders of their "early extinction."[6]

The chiefs' alliance with the Sandwich Islands Mission grew sufficiently strong for the latter to declare a New England–style "Great Awakening." It was short-lived, the fervor limited to portions of the Big Island and O'ahu. However, a broader awakening was occurring simultaneously. Hawaiians were awakening to the reality of their long-term decline due to disease, low fertility, and poor health. In fact, the Great Awakening and the Great Fatalism were linked phenomena, as American missionaries offered Islanders an alternative to their current life of suffering by promising them a better life in the present or, short of that, in the afterlife.[7] Christianization was thus achieved by a spirit of fatalism following five decades of poor health, premature death, and declining fertility.

GRASS FIRES

"Within three to five years" of the missionaries' arrival, many had "turned to God," and there was no region, Kamakau wrote, "where the people did not turn and repent."[8] That was an exaggeration. Public acceptance of the "prayer priests" (*kāhuna pule*) and their program was one thing, repentance something else altogether. Islanders kept their family gods and observed various local rituals without interference from missionaries or island authorities. Commoners also continued to rely on medical kāhuna while experimenting with and incorporating foreign medicine. In all likelihood, religious and medical practice, at least in the countryside, looked little different in 1825 than 1778.

---

[6] Hill, *Travels in the Sandwich and Society Islands*, 114. As late as 1862, newspaper editor Abraham Fornander (married to a Moloka'i chiefess) wrote of "some undefined impending woe pervading the people" ("Let us look the situation . . .," *Polynesian*, Aug. 2, 1862). The rhetoric of Hawaiian decline was skillfully marshaled in the '50s by American filibusters, annexationists, anti-annexationists, physicians, and others; see Chapter 6.

[7] Notions of the afterlife varied considerably. The "most learned" ancients, according to Kamakau, identified three possibilities for the soul (*'uhane*): the realm of "homeless" or "wandering" souls," akin to the hungry ghosts in Buddhism; the realm of ancestral spirits (*ao 'aumākua*), which included a number of "heavenly" realms; and the realm of "endless darkness" (*po pau 'ole*), an underworld also known as the realm of Milu. Many, if not most, of these spirit realms had actual physical or geographical locations or "gateways," e.g., a cliff from which the soul would leap into the next realm. Unlike Protestantism, island religion provided "many doors by which to enter the *'aumakua* realm" (Kamakau, *Ka Po'e Kahiko*, 47–53, esp. 47–49). See also Kamakau, *Ruling Chiefs*, 214–15.

[8] Kamakau, *Ruling Chiefs*, 248. The failed ABCFM mission to the Marquesas offers an interesting contrast; see Richard Armstrong journal, July–Dec. 1833, HMCS.

This is not to say that life was unchanged. Among makaʻāinana, squalor as well as disease were reported throughout the '20s. American missionary Charles S. Stewart recorded devastating scenes of Hawaiian poverty. He did so, in part, to provide evangelical readers with evidence of Hawaiians' degraded condition, their native savagery, and the necessity of Christianity and civilization. Yet the health implications cannot be ignored. On southern Oʻahu, Stewart observed makaʻāinana nitpicking and ingesting fleas off their pets and lice from their own hair, suggesting subhuman degradation.[9] The report would hardly be worth recounting were it not for the fact that fleas and lice spread disease and the possibility that impoverished commoners had resorted to eating the vermin because of malnourishment or chronic hunger.[10] The famine – if such it was – had resulted from a sandalwood harvesting frenzy on Oʻahu. Laborers in the mountains "suffered for food" and resorted to leaves and herbs, which earned them the nickname "excreters of green herbs (*hilalele*)." Others simply "died and were buried there."[11] It is not clear whether makaʻāinana subsistence patterns had been affected on other islands.[12]

Rev. William Richards noted the psychological power that ʻanāʻanā continued to hold. When a young friend of the king fell ill with flu-like symptoms and cold extremities, local people suggested he had fallen victim to a sorcerer, since another boy had recently died under mysterious circumstances. The consensus seemed to be that the same sorcerer had designs on the young friend of the king and that this boy would die no matter what "remedies should be used" upon him. Richards and his fellow missionaries administered opium and bottles of hot water for the boy's hands and feet. The following morning, the boy woke, "surprised" to find himself "nearly well." Hawaiian opinions about the boy's recovery differed: "Some [thought] there was an extraordinary efficacy in our

---

[9] Stewart, *Journal of a Residence*, 151–52. For the author's depiction of a chiefess sharing a bone with a dog, see ibid., 129.

[10] There has been no research on endemic, flea-spread murine typhus in nineteenth-century Hawaiʻi; untreated, this debilitating disease can be fatal to people with compromised immune systems. Islanders were apparently preserved from the more dangerous Old World typhus thanks to the absence of the bacteria *Rickettsia prowazakii* in the islands' resident body louse. The first outbreak of bubonic plague was recorded in 1899. See Bushnell, *Gifts of Civilization*, 51.

[11] Kamakau, *Ruling Chiefs*, 252. For earlier "famines" induced by sandalwood harvesting on the Big Island, see ibid., 204.

[12] See Sahlins, *Anahulu*, 1:4, 41; Schmitt, "Famine Mortality in Hawaii."

medicine," while others supposed the sorcerer had simply left off terrorizing the boy.[13]

A case in Richards' own household served as further evidence. When Richards sent some Hawaiian boys to recover a bolt of cloth that had been stolen from his yard, the boys located the thief and, in the process of taking back the cloth, ripped his clothes. In response, the thief "threatened to pray them to death." One of the children, according to Richards, was convinced that "there was no hope for him" unless he managed to regain the favor of the sorcerer-thief. Within three days the child took ill, believing death to be near. Unable to identify physical symptoms, Richards forced the boy to engage in physical work, and within a few hours, the cure took; discovering that he was not sick, the boy "concluded that not only foreigners, but also the [Hawaiian] men who live with him, are proof against" sorcery. Perhaps, though no one bothered to track the boy's views on 'anā'anā after the brief illness. And even if he had ceased to believe the power of 'anā'anā, the thief-sorcerer continued to cause havoc in Lahina in spring 1824, and Richards himself admitted that fear of 'anā'anā remained "nearly universal here."[14]

Two prominent ali'i were victims of sorcery that same month. Kiliwehi, daughter of Kamehameha I and wife of Chief Minister Kalanimoku, took ill with undisclosed symptoms. Kiliwehi's half-brother Kaiko'okalani then came down with the "same disease," according to Richards. Both ali'i seemed, to Richards, to believe that a kahuna 'anā'anā was using sorcery against them. When Kiliwehi appeared to have recovered, she visited her brother. After a swim in the ocean, she died "without a moment's notice." Kaiko'okalani had immediately called on a kahuna to save his sister. When the kahuna's prayer failed to be "answered," Richards editorialized, the kahuna "determined to pray to [the akua] no more. [He] is now attending the *palapala*, and prays to Jehovah every morning and evening."[15] Of course Richards provides just one perspective on these events; few Hawaiians were recording their thoughts in writing as yet. Yet some people seem to have been questioning the efficacy of the kāhuna 'anā'anā and other Native practitioners as early as 1824 while simultaneously noting the relative efficacy of some Western medicine.

One thing was clear to Richards: there had been an "unusual mortality among the chiefs" over the past two years. Among other proposals to stop

---

[13] "Sandwich Islands: Lahaina; Extracts from the Journal of Mr. Richards" (March 20, 1824), *Missionary Herald* 23 (May 1827): 143.
[14] Ibid.   [15] Ibid.

the spread of illness, according to Richards, was that the king should stop studying and instead go on a cock-fighting tour of the islands. This proposal had come from a boy who dreamed that "the sickness [was] owing to the prince's confining himself so closely to study." Another Hawaiian dreamed that the sickness had been caused by an infestation of the gods in local homes. The suggested remedy was to burn all the houses. Upon hearing this proposal, the boy-king Kauikeouli observed that setting little fires *next* to each house would serve the same purpose by scaring away the akua. According to Richards, it was "but a moment before all Lahina was illuminated" with small grass fires.[16]

Given the long odds of survival, the ruling chiefs decided that the Sandwich Islands Mission offered the better of two options for a Hawaiian future. From one angle, the choice was obvious: the liquor, tobacco, silks, and other trade goods provided by foreign merchants and beachcombers had done nothing to help Hawaiians live or thrive. At the same time these commodities had trapped the ali'i in a spiral of debt, largely by their buying goods on credit.[17] 'Ai'ē (debt) means "to eat beforehand," that is, before paying; it is clear from extant records that the chiefs had been "eating beforehand" for more than a decade by 1825. Debt required an ongoing relationship with the merchant community that could not be gainsaid. Few ruling chiefs opted for a return to traditional political, economic, or religious practices in the face of dire new challenges. Only a small-scale rebellion on Kaua'i in 1824, quickly quashed by Island Carver Kalanimoku, advocated the removal of foreigners and a return to traditional practices. This is not to suggest that "everyday resistance" was not standard practice, particularly on the local level.[18] Yet the way forward would include foreigners and foreign influence.

And they continued to come. When Baltic German navigator Otto von Kotzebue met with Kalanimoku in January 1825, the latter's health was failing and his views on the future of the kingdom struck a dismal note. While adoption of Christianity had been positive, Kalanimoku believed that some commoners did not "understand its superiority; and strong measures are necessary to prevent their relapsing into idolatry." The overarching problem was that Liholiho had too quickly "annihilated all that [the people] held sacred ... How all will end, I cannot foresee; but

[16] Ibid., 143–44.
[17] See Rosenthal, "Hawaiians Who Left Hawai'i," chap. 1. Cf. Arista, "Histories of Unequal Measure," chap. 2; Rifkin, "Debt and the Transnationalization of Hawai'i."
[18] Scott, *Weapons of the Weak*.

I look forward with fear. The people are attached to me, and I have influence over them; but my health declines, and the Government, which I have scarcely been able to keep together, will probably not survive me." Other ali'i apparently agreed with Kalanimoku. According to Kotzebue, many ali'i were "persuaded that the monarchy [would] be dismembered" at Kalanimoku's death.[19]

A few days later Kotzebue received via messenger a letter from Lydia Nāmāhāna Pi'ia, one of the widows of Kamehameha. Kotzebue had first met "Queen Nomahanna" during his extended visit of 1816. More recently Kotzebue had spent some time with Nāmāhāna Pi'ia upon his arrival at the royal compound in Honolulu. The two had discussed the passing of Kamehameha and the introduction of Christianity to the islands, among other topics. Kotzebue sent for longtime foreign resident and ali'i Francisco de Paula Marín to translate. After niceties – "I salute thee, Russian!" – Nāmāhāna Pi'ia's tone shifted:

Thou wilt find all here much changed. While [Kamehameha] lived, the country flourished; but since his death, all has gone to ruin. The young King [Liholiho] is in London; and Chinau [Kahō'anokū Kīna'u, a son of Kamehameha], who fills their place, has too little power over the people to receive thee as becomes thy rank. He cannot procure for thee as many hogs and sweet potatoes, and as much tarro as thou hast need of.[20]

In their earlier conversation, Nāmāhāna Pi'ia had expressed to Kotzebue her concern about the future: with the passing of Kamehameha the people had lost "a protector and a father. What will now be the fate of these islands, only the God of the Christians knows." Nāmāhāna Pi'ia was not the only ruling chief who viewed Kamehameha's rule as Hawai'i's golden era. Kalanimoku and others made similar laments to visitors from various countries. Like Kalanimoku, Nāmāhāna Pi'ia also voiced regret about the current state of the kingdom. Having apologized for her poor reception of Kotzebue and his men at O'ahu, Nāmāhāna Pi'ia requested that Kotzebue "carry my salutations to thy whole nation.

[19] Kotzebue, *New Voyage*, 2:229. Kalanimoku was suffering from partial blindness and dropsy. By summer 1826 he required "constant watching, & frequent opperations ... to keep him alive" (Abraham Blatchley to J[eremiah] Evarts, July 26, 1826, ABCFM Papers). He was apparently "unable to rise from his bed," yet his mind was still "active and unimpaired" (Beechey, *Narrative of a Voyage*, 1:317–18).
[20] Kotzebue, *New Voyage*, 2:234–36. The letter has not survived but was written in Pi'ia's own hand in Hawaiian; Kotzebue gathered that she had worked on it for "many weeks" (ibid., 236). At least two ali'i named Kīna'u, male and female, were on the scene at this time; the chiefess Kīna'u who became kuhina nui is discussed later.

Since I am a Christian, and that thou art also such, thou wilt excuse my indifferent writing."²¹

Nāmāhāna Piʻia was, according to Kotzebue, proud of her new religion. She was certainly quick to put it on display whenever a European or American ship captain was in town. Yet her exchange with Kotzebue illustrates how some ruling chiefs viewed the new religious program. When Kotzebue inquired "how far she had been instructed in the religion" and the "grounds of her conversion," Nāmāhāna Piʻia suggested he talk to Bingham. Yet she was quick to add that if Christianity "should be found unsuited to our people, we will reject it, and adopt another."²² Kotzebue, to be sure, was no fan of the missionaries.²³ Yet Nāmāhāna Piʻia's comment – a striking example of realpolitik in the chiefly posture toward Christianity – was not unique. Only time could tell whether New England religious law would be a good fit for Hawaiʻi.

ALOHA FOR JEHOVAH

Hawaiʻi's future as a Christian nation appeared set by 1825. In a private letter to the London Missionary Society marked "Not to be published," William Ellis declared that the deaths in London of King Liholiho and Queen Kamāmalu, while "lamentable indeed," would not adversely affect the kingdom, "nor in any way retard the advancement of the missionary work," which had been progressing "most prosperously."²⁴ Bingham agreed completely. If still young, the king and his sister Nāhiʻenaʻena seemed to Bingham "very favorably disposed" to Christianity.²⁵

If it was hard to imagine things getting worse for the Aliʻi, overlapping outbreaks of influenza, whooping cough, and perhaps other respiratory ailments took a further toll. None of these epidemics is well documented, and even people well positioned to record morbidity and mortality mostly resorted to generalization. The scattered accounts reveal that Hawaiian disease and population loss were hardly news by the mid-'20s. "Many people sick," Spanish aliʻi Francisco de Paula Marín recorded on Feb. 20, 1824. "Many deaths & many coughs" (May 20, 1824); "many sick – few deaths" (May 29, 1824); "many deaths" (June 6, 1824); "many catarhs & deaths" (Jan. 11–16, 1825); "many sick of fevers & colds & many dying"

---

²¹ Ibid., 2:208, 235–36.   ²² Ibid., 2:208–9.
²³ See Ellis, *Vindication of the South Sea Missions.*
²⁴ W[illia]m Ellis to G[eorge] Burden, May 16, 1825, CWM/LMS Papers, box 5A, folder 4.
²⁵ Bingham to Burden, June 8, 1825, CWM/LMS Papers.

(Feb. 1, 1825); "much illness & many deaths" (Feb. 15, 1825).[26] Outside observers were hardly more specific. Regarding the flu-like outbreak in the winter of 1825, Kotzebue recorded only that "death generally followed the attack within a few days." In Honolulu, where Kotzebue saw "many corpses daily carried to their burial," it seemed to him that the chances of "recovery from serious illness" were nowhere "so improbable as here."[27] In a brief address to the people later that year, Kaʻahumanu wrote that the "axe is laid at the base of my tree; the day is not known when the Lord shall take away my spirit."[28] In fact she would live another seven years, but no one would have guessed it from the grim mood of her missive.

A few weeks after the state funeral for King Liholiho and Queen Kamāmalu, Scottish botanist James Macrae and a fellow HMS *Blonde* officer crossed paths in Honolulu with Kaʻahumanu and a fellow queen – either her sister Lydia Nāmāhāna Piʻia or her cousin Wahinepio (also known as Kahakuhaʻakoi and Kamoʻonohu), both of whom were also widows of Kamehameha I.[29] The two queens were on their way to bathe in a nearby fishpond. Upon meeting the British officers, the women were, according to Macrae, "very inquisitive to know if Mr. Forder and I were married men." The Britons responded that they were. The queens then "wanted to know the number in our families." Forder said that he had six children but that Macrae had none as yet. The queens then pointed out to the men that Macrae "could only have one wife." It is not clear whether the chiefesses were stating the obvious, identifying a flaw in British law, or simply teasing Macrae. "After a few more questions," the women continued on their way.[30]

Although Macrae made nothing of this exchange, the queens' inquiry about family size was no small talk – or if it was, it was small talk in

---

[26] Gast and Conrad, *Don Francisco de Paula Marin*.

[27] Kotzebue, *New Voyage*, 2:243–44. Among those who perished in these outbreaks was twenty-seven-year-old George Prince Humehume, son of Kauaʻi mōʻī Kaumualiʻi. Humehume's earlier role in the Kauaʻi rebellion precluded his receiving either a Christian or traditional aliʻi burial; he was interred like a commoner in Honolulu where he was being held prisoner.

[28] Elisabeta Kaahumanu (Dec. 20, 1825), in *Ka Manao o na Alii* [Thoughts of the Chiefs], 5. The first half of the statement is from *Matthew* 3:10; see *Ka Palapala Hemolele*, 2.

[29] All of the ruling chiefs attended the state funeral, as did the *Blonde* officers, whose voyage was predicated on the return of the royal bodies (Bingham, *Residence*, 265). Macrae identified the queen as "Pio," which the editor took to be Lydia Nāmāhāna Piʻia, but Wahinepio is also a possibility (Macrae, *With Lord Byron*, 41). Both chiefesses were apparently living in Honolulu at this time. For British sightings of Nāmāhāna Piʻia on this visit, see Bloxam, *Diary of Andrew Bloxam*, 48; Byron, *Voyage of H. M. S. Blonde*, 110.

[30] Macrae, *With Lord Byron*, 41.

a particular, Hawaiian key. Kaʻahumanu was about fifty-seven years old at this time, childless, and lacking an heir. Her companion, if Nāmāhāna Piʻia, was about thirty-eight and also childless; Wahinepio had two surviving children in 1825, though she would die, along with her son and grandson, of whooping cough the following April. This was not the extent of the women's kinship ties – among other things they were *punalua* (plural wives) to each other, having shared Kamehameha as husband – but their exchange with Macrae and Forder suggests that the queens were thinking about how a family could be sustained in the face of infertility. They asked about family *size*, as opposed to pedigree or gender composition or the nature of family life itself.[31]

Yet if Islanders understood Britons to be fecund, they also believed Britain itself to be an unhealthy place for themselves. Understandably to Capt. Richard Beechey, the Hawaiian delegates who had survived the trip to Britain had a "great dread of the diseases of our country." Many Hawaiians, he noted, considered Britain "very unhealthy." Beechey was happy to learn that these concerns had no bearing on their admiration for the people and government of his native country. Still, it would be very unlikely that the survivors would "risk another visit."[32] When a Dutch captain agreed to take aboard a boy ("barely eight years old") who had begged to join the crew, the child's mother swam out to the ship just before departure to give her son "some herbs that these islanders use as medicine in case of certain illnesses." The captain did not name the herb or elaborate on which illnesses it was used to treat. Probably he did not know. "With a flow of tears" and wailing that "resounded" throughout "the whole bay," the woman bid her young son farewell.[33]

Three days after the chance meeting between the queens and British officers in Honolulu, a cast of ruling chiefs and some one hundred others presented themselves to the Sandwich Islands Mission for baptism. The chiefs included Kalanimoku, Big Island chiefess Kapiʻolani, and the sister-queens Kaʻahumanu, Nāmāhāna Piʻia, and Kalākua Kaheiheimālie, along with their husbands. For mission leader Hiram Bingham it was clear that the death of the king and queen had drawn the chiefs into the bosom of

---

[31] In light of fertility problems, it may be significant that none of Kaʻahumanu's new kapu touched on sex despite missionaries' constant harping on adultery, fornication, polygamy, and prostitution. One chief's decision to retain his three wives, for example, seemed to missionaries to slow the progress of Christianity in Hilo ("Journal of Mr. [Artemas] Bishop, While on a Tour to Hiro [Hilo]," *Missionary Herald* 23 [Feb. 1827]: 52).

[32] Beechey, *Narrative of a Voyage*, 1:318–19.   [33] Boelen, *Merchant's Perspective*, 72.

the church.[34] Yet the process was not so precipitous or straightforward. Binding the high chiefs to the mission was the result of nearly five years of missionary labors. As it happened Bingham refused to baptize any who could not prove that their desire to join the church stemmed from a conversion experience "born from above."[35] Most ali'i supplicants would have to wait until the end of 1825 for the sacrament. Nevertheless, the mission published an eight-page pamphlet in Hawaiian to advertise the ruling chiefs' acceptance of the faith. *Thoughts of the Chiefs* began with a posthumous letter by Liholiho from January 1823. "Hear correctly" the word of God, he commanded, so that "our spirits shall live and our bodies shall be well."[36] The king's words were followed by devotional statements by Kalanimoku, Ka'ahumanu, Nāhi'ena'ena, Boki, and the twelve-year-old King Kauikeaouli, all from 1825. It is difficult, perhaps impossible, to know which of the ruling chiefs assented to these words. Boki's "thoughts," for example, are out of sync with his actions and other statements.[37] Yet his brother Kalanimoku's thoughts were consistent with remarks made in private correspondence: "I have abandoned the old mind [or heart]," he wrote to the people. "I am here with the new mind [heart]."[38] The boy king, in a statement that was probably composed for him, echoed his deceased brother in applauding the "word of God ... through which our bodies and souls shall live."[39]

NEW MALADIES

When a Dutch merchant ship came in sight of the Big Island in 1827, crewmen spotted a drifting corpse. It looked "like a man," the boatswain

[34] Bingham, *Residence*, 267–68. Bingham's perspective, geared for public consumption, may have developed in hindsight; see, by comparison, H[iram] Bingham to Geo[rge] Burden, June 8, 1825, CWM/LMS Papers, box 5A, folder 4. Historians have too closely adhered to Bingham's published comments of this event (Daws, *Shoal of Time*, 74–75).

[35] Bingham, *Residence*, 268. The mission had baptized only two Hawaiians as yet: Keōpūolani in 1823 and Pua'aiki in 1825. For Pua'aiki, see Chapter 6.

[36] Liholiho (Jan. 1823), in *Ka Manao o na Alii*, 1, trans. Lōkahi Antonio. See also Tamehameha [Liholiho] to "*Ka poe* American Board" [ABCFM], March 18, 1823, ABCFM Papers.

[37] E.g., Beechey, *Narrative of a Voyage*, 1:319.

[38] "*Ua haalele i ka naau kahiko; eia wau ma ka naau hou*" (Kala[n]imoku [Dec. 16, 1825], in *Ka Manao o na Alii*, 3 [my translation]). *Na'au* is intestines or bowels; digestive organs were considered to be the seat of the emotions. For his earlier remarks, see Karaimoku [Kalanimoku] to Jeremiah Evarts, March 16, 1825, ABCFM Papers.

[39] Kauikeaouli (Nov. 20, 1825), in *Ka Manao o na Alii*, 1–2, trans. Lōkahi Antonio. Ballou and Carter suggest that this pamphlet, which had a print run of 3,000 copies, "was not valued by the people, nor read much" ("History of the Hawaiian Mission Press," 21).

reported to Capt. Jacobus Boelen, "dressed in a short morning coat and a pair of trousers." With no other sea craft in sight, Boelen could not imagine that a corpse would be floating on the open sea so many miles from land. Finally, he decided the sailors were hallucinating.[40] Perhaps he was right. But the past few years had been particularly deadly on the Hawaiian Islands. Influenza, whooping cough, and perhaps other respiratory diseases had taken countless lives. A keen Dutch sailor may well have interpreted the sight of a floating corpse off Hawai'i as a kind of emblem of the peoples' struggles.

Whooping cough took a number of lives, including two dowager queens. Wahinepio was sister to Kalanimoku and Boki, cousin to Ka'ahumanu, and widow of Kamehameha; Pauahi (also known as Kalanipauahi) was widow (and niece) of Liholiho. Also killed were the royal governor of Kauai, Kahalai'a Luanu'u, and his young son.[41] In the midst of these scourges, octogenarian British ali'i John Young wrote the ABCFM to say that the Big Island – "filled with inhabitants" at his arrival in 1790 – had "dwindle[d]" through warfare and disease "to its present few." Young was convinced that "nothing but Christianity" could save the people from "total extinction." It is a striking statement from a man who showed no religious inclinations and had lived as a Polynesian chief for forty years. While Young probably had diplomatic reasons to laud Christianity in a letter to mission headquarters and while the letter itself is in the hand of a scribe, Young signed in a characteristically elderly hand. Still powerful in 1826, Young had his wits about him and would live for another decade. Anticipating Christian laws and ethics for Hawai'i was, for the old chief, the "only hope that brightens my prospects as I descend down to the grave."[42]

The Maui chiefs' incorporation of that program, however, was neither uniform nor consistent. Liholiho was a particular source of disappointment due to his drinking and indifferent attention to the palapala. Yet even the most important allies did not behave as missionaries expected them. Maui governor George Cox Ke'eaumoku, brother of Ka'ahumanu and critical ally to the mission, had enjoyed days-long binges with his retinue in the summer of 1822.[43] Big Island governor John Adams Kuakini, while

---

[40] Boelen, *Merchant's Perspective*, 10.
[41] Kahalai'a Luanu'u was the husband of Kīna'u, Kamehameha's daughter and Liholiho's widow and half-sister. Their son's name was apparently unrecorded.
[42] John Young to ABCFM, Nov. 27, 1826, ABCFM Papers.
[43] Mathison, *Narrative of a Visit*, 392–407.

eager for missionary instruction, also continued to indulge in strong spirits. Various chiefesses whiled away the hours, as missionaries saw it, drinking and playing cards.[44] Foreigners' anecdotal accounts of aliʻi consumption of liquor and tobacco are legion but do little to draw conclusions about particular health effects. In the case of Liholiho, alcohol consumption compromised his health between 1820 and 1823, bringing on "fits" of delirium tremens.[45] (His brother Kauikeaouli would later die of alcoholism.) Yet even if we knew the volume of liquor and tobacco traded to the chiefs, it would be impossible to determine actual consumption, much less specific health problems exacerbated by substance abuse, though tuberculosis would be a good candidate. A Tahitian missionary on the Kona coast noted that drinking was the "main amusement in Kailua these days" and that the people "of Kona from one end to the other indulge."[46] Kamakau wrote that liquor consumption during Liholiho's rule was "extravagant" among chiefs and commoners alike: "They almost bathed in it."[47] Beyond such statements, the health toll of liquor and tobacco in the '20s is difficult to assess.

In February 1827, after years of being "tapped" by visiting surgeons to drain fluids, Island Carver William Pitt Kalanimoku died from complications of edema.[48] At fifty-eight, he was old for a Hawaiian. While no one could have known, the Island Carver's family line would shortly run out. Kalanimoku had married four times, but only one wife, Kiliwehi, bore a surviving child before succumbing to an unidentified illness in 1824 (possibly the respiratory epidemic that killed so many aliʻi at court). The surviving child was William Pitt Leleiohoku I, who became royal governor of Hawaiʻi Island as a young man. William Pitt Leleiohoku I first

---

[44] See, e.g., Sybil Moseley Bingham journal, March 14, 1822, HMCS; Kotzebue, *New Voyage*, 2:218–19. The first missionaries did not themselves abstain from alcohol, but they were fierce teetotalers when it came to Islanders.

[45] For "fits," see Sybil Moseley Bingham journal, Feb. 19–20, 1823, HMCS. For "delerium tremens," see Marín journal (March 1, 1822), in Gast and Conrad, *Don Francisco de Paula Marin*, 262, 313n68. It is possible that a compromised immune system hampered Liholiho's recovery from measles in London.

[46] Barrère and Sahlins, "Tahitians in the Early History," 29.

[47] Kamakau, *Ruling Chiefs*, 250. Mykkänen considered the eventual bans on intoxication as Kaʻahumanu's "usurpation of Liholiho's symbolic space," yet it is not clear whether she approved these laws before his death (*Inventing Politics*, 46).

[48] Lydia Nāmāhāna Piʻia died of edema two years later. For both chiefs, obesity may have been the cause of organ failure that in turn led to edema. Note that edema was probably limited at this time to those who could afford to eat prodigiously and live a sedentary lifestyle. See J. Worth Estes, "Dropsy," in Kiple, ed., *Cambridge World History of Human Disease*, 689–96.

married the princess (and daughter of Kamehameha) Nāhiʻenaʻena, who died along with her newborn from complications of childbirth at the age of twenty-one in 1836. Gov. Leleiohoku then married a *grand*daughter of Kamehameha, Ruth Keʻelikōlani, who – as with Kiliwehi the previous generation – bore a single surviving son. Gov. Leleiohoku himself perished in the measles epidemic of 1848 at the age of twenty-seven. Gov. Leleiohoku's surviving son with Ruth Keʻelikōlani was William Pitt Kīnaʻu, who died at the age of sixteen in what was reported variously as an accident, poisoning, and, what is most likely, consumption.[49] Thus, the exalted line of William Pitt Kalanimoku, the "Iron Cable" of the kingdom, came to a close.[50]

Few aliʻi thought in soulless terms of the reproductive capacity of the class and life expectancies, yet even the luckiest couples faced difficult odds of their children surviving to adulthood. It is important to note that Islanders did not reckon family relations exclusively by biological descent and that the Hawaiian cultural toolbox had mechanisms for cushioning the blow of unusual mortality within a family.[51] In addition to the complex kinship system to which polygamous unions contributed, hānai enabled elite families to carry on their "lines" in cases of early death or the infertility of would-be parents. Indeed, the third generation of Kalanimoku's family (see earlier) did just that. After the death of her teenaged son William Pitt Kīnaʻu in 1859, Ruth Keʻelikōlani adopted William Pitt Leleiohoku Kalahoʻolewa, who shortly became known as William Pitt Leleiohoku II. Yet he too died as a young man (age twenty-three), and Ruth Keʻelikōlani lived out the final years of her life without children. Some historians have suggested that the aliʻi practice of close endogamous marriage (inbreeding) may have contributed to the decline of elite families such as that of Kalanimoku.[52] In fact, some aliʻi couples probably faced decreased odds of conception because of consanguinity;

---

[49] For "accident," see Silva, "Princess Ruth Keʻelikōlani," 1; for poisoning, see Taylor, *Under Hawaiian Skies*, 200; for consumption, see "Death of a High Chief," *Pacific Commercial Advertiser*, Sept. 17, 1859.

[50] Del Piano, "Kalanimoku." The office of kālaimoku apparently expired with Kalanimoku. Missionaries later reported that Kalanimoku's death was a blow to Kaʻahumanu and that her bereavement "affected her health, and shortened her career," but the claim is unsubstantiated (Anderson, *History of the Mission*, 78).

[51] Yet talk of "blood" descent was not – and is not – uncommon (Kamakau, *Ruling Chiefs*, 259–60; Liliʻuokalani, *Hawaii's Story*, 25, 83, 148, 173, 360, 373; Handy and Pukui, *Polynesian Family System*, 48–51, 65; Young, *Rethinking the Native Hawaiian Past*, chap. 2; Snow, "Pihana," 26).

[52] Bushnell, *Gifts of Civilization*, 27–29.

TABLE 5.1 *Chiefs' age of death over time*[53]

yet the phenomenon that geneticists refer to as "pedigree collapse" does not seem to have occurred in nineteenth-century Hawai'i.[54] Rather, the problems seem to have been chronic low fertility, premature death, and infant mortality.

Not all ali'i families followed the pattern of Kalanimoku. Yet even in numerically exceptional ali'i families, life expectancy and average life span were low. The patriarch Caesar Kapa'akea and matriarch Analea Keohokālole – cofounders of what came to be known as the House of Kalākaua – had as many as ten children (including the aforementioned William Pitt Leleiohoku II, hānai son to Ruth Ke'elikōlani) over the course of a remarkable thirty-three-year union. Their firstborn, James

---

[53] The graph shows the relationship between the year of birth and the age of death for each individual, based on vital statistics for 120 chiefs collected by the author. Age at death declined between the period 1729 and 1858, as displayed in the fitted line. Both parametric (Pearson) and non-parametric (Spearman) correlations show a negative correlation (−0.46 and −0.44 respectively) between the year of birth and the age at death. Both correlations reveal significant results (p≪0.001). Thanks to Rodrigo Retamal of the University of Chile for producing the graph and rendering the figures.

[54] There is no record of profound physical and mental disabilities such as those suffered by the inbred Spanish Habsburgs, who also struggled with infant mortality and low fertility (Langdon-Davies, *Carlos*).

Kaliokalani, died at the age of seventeen in 1852 of unknown causes. As many as four other children of Kapaʻakea and Keohokālole died even younger, including Kaʻiminaʻauʻao, who died in the measles epidemic of 1848 at the age of four. Yet four children survived to adulthood, and two of those individuals, David Kalākaua and Lydia Liliʻuokalani, became monarchs. (William Pitt Leleiohoku II died of rheumatic fever at the age of twenty-three; Miriam Likelike died of unknown causes at the age of thirty-six.) Of the "Four Sacred Ones of Hawaiʻi," as these surviving adult siblings of the House of Kalākaua were known, only one, Princess Miriam Likelike, produced offspring.[55]

Only Queen Keōpūolani is thought to have borne more children than Analea Keohokālole. By way of comparison, three of Keōpūolani's eleven children survived into adulthood (each, as it happens, fathered by Kamehameha): Liholiho lived to twenty-six, Nāhiʻenaʻena to twenty-one, and Kauikeaouli to forty-one. As with the surviving children of Analea Keohokālole, two of Keōpūolani's surviving children became monarchs. The challenges faced by aliʻi families in producing heirs were real, and Hawaiians of all classes were aware of the problem by 1827. Various aliʻi were desperate to have children, not only to keep the kingdom viable but also – and which became at least as important – to keep foreign residents from taking over the islands.

A few months after Kalanimoku's death, three Catholic missionaries – two French, one Irish – settled in Honolulu. Boki's earlier baptism by a French priest aboard the *Uranie* probably had little if anything to do with the alliance he shortly forged with the priests. Instead, the newcomers provided Boki and other disgruntled chiefs an alternative to Kaʻahumanu and the American Protestants. An impressionable fourteen-year-old Kauikeaouli was swayed by Boki, and for a short time, the "Catholic" chiefs appeared to be viable contenders to the Maui chiefs. Francisco de Paula Marín seems to have played a role in this schism. Whether he had maintained his preference for Catholicism over the course of two decades or, like Boki, preferred an alternative to Kaʻahumanu and the Protestants, Marín welcomed the priests. The first Catholic baptisms were conducted in Marín's house, and Marín himself seems to have secured a safe haven for Catholicism. By January 1828 the new foreign priests had erected a chapel

---

[55] Princess Kaʻiulani was born to great fanfare in 1875 but died at the age of twenty-three of "inflammatory rheumatism" ("Princess Kaiulani Dead," *New York Times*, March 18, 1899). Note that like other childless aliʻi, both Kalākaua and Liliʻuokalani raised hānai children, and Liliʻuokalani herself had been hānai daughter to Abner Pākī and Laura Kōnia.

in Honolulu, and horrified American Protestants began a campaign to sway Ka'ahumanu to banish the "Papists."[56]

Other issues pressed on the kingdom. Between 1827 and 1829 Ka'ahumanu announced a series of new laws including bans on murder, theft, adultery and prostitution (*kāma'i*), gambling, amusements on the Sabbath, and the manufacture, sale, and consumption of liquor. Foreign influence was clear from the first words: "We assent to the request of the English [foreign] residents; we grant the protection of the laws; that is the sum of your petition."[57] Kamakau later noted that the new kapu were supported by chiefs across the islands, but evidence suggests otherwise. While Boki – upon surviving the journey home from England – had allegedly stated that "the Lord Jehovah [was] his God" and that the "chiefs and people [ought] to obey His precepts which are just and good," in fact he was far from joining the missionaries.[58] Against Ka'ahumanu's orders, he kept a brothel in Honolulu supplying women and girls to visitors.[59] Male ali'i were not the only procurers. In 1825 the royal governor of Maui, Wahinepio, sold a girl named Leoiki to British captain William Buckle to be his "wife" at sea. According to high chief Ulumāheihei Hoapili, Leoiki "wept on account of her unwillingness to go." (Wahinepio, whose assumed name ironically translates as "captive woman," was herself mother of a twenty-year-old daughter when she accepted Buckle's gold pieces in exchange for Leoiki.) When the young woman returned five months later, she was pregnant and shortly gave birth, presumably to Buckle's child.[60]

---

[56] Yzendoorn, *History of the Catholic Mission*, 40–41.

[57] "These are the Names of the King of the Islands and the Chiefs in Council" (Kauikeaouli's Proclamation), Oct. 7, 1829, HSA. See also Kauikeaouli, "*He Olelo No Ke Kanawai*" [A Word about the Law], Series 418, HSA. The kapu were printed in Hawaiian and English on a single broadside. According to Kamakau, this was an era when "innumerable laws were made," and "there was no peace [but] bitterness everywhere" (*Ruling Chiefs*, 288). Mykkänen characterizes ali'i–missionary efforts to ban prostitution as the "invention" of Hawaiian politics (*Inventing Politics*, 89–177, esp. 97–98).

[58] Journal of Elisha Loomis, May 6, 1825, HMCS. See also Bingham, *Residence*, 262–64; Ellis, *Narrative of a Tour*, 466–68. Boki had settled in Honolulu, where he cultivated taro, had roads built, and studied Native medicine, surrounding himself with leading diagnosticians (Kamakau, *Ruling Chiefs*, 291).

[59] For this reason Boki was showered with praise in American and British newspapers. Forced labor regimens for people convicted of prostitution began as early as 1826 (Gast and Conrad, *Don Francisco de Paula Marin*, 303). If Catholic priests knew about Boki's flesh trade, they probably felt obliged to turn a blind eye, given their precarious position.

[60] H[iram] Bingham et al., to Jeremiah Evarts, Oct. 15, 1825, CWM/LMS Papers, box 5A, folder 4; "Certificates of several persons respecting Capt Buckle's purchasing a mistress to accompany him on a sea voyage," Nov. 1827, ABCFM Papers. (Malo and Tahitian

FIGURE 5.2 British sailor negotiates the release of Hawaiian woman (kneeling) from her family. "View near the Town of Honoruru, Sandwich Islands; From the Tara [Taro] Patches."
Richard Brydges Beechey, 1826. Courtesy of Peabody Essex Museum, Salem, Massachusetts (M12467).

With a potential civil war brewing between the Protestant- and Catholic-allied chiefs in 1829, Boki, in a desperate move to relieve debts to foreign traders, prepared a massive sandalwood expedition to Vanuatu some 3,500 miles to the southwest.[61] Boki allegedly gave his people a "parting charge," explaining that he had been "foolish" in "disregarding the laws of God" but was now "resolved to take a stand on the side of truth & righteousness & wished them to obey his precepts, as coming from the word of God."[62] To the end Boki played a double game. Even if sincere in his parting charge, it was not clear which "precepts" (Catholic or Protestant) Boki meant the people to follow. The chiefs were more concerned about Boki surviving at all. His wife Liliha, the queens Kīnaʻu and Kekāuluohi, and the king Kauikeaouli all pleaded with him not to go. The *Kamehameha*, with Boki aboard, was lost at sea and never heard from again. The *Keokoʻi* returned to Hawaiʻi some months later, with seven or

missionary Tauʻā both reported that Leoiki had become a Christian before being sold.) For more on this event, see Arista, "Listening to Leoiki" and "Captive Women in Paradise."
[61] For "war footing," see Yzendoorn, *History of the Catholic Mission*, 58.
[62] Diary of Delia Bishop (typescript), Nov. 30, 1829, Hawaii-Bishop Collection, HL.

eight survivors out of a crew of two hundred. The story – as told by survivors and recorded by Kamakau – was that the ships had separated after taking on provisions at Rotuma Island, north of Fiji. The *Kamehameha* sailed ahead, and when the *Keoko'i* arrived at Vanuatu, their sister ship was nowhere to be found. Waiting for the *Kamehameha* to turn up, the crew of the *Keoko'i* were "stricken with an epidemic" that killed "almost the entire company." Two of the survivors who returned to Hawai'i were suffering from "swollen stomachs and falling hair." No other symptoms were recorded.[63]

Back in Hawai'i, Boki's widow Liliha replaced him as royal governor of O'ahu and guardian of the young king. Like her husband, Liliha had long resisted the missionaries; more recently she had cultivated a relationship with the three Catholic priests. High chief Ulumāheihei Hoapili, firmly attached to the mission, played a key role in containing his daughter and ultimately stripping her of her power and property.[64] In the end, Boki's death and Hoapili's control over Liliha eliminated the principal impediment to the Protestant chiefs' hegemony, thus securing the long-term stability of the mission. Boki and Liliha's followers on O'ahu were shortly deposed and their lands confiscated. Foreign and Hawaiian Catholics alike faced persecution by Ka'ahumanu's government for two years before the priests were banished to California in 1831 and Catholicism essentially outlawed on the islands.

While the Catholic controversy was playing out, Ka'ahumanu canvassed the islands to announce yet another set of new laws: six prohibitions (kapu) and an appeal to "seek after truth and keep the words of God." There was considerable overlap with the first set of printed laws. The kapu of 1830 prohibited (1) murder; (2) adultery, prostitution, and polygamy; (3) idol worship, including worship of the akua, 'aumakua, and other "untrue gods"; (4) hula, traditional songs, and nude bathing by women; (5) planting and consumption of 'awa; and (6) manufacture of liquor.[65] A ban on brothels was added in 1831. With the exception of murder and bans on cultural expression, Ka'ahumanu's kapu can be classified as heresy, temperance, and sex laws. The three categories would be hallmarks of island law to century's end. Hula – the inimitable form of Hawaiian cultural expression – would be contested for decades to come.

---

[63] Kamakau, *Ruling Chiefs*, 296.

[64] For Liliha as hānai daughter to Ulumāhehei Hoapili, see Kapiikauinamoku, "Story of Maui Royalty," 34.

[65] Kamakau, *Ruling Chiefs*, 298–99. It is not clear whether Ka'ahumanu knew about the Tahitian monarchy's efforts to control sexual commerce in the 1810s and '20s (O'Brien, "Think of Me as a Woman," 110–11).

"MY BODY IS GOING"

It would be easy to characterize the earliest Protestant and Catholic Hawaiian chiefs as opportunists. Indeed their political actions constitute our primary means of knowing them, and they were certainly no less opportunistic than political leaders elsewhere. Yet to reduce the chiefs' new religious affiliations merely to political expediency would be a mistake. More than a few converts offered their views about the superiority of Christianity to the kapu system, and some were devout Christians whom missionaries could recognize, admire, and even emulate.[66] For instance, high chief 'Aikanaka, grandfather to two future monarchs, was apparently suffering an advanced illness when he wrote the following brief letter, in his own hand, in Hawaiian, to the mission's business agent. The letter reads, in full:

Here is my thought to you all. My body is going. I love you all, but my main thought is on the cross of Jesus where is my great affection. I live for Him, the Forgiver of my sins who washed them in his blood, that my body and spirit may live. He leads my thoughts in His work. This is my desire.[67]

There is no record of 'Aikanaka receiving missionary guidance in the composition of this letter; even if he did, there is no evidence to suggest that the sentiments were not his own. Women and non-elite men also gave expression to religious feelings.[68] In the 1830s an O'ahu woman of unknown social class wrote to thank the ABCFM for sending missionaries. Ana Waiakea looked forward to meeting the New England Christians on judgment day, along with Jesus, "that great friend who caused us to become one family." While Ana felt afraid to stand in the presence of God, she noted that "he it is that knows the infirmities of the mind." She added, gratefully, that "God has taken care of my body."[69]

To be sure, converts' religious practices and beliefs were far from orthodox Protestantism. This gap extended to daily life. When kuhina nui Kīna'u – leader of Protestant Hawai'i – struggled through a difficult birth in 1830 and was offered the choice of a Native or foreign physician,

---

[66] For an ali'i convert who ardently promoted Christianity after 1825, see Brown, *Facing the Spears of Change*, esp. 57.

[67] Aikanaka to Levi Chamberlain, June 28, 1830, trans. Henry Pratt Judd, HMCS.

[68] For a non-elite man, see Davida Malo to "All Those Who Love the Lord Jesus Christ" [ABCFM], Oct. 6, 1828, ABCFM Papers.

[69] Ana Waiakea to ABCFM, no date, trans. Levi Chamberlain, HEA Archives, HMCS. Ana Waiakea seems to have died in Honolulu in 1850 ("Notice," *Polynesian*, Oct. 12, 1850).

she chose the latter.[70] And for every devout ali'i, another played missionaries and other foreigners off each other or simply refused to go along with
the mission. The teenagers King Kauikeaouli and Princess Nāhi'ena'ena
(the king's full sister) fit this model and help to illustrate the complicated
dealings of ali'i with the mission.

After Ka'ahumanu's 1832 death from intestinal illness, Kauikeaouli
"abandoned all restraint," passing his days in gambling, drinking, and
carousing with his friends and attendants the *Hulumanu* (Bird Feathers).[71]
According to Kamakau, the Hulumanu were notorious for "wasting their
substance" on women. (The double entendre may be intended.) While
staying at the village of Waolani on O'ahu, the men contracted a skin disease
"resembling the oozing white sores of the sandalwood tree." This earned
them a new nickname: Foul-Feathered Birds.[72] At least one observer suggested that Kauikeaouli himself was syphilitic.[73]

A lapsed Protestant and son of a Hawaiian father and Tahitian mother
earned considerable blame for leading the king astray. Scant attention has
been paid by historians to Kaomi, which is surprising given that
Kauikeaouli referred to him as "joint king" and "joint ruler" (*mō 'ī ku'i,
aupuni ku'i*).[74] In fact, Kaomi seems to have been in charge during
Kauikeaouli's more protracted binges. Kaomi had gained influence with
the king "not because he was well-educated and intelligent" but because
he was skilled in the art of healing. Kaomi was a kahuna hāhā, a hands-on
diagnostician, and was also adept at prescribing medicine. When Kaomi's
medical advice proved "successful," the king "conceived a great liking for

---

[70] Kamakau, *Ruling Chiefs*, 304. The child, Lot Kapuāiwa, later became Kamehameha V.
[71] Sinclair, *Nāhi'ena'ena*, 128. See, e.g., diary of Sarah Joiner Lyman, Feb. 23, 1833, in
Martin, ed., *Lymans of Hilo*, 53. For the death of Ka'ahumanu, see Richard Armstrong
journal, June 5, 1832, HMCS; [Hiram Bingham], "Sandwich Islands: Extracts from the
General Letter of the Mission Dated June 23, 1832," *Missionary Herald* 29 (May 1833):
165–68.
[72] Kamakau, *Ruling Chiefs*, 279.
[73] In 1828 the king's face was "swollen, and disfigured by the smallpox," reflecting the
"degree to which this young prince had already become acquainted with some of the lusts
harmful to youth" (Boelen, *Merchant's Perspective*, 52). "Lusts" of "youth" suggests
venereal disease. (Smallpox did not arrive until 1853; leprosy was not observed until the
mid-'30s.) Advanced syphilis might have left facial scarring, but congenital venereal
disease is more likely for a boy. Yet there is no evidence of either Kauikeaouli's father
(Kamehameha) or mother (Keōpūolani) carrying either disease. In any case, the king
would never enjoy good health during his relatively long life.
[74] Kamakau, *Ruling Chiefs*, 335. Kame'eleihiwa identified Kaomi as Kauikeaouli's
aikāne, yet there is no evidence that he filled this capacity in the traditional sense
(*Native Land*, 157).

FIGURE 5.3 Honolulu, looking toward Diamond Head, with Kauikeaouli's compound in foreground. "The South Eastern Part of the Town of Hanarura at Oahu, Sandwich Islands." Frederick William Beechey (attributed), 1826. Courtesy of Hawaiian Mission Children's Society Library.

him." More than that, Kauikeaouli outfitted Kaomi with bodyguards and warriors. Kaomi was empowered to dispense land grants, clothing, and "anything else that man might desire." He even granted loans from the kingdom's treasury. Meanwhile, the "evil ways" that had been largely "stamped out," according to Kamakau, returned with a vengeance under Kaomi and Kauikeaouli. Hula, liquor distilleries, and prostitution – all the "natural impulses" of the past – returned.[75]

In December 1832 the nineteen-year-old king held an enormous hula festival with traditional games that had been banned by Ka'ahumanu one year earlier. A few months later Kauikeaouli repealed all the laws of the kingdom except those against murder and theft. The king and his supporters were on a collision course with Kīna'u and the mission. Having inherited Ka'ahumanu's mantle as kuhina nui, Kīna'u would effectively rule – and struggle against Kaomi – while Kauikeaouli courted chaos. The king and Kaomi were not, however, Kīna'u's only problem. In October 1831, according to the mission's secular agent, Kīna'u was

---

[75] Kamakau, *Ruling Chiefs*, 335. For an unapologetic view of Kauikeaouli and the Hulumanu, including allegations of gang rape, see Brown, *Facing the Spears of Change*, 69–77. Kaomi died some time before 1839 (Dibble, *History and General Views*, 110).

beaten by her husband Mataio Kekūanāoʻa, whom she outranked. Kekūanāoʻa's wrath had been kindled by Kīnaʻu's too close intimacy with her half-brother (and brother-in-law) Kauikeaouli, the man against whom she was supposedly protecting Hawaiʻi.[76] Kīnaʻu, it seems, could not win.

As for Kauikeaouli, his relationship with the mission was complicated by the desire to be with his sister Nāhiʻenaʻena – an effort, at least in part, reclaim his status as mōʻī and aliʻi nui. (Nāhiʻenaʻena's views on the matter are obscure.) While their mother Keōpūolani had been the off-spring of a full-sibling marriage – and had proceeded to marry her uncle Kamehameha – the royal siblings under the new order were forbidden from such attachments. Kīnaʻu and the Protestant chiefs suggested the king instead marry Kamanele, daughter of Gov. John Adams Kuakini; but as preparations for a royal wedding were under way in 1834, Kamanele died of unknown causes at the age of twenty.[77] Meanwhile, the intended husband of Nāhiʻenaʻena, twenty-year-old chief Keolaloa Kaʻōleiokū, also perished of unknown causes. In this way, both young monarchs saw equally young fiancés off to early graves.

Kauikeaouli's rebellion reached its apogee in his effort to couple with his sister. When he sent a ship from Oʻahu to Maui to collect Nāhiʻenaʻena in early June 1834, she refused to come to him. Later that month Kauikeaouli, still drinking heavily, reportedly tried to take his own life. Details will probably never be known, but the young monarch apparently was *in extremis* at this time. Missionaries reported on the king's attempted suicide in their personal journals but were careful not to publish the news for fear of compromising the standing of the mission.[78] Having stabilized himself, Kauikeaouli determined to be a mōʻī. In the house of close friend Abner

---

[76] Levi Chamberlain journal, Oct. 21, 1831, HMCS. (Chamberlain did not elaborate on the incident.) For possible domestic violence in the Pōmare dynasty in the 1840s, see O'Brien, "Think of Me as a Woman," 123, 125, 127n112.

[77] A mission wife claimed that the young chiefess had been "for a considerable time, given up to wickedness – drinking, &c," and that she had "died in consequence of wicked conduct" (Clarissa Armstrong journal, May 23 [27?], 1834, HMCS). Out of concern for the reputation of the mission, Armstrong added that "this must never be told in print – remember."

[78] Clarissa Armstrong wrote that the King had "attempted taking his own life – Upon peril of live [life] do not publish this hint ... It is dangerous to have any thing published that is unfavorable to the foreign residents here, or to the natives, because it is used to injure the progress of Christ's course" (ibid., June 29, 1834). An American merchant noted that "all guessed, none knew" the circumstances of the king's attempt on his own life (Stephen Reynolds journal, July 22, 1834, qtd. in Sinclair, *Nāhiʻenaʻena*, 142; see also Daws, *Shoal of Time*, 93–94).

Kuhoʻoheiheipahu Pākī, the king and princess slept together. Word spread quickly. While it is impossible to recover what either Kauikeaouli or Nāhiʻenaʻena were thinking – neither left written records of a personal nature – the public reception of this ancient practice was deeply significant. Aliʻi sibling coupling symbolized the old ways, suggesting that Protestantism and the mission might be rendered obsolete.[79] At the very least, royal incest and the revival of hula and traditional games suggested a changed route after the death of the Christian queen Kaʻahumanu.

In the event, the kingdom-mission breach was short-lived. Kauikeaouli continued his "dissolute" ways through 1834, at which time a missionary physician reported him to be "a drunkard" whose "bloated visage" was testament to the "the number of ... days" that remained to him.[80] The king and princess seem to have carried on their sexual liaisons as well. Then a shift occurred. Still unmarried at the age of twenty-two, the king settled down and made his peace with the mission. The reasons are unclear.[81] Still reeling from the incestuous union, missionaries arranged for Nāhiʻenaʻena to marry fourteen-year-old chief William Pitt Leleiohoku I, son of the late Island Carver Kalanimoku. Kīnaʻu and the Protestant chiefs were amenable to the match. Reports of Nāhiʻenaʻena's "miserable and cast down" mood in 1835 suggest dissatisfaction.[82] Yet missionary attempts to bar church members from associating with the princess until she accepted the mission program could also have fed her isolation.[83]

Nāhiʻenaʻena shortly became pregnant – perhaps by her teenage husband, perhaps by Kauikeaouli who claimed the child was his. (The timing of conception makes this a possibility.) It was the princess's first reported pregnancy. Missionaries wrote from Maui that the king and princess continued to indulge in heavy drinking through the spring of 1836, Nāhiʻenaʻena's second trimester.[84] In the summer, Kauikeaouli, Nāhiʻenaʻena, and her fifteen-year-old husband Leleiohoku removed to Honolulu in preparation for the royal birth. Nāhiʻenaʻena delivered the

---

[79] For discussion, see Kameʻeleihiwa, *Native Land*, 161–65; Sahlins, *Anahulu*, 1:122.

[80] Alonzo Chapin to Samuel Ruggles, Sept. 30, 1834, HMCS.

[81] See "Sandwich Islands: Extracts from the Annual Report of the Mission, Dated July 3d, 1835," *Missionary Herald* 32 (March 1836): 104. See also Daws, *Shoal of Time*, 94. Dibble dates the king's change to the 1836 death of Nāhiʻenaʻena (*History of the Sandwich Islands*, 288). There is some evidence that Kauikeaouli in the early '30s was trying to emulate his father's rule (Kuykendall, *Hawaiian Kingdom*, 1:135).

[82] Richard Armstrong, qtd. in Sinclair, *Nāhiʻenaʻena*, 156.

[83] Sinclair, *Nāhiʻenaʻena*, 154. [84] Ibid., 156.

baby, a son, who lived only a few hours. The child would have been next in line for the throne. Nāhiʻenaʻena herself apparently never regained her strength and remained ill through autumn 1836. On December 30, she died in the presence of her husband Leleiohoku, Kauikeaouli and Kīnaʻu, and missionary physician Gerrit Judd and his wife Laura Fish Judd. The cause of her death was reported as complications from childbirth. A foreign surgeon on hand for her illness noted that the princess had, for instance, "imprudently indulg[ed] in a cold bath" soon after giving birth.[85] Yet a letter composed by American missionary physician Alonzo Chapin in fall 1834 suggests that complications of childbirth were not the whole story. From Lahaina, where Nāhiʻenaʻena was living at the time, Chapin wrote to Rev. Samuel Ruggles, who had recently returned home to New England after thirteen years with the mission. "You have probably been shocked to hear of the down fall of the princess," Chapin began.

She has fallen, like Lucifer, we fear. She has been enlightened and has tasted of the good word of God, but has fallen away, and ... is following that which is destructive to her body and soul. She is now under the physician's care in consequence of disease contracted by her vicious course.[86]

The coded language was for missionary readers. The well-trained Chapin likely knew the nature of the "disease." While not unlikely, syphilis is impossible to prove. Either way, Chapin's letter casts the death of mother and child from "complications in childbirth" in a different light. No additional hints about the nature of Nāhiʻenaʻena's 1834 disease have surfaced (Fig. 5.4).

With Nāhiʻenaʻena gone, King Kauikeaouli chose for a wife Kalama, daughter of a low-ranking chief and harbor pilot. The king's choice was a great disappointment to some ruling chiefs, including his half-sister Kīnaʻu, who considered Kalama's rank unbefitting a king. Yet Kauikeaouli had not put Nāhiʻenaʻena out of his mind. In Lahaina he

[85] W. S. W. Ruschenberger, qtd. in ibid., 157. Mission agent Levi Chamberlain wrote that the princess "appear[ed] quite low" seven weeks after delivery in early November. Chamberlain "conversed with her a little and exhorted her to repentance." Though ill at this time – perhaps seriously so – she still had control of her faculties but could not "be much awakened with a sense of her condition" – by which Chamberlain presumably meant the "condition" of her soul (Levi Chamberlain journal, Nov. 7, 1836, HMCS). For the possibility of syphilis among the Pōmare dynasty at this time, see O'Brien, "Think of Me as a Woman," 111, 124–25.
[86] Alonzo Chapin to Samuel Ruggles, 30 Sept. 1834, HMCS. Nāhiʻenaʻena was not the only prominent apostate at this time. A Hawaiian who sailed with the sixth company of New England missionaries deserted the mission, found a wife, and succumbed to tuberculosis within a year (Journal of Clarissa Chapman Armstrong, May 27–July 2, 1834, HMCS).

FIGURE 5.4 *Left,* Nāhiʻenaʻena at the royal funeral for Liholiho and Kamāmalu
("Nahiʻenaʻena, Sister of Kamehameha III"); *right,* Nāhiʻenaʻena the year she died
(*"Nahienaéna, Soeur germaine du Roi des Iles Sandwich Taméhaméha III"*).
Robert Dampier, 1825, courtesy of Honolulu Museum of Art (#1067.1);
Barthélémy Lauvergne, 1836, courtesy of Bishop Museum (SXC127397).

built a large stone house with a mausoleum on the top floor for his mother
Keōpūolani, his sister – and, as he seems to have considered her, first wife –
Nāhiʻenaʻena, and their infant child.[87] It is difficult to know whether he
interpreted these losses as the "ultimate divine sanction of Jehovah against
his way of life" or as proof that the akua had "forsaken him," yet he
would not rebuff the missionaries for the remainder of his rule.[88] With his
new wife Kalama, he retreated to Lahaina, leaving the kuhina nui Kīnaʻu
in charge of Honolulu. By November 1836, a British consul described
Kīnaʻu as holding the "reins" of the kingdom but "entirely governed by
the American Missionaries who through her govern the Islands with
unlimited sway."[89] That was hyperbole, but it is true that Kauikeaouli

---

[87] Sinclair, *Nāhiʻenaʻena,* 161.   [88] Kameʻeleihiwa, *Native Land,* 165.
[89] Richard Charlton to Lord Palmerston (Nov. 23, 1826), qtd. in Kuykendall, *Hawaiian
Kingdom,* 1:136. See also Simpson, *Sandwich Islands,* 68. American missionaries were
not averse to meeting their objectives through commercial means. A substantial portion
of their expenses were borne by Native Hawaiians in the form of labor and "products of
the island[s]" (Edwards, *Missionary Gazetteer,* 336). See also Dwight Baldwin to Rufus
Anderson, Aug. 10, 1832, and Artemas Bishop to Anderson, Oct. 16, 1836, ABCFM
Papers. Missionaries also kept Hawaiians as house servants. Such contributions, they
reasoned, gave Islanders a stake in their education and Christianization.

had deferred to Kīnaʻu, and it also is true that the kāhuna of Kīnaʻu were now all foreign Christians. The path forward for Hawaiʻi would be the one outlined by the chiefesses Keōpūolani and Kaʻahumanu a decade earlier. Their kinswoman Kīnaʻu would lead the way.

It was in this context that the mission celebrated a changed relationship with the chiefs around 1837. Never averse to hyperbole, missionaries called it a Hawaiian "Great Awakening." In hindsight, the transformation can be seen as a gradual warming to the new kāhuna, as one after another chief was laid in the grave. While the mission won a number of converts, most came from southern Oʻahu and the Kona coast of the Big Island. The Great Awakening was thus neither "great" in scale nor an "awakening" of a dramatic nature.[90] The enthusiasm was also short-lived.[91] Nevertheless, Hawaiʻi was quickly becoming a Christian nation. Yet a new state religion did not prevent people from choosing a different path. In Puna district on the Big Island, a teenager educated at one of the Protestant missionary schools drew wide attention for her prophecy and ability to cure diseases. Across the Big Island, seekers made pilgrimages to meet her in 1831. When Hapuʻu (or Kahapuʻu) died a year later, a syncretic, apocalyptic religious movement arose that observed three gods: Jehovah, Jesus Christ, and Hapuʻu herself. Only the last of these gods could protect the people from the looming destruction.[92]

LARGE FISHES

The Sandwich Islands Mission was shaped in significant part by Hawaiian health problems and concerns about population loss. Missionaries expected to focus on the conversion and instruction of Islanders; instead they spent a great deal of time ministering to the sick. Christianization

[90] Rev. Titus Coan is said to have baptized 1,705 residents of Hilo coast in one day in 1838 (Musick, *Hawaii: Our New Possessions*, 46). No study has been conducted on the Hilo church's retention of parishioners.

[91] For apostasy after 1839, see, e.g., Levi Chamberlain journal, March 1, 1841, HMCS. See also Daws, *Shoal of Time*, 102–5.

[92] Dibble, *History and General Views*, 107–9; Dibble, *History of the Sandwich Islands*, 282–84; Yzendoorn, *History of the Catholic Mission*, 83–85. The cause of Hapuʻu's death is unknown. "Hapuuism" apparently lasted until 1841 when its adherents became Catholics; Yzendoorn speculated that Catholic converts had been instrumental in Hapuʻu's development as a prophet (*History of the Catholic Mission*, 84). See also Ralston, "Early Nineteenth Century Polynesian Millennial Cults," 324–25. For syncretic and prophetic movements in Tahiti and New Zealand, see Newbury, *Tahiti Nui*, 60–63; O'Malley, *Meeting Place*, 174–75.

thus followed a pattern set earlier in the Americas where Indigenous people shaped the process out of sheer need. In Hawai'i that need was widespread. In 1833 newly arrived mission wife Ursula Emerson reported "a great many" Natives had been sick at Waialua on the north shore of O'ahu: "[M]any come every day for medicine." Still more distressing to Emerson were the "many sick babies" brought to the mission house, some of them covered with "sores." With no physician to serve the newly established post, Emerson explained that her untrained husband had taken it upon himself to prescribe medicines – of what type, she did not say. Fortunately for the Emersons and their children, the climate at Waialua was "a healthful one for ourselves." The chronic health woes of the people were a function, she believed, of "their irregular habits of living."[93] Two years later, missionaries reported that childlessness in Hawai'i "scarcely find[s] a parallel in any other nation."[94] From Kaua'i a missionary implored the ABCFM, "[W]hat we do for this perishing people, must be done quickly. Since I came to this island, fifteen years ago, one whole generation have gone down to the grave."[95]

From early on New England evangelical mores affected medical care on the islands. The physicians who accompanied American missionaries were themselves full members of the mission; thus, their primary concern was Hawaiian souls rather than bodies. Physicians or not, most missionaries viewed Hawaiians' physical afflictions as God's punishment for "licentiousness." The Hawaiian covert William Beale provides an example. Son of an unidentified American father and a Hawaiian mother, Beale lived with Hiram and Sybil Bingham and was celebrated in the missionary press for his "singular attainments" of civilization and his grasp of English. In the summer of 1822, after two years of missionary instruction, Beale was chosen by Ka'ahumanu as her personal teacher.[96] When Beale

[93] Ursula Sophia Newell Emerson journal, Jan. 28 and April 8, 1833, in Emerson, *Pioneer Days in Hawaii*, 66–67, 70–71. See also John S. Emerson to Anderson, Aug. 21, 1834, ABCFM Papers. It is not clear whether maka'āinana believed missionaries were spreading disease by prayer and hymn singing (foreign sorcery), as some Tongans apparently did (Campbell, *Island Kingdom*, 43).

[94] "Sandwich Islands: Letter from Messrs. [Asa] Thurston and [Artemas] Bishop, Dated at Kailua, Nov. 10, 1835," *Missionary Herald* 32 (Oct. 1836): 385.

[95] [Samuel Whitney], "Sandwich Islands: Letters from Missionaries on Kauai" [Oct. 15, 1835], *Missionary Herald* 32 (Nov. 1836): 428. See also William P. Alexander, Kaua'i Mission Station Report (1835), qtd. in Stannard, "Disease and Infertility," 331. Ballantyne reads such sentiments in the context of "humanitarian narratives" popular among evangelicals at this time (*Entanglements of Empire*, chap. 6).

[96] Bingham, *Residence*, 172.

died in 1824, the mission's physician wanted to set the record straight: "It has gone to you in manuscript . . . that he died of a liver infection . . . [I]n fact he died a victim to a disorder contracted by following the multitude in a wicked course – This I affirm for he was under my care for a long time before his death." The language is almost identical to Chapin's description of Nāhiʻenaʻena's "vicious course" a decade later. In Beale's case, as in Nāhiʻenaʻena's, the cause of death is unknown; likely possibilities for a fatal "disorder" stemming from "wicked" behavior include venereal disease and alcohol abuse. Blatchley also complained of "another boy . . . named in our public journal in much the same way [as] Wm Beale . . . [T]here is not a boy that I know of whose customs & manners & habits in the streets is more nature like than his." Given these disappointments, Blatchley implored the ABCFM to be more cautious in its Sandwich Islands propaganda. Promoting false Christians and uncivilized Islanders was bound to embarrass the mission or worse: tithing churchgoers in New England might withhold their hard-earned wages. "For more reasons than I have time to state here," Blatchley concluded, "there is little doubt but that the sums contributed for the support of children or youths in the mission families can be better applied in some other country than here."[97]

Missionary physicians' fierce resistance to the kāhuna lapaʻau should come as no surprise. Indeed, it might have been difficult to find a regular physician in all of New England to defend Hawaiian medical practices, although Gerrit Judd reported that other foreigners ("and men of information too") trusted Native physicians and regularly resorted to their treatments.[98] Yet missionaries' opposition to Native medicine ran deeper still, as kāhuna were more than medical practitioners. They were also important advisors to the chiefs and monitors of the Hawaiian body politic. For the same reason, aliʻi were predisposed to trust foreign physicians, as we have seen, and to lean on them as advisors. While missionary reservations about Native medicine had more to do with their own evangelical goals, they also objected to the particulars. The mission's first physician opined that the kāhuna lapaʻau knew "little or nothing of distinguishing one disease from another." When a patient under their

---

[97] Blatchley to Evarts, [no month] 15, 1824, ABCFM Papers. For a similar appeal for discretion, see Thigpen, *Island Queens and Mission Wives*, 98. For more on William Beale, see Sybil Moseley Bingham journal, Oct. 9, 1823, HMCS.

[98] G. P. Judd, "Remarks on the Climate of the Sandwich Islands," *Hawaiian Spectator* 1 (1838): 22.

care died, physicians "suppose[d] him to have been prayed to death by some enemy."[99] Rev. Richard Armstrong considered "much" of Native medicine to be "little else than mere *manslaughter.*"[100]

Unfortunately for ill Hawaiians, some kāhuna lapaʻau eschewed treatment of diseases introduced by Westerners, on the logic that illnesses of foreign origin required treatment by foreign physicians.[101] Most Native physicians worked with what they had, adding new treatments and practices to their arsenal as they became available.[102] Yet neither a strict course of the latest New England medicine nor an enlightened view of the *materia medica* of the kāhuna lapaʻau would have affected the general contours of Hawaiian epidemiology in the nineteenth century. Until the acceptance of germ theory and the development of penicillin, chronic and acute infectious diseases such as syphilis, measles, and smallpox were going to exact their toll. Medically speaking, the early nineteenth century was still an age of purgatives and emetics, heavy metals, and bloodletting. Nevertheless, it is surprising that missionaries and physicians, while assiduously monitoring Hawaiian population loss, failed to make American medicines (such as they were) available to more people.

Even more surprising are the conclusions mission doctors drew about Hawaiian epidemiology and depopulation. In the anatomy book he published for Hawaiian students, Judd described syphilis as the "sickness that God gave us as punishment to adulterous people."[103] Alonzo Chapin, who served as missionary physician in the mid-'30s, agreed that venereal disease was "sent as a punishment for transgression."[104] Nevertheless, both Chapin and Judd treated syphilis and gonorrhea victims. They had

---

[99] Thomas Holman to ABCFM, Nov. 21, 1820, ABCFM Papers.

[100] Armstrong et al., *Answers to Questions*, 48. Similarly, Chapin described island medical practice as "a mixture of absurdities the most ridiculous, and often dangerous" ("Remarks on the Sandwich Islands," 55); Judd called the kāhuna lapaʻau "a miserable set of quacks who often shorten the lives of their patients by their remedies" (Judd, *Dr. Judd: Hawaii's Friend*, 87).

[101] Pukui et al., *Nānā i ke Kumu*, 2:95.

[102] Bushnell, *Gifts of Civilization*, 97, 104–6, 114; Gutmanis, *Kahuna Laʻau Lapaʻau*, 54, 78, 86–87. Morning glory (*Ipomoea* spp.) and various other herbal remedies (taken internally and applied to skin) were used by Native physicians, in addition to the "white man's syphilis medicine" ("Records of medical work done by Dr. Ohule," Sept. 2, 1870, Hawaiian Ethnographic Notes 1:1519, BM). There is also evidence in kāhuna records of gender-specific remedies for syphilis and gonorrhea (ibid., Oct. 26, 1870, May 3, 1871). See also "A Concoction for Venereal Disease in Men," HEN Archives 68–69, BM. The earliest reference to potassium iodide for venereal disease that I have encountered is from 1860 (Pukui et al., *Nānā i ke Kumu*, 2:99).

[103] Judd, *Anatomia, 1838*, 20.   [104] Chapin, "Remarks on the Sandwich Islands," 50.

little choice: the most frequent application for their services was for the "relief of the venereal."[105] In 1837 missionaries expanded their reporting on Hawaiian health and depopulation beyond mission publications. At Kailua-Kona, Rev. Artemas Bishop collected data on the number of fatalities and suspected causes of death, which had been compiled starting in 1825. He agreed with other missionaries that civilization was not to blame but rather "civilized vices": the "savage" drinks these "like water, without knowing that their attendant diseases are cutting the tendrils of his heart, and drawing away his life's blood." With the Hawaiian population in 1836 at 110,000, down from 400,000 in 1778 (the accepted estimate at the time), Bishop calculated it would take "but fifty or sixty years to extinguish every vestige of aboriginal blood in the land." This regrettable state of affairs had resulted from Islanders' "looseness of morals" providing a "ready conductor for the disease … introduced by the first ship that touched here."[106] Bishop's concern about Hawaiians' future overlapped considerably with his own. While still serving as a missionary, he had one of the first sugar mills on Oʻahu constructed. Powered by Islanders, Bishop's mill produced between forty and fifty tons of sugar in the year 1840 alone.[107] Population loss, he knew, would affect earnings in this labor-intensive industry.

Bishop's main contribution to the question of Hawaiian morbidity and depopulation was his observation that syphilis had contributed to low birth rates and increased infant mortality.[108] Hawaiian students at Lahainaluna Seminary seemed to agree, ranking sexual intercourse with foreigners as the leading cause of population loss.[109] In two articles on the subject, Chapin highlighted the effects of advanced syphilis: tooth decay and oral infection, malnutrition, blindness, and "visages horridly deformed." In some cases, the "entire front of the thorax would be covered" with syphilitic ulcers. Other victims had lost their genitalia completely. In one advanced case, Chapin reported, the patient's skull had been "perforated to the brain with numerous fistulas." While Chapin claimed to have helped one patient suffering from secondary syphilis with a course of mercury, he believed there was no prospect of the epidemic letting up, as the people had "no means which will control it." Only a few

---

[105] Chapin, "Remarks on the Venereal Disease," 90.
[106] Bishop, "Inquiry into the Causes of Decrease," 53, 59, 61. For a similar report on the Māori this same year, see Ballantyne, *Entanglements of Empire*, 231–34.
[107] Kashay, "Agents of Imperialism," 295.
[108] Bishop, "Inquiry into the Causes of Decrease," 61, 63.
[109] Kahananui, *Ka Mooolelo Hawaii*, 233.

Hawaiians had "access to foreign physicians, and many within reach appear too indifferent to their condition to make application."[110] Like Bishop, Chapin recognized that venereal diseases had diminished fertility, and he figured that Islanders' days were numbered. In some respects, they were already gone, as the "superfluous wants" generated by contact with foreigners had "destroy[ed] their native character" and made them an "artificial and degenerate race."[111] Some missionaries would have rejected Chapin's language, though not his condemnation of Native lifestyles and consumption patterns.

In 1839 Hawaiian scholar and convert Davida Malo published an article on the subject of disease and depopulation. An early and ardent Christian, Malo had been educated at Lahainaluna Seminary and had previously lived at Kuakini's court on the Kona coast. He probably had some contact with Tahitian and British missionaries and was a trusted advisor to Keōpūolani in her last years. In the early '30s he would have been in close contact with Kauikeaouli and Nāhiʻenaʻena at Lahaina. He witnessed the princess's fall from grace and may have been on hand for her death in 1836. Regarding the population crisis, Malo identified various factors including warfare, abortion and infanticide, and poor medicine, but most critical were the "illicit intercourse of Hawaiian females with foreigners[,] ... the sloth and indolence of the people at the present time[,] ... [and] the disobedience of the chiefs and people to the revealed will of God." Ongoing population loss seemed inevitable: "The kingdom is sick, – it is reduced to a skeleton, and is near to death; yea, the whole Hawaiian nation is near to a close." Barring a miracle, the "diminishing of the people will not cease."[112] A year earlier, Malo suggested in a letter to the kuhina nui Kīnaʻu and her husband that the aliʻi consult frequently with their advisors to prevent foreigners from doing harm to the kingdom.

---

[110] Chapin, "Remarks on the Sandwich Islands," 51; Chapin, "Remarks on the Venereal Disease," 90.

[111] Chapin, "Remarks on the Sandwich Islands," 55–57. Like Chapin, Armstrong believed that Hawaiians' "artificial wants" helped to explain "why they decrease" (Armstrong to David Greene, Nov. 11, 1845, ABCFM Papers).

[112] Malo, "On the Decrease of Population," 125, 130. See also [Sheldon Dibble], ed., "Ka Mooolelo Hawaii," *Hawaiian Spectator* 1 (1838): 446–47; Kahananui, *Ka Mooolelo Hawaii*, 233. For similar sentiments expressed by foreigners a decade later, see Armstrong et al., *Answers to Questions*, 6–13, 30–35, 47–50. Malo later served as superintendent of schools and earned one of the few preaching licenses granted to Hawaiians (Noelani Arista, "Davida Malo, A Hawaiian Life," in Malo, *Moʻolelo Hawaiʻi*, 108–9). Chang observes that stadial theory and racialist thinking dominated Malo's missionary education (*World and All the Things upon It*, 118–21).

To emphasize his point, Malo employed a metaphor from the natural world:

If a big wave comes in, large fishes will come from the dark Ocean which you never saw before, and when they see the small fishes they will eat them up; such also is the case with large animals, they will prey on the smaller ones. The ships of the white man have come, and smart people have arrived from the great countries which you have never seen before, they know our people are few in number and living in a small country; they will eat us up, such has always been the case with large countries, the small ones have been gobbled up.[113]

One month later Malo wrote the ali'i nui again. This time he was brief: "I think we are a dying people."[114]

In fact, the population had plummeted over the previous four years. As many as 22,000 lives were lost between 1832 and 1836, with no reported epidemic.[115] The timing of Malo's article was not coincidental. Yet his fatalism was not temporary. When Gov. John Adams Kuakini died five years later, Malo published an obituary in a Hawaiian-language newspaper. The elegy was not for Kuakini alone: "Alas for us, oh chiefs, death comes swiftly upon us the Hawaiian people, and upon you the chiefs. Perhaps we will be laid waste [consumed] and this race of people disappear."[116] One consolation for Christians like Malo was the promise of an afterlife; how much solace it provided is not clear. Some surely wondered, what was the point of eternal life without the bone, flesh, and blood of kin?

Fatalism was central to the Christianization of Hawai'i. By 1840 neither Hawaiians nor foreigners offered a viable solution to the problem of disease and population decline. At the same time, the chiefs were trapped in a cycle of debt, shortened lives, low fertility, and increasing dependence on American allies. For foreigners, Christianity and Western law created real opportunities: New England missionaries rose to positions

---

[113] Kuykendall, *Hawaiian Kingdom*, 1:153. For similar metaphors employed by Native North Americans at this time, see Haake, "'In the Same Predicament as Heretofore',", 62–63, 67–69.

[114] "*Ke manao nei au he poe make kakou a pau*" (Malo, *Mo'olelo Hawai'i* [trans. Noelani Arista], 96).

[115] Schmitt, *Historical Statistics of Hawaii*, 8–9.

[116] Malo, *Mo'olelo Hawai'i* (trans. Noelani Arista), 118. "Perhaps we will be consumed" is an alternative translation of "*e pau ana paha kakou*." For the original obituary, see Davida Malo, "*Ka Make o Kuakini*," *Ka Nonanona*, Dec. 21, 1844.

of power and permanent influence. Soon they would be awarded significant landholdings to match. In the long run, the chiefs' alliance with the kāhuna pule and their families reestablished state religion on the islands and set the kingdom on a path toward domination by the United States.

6

The Wasting Hand

Lots of our folks in Waianae died, 84 in all ... All new born infants died, 27 in all.
—S. Waimalu, Oʻahu, 1848

The Hawaiian people welcome the stranger freely; rich and poor, high and low give what they can. The strangers call this love ignorance and think it is good for nothing.
—Samuel Kamakau, 1869

In 1840 Hawaiʻi became a constitutional monarchy with mechanisms for universal male suffrage and the protection of religious liberty. This was no small change. For the first time, the king's authority was limited by a governing structure put in place to separate kingdom from king.[1] For those positioned to navigate it, the new legal structure provided genuine opportunities. But a constitution and new laws did little to improve life for the vast majority of Hawaiians. Poverty, decreased fertility, and premature death continued to plague the makaʻāinana, while the influence of the aliʻi shrank dramatically. The kingdom naturalized foreigners and opened up the crown lands for purchase. Shortly, foreigners built a plantation complex and jockeyed for position in the highest ranks of government. Overwhelmingly destitute, common Hawaiians now were landless as well.

By the 1850s the question for many was not whether the islands would pass into American hands but rather what kind of American Hawaiʻi

[1] Banner, *Possessing the Pacific*, 139.

would prevail. As in the US acquisition of the Oregon Country and half of Mexico, manifest destiny exerted a powerful pull for Americans of all stripes. Whigs and Democrats; filibusters, annexationists, missionaries, and Argonauts; Free Soilers and the slave power: everyone dreamed big about Hawai'i.[2] While they disagreed vehemently about what society should be created on the islands, almost no one questioned the wisdom of creating it, and few failed to overlook the critical factor that made possession possible: Native depopulation.

Population decline became a principal concern of the chiefs and naturalized foreigners who together ruled the kingdom to midcentury. Maka'āinana – the islands' labor force – came to be seen by island elites as the last bulwark against conquest or incorporation by more powerful nations. Understanding this preoccupation helps explain the various laws and reforms enacted by the kingdom; in particular, the privatization of lands and legal efforts aimed at reforming Hawaiian life, including marriage and sexuality. Missionaries and other foreigners were instrumental in creating this new legal regime, but reforms could only be enacted with the backing of the ruling chiefs. As a group, these elite Hawaiians determined that improved Hawaiian health and population growth required new approaches to island society.

Landed or landless, policed or left to their own devices, the Native population continued to decline. By 1855, a newly anointed King Kamehameha IV identified the "decrease of our population" as a subject "in comparison with which all others sink into insignificance." Throwing down the gauntlet, the king exhorted legislators to address the crisis: "Our acts are in vain unless we can stay the wasting hand that is destroying our people."[3] He was hardly alone. Sensing an opportunity, newcomers adopted the rhetoric, if not always the policy, of improving Islander health and aiding their survival. To say that the islands and their government were ill-equipped for the health challenges that lay ahead is, as one scholar noted, a vast understatement.[4]

The political history of the Hawaiian kingdom has been well covered by historians, yet the role of Native health in fundamentally shaping political and social change has not. Among other factors affecting the islands was a new direct sea route from San Francisco, enabling the arrival of destructive new diseases and aggressive filibusters. Historians have

---

[2] Greenberg argues that American "enthusiasm" for the islands "dramatically increased" after the US–Mexico War (*Manifest Manhood*, 240).
[3] Kamehameha IV, *Speeches of His Majesty*, 15.   [4] Osorio, *Dismembering Lāhui*, 47.

increasingly recognized the important economic and political factors that drew Hawai'i closer to the American West and, by extension, into the US geopolitical sphere. Yet rarely do Islanders play a leading role in that story. This is odd given that Hawai'i's polyglot society today is a direct consequence of Hawaiian health struggles and the responses by island leaders. The time is overdue for a consideration of both.

"SOMETIMES PROVES MORTAL"

In April 1839 the kuhina nui and dowager queen Kīna'u died from complications of the mumps. The course of her illness was apparently rapid. Mission agent Levi Chamberlain first noted it on March 30, and by April 4 the thirty-three-year-old chiefess was gone.[5] Missionary physician Gerrit P. Judd was dismayed. For Judd, mumps was a childhood disease that required "little" treatment. Hoping to alleviate fears about yet another new infectious disease, Judd reassured people in Honolulu that mumps was a mild disease that shortly would run its course. He soon learned otherwise: "In many instances" the disease became "rather serious." Among other consequences Judd reported were organ failure and "inflammation" of the "general system."[6] Like other new pathogens, mumps exhibited uncharacteristic virulence among Islanders. Arriving on an American vessel in 1838, the disease spread from southern O'ahu across the archipelago, infecting "both young and old," yet Kamakau noted that "few died of it."[7] In fact no deaths of newborns were recorded

[5] The Hawaiian term for mumps (*auwae pahāha*, "swollen chin") highlights its distinctive feature: painful swelling of the salivary glands. Other symptoms are generically flu-like. In modern populations, 15 to 27 percent of cases will display no symptoms or nonspecific symptoms, which of course serves to facilitate the spread of the disease (Immunization Action Coalition, "Mumps: Answers and Questions," www.immunize.org/catg.d/p4211 .pdf). It is not clear whether asymptomatic mumps is less common in populations for which the disease is new.

[6] Gerrit P. Judd 1839 report to the Sandwich Islands Mission (typescript), U178, HSA. Judd spent most of 1838 practicing medicine instead of editing his newspaper as he would have liked.

[7] Kamakau, *Ruling Chiefs*, 346. Sources disagree as to the vector. Judd identified the *Rasselas*, which arrived from San Francisco in early December (1839 report to Sandwich Islands Mission; Levi Chamberlain journal, Dec. 3, 1838, HMCS). Kamakau, who identified the New England ship *Don Quixote* that called at O'ahu in mid-November, may have confused two events (*Ruling Chiefs*, 345). In 1841 Hawaiian sailors aboard the *Don Quixote* contracted smallpox at Valparaiso, Chile. Two of seven Hawaiians had apparently been vaccinated for smallpox; the other five perished. The *Don Quixote* proceeded to spread smallpox to Tahiti killing hundreds or more. See "Tahiti," *Sydney Herald*, Nov. 19, 1841; Igler, *Great Ocean*, 64–65.

in this first outbreak.[8] Yet at least one other high chief succumbed. Royal governor of Kaua'i, Kaikio'ewa, was in his seventies and may well have been frail when exposed to the virus.

Mortality among Hawaiian commoners in the early '40s was equally high.[9] In May 1846 the kingdom's new Minister of Foreign Affairs, recently arrived Scottish businessman Robert Crichton Wyllie, submitted a survey of 116 questions to American missionaries stationed across the islands. The goal of the survey was to better understand and ultimately reverse the decline of the Hawaiian population. Someone in the government believed that the missionaries knew a great deal about the state of maka'āinana life; in spite of evident biases, their answers bore that assumption out. It is not clear how many missionaries received the survey, but twelve respondents from the five largest islands submitted answers. Responses to Minister Wyllie's survey revealed a great deal more than demographic trends. While the various responses offered no workable solution to the problem Native population loss, they documented a range of ailments and challenges faced by the maka'āinana in the '40s.

Wyllie's query about "Diseases prevailing continuously or epidemically in the district" drew consistent answers. Rev. Titus Coan explained that the major diseases at Hilo on the Big Island were "of the venereal, scrofulous and cutaneous character" – in other words, sexually transmitted infections, tuberculosis and other lung diseases, and skin diseases. "Diseases of the liver, influenza, asthma, palsy, fevers, rheumatisms," and consumption also prevailed "to some extent." Jonathan S. Green believed that people in central Maui had been "exempted from such diseases to a remarkable extent" since his arrival in 1842, but he had to admit that

---

[8] Real figures for overall morbidity and mortality are also lacking. Royal advisor John Papa 'Ī'ī and his wife Sarai Hiwauli both contracted mumps and survived (Brown, *Facing the Spears of Change*, 76). Although Stannard suggested that as many as a third of Hawaiian males who contracted the disease were rendered infertile ("Disease and Infertility," 343), male sterility in fact is "extremely rare" in mumps because the disease – when it affects the testicles at all (20 to 30 percent of cases in males) – does so bilaterally, involving the inflammation of only one testicle and thus having a negligible effect on sperm count (Robert J. Kim-Farley, "Mumps," in Kiple, ed., *Cambridge World History of Human Disease*, 888).

[9] For all the scholarly attention to leprosy (or Hansen's disease) in Hawai'i, overall morbidity and mortality were exceedingly low relative to other introduced diseases. Leprosy was apparently present on O'ahu by 1840 (Nathaniel Bright Emerson, "Ahia, the First Leper in Honolulu," c. 1880, N. B. Emerson Papers, HL; Mouritz, "*Path of the Destroyer*," 30). A Chinese vector has not been ruled out; Islanders referred to the disease as *ma'i Pākē* (Chinese disease). In 1865 infected Hawaiians were forcibly removed to the notorious leper colony on Moloka'i (Inglis, *Ma'i Lepera*; Law, *Kalaupapa*).

"occasionally the influenza prevails." Benjamin Parker at Kāne'ohe, O'ahu, noted that "colds and influenzas" were common, as were asthma and venereal and skin diseases. At 'Ewa, O'ahu, Artemas Bishop listed cutaneous diseases ("very prevalent and distressing"), influenza ("sometimes proves mortal"), and fevers ("frequent but of a mild type"). Bishop had written extensively about this subject in an 1838 article for the *Hawaiian Spectator*. Then as now he judged "the most prevailing and mortal" diseases to be those "consequent upon the venereal corruption of the blood." Missionary instructor Edward Johnson at Hanalei, on the north shore of Kaua'i, and Rev. John S. Emerson at Waialua, O'ahu, both listed venereal diseases at their districts, while Emerson added "the itch" (probably scabies).[10] From Hilo to Hanalei, then, commoners continued to struggle with respiratory diseases, venereal infections, and other skin conditions.

Syphilis and gonorrhea had proven their staying power. As late as 1847, apothecaries in Honolulu and Lahaina reportedly did two-thirds of their business in venereal remedies.[11] Green and other missionaries believed that prostitution had been on the rise since 1843. Anti-missionary writers did not disagree. According to the opposition *Sandwich Islands News,* every local vessel that came into Lahaina was "crowded with native women from the other islands." When the ships departed, they returned to their villages, "their persons all filled with diseases."[12]

With one exception, missionaries reported that deaths exceeded births by a factor of two. Coan reported the annual number of deaths in Hilo at "about four hundred," with "about two hundred" births. Parker at Kāne'ohe reported similar rates: 160 deaths, 75 births. Central Maui again proved an exception: Rev. Ephraim Clark reported that deaths only "somewhat exceed[ed]" births at Wailuku, though he failed to collect figures; at neighboring Makawao, Green reported sixty-four births and thirty-one deaths for the year 1846, nearly the inverse of the reports from O'ahu and the Big Island. The Makawao figures would seem to confirm Green's claim that people in central Maui had been comparatively healthy. As for Wyllie's question about "Instances of great longevity," three of six missionaries responded that there were no such cases in

[10] Armstrong et al., *Answers to Questions*, 19–20. None of the respondents had seen the effects of the 1848–49 epidemics. For Green's arrival in Makawao, see Maly and Maly, *He Mo'olelo 'Āina*, 18. For the rising sex trade at Hilo, see O'Brien, *Pacific Muse*, 110.

[11] Quidam, "Island of Maui," *Sandwich Islands News*, June 23, 1847.

[12] *Sandwich Islands News*, March 10, 1847, qtd. in Linnekin, *Sacred Queens*, 186. For a similar complaint in 1862, see F. W. Hutchison to R. C. Wyllie, *Polynesian*, Aug. 2, 1862.

their district, while Clark noted that such cases at Wailuku were "not numerous."[13]

Living conditions for maka'āinana were universally reported as grim. Green believed that commoners' homes and clothing had become "more prejudicial to health" since the arrival of missionaries.[14] Across the islands infant mortality was unusually high. At Waialua, O'ahu, moreover, many surviving children were infected with venereal disease.[15] If central Maui had proved an exception to the general ill health and high mortality across the islands in the mid-'40s, maka'āinana suffered regardless. Green wrote the *Polynesian* to express his concerns about the "rapid" increase of young Maui men joining the whalers. While small numbers of young men in Lahaina, Honolulu, and Hilo had boarded ships for years, Green noted that central Maui was now losing many of its "most promising" young people. (This marked the high point of whale ships calling at the islands.) The problem was not limited to loss of labor: "How are their families supported?" How many wives of seamen had been forced to "sell themselves for the means of subsistence"? Was seafaring even profitable for Hawaiian men – any more so than "industrious[ly] . . . cultivating the soil" at home?[16] No answer would be forthcoming in the *Polynesian*.

Missionaries offered many causes for population loss. The Native medical profession was implicated by at least three respondents. Clark did not attack the kāhuna directly but complained of a "want of suitable medical aid, and other comforts for the sick." Rev. Richard Armstrong was more direct: infants were dying at disproportionate rates due to the "want of medicine and medical skill," while the whole nation was subject to "injur[y]" by Native medicine and "quacks."[17] As for solutions, missionaries suggested incentives for families, such as land grants and tax breaks for parents with multiple children. Some prominent Hawaiians complained that taxes were onerous and that forced labor regimes were burdensome and unjust. Hopu, who had introduced the first missionary delegation to the monarchs in 1820, proposed a new system of taxation, arguing in a letter to King Kauikeaouli that above all

---

[13] Armstrong et al., *Answers to Questions*, 43–44.   [14] Ibid., 47.
[15] Ibid., 34. For the possibility of famine following an 1845–46 drought in Ka'ū district, Hawai'i Island, see Handy and Pukui, *Polynesian Family System*, 239.
[16] J. S. Green letter to the editor, *Polynesian*, May 23, 1846. Kuhina nui John Kalaipaihala Young II (known as Keoni Ana) estimated that as many as 2,600 men between the ages of fifteen and thirty were abroad or at sea in 1846 ("Report of the Minister of the Interior," *Polynesian*, Aug. 8, 1846). See also Armstrong et al., *Answers to Questions*, 78.
[17] Armstrong et al., *Answers to Questions*, 48.

else the land needed to be "filled again with people."[18] Bishop recommended the establishment of drug dispensaries in "every district," furn-
ished with medicines for children in particular. He also identified what
seemed to him an inordinate number of parents who gave away their
offspring to loved ones in hānai. Emerson recommended a medical
school to train "native doctors and midwives" but noted that success
would depend wholly on government patronage.[19]

No one suggested public health laws. Kīna'u had instituted the kingdom's first public health measure in 1836: inspection and quarantine of
ships entering Honolulu harbor.[20] The measure remained on the books
through the '40s. But no other health measures were considered that did
not also involve remaking Hawaiian life, labor, and society as a whole.[21]
All agreed that the "Christian education" and the inculcation of Protestant
"habits of industry" in the Native character would be indispensable to
reversing depopulation.[22] Still, solutions could be too little too late. The
general consensus among the missionaries was that "the nation is *rusting
out*."[23]

Throughout the '40s Hawaiian requests for medical assistance were a
"perpetual burden" and "hindrance" to missionary labors.[24] "I was sick
one month and many Dr's attended me," Prince Lot Kapuāiwa's journal
begins: "Dr Judd Dr Gibson Dr W[y]llie and Dr Gordon."[25] Once the
fourteen-year-old prince recovered, his younger brother Alexander
Liholiho was plagued by a throat abscess (quinsy) for which Judd outfitted
him with a therapeutic collar.[26] "How strange and afflicting have been the

---

[18] Toma Hopu to Kauikeaouli, May 21, 1838, Interior Department Box 140, HSA. Later
that year, a vagrancy law criminalized non-work, with different punishments for women
and men ("Instructions in regard to those who have no money," Nov. 26, 1838, Ser. 418,
HSA). Big Island governor John Adams Kuakini was suspended by the Mission in 1840
for "oppressi[ng]" the people and "seeking his own interests in opposition to theirs" (Asa
Thurston [1840], qtd. in Ralston, "Hawaii, 1778–1854," 38–39).
[19] Armstrong et al., *Answers to Questions*, 52.
[20] Kīna'u, Auhea, and Pākī, "To the Pilot at Honolulu," Laws of the Hawaiian Kingdom,
Ser. 418, Box 1, HSA.
[21] Missionaries advocated improved ventilation and sanitation in Native homes (Armstrong
et al., *Answers to Questions*, 21–22).
[22] Ibid., 53–54.   [23] Ibid., 6.
[24] Dwight Baldwin to Rufus Anderson, July 18, 1842, ABCFM Papers; Baldwin to
Anderson, Dec. 1, 1843, ibid. In 1844 Baldwin pleaded with the ABCFM for "medical
aid" at Lahaina to be supplied "from some other source than me" (Baldwin to Greene,
Dec. 10, 1844, ibid.).
[25] Lot Kapuiāwa journal, May 30, 1844, HMCS.
[26] Ibid., June 20, 1844. Alexander Liholiho also suffered from chronic asthma.

dealings of God with the Hawaiian chiefs," Armstrong wrote to the ABCFM a few months later. "Not one of the old stock now remain. One by one they have been laid in the grave, until they are all gone."[27]

While the princely brothers had their best years ahead of them, the chiefs to whom Armstrong referred comprised a long list. Royal governors of Maui, Kalākua Kaheiheimālie (also known as Hoapiliwahine, "Hoapili's wife") and her husband Ulumāheihei Hoapili, both perished. They had been early converts to Protestantism and important allies of the Sandwich Islands Mission.[28] Kaheiheimālie's brother also died: John Adams Kuakini had been royal governor of Hawai'i Island. Married four times, Kuakini had only one surviving child, Mary (Mele) Kamanele Kuakini. Betrothed to Kauikeaouli, twenty-year-old Mele died of unknown causes in 1834 before the marriage could take place. Kaheiheimālie's daughter Miriam Kekāuluohi, kuhina nui and widow of two former kings (Kamehameha and his son Liholiho), also died in 1845, reportedly of influenza.[29] Miriam Kekāuluohi had one son, William Charles Lunalilo, who would later serve a one-year term as king before dying prematurely in 1874. Finally, Big Island chiefess Kapi'olani – who famously defied the volcano goddess Pele in 1824 – died from complications of a lumpectomy performed by Gerrit Judd.[30]

For missionaries, an equally significant loss was that of "Blind Bartimaeus" (Pua'aiki), the first Hawaiian minister trained on the islands. Pua'aiki ("little pig") was said to have been abandoned as an infant and may have suffered a congenital disorder. Partially blind, he walked hunched over and was reported to be small "almost to deformity."[31] In the early 1820s Pua'aiki gained employment as a jester and hula dancer in the court of Queen Kamāmalu. Some time after 1822 he met the Hawaiian Protestant John Honoli'i (educated and Christianized at the Foreign Mission School in Connecticut), who won him over to the faith. Along with the Tahitian Protestants at the court of Keōpūolani, Pua'aiki

---

[27] Richard Armstrong to David Greene, Nov. 11, 1845, ABCFM Papers.
[28] A founding member of the House of Nobles, Kalākua Kaheiheimālie (sister of Ka'ahumanu and onetime wife of Kamehameha) in 1840 replaced Hoapili as royal governor of Maui, a post she held until her death in 1842. Hoapili's daughter Liliha, Royal Governor of O'ahu and widow of Boki, died in 1839, allegedly poisoned. Daws notes that the deaths of Hoapili and Kalākua Kaheiheimālie were instrumental in opening Maui up to whalers and thus to liquor and prostitution (*Shoal of Time*, 166–67).
[29] Brown, *Facing the Spears of Change*, 98.
[30] Levi Chamberlain journal, March 23, 1841, HMCS. See also Judd, *Dr. Judd: Hawaii's Friend*, 89–90.
[31] Stewart, *Private Journal*, 250.

FIGURE 6.1 Pua'aiki. "Bartimaus [*sic*], Wailuku, Maui."
Clarissa C. Armstrong, 1847. Courtesy of Hawaiian Mission Children's Society
Library.

preached in the vicinity of Lahaina and was admitted to the Church in
1825, later becoming a licensed minister.[32]

Relishing in Pua'aiki's transformation from a deformed outcast to a
devout man of God, missionaries spun elaborate tales of Pua'aiki's spiritual awakening. The ABCFM rendered him a kind a saint. Mission wife
Clarissa C. Armstrong offered a less partisan view in a sensitive portrait
she painted four years after his death (Fig. 6.1).

This rash of mortality left only one prominent ali'i from Ka'ahumanu's
generation. Niece of Kamehameha I, Kuamo'o Ka'ōana'eha (later known
as Mary or "Mele" Kuamo'o) was born around 1780 and married British
seaman John Young in 1805 (his second wife), with whom she had four
children. Meanwhile, from the next generation (born 1785 to 1795), no

---

[32] Green, *Notices of the Life of . . . Puaaiki.* Fueling the missionary campaign against a
perceived crisis of infanticide, Green claimed that Pua'aiki's mother had tried to bury him
alive as an infant (ibid., 5–6).

more than ten prominent ali'i remained by 1845. These included the Royal governor of O'ahu, Mataio Kekūanāo'a; Honolulu armory manager 'Aikanaka; high chief and royal advisor Ho'oulu; and the scholar Davida Malo. No one surveyed them about their sense of Hawai'i's future; if Malo's comments are any indication, prospects seemed grim.

REVOLUTIONS OF 1848

With a constitution and written laws came new leaders for the kingdom. Two legislative bodies had been created in 1840, a House of Nobles (fifteen members) appointed by the king and a smaller House of Representatives (five to seven members) elected by voters. A Supreme Court consisted of four judges appointed by the Representatives, along with the king and his kuhina nui (often referred to as premier), who in 1840 was the chiefess Kekāuluohi. Along with three other ali'i women, Kekāuluohi also served in the House of Nobles, though it is not clear whether these chiefesses participated in the proceedings.[33] Despite continuing to hold the office of kuhina nui, ali'i women's roles would gradually be suppressed by patriarchal laws, including a coverture law, imported from New England. By 1855, only one female Noble remained, and no others held government office.[34] While women of all classes were stripped of customary rights under the new legal regime, there is little evidence to suggest that their diminished political role affected their standing in local communities or the household.[35]

Foreigners were few in number but enjoyed outsized influence in the government.[36] Given the makeup of the voting population in this period, a leading scholar notes, Hawaiians in significant numbers must have voted for these haole to represent them.[37] A key development was détente among foreigners. For all the earlier vitriol between missionaries and merchants, the two factions had come to agree on a set of shared concerns by 1840. The US financial panic of 1837 was a major cause. Missionaries warmed to commercial principles as contributions to mission headquarters in Boston dried up and as their own property grew in value. Pocketbook concerns steered missionaries into the government. The author of the

---

[33] Greer, "Honolulu in 1847," 79; Osorio, *Dismembering Lāhui*, 45, 66.
[34] Osorio, *Dismembering Lāhui*, 109.   [35] Merry, *Colonizing Hawai'i*, 227.
[36] Of a few hundred Americans resident on the islands in 1840, seventy-nine were missionaries. By 1844 fourteen foreigners were employed in government as cabinet members or legislators; by 1852, the number had risen to forty-eight (Daws, *Shoal of Time*, 108).
[37] Osorio, *Dismembering Lāhui*, 70. There was "really no way of getting rid of the haole" by 1845 (ibid., 41).

1840 Constitution, William Richards, himself resigned from the mission to serve the kingdom.

In 1845 a series of Organic Acts established four cabinets for the kingdom – Interior, Foreign Affairs, Finance, and Education – as well as the position of attorney general.[38] Of these five prominent offices, only one was held by a Hawaiian, John Kalaipaihala Young II (known as Keoni Ana), who served as Minister of Interior. The other four were occupied by foreigners. Two former missionaries – Richards and Judd, both fluent in Hawaiian – held enormous sway.[39] The king placed his confidence in foreigners who "worked with vigor as is the haole way, quickly deciding what was for our good and what should be done," as he wrote to the recently deposed queen of Tahiti.[40] One historian pointed out the obvious "paradox" in this strategy: a new legal regime required foreigners to run it, but foreigners in government were a major threat to sovereignty.[41] Yet it bears repeating that Hawaiian elites made up the majority of both houses of the legislature in this period and also served as judges in district and Supreme courts. The government was mixed, if not by design then at least as a stopgap measure to preserve sovereignty.

By 1848 the House of Nobles consisted of seventeen members, including the half-brothers Keoni Ana and James Young Kānehoa, both sons of British sailor-turned-aliʻi John Young. Kānehoa also served as governor of Maui and on the Board of Land Commissioners that oversaw land reform. Keoni Ana was Kauikeaouli's right-hand man and the first male to serve as kuhina nui (1845–54). Both Kānehoa and Keoni Ana had multiple Hawaiian wives, and one of Kānehoa's wives was, like him, hapa haole. While there is no evidence that either brother identified as anything but *Hawaiian* aliʻi, both were occasionally identified after annexation as villains. In any case, hapa haole rulers were hardly necessary for capitalist development and the displacement of makaʻāinana from their hereditary lands, much less the increase of foreigners in government. The dramatic political changes that took place in this period were coordinated efforts by the monarchy, legislature, former

---

[38] A Privy Council was also established, consisting of the cabinet ministers and the islands' four governors. The capital was moved from Lahaina to Honolulu.

[39] Kameʻeleihiwa called them "de facto" rulers of the kingdom (*Native Land*, 186).

[40] Kauikeaouli to Queen Pomare, qtd. in Osorio, *Dismembering Lāhui*, 37. Osorio suggests that Kauikeaouli may have seen his duty as "mediat[ing]" the power of foreigners, as earlier mōʻī had mediated the akua (ibid., 38).

[41] Kuykendall, *Hawaiian Kingdom*, 2:89.

missionaries, a handful of foreigners, and other elites, the vast majority of them Hawaiians.

The Māhele, or privatization of the crown lands, was the most consequential political event of this period. With the gradual decline of whaling, plantation agriculture appeared to foreigners and ali'i the obvious way forward. But agricultural productivity had fallen dramatically as the number of laborers declined. The ali'i, as principal landholders, stood to gain by opening up lands for purchase and development. The only question was who would work the fields. For some ali'i, profit was a sufficient motive for land reform; others hung their hopes on immigrant labor bolstering the Hawaiian population through marriage and ultimately saving the race. The Māhele had three immediate causes: the kingdom's need to naturalize (and thereby control) foreigners, haole desire for profitable agriculture and protection of their private property, and the chiefs' desire to preserve their land wealth in case of annexation. Each will be discussed in turn.

Threats posed by foreigners were as various as the group itself. Naturalization, it was hoped, would win the allegiance of many of them, or at least their obedience to the law.[42] Foreigners holding government office was a different problem. Some historians underestimate advisors' cynical manipulation of the chiefs, including consuls who stoked the monarchy's fears about conquest.[43] Yet threats to sovereignty were real, and many believed that Western laws and land policy would protect the kingdom by establishing its legitimacy. Under duress in 1843 Kauikeaouli had signed the kingdom over to a British naval officer. While Great Britain revoked the deal six months later, imperialists everywhere smelled blood in the water. Kingdom debts continued to be used as a justification for imperial coercion, yet European and American demands of extraterritoriality were also invoked.[44] In August 1849 a French naval expedition attacked Honolulu in hopes of taking the islands, a remarkable act of bravado given that there were only twelve French nationals and a handful of priests on the islands at this time.[45] Two years later an American no one

---

[42] The plan did not succeed. Only 676 of some 1,600 haole were naturalized by 1851, with the rest remaining as foreign nationals (Osorio, *Dismembering Lāhui*, 52–53).

[43] Banner, *Possessing the Pacific*, 128–62. Such manipulation dates from the mid-'20s or earlier: "The English Consul says to Kauikeouli [*sic*], 'If you establish laws, your lands are gone. But if you will first give information to England[,] and King George establish [*sic*] laws, then that will be right['"] (Translation of [Davida] Malo's letter to Mr. [Elisha] Loomis, Dec. 11, 1827, ABCFM Papers).

[44] For a bigamist US Consul's refusal to yield to government authority, see Kīna'u to Martin Van Buren, Jan. 12, 1839, HMCS.

[45] Daws, *Shoal of Time*, 136.

had ever heard of used his California gold rush earnings to plan a coup. While Sam Brannan's plan came to nothing, the kingdom was worried enough to organize a standing army.[46] As late as 1854 there were rumors of filibusters and plots being hatched in Honolulu.[47]

Missionaries had been concerned about private property since the '30s.[48] Foreigners invested years of sweat equity in their homes and in lands held at the pleasure of the king. They wanted outright ownership and a reliable labor force that could turn a profit. Concerns about labor shortages appeared in the Honolulu press by 1847.[49] With thousands of acres across the islands laying fallow in 1850, Kauikeaouli demanded "greatly increased cultivation of the soil," a bid that he acknowledged would rely upon the "aid of foreign capital and labor."[50] Two years later the kingdom imported some 300 contract laborers from China. Historians have tended to view this turn to immigrant labor as the exclusive desire of American planters and business interests. Yet Hawaiian elites were clearly concerned about the massive losses in the labor force (including some 10,000 lives in 1848–49 alone). Long before the kingdom looked abroad for plantation labor, that is to say, it contemplated the challenge of Native health. What could be done to stanch disease spread, increase fertility, and improve living conditions so that a *Hawaiian* kingdom might survive? Land reform was one option.

Addressing the king in 1847, Judge William Little Lee acknowledged that land reform would be attended with a "Multitude of difficulties." Nevertheless, it would be necessary to raise the people from a state of "hereditary servitude" to that of a "free & independent right in the soil they cultivate." Privatization, Lee assured the king, would "promote industry and agriculture, check depopulation," and ultimately prove

[46] Richard Armstrong journal, Nov. 7, 1851, HMCS. See also Daws, *Shoal of Time*, 137–38; Greenberg, *Manifest Manhood*, 235–38.

[47] Diary of Sarah Joiner Lyman (July 21, 1854), in Martin, ed., *Lymans of Hilo*, 135. *Putnam's Monthly Magazine* (New York) and *De Bow's Review* (New Orleans and Washington, DC) were influential organs of annexation and filibustering focused on Hawai'i; see Greenberg, *Manifest Manhood*, 231–61.

[48] "Sandwich Islands: Statements Relative to the Population and the Progress of the Mission," *Missionary Herald* 32 (Sept. 1836): 358–59.

[49] Greer, "Honolulu in 1847," 70.

[50] Kuykendall, *Hawaiian Kingdom*, 1:329. See also Schmitt and Nordyke, "Death in Hawai'i," 11. Starting in 1847 the kingdom offered tax relief to those who cultivated "undeveloped" lands, a scheme that Osorio argues was about more than profits or capitalist expansion: cultivation of the 'āina had long been the "basis for, and also a sign of, a healthy and prosperous" nation (*Dismembering Lāhui*, 47).

the "Salvation of Your People."[51] Most missionaries (and former missionaries, now in government) agreed that granting Islanders real property in cultivable land was their best chance of survival in the long run.

Maka'āinana feared the worst. In the thousands, they petitioned the monarchy to prevent the Māhele. Foreigners hungry for land arrived with hard currency, but commoners lacked the means. Maui Islanders implored Keoni Ana to protect their "right of being *kamaaina* [children of the land] of Waiohuli." Without his support they feared the 'āina would be "taken by strangers ... and we and our children ... become wanderers in the land."[52] Under the new regime, "we shall immediately be overcome," read a petition from Lahaina. "The native is disabled like one who has long been afflicted with a disease upon his back."[53]

These concerns proved legitimate. Corruption was rife in the Māhele, and some chiefs prevented commoners from filing land claims. Many more lacked the requisite information to make claims they were entitled to. By 1854, maka'āinana, comprising perhaps 95 percent of the population, owned just 1 percent of the land, while kingdom officials enjoyed enormous wealth.[54] While privatization was orchestrated in large part by haole in the kingdom, a number of ruling chiefs were on board, not least because they feared being left with nothing should the islands be annexed by a foreign power.[55]

Land reform also had cultural effects. For one thing, the ties that bound ali'i and maka'āinana were permanently torn. For another, all Hawaiians were rendered "competitors" rather than "caretakers of the 'āina," a considerable shift in orientation.[56] Henceforth, it would be impossible for maka'āinana to "subsist on the land without participating in the market economy."[57] In the revised Constitution of 1852, adult male subjects (that is, Hawaiians and naturalized foreigners) were granted the right to vote for their Representatives, though not for Nobles. Political

[51] William Little Lee (Dec. 18, 1847), qtd. in Kame'eleihiwa, *Native Land*, 215. Later, Lee protected Hawaiian sovereignty by adding a clause to the US treaty of annexation that would have made Hawai'i a state rather than a territory, with Hawaiians enjoying the full rights of citizens. An anti-annexationist, Lee knew that racist American congressmen would flatly reject the treaty on this basis, which they did (Daws, *Shoal of Time*, 152–53).
[52] Sahlins, *Anahulu*, 1:137.
[53] Kenui et al., "Concerning Foreigners Taking the Oath of Allegiance," *The Friend*, Aug. 1, 1845 (translated from the original in *Ka Elele Hawaii*).
[54] Brown, *Facing the Spears of Change*, 151–52.
[55] Banner, *Possessing the Pacific*, 146–62. [56] Osorio, *Dismembering Lāhui*, 55.
[57] Linnekin, *Sacred Queens*, 195.

reform thus saw the triumph of capitalism and limited representative democracy.

What role did Hawaiian health play in the Māhele? Disease and population decline created a perfect storm for the Māhele to have maximum impact. Three epidemics struck the islands in the midst of reforms. Measles entered Hilo in 1848, apparently on a US ship from Mazatlán.[58] Around the same time, a new strain of whooping cough entered Oʻahu via California. In December, influenza struck Islanders across the archipelago and carried off a number of elderly people. A particularly cold and stormy season seems to have exacerbated the flu and whooping cough. Measles, for its part, killed scores and was attended by potentially fatal diarrhea, especially for young children. Dwight Baldwin claimed that "thousands" in western Maui were afflicted by diarrhea.[59]

Taken together, the disease outbreaks of 1848–49 were the most costly in human life since the eighteenth century. While some missionaries and government officials had gained useful experience treating victims of infectious disease, there was no vaccine for measles and little to be done for either of the respiratory diseases. Missionary Amos Cooke and legislator John Papa ʻIʻi distributed arrowroot pills as antidiarrheals, with Cooke reporting that some were "made better" by it but others "refused" his medicine.[60] How many died of measles-induced diarrhea is not known. To make matters worse, some kāhuna lapaʻau and imposters charged victims extortionary prices for medicine and healing treatments.[61] "Never was I more depressed in regard to the natives," wrote Armstrong from Honolulu. "It w[oul]d seem to be the delight of God to blot them from the face of the earth. Almost the entire population has been prostrate &

[58] "Sickness," *Polynesian*, Oct. 14, 1848. Measles and whooping cough were reported in Honolulu and Hilo in Oct. 1848. I have been unable to find references to measles in the Hawaiian-language press before 1867 ("*No ka mai Ulalii*," [On Measles], *Ka Nupepa Kuokoa*, Nov. 9, 1867).

[59] D. Baldwin to E. B. Robinson, qtd. in Schmitt and Nordyke, "Death in Hawaiʻi," 6. Like influenza, mumps, and the common cold, the measles virus is spread through the air, but it can also survive on objects such as bedding. The virus is highly contagious. An asymptomatic incubation period of ten days enables further spread. Measles in the nineteenth-century developed world was primarily an endemic disease of childhood like mumps and whooping cough (Robert J. Kim-Farley, "Measles," in Kiple, ed., *Cambridge World History of Human Disease*, 871–75).

[60] Richards, *Chiefs' Children's School*, 316. One-time advisor to Liholiho, ʻIʻi was now a Noble.

[61] S. Waimalu to D. Baldwin, July 24, 1849, trans. Mabel K. A. Awai, HEA Archives, HMCS.

great numbers die daily in this place."[62] In early December the monarchy announced a day of "fasting, humiliation, and prayer." Never before, another missionary observed, had "God laid his Hand so heavily on these people."[63] The census of 1849 recorded 1,478 births total (foreigners and Hawaiians) and 7,943 deaths. The overall death toll from the combined epidemics may well have reached ten thousand, one-tenth of the islands' population.[64]

As terrible as these epidemics were, tuberculosis was the leading cause of death by midcentury. A chronic and slow-moving killer, the disease typically failed to make news. Yet not only did tuberculosis play a larger role in population decline than other diseases, it may have also discriminated by sex. Scholars have posited various explanations for the dearth of females in nineteenth-century Hawai'i; tuberculosis rarely enters the discussion. Perhaps the best case to be made for tuberculosis disproportionately affecting women and girls is the fact that censuses in Fiji, New Zealand, the Cooks, and the Marquesas – all struggling with the disease – also counted fewer females than males.[65] Further study will be required to understand the causes of skewed sex ratios in Hawai'i and other Polynesian societies in this period. One thing is clear: Hawaiian sex disparities were no statistical error or fiction.

MANA OF THE GODS

Infant mortality and infertility (among both women and men) were major causes of the staggering population decline on the islands to midcentury.

---

[62] Richard Armstrong journal, Nov. 12, 1848, HMCS.

[63] D. Baldwin to E. B. Robinson, qtd. in Schmitt and Nordyke, "Death in Hawai'i," 9.

[64] *The Friend*, March 1 and Nov. 15, 1849. Chiefs perishing in 1848–49 included William Pitt Leleiohoku I, Gideon P. La'anui, Aarona Keali'iahonui, Moses Kekūāiwa, Keaweamahi, Ka'imina'au'ao, George Na'ea, and the hapa haole chiefesses Elizabeth Peke Davis and Theresa Owana Kaheiheimalie Rives.

[65] Gilson, *Cook Islands*, 35–36; Pool, *Te Iwi Maori*, 42–53; Luker, "Mothers of the Taukei," 22–25; Dening, *Islands and Beaches*, 280. In late-'40s Rarotonga, the largest of the Cook Islands, the ratio of unmarried adult men to women was as high as two to one. For earlier discussions of sex disparities in nineteenth-century Hawai'i, see Plews, "Charles Darwin and Hawaiian Sex Ratios"; Linnekin, *Sacred Queens*, 207–12; Crosby, "Hawaiian Depopulation as a Model." Female infanticide was common in the nineteenth century worldwide, but there is insufficient evidence of it in Hawai'i to account for the sex ratios (cf. Crosby, "Hawaiian Depopulation as a Model"). Stannard, however, overstated his case by characterizing infanticide as a "political myth" ("Recounting the Fables of Savagery"). Abortion and infanticide probably occurred at rates comparable to other Indigenous Pacific societies in this period (e.g., Pool, *Te Iwi Maori*, 47–48).

Strictly speaking, there are no statistics on reproduction and infant mortality in this period. Nevertheless, change can be traced in more than an impressionistic way. Among ali'i, it is known who managed to have children, who did not, and the fate of most offspring who survived infancy. Local rates of reproduction and infant mortality among maka'āinana can be gleaned from missionary censuses. For many Islanders, childlessness and infertility were the norm rather than the exception. Cultural iterations of the phenomenon are abundant in the historical record.

Recognizing the low rate of reproduction soon after his arrival on the Big Island in 1837, missionary physician Seth Andrews began to compile statistics, which he reported both to the ABCFM and to other visitors. In a sample of ninety-six married women on the Kona coast ("nearly all" of them under the age of forty-five), Andrews found that twenty-three had no children. The remaining seventy-three had a total of 299 children, yet 152 of these did not survive past two years of age; another six died between the ages of two and ten, and fourteen died at age ten or older.[66] Since it was clear to Andrews that the climate of Hawai'i was healthy "even to the tender infant," he concluded that the high rate of infant mortality must be due to Hawaiians' "insufficient clothing . . . improper food & want of cleanliness."[67]

Other observers provided more subtle explanations. Former legislator and judge Samuel Kamakau wrote of a cousin who had struggled for twenty-five years to become pregnant, finally managing to do so at age forty-five. Kamakau attributed this happy fact to the intervention of the couple's elders: the couple had "asked their old folks for a child, and were told they would have a child, a daughter, and they did have a daughter."[68] Kamakau did not need to explain that his cousin's "old folks" likely had first right of refusal to this newborn, according to the custom of *kupuna* (grandparent) kinship, where children were commonly adopted by older relatives to reinforce familial ties.[69] What is surprising is that Kamakau's cousin and her husband were devout Christians, having been married by the leader of the New England Protestant mission in the '20s and having lived out their childless quarter century "under proper marriage conditions," that is, in monogamous Christian matrimony.[70] Other childless

---

[66] Seth L. Andrews to Anderson, Aug. 22, 1840, in ABCFM Papers; Wilkes, *Narrative of the United States Exploring Expedition*, 4:95–96.

[67] Andrews to Anderson, Aug. 22, 1840, in ABCFM Papers. For comparable infant-mortality figures a decade later at Lahaina, see Stannard, "Disease and Infertility," 334.

[68] Kamakau, *Ka Po'e Kahiko*, 99.   [69] Sahlins, *Anahulu*, 1:196–208.

[70] Kamakau, *Ka Po'e Kahiko*, 100.

Hawaiian couples, making note of missionary fecundity, sought out Christian matrimony. "The circumstance was so manifest," one observer wrote, "that women as old as [the Biblical] Sarah called on the missionaries, requesting to be re-united to their husbands according to the christian ceremonial, hoping thereby to be made fruitful."[71]

Yet try as they might, missionaries were unable to enforce what were to them clear boundaries between "degenerate heathenism" and the true path of the righteous God. Hawaiians everywhere selectively added elements of the new religions to their own ideological arsenal and daily rituals. And wherever Native religious ritual continued to serve a function – reinforcing social hierarchies, connecting people to their ancestors or kin, or simply easing an anxious mind – it could not, and would not, be rooted out. Thus it was that a childless, aging, devoutly Christian couple sought intervention from their elders and from the "mana of the gods" to become fruitful. In short, neither Christian practice nor the kāhuna could make an exclusive claim on Islanders, whether ali'i or maka'āinana.

To some historians, it is clear that common Hawaiians shared their monarchs' concerns about the population crisis: the people were "desperate to have ... children who survived, and they did everything in their power to counter the devastating effects of introduced disease on their low birth rates and on their high levels of infant mortality."[72] Kamakau's stories are more equivocal. Hawaiians who wanted children did everything they could to perpetuate their lines. But they also continued to practice family planning as they had for centuries.[73] Hawaiians were aware of population decline; they saw it everywhere. They were aware, too, of the growth of the foreign population, and of foreigners' increasing role in government. But it does not follow that the fertility crisis was an existential concern to individuals or that they took it upon themselves, in any significant numbers, to fix it. Certainly high-ranking chiefly families who hoped to perpetuate their status and maintain a form of Hawaiian

---

[71] Chapin, "Remarks on the Venereal Disease," 92.

[72] Stannard, "Recounting the Fables of Savagery," 404. See also Stannard, "Disease and Infertility," 334.

[73] For a childless woman who sought out a Native fertility specialist (*kahuna ho'ohapai keiki*), bore more than ten children, and then resorted to abortion and other means of family planning, see Kamakau, *Ka Po'e Kahiko*, 100–1. Among other fertility aids were morning glory (*koali*) blossoms inserted into the vagina before intercourse ("Fragments of Hawaiian Methods for Treating the Sick," n.d., Hawaiian Ethnographic Notes, 6:1629, BM). See also Pukui et al., *Nānā i ke Kumu*, 2:102.

rule, however attenuated, were concerned about their own subfecundity. But among commoners, it is likely that abortion and infanticide continued as usual, possibly increasing due to illness and poverty, at the same time that the population plummeted and their monarchs implored them to reproduce. This is not to say that family planning played a significant role in population decline.[74] After complaining about child neglect and infanticide through the '20s, not one of the eleven missionaries surveyed in 1846 believed infanticide or abortion to be a serious problem in their district.[75]

Solutions were hard to come by. Discovering that population loss was not unique to Hawai'i was of no help. Hawai'i-based ABCFM missions to the Marquesas in the '50s discovered population loss on those islands that mirrored their own. While the causes of decrease on the Marquesas were not limited to disease, Hawaiian missionary Samuel Kauwealoha highlighted smallpox, measles, typhoid fever, and dysentery as major culprits.[76]

For many, the pressing question was how to repopulate the land and bolster the kinship ties that were the bedrock of society. In the late '40s evidence surfaced of Native religious and medical practice among the maka'āinana. In response to Minister Wyllie's question about the "number of idolators or heathen still remaining" in their districts, most missionaries identified few, yet their answers suggested that interest in these activities was great. In Makawao district in central Maui, Green noted that there were "some superstitious doings" which were "in some way mixed up with their medical prescriptions." Armstrong in Honolulu noted that "many" people, especially older folks, "adhere to some idolatrous customs," while "others connect some mysterious rites with the healing art." Parker considered idolatry to be common in central Maui, where the people maintained a belief in 'anā'anā. At Waialua, O'ahu, Emerson noted that few would "avow idol worship" publicly; on the other hand, there were hundreds of people gathering on the north shore of O'ahu (at the very moment Emerson was writing) to visit a man who "has the power to heal diseases miraculously." Nor was this a unique case. There had been "several" such healers during the past year, Emerson noted, who had "received attentions from many." Interestingly, some

---

[74] Cf. Malo, "On the Decrease of Population"; Bushnell, *Gifts of Civilization*, 293.
[75] Armstrong et al., *Answers to Questions*, 65. See also Wilkes, *Narrative of the United States Exploring Expedition*, 4:63.
[76] Dening, *Islands and Beaches*, 259.

female healers on Oʻahu claimed the ability to channel the mana of the current Queen, Kalama, and the deceased high chiefess Nāhiʻenaʻena. "Such kind of idolatry as this is abundant," Emerson concluded.[77]

Interest in traditional religious practices and ideology was hardly short-lived. In the wake of the 1848–49 epidemics, Hawaiian Protestant minister S. Waimalu wrote a series of short letters to Dwight Baldwin in Lahaina describing conditions among his parishioners in the Waiʻanae district of western Oʻahu. Among other problems Waimalu identified was renewed interest in Native medicine and declining participation in his church. "The deacons all have left the work of the Lord," Waimalu reported, "gone after money by fishing" instead.[78] Many still believed in the "old Hawaiian medicine and Hawaiian idols." The "Lord's work in Waianae," he concluded, was "rather weak."[79]

Low fertility alone might have been endured; high mortality and premature death among aliʻi ranks could not. The unremitting nature of their losses in this period is amply illustrated in the House of Nobles. The upper house of government consisted of fifteen to eighteen members appointed for life. All but a few Nobles were Hawaiian aliʻi. Between 1841 and 1852 fourteen of them perished in office.[80] When family members were available, they were tapped as replacements. Otherwise, haole were happy to keep the seats warm. The most powerful woman in the kingdom at this time, the kuhina nui Kekauʻōnohi, was married four times during her life, each time to a Hawaiian aliʻi (Fig. 6.2). She bore just one child, who died young, perhaps in infancy. (The child, William Pitt Kīnaʻu II, would have become king.) Kekauʻōnohi herself died in 1851 of unknown causes at the age of forty-six. Because she was without children, she became foster parent to two hānai children. In this, she followed a pattern set by the earlier childless queen, Kaʻahumanu. Kekauʻōnohi would be in good company in the decade ahead: the 1860 census revealed one birth for every eleven and a half women.[81]

---

[77] Armstrong et al., *Answers to Questions*, 59. In private correspondence, missionaries were even more pessimistic about Native idolatry and the prospects for Hawaiian Christianity. See letters between Artemas Bishop and his son Sereno Bishop, 1845–52 (Sereno Edwards Bishop Collection, Box 1, HL).

[78] S. Waimalu to Dwight Baldwin, July 25, 1849, trans. M. K. A. Awai, HEA Archives, HMCS.

[79] S. Waimalu to Dwight Baldwin, Dec. 22, 1848, trans. M. K. A. Awai, HEA Archives, HMCS. For the epigraph that heads this chapter, see ibid.

[80] Osorio, *Dismembering Lāhui*, 88.

[81] [Abraham Fornander], "Let us look the situation ...," *Polynesian*, Aug. 2, 1862. This subject was close to home for Fornander, whose wife had lost four of their five children in

FIGURE 6.2 Kekau'ōnohi.
Henry L. Chase, no date. Courtesy of Bishop Museum (SP96920).

SEX LAWS, SMALLPOX

Under missionary influence in the '40s and '50s, the kingdom aspired to render positive changes in Native life. Reform efforts targeted sexual behavior, drinking, gambling, public disorder, and failure to work. Native sexuality had long been a concern of missionaries trying to root out what they viewed as sinful practices. With the help of the ruling chiefs,

infancy; Pinao Alanakapu herself died from complications of childbirth in 1857 (Fornander, *Thirteen Letters*, 9–11).

sex laws – specifically, prosecution of adultery, fornication (sex between unmarried people), and prostitution – gained traction. While some Hawaiian Christians seemed genuinely to condemn *moe kolohe* ("mischievous sleeping"), they did so as often for religious or political reasons as for health.[82]

Practically no foreigners were prosecuted for sex crimes; cases against Hawaiians clogged the courts. Twenty-nine percent of *all* cases in Honolulu District Court in 1844–45 involved sex crimes. In Kaua'i, the following year: 63 percent. On the Big Island from April 1852 to December 1853: 44 percent. The vast majority of cases involving sex crimes ended in conviction. Interestingly, 90 percent of these cases involved adultery or fornication, which suggests that policing prostitution had taken a backseat to reform of Islander sexual behavior more broadly. For anthropologist Sally Engle Merry, sex laws were part of a missionary effort, motivated by notions of sin, propriety, and the liberal state, to reform the Hawaiian family and to manage Native bodies.[83] Yet missionaries firmly believed that reforms of this nature would improve Hawaiian health.

Social reform held little interest for most chiefs. Fewer still were concerned about the peoples' sexual practices. So why play along? In the first place, sex laws, like all laws, proved to the outside world that Hawai'i was a civilized, deserving nation.[84] Westernization, the chiefs hoped, would inoculate them against conquest. Sex crimes also generated useful forms of labor, as the convicted were set to building roads and other infrastructure without compensation. A single adultery conviction could result in as much as half a year's labor for maka'āinana.[85] In this way, Protestant law reinstated valuable forms of coerced labor that the ali'i had lost with the fall of the kapu. Whether any ali'i "accepted the missionary view" that reforming marriage and sex through legal measures would reverse or stem depopulation, as Malo and other converts did, is

---

[82] For a possible condemnation of fornication for health reasons, see S. Waimalu to Dwight Baldwin, Dec. 4, 1853, trans. M. K. A. Awai, HEA Archives, HMCS. Adultery and fornication were common causes of suspension of church membership.

[83] Merry, *Colonizing Hawai'i*. For the data cited above, see ibid., 222–25. The ratio of adultery and fornication cases to prostitution cases on Hawai'i Island in 1851 was nine to one (ibid., 223–24). Greer suggests that sex workers outnumbered police in 1847 Honolulu by "at least ten to one" ("Honolulu in 1847," 79).

[84] Merry, *Colonizing Hawai'i*, 221.

[85] Ibid., 251. Constables did much of the apprehending and enjoyed a cut of the proceeds derived from fines.

difficult to determine.[86] Yet they were certainly party to the criminaliza-
tion of maka'āinana sex.

And not only maka'āinana sex. Reform efforts extended to ali'i children. At the Chiefs' Children's School, missionaries enforced strict rules to
keep students separate. When that failed to prevent sexual encounters,
proprietors Amos and Juliette Cooke forced students to sign a "purity
pledge." Eventually, the school was closed after the epidemics of 1848–49
reduced their students to zero. In a letter to the ABCFM, Amos Cooke
regretted that few if any of the chiefs' children had been truly converted to
Christianity. One problem was that the students' health problems and
lack of practical skills distracted missionaries from spiritual work. As
Cooke put it, "our great care for their bodies and their progress in knowledge" constrained the work of evangelism among the young ali'i.[87] This
was distressing to the ABCFM, which viewed the uncertain political
environment and economic slump on the islands as threatening to undo
a quarter century of efforts. Missionaries were instructed to redouble their
efforts to raise up Hawaiian pastors to take the reins as quickly as
possible. In an exasperated letter to missionaries, the ABCFM secretary
argued that Islanders were "in danger of being excluded from all important offices and responsibilities, *both in church and state* . . . Nothing will
save the native government but a native ministry placed over the native
churches."[88]

The 1848–49 epidemics coincided with news of gold in California.
With Hawaiian men already boarding whale ships in large numbers, the
draw of the gold fields threatened to exacerbate the problem. To head off
massive emigration, the legislature passed an "Act to Prohibit Natives
from Leaving These Islands," signed by Kauikeaouli and Keoni Ana, the
kuhina nui and Minister of the Interior.[89] Many argonauts found ways
around the act. But the measure itself was aimed at putting the brakes on
population loss stemming from the recent epidemics and maintaining a
labor force for a promising new market in agricultural produce to supply
California.[90] With similar goals in mind, the legislature established the

---

[86] Ibid., 245. No restrictions were placed on interracial marriage. An interesting counter-
factual is whether Anglo-American missionaries would have created a tiered legal system,
such as apartheid, had the Native monarchy not endured to 1893.

[87] Menton, "Christian and 'Civilized' Education," 233.

[88] Rufus Anderson to Sandwich Islands Mission, April 10, 1846, qtd. in Kuykendall,
Hawaiian Kingdom, 1:337.

[89] See "An Act to Prohibit Natives from Leaving the Islands," *Polynesian*, Sept. 7, 1850.

[90] Daws, *Shoal of Time*, 173.

kingdom's first Board of Health in May 1851, with Keoni Ana as president. The board's explicit purpose was to prevent epidemics, by monitoring quarantines in port, inspecting houses where disease might be present, and managing gravesites.

That autumn, the man who had orchestrated the Māhele wrote to a former US Consul to Hawai'i about his perceptions of the Hawaiian people. Chief Justice and House Speaker William Little Lee had recently completed a seven-week tour of the islands amid an economic downturn. It is difficult to know whether a struggling economy colored his impressions. For all their good traits, Lee wrote, the people lacked the "elements necessary to perpetuate their existence." "I consider the doom of this nation as sealed," he concluded, "though I will labor on without ceasing, hoping for the blessing of heaven to bring some change."[91] A few months later the *Polynesian* printed an "Important Correction." The paper had printed faulty vital statistics in its previous issue: 5,792 deaths across the islands in 1851 (the proper figure was 2,792). With 2,424 births, the corrected ratio suggested a marked improvement from previous years. An exuberant editor anticipated a 5 or 6 percent annual increase in the Native population.[92]

Then smallpox arrived. Thousands of Hawaiians took ill, and as many as 6,000 died across the islands within a year.[93] Quarantine laws in effect since 1839 were no match for the volume and increased speed of ships crossing the eastern Pacific.[94] Among others who arrived aboard those fast ships were Mormon missionaries from the unrecognized State of Deseret (Utah). Unaffiliated with the kingdom and unattached to local people through kinship networks, the newcomers nevertheless provided illuminating accounts of the epidemic.

After two years on the islands with little to show for their evangelical efforts, a handful of "Saints" spent the summer of 1853 ministering to those who would allow them to come near and arguing with Protestants

[91] W. L. Lee to Joel Turrill, Oct. 11, 1851, in "Turrill Collection," 47. Lee was in the process of drafting the revised Constitution of 1852.

[92] "Important Correction," *Polynesian*, May 8, 1852. Below this article appeared an obituary for ali'i James Kaliokalani, who had died in Lahaina, aged sixteen ("Died," ibid.).

[93] Greer, "Oahu's Ordeal," 261. The virus arrived on the *Charles Mallory* from San Francisco.

[94] Kīna'u, "*He Kanawai No Ka Mai Puupuu*" (A Law Regarding Smallpox), Board of Health Papers, HSA.

over their right to treat the sick.[95] Many Hawaiians who had expressed an interest in the new missionaries disappeared from sight; others requested baptism and especially faith healing, the Saints' signature rite. Yet reports from the field were grim: an Oʻahu man who had been ordained a Mormon priest and was "well and hearty to all appearances" weeks before was now "so disfigured with the small pox that no traces of his countenances [*sic*] were discoverable & his throat was so stopped up [with lesions] that his voice was scarcely audible."[96] Another "Saint" had lost most of the skin on her face and was "so far gone" in her illness that she could not recognize the missionaries. "Scarcely a day" passed without "someone of the Brethren or sisters . . . dying of" smallpox.[97] As many as a third of the Hawaiian Saints on Oʻahu died. More destructive to the Mormon cause itself was Hawaiian apostasy in its wake.

Honolulu became a charnel house. Government wagons carted the sick and dead through town, and yellow flags hung in doorways.[98] On Maui, legislator and judge Samuel Kamakau, who had no medical training, busied himself administering vaccines. Some infected residents were sent to Oʻahu to be "placed in hospitals," he noted, but many others died of "ignorance" or "stupidity" by failing to take precautions or following improper treatments. In the small village of Hana alone, thirty-nine had perished by September. Kamakau estimated that one-eighth of those who contracted the disease in eastern Maui recovered, but "most ha[d]" died.[99] In fact, overall mortality rates for infected Islanders may have approached 50 percent locally.[100]

---

[95] See W. Farrer diary, July–Aug. 1853, HBLL. A few of these cases actually went to court. A three-day quarantine imposed by Mormon missionaries on converts traveling from Honolulu to Lahaina probably did little to prevent infection (W. Farrer diary, Oct. 1, 1853, HBLL).

[96] Ibid., June 28, 1853. Kamahiʻai, who was a priest, died the evening of July 1 (ibid., July 2, 1853). Farrer himself developed symptoms of smallpox, including its characteristic blisters, but was restored within days (ibid., July 16, 1853).

[97] Ibid., Aug. 23 and 26, 1853. Vaccination campaigns had been poorly executed by foreigners in the government, and some Islanders resisted vaccination when offered (E. Green diary, June 13, 1853, HBLL; Greer, "Oahu's Ordeal"; Kenney, "Mormons and the Smallpox Epidemic"). There has been no study on fertility and the smallpox epidemic; cases elsewhere indicate a possible decline in male fertility (Stannard, "Disease and Infertility," 343).

[98] Daws, *Shoal of Time*, 141.

[99] Kamakau to Dwight Baldwin, Sept. 14 and 19, 1853, trans. Henry P. Judd, HMCS. A March 1854 report for Maui listed 280 cases total and 124 dead (Greer, "In the Shadow of Death," 315).

[100] Greer, "Oahu's Ordeal," 261; Greer, "In the Shadow of Death," 321. Kamakau recorded a few local remedies for smallpox (*Ka Poʻe Kahiko*, 25).

FIGURE 6.3 Honuakaha smallpox cemetery, Quinn Lane, Honolulu. Hundreds are believed to be buried under the Kaka'ako Fire Station parking lot, rear of photograph.
Courtesy of the author.

Like Kamakau, former missionary Richard Armstrong, now Minister of Education, blamed the epidemic on Islanders' carelessness, "ignorance[,] and stupidity."[101] He then called an emergency meeting of the Privy Council to urge a day of "humiliation, fasting and prayer that the Almighty may remove from among us the smallpox now spreading everywhere." The council passed Armstrong's proclamation, but not without strident criticism from the less supernaturally inclined non-missionary press.[102] Other missionaries and at least one mission doctor were too busy trying to save

[101] Greer, "Oahu's Ordeal," 235.   [102] Ibid., 227.

lives to bother with proclamations and finger-pointing.[103] Nevertheless, in the wake of the disaster, Judd, Minister of Finance and the islands' leading physician, was widely blamed for lack of planning. Immunization of Hawaiians had been piecemeal before 1853, and the vaccine matter that had not already expired was in short supply when needed most. Worst of all, Judd had rejected a proposal by Honolulu physicians just before the outbreak to inoculate Islanders on Oʻahu at government expense (ten cents per person).[104] Few Native Hawaiians had been inoculated or vaccinated against what seems in hindsight the inevitable introduction of the smallpox *variola*.[105]

In the summer of 1853, the Royal Commissioners of Health posted a notice around Honolulu, attesting to the problem of unburied corpses. Public Notice No. 5 announced that henceforth "all able-bodied men ... recovered from the Small Pox" were "liable to be called on to render assistance in burying the dead, without remuneration."[106] After the epidemic, a meeting of prominent foreigners was called and a petition circulated, signed by Hawaiians and foreigners alike, accusing Judd of "criminal parsimony and neglect," "selfish cupidity," and "malfeasance in office." Judd was shortly ousted from both Finance and the Privy Council, although his supporters – again, both foreigner and Native – cried foul.[107]

The monarchy had escaped smallpox – a crowd disease, like measles – mostly unscathed. But their health was not good. In summer 1854, Kamakau reported to missionary physician Dwight Baldwin that while the king had recently enjoyed good health and was drinking less, Keoni Ana had been "very ill caused by much drinking."[108] Earlier that spring, legislators had debated multiple bills on the sale of liquor and public intoxication. Kamakau reported as many as "400 drunkards" in Lahaina and decided that it would be "better to forbid" the sale of alcohol entirely. "My idea," he wrote to Baldwin, "is that Lahaina should be

---

[103] Baldwin vaccinated some 2,000 residents of Maui against smallpox in 1842. During the 1853 outbreak, he worked "in a flurry" to vaccinate people in eastern Maui and on Lānaʻi, likely saving hundreds of lives (Alexander, *Dr. Baldwin of Lahaina*, 232–40; Greer, "In the Shadow of Death," 312–15).

[104] Greer, "Oahu's Ordeal," 250.

[105] Compare this to New Zealand, where Māori were inoculated in significant numbers before the arrival of smallpox (Dow, *Maori Health*, 47–56).

[106] Halford, *9 Doctors & God*, 210.

[107] Judd, *Dr. Judd: Hawaii's Friend*, 203–4. To be sure, anti-Judd sentiment was at least as old as the Paulet affair; see, e.g., Simpson, *Sandwich Islands*, 56–58.

[108] Kamakau to Dwight Baldwin, July 28, 1854, trans. H. P. Judd, HMCS.

peaceful."[109] Then, in December, after years of poor health and increasing fits of delirium tremens, Kauikeaouli died.[110]

WEST INDIES OF THE PACIFIC

Many assumed that a struggling Hawaiian kingdom would collapse with the death of its king.[111] In fact, transfer of power to Kauikeaouli's brother Alexander Liholiho (Kamehameha IV) went off without a hitch (Fig. 6.4).[112] When the US formally rejected plans to annex the islands in 1855, two major crises, it seemed, had been averted. Yet Hawai'i's rulers were aware that a single vote in a foreign legislature could spell the end of the kingdom. For this reason Kauikeaouli's diplomats carried blank documents with his signature in case an agreement of protection or outright annexation became necessary.[113] The diplomats themselves were all haole.

It is not clear when government officials began to think about immigrant labor as a solution to the population problem as opposed merely to labor shortages. But when some 300 Chinese contract laborers arrived on Maui sugar plantations in 1852, a pattern was quickly established.[114] Many stayed on past their contracts, and most of these men found Hawaiian wives. While Islanders in considerable numbers continued to work in sugar through the '60s, imported labor for plantation agriculture appeared to be Hawai'i's future.[115]

Observers quickly noted the health implications of intermarriage. In an article for the *New-York Journal of Medicine,* missionary son and physician Luther H. Gulick wrote that the "children of alliances between natives and Chinese, or negroes, or any of the European nations, are far more healthy, and are better physically developed than those of pure Hawaiian blood." Gulick was not sure whether this development was due to the "exhaustion" of native "blood" or simply superior parenting by the foreign half. While the hapa haole population was still small, there was reason to think it would grow rapidly. Besides the benefits of racial

---

[109] Kamakau to Dwight Baldwin, April 26, April 29, and May 3, 1854, trans. H. P. Judd, HMCS. Temperance reforms began in the mid-'20s. At the movement's peak, temperance meetings were mandatory for young ali'i at the Chiefs' Children's School (Lot Kapuāiwa diary, Aug. 5, 1844, HMCS).

[110] William Richards journal, Dec. 24, 1854, HMCS.   [111] Daws, *Shoal of Time,* 112.

[112] S. J. Lyman diary (March 5, 1855), in Martin, ed., *Lymans of Hilo,* 135.

[113] Daws, *Shoal of Time,* 135.

[114] Char and Char, "First Chinese Contract Laborers," 128. Few Asian women immigrated before 1870, but many later joined men on the plantations.

[115] Kuykendall, *Hawaiian Kingdom,* 2:125; Kessler, "Plantation upon a Hill."

FIGURE 6.4 From left, Queen Kalama, Alexander Liholiho (Kamehameha IV), Kauikeaouli (Kamehameha III), Lota Kapuāiwa (Kamehameha V), Victoria Kamāmalu. The three siblings were all children of Kīna'u and Mataio Kekūanāo'a; Kauikeaouli and Kalama were childless. "The Kamehameha Royal Family." Hugo Stangenwald, ca. 1853. Courtesy of Bishop Museum (SP41657).

mixing, Gulick observed, the islands' "almost unparalleled salubrity [would] rapidly make them a noted resort for the united objects of pleasure and health." This was particularly to be expected as the islands continued to be "populated by a race of higher civilization, and as the luxuries of life are multiplied and diffused." Gulick could not pretend that the islands were free from the ravages of disease; to him, however, such woes were the exclusive reserve of Native Hawaiians and a direct result of "their miserable modes of living."[116]

Intermarriage, to Gulick's thinking, would save Hawaiians while also raising the racial stock of island society. This mattered to Gulick because

---

[116] Gulick, "On the Climate, Diseases and Materia Medica," 191, 169, 178, 194. News of the smallpox epidemic clearly had not reached Gulick in Micronesia: "*Small-pox* has never spread among the [Hawaiian] people, and should it now arrive they are probably quite well prepared for it by vaccination" (ibid., 194).

Hawai'i itself mattered. The islands' produce and their healthfulness (for foreigners) promised to make Hawai'i an appendage of the United States. Politicians would sort out the particulars, but Hawai'i *would* become American. Portions of Gulick's article were shortly reprinted in the *American Journal of Pharmacy,* published in Philadelphia. In a prefatory note to the article, the journal's editor (a professor at the Philadelphia College of Pharmacy) emphasized the "great importance" of Hawai'i's "tropical productions." These products – sugarcane, coffee, arrowroot, and salt – should be "increased and encouraged," the editor argued, so that Hawai'i could "become to the Pacific states what the Bahamas and Cuba at present are to the Atlantic region," namely, "a perennial fruit garden and salubrious resort to the invalid."[117] Gulick, the professor, and tens of thousands of Americans would get their wish.

Even after the kapu were abolished, it was not unusual to see "old men and women ... wrinkled and flabby-skinned, with eyelids hanging shut," Kamakau wrote in 1867. "One does not see such people today."[118] Despite the growth of the foreign population, the islands reached a new low in 1850 of 86,000 persons, a decrease of more than 80 percent since the arrival of Cook. Smallpox killed as many as six thousand more. Ordinary Hawaiians were increasingly torn from their loved ones by disease-induced mortality and from the land by the rise of a capitalist economy. The Māhele had proved a disaster for common Hawaiians, rendering them largely landless and voiceless in a kingdom where foreigners wrote the laws and their chiefs were more vulnerable than ever. In a cruel twist, the loss of so many Hawaiian lives made even more lands available for foreigners. A major concern of officials was how to keep the Hawaiian people from disappearing, as they saw it, off the face of the earth. The turn to immigrant labor, though never without controversy, would prove the major influence in reshaping Hawaiian society to the end of the century.

---

[117] [William Procter, Jr.], prefatory note to "On the Materia Medica of the Sandwich Islands," by Luther H. Gulick, *American Journal of Pharmacy* 27 (1855): 234–35. See also Armstrong et al., *Answers to Questions,* 15–17. An excitable and unquenchable US empire also eyed Japan and Latin America in the '50s (Greenberg, *Manifest Manhood,* 231–68).

[118] Kamakau, *Ruling Chiefs,* 172. For the original passage in Hawaiian, see *Ka Nupepa Kuokoa,* June 8, 1867.

Conclusion

Lele wale aku la. (It has flown.)[1]

Celebrations marked the birth of a prince in 1859. The first surviving child born to a sitting monarch in more than forty years, Prince Albert symbolized not only hope for a Hawaiian future but also the salvation of the kingdom. When Albert died suddenly at the age of four, the national mood shifted. A year later, Albert's father, twenty-nine-year-old Kamehameha IV, died from complications of asthma. Eighty years after the first venereal scourge unleashed by Cook's men, it was clear that health problems continued to vex commoners and chiefs alike.

A decade later, in an 1872 legislative session, Rep. Samuel Kamakau delivered "fecundity instructions," complete with prayer instructions to the akua Kū and Hina, to the assembled chiefs.[2] Meanwhile, government officials scoured the western Pacific and Southeast Asia for "cognate races" to import for industrial sugar production.[3] The key, according to missionary son Sanford B. Dole – uncle of the man who later founded the Pacific's largest fruit empire – was not to "displace" Hawaiians but rather to "supplement" them.[4] This future President of the Republic of Hawai'i stressed the importance of incorporating immigrants as "settlers and citizens" rather than as "convicts and coolies." Families, concluded

---

[1] Closing to a Hawaiian prayer.
[2] Spencer, ed., *Buke 'Oihana Lapa'au*, trans. Justin Kepo'o Keli'ipa'akaua, 18.
[3] Kuykendall, *Hawaiian Kingdom*, 2:177–95, esp. 182.
[4] S. B. Dole, "The Problem of Population," *Pacific Commercial Advertiser*, Sept. 28, 1872.

Dole, not plantations, "constitute the true basis of state prosperity and therefore the first object of our needs."[5]

Debates about immigration policy and population decline were already decades old when Dole published those opinions. The "solutions" worked out in the second half of the nineteenth century – a plantation complex fueled by immigrant labor; the Bayonet Constitution and overthrow of the monarchy; and annexation by the US – can all be traced in some way to the dual problems of Native health and population loss. Yet practically no memorials to Native health struggles can be found on the islands today. When I went searching for a smallpox memorial in Honolulu in 2013, I cycled past the site three times before realizing that the entrance, down a narrow alley, was obstructed by discarded mattresses, a soiled recliner, and other rubbish. Beneath the small commemorative plaque to "This Sacred Site" sat an air-conditioning unit and a broken television.

This book has suggested that the time is overdue for health to be incorporated into our narratives of Indigenous and colonial history. In Hawai'i the saga began when British men introduced syphilis, gonorrhea, and probably tuberculosis, setting the stage for decades of social discord. The "seeds" that Cook and his men "planted," in Kamakau's terms, "sprouted" and grew, presaging the arrival of other "things which weaken the body."[6] By the 1790s women and girls were being exploited in a sex trade, while maka'āinana became subject to the chiefs' self-aggrandizement amid trade colonialism. By 1800 the birth rate had fallen precipitously. While people continued to practice Native medicine and to seek out trusted kāhuna, the religious laws that bound together island society fractured. Chiefesses in search of a new life nullified the kapu system and shortly allied with fecund Protestant missionary families, hoping the effect was contagious. By the 1830s a spirit of fatalism pervaded island life, with many Hawaiians anticipating their demise in the face of foreign onslaught. In the '40s missionaries infiltrated the kingdom's governing structures and created a new system of laws constraining women's freedoms and policing the sexual and other behavior of Islanders. Weakened by these outside forces, the kingdom also struggled to perpetuate itself by generating new offspring. The combined result was a monarchy hanging on by a thread. Eventually, American planters and businessmen executed a coup, and Hawaiian sovereignty was

---

[5] S. B. Dole, "Immigration," *Pacific Commercial Advertiser*, Oct. 26, 1872.
[6] Kamakau, *Ruling Chiefs*, 104.

extinguished. But the struggle continues, and Hawaiian culture thrives today in spite of what many view as an illegal occupation by the United States.

The illustration on the cover of this book suggests why. A woman holds a toddler to her breast.[7] She is the child's mother, though perhaps not biologically, given the custom of close-family adoption (hānai). She faces a man wearing a malo and a tattered sailor's coat. His body displays traditional tattoos and newer designs, like the rifle on his thigh. Perhaps the couple is married. If so, either person could be one of multiple spouses to the other. Or maybe they are siblings, in which case the man bears considerable responsibility for the child. The image highlights various aspects of cultural survival: Islanders' strategic incorporation of foreign commodities, the power of kinship and *kōkua* (help, care, aid), and the preservation of the lāhui (nation, people) through culture. Hānai is perhaps the best example. This age-old Polynesian institution took on increased importance amid rising mortality, decreased fertility, and precipitous population decline. Hānai protected vulnerable children, perpetuated kinship ties, and maintained Hawaiian families in the most trying of circumstances.

Hawai'i today is routinely crowned the healthiest US state, with low rates of obesity, diabetes, and cardiac disease.[8] Yet 240 years after Cook, Native Hawaiians suffer the worst health outcomes and lowest life expectancy of any group that calls the islands home.[9] The glaring fact that Hawai'i's Indigenous people cannot be counted among the Aloha State's healthy residents is only heightened by the constant presence of leisured global visitors who stroll its beaches and patronize its tiki bars. Beyond physical health, Native Hawaiians face a broad set of social challenges, from educational attainment and employment opportunities to household

---

[7] O'Brien demonstrates the nineteenth-century French fad of depicting the "natural woman" of the Pacific, often in nursing scenes (*Pacific Muse*, chap. 4).

[8] United Health Foundation, "America's Health Rankings 2016 Annual Report," www .americashealthrankings.org/learn/reports/2016-annual-report. The state has claimed the top spot for five straight years and has never been ranked lower than six since the study began in 1990; in 2016, Hawai'i scored "far better" than the "other top-five states" (ibid., 5).

[9] Blaisdell, "Health Status of Kanaka Maoli"; Johnson et al., "Papa Ola Lōkahi Hawaiian Health Update." The achievements of Papa Ola Lōhaki (the Native Hawaiian Health Board) and other island-based Indigenous health advocates should not be overlooked. Since 1988 Papa Ola Lōkahi has built an archipelago-wide Native health infrastructure while also training Native health professionals and educating the public. For the federal Native Hawaiian Health Care Improvement Act (NHHCIA) of 1988, see Papa Ola Lōkahi, *Ka 'Uhane Lōkahi*, 118–39. The NHHCIA was reauthorized as part of the 2010 Patient Protection and Affordable Care Act through 2019.

income, mental health and substance abuse, and incarceration. One in four Native Hawaiians on the islands lives in poverty.[10] In all this, they are not alone among Indigenous populations whose ancestral lands are now claimed by the United States. And not only the US; wherever data exist, Indigenous people worldwide tend to be poorer, less healthy, and shorter-lived than the non-Indigenous people who reside on their lands.[11] Meanwhile, Native peoples from the Amazon basin to the Indian Ocean continue to struggle with epidemiological intrusions not unlike those described in the early chapters of this book. The ongoing problems of colonialism and Indigenous health are thus hardly academic.

While solutions do not lie in the past, the more we learn about the history of Indigenous health, the better our chances of understanding the profound and lasting consequences of colonialism. Historians of health can also help Indigenous communities recover aspects of their past that go unrecognized or reinterpret aspects that are mischaracterized in received narratives. Finally, raising awareness about Native American and Indigenous health disparities may be one way to reenergize tired debates about federal and state obligations to Native nations and about the broader social safety net. Above all, the fact of Indigenous health struggles – past and present – underlines the profound resilience of Indigenous peoples and of their cultural survival against the odds.

---

[10] Native American poverty and health disparities are broadly recognized if little addressed by policymakers. For Hawaiian cases, see S. M. Kanaʻiaupuni et al., *Income and Poverty among Native Hawaiians* (Honolulu: Kamehameha Schools, 2005), www.ksbe.edu/_asse ts/spi/pdfs/reports/demography_well-being/05_06_5.pdf; *Native Hawaiian Educational Assessment Update 2009: A Supplement to Ka Huakaʻi 2005* (Honolulu: Kamehameha Schools, 2009), www.ksbe.edu/_assets/spi/pdfs/kh/KH_Supplemento9.pdf; David E. Stannard, "The Hawaiians: Health, Justice, and Sovereignty," in Fujikane and Okamura, eds., *Asian Settler Colonialism*, 161–69; Healani Sonoda, "A Nation Incarcerated," ibid., 99–115.

[11] Kunitz, "Globalization, States, and the Health of Indigenous Peoples," 1531; Jones, *Rationalizing Epidemics*, 227–28.

APPENDIX A

Hawaiian Terms for Venereal Disease[1]

Term	Alternates	Condition/translation	Source
ʻako	ʻakoʻako	infectious venereal disease, in females only? (*lit.*, "itch"; *fig.*, lust?); "name of a disease of females of bad character" (Andrews)	Andrews, Handy, PE, Kent
ʻaukoʻi	ʻanokoʻi	venereal tumor; bubo; swelling in groin; "a disease in the groin, resulting from pollution" (Andrews)	Andrews, PE, Kent
auwaihiki	awaiāhiki, ʻāwai, ʻēwai	swelling in groin; bubo; "a running disease in the groin from impure habits" (Andrews)	Andrews, Handy, PE, Kent
hahaʻi		swelling in groin; bubo; "name of a disease on the upper part of the thigh or groin, occasioned by impure connections and habits" (Andrews)	Andrews, Handy, PE, Kent
hoakakakala		stage of venereal infection	Handy

(continued)

---

[1] The contemporary term *maʻi lele ai* (sexually transmitted infection, *lit.*, "contagious intercourse sickness") was apparently not used in the nineteenth century; see Kōmike Huaʻōlelo et al., *Māmaka Kaiao*, s.v. "ai₁."

Term	Alternates	Condition/translation	Source
hilo²	maʻi hilo, ule hilo	gonorrhea; running sore (*ule* = penis)	KPH, Judd1, Andrews, Judd2, BOL, Handy, PE, Kent
hua ʻole		infertile (*hua* = fruit, testicles; thus, *lit.*, "no fruit")	Andrews, PE
ihu ʻole		syphilitic saddlenose (*lit.*, "no nose")	Kamakau, PE, Kent
kamaiowa		disease of genitalia in females (including nonvenereal conditions?)	Handy
kaokao³		syphilis	BLL, Andrews, Judd2, Kamakau, PE, Handy, Kent
kio		bubo, a manifestation of syphilis	Andrews, Handy, Kent
kohe ʻako	koheʻaka	venereal disease in females (*lit.*, "itching vagina")	Andrews, Handy, PE
kohekohe papa		stage of syphilis, in females?	Andrews, Handy
kohepopo		venereal disease in females, characterized by discharge (*lit.*, "rotten vagina")	BOL, HEN, Handy, PE
kōhoko	kohoko	syphilitic infection (nonspecific syphilis); a disease of the womb	Andrews, Handy, PE, Kent
kua nanaka	kuanaka	confluent syphilitic lesions on the back (could also refer to Hansen's disease)	Andrews, Kamakau, Handy, Kent
kulu⁴		gonorrhea, dysentery ("to drip, leak, trickle"; *fig.*,	BLL, Andrews, Handy, PE, Kent

(continued)

² Ship surgeon David Samwell seems to have heard *hilo* as "herore" in 1779; he translated it as "the Pox" (Beaglehole, *Journals*, 3:1233).
³ Missionary physician Gerrit P. Judd mistakenly believed *kaokao* to be distinct from both syphilis ("*pala*") and gonorrhea ("*ule hilo*"); *kaokao* was, he believed, "not brought from the foreign countries" (Hawaiian-language medical book, HMCS).
⁴ See discussion in Chun, *Hawaiian Medicine Book*, 61.

Term	Alternates	Condition/translation	Source
kuna	kunakuna	disparaging term for a chief whose mother was said to be a commoner; discharge from genitals) venereal disease in men (or scabies); "a dangerous sore; a species of itch difficult to cure" (Andrews 1865)	BLL, Andrews, PE
kūʻoha	hoʻokūʻoha	venereal disease of genitalia, either sex	Andrews, Handy, PE, Kent
lolena		impotent, incapacitated; infertile, barren, unproductive	Andrews, PE
maʻi ʻawa		infertility (*lit.*, "sour genitalia")	PE
maʻi ʻino		venereal disease (*lit.*, "sinful disease")	PE
maʻi kakai	hoakakai, hoakakakai	syphilitic infection	Andrews, Handy, Kent
ʻōpikopiko		manifestation of syphilis in which skin becomes spotted	Andrews, Handy, PE, Kent
ʻōpūlauoho[5]		congenital venereal disease? (*lit.*, "stomach hair," for capillaries on stomach of newborn)	HEN, PE, Nānā, Kent
pā		infertile, of females	Andrews, Handy, PE, Kent
pala	pala hao, pala lalo, pala kio	syphilis; venereal disease; manifestation of gonorrhea (*lit.*, "rotten"; *pala hao* = "hard	Judd1, Andrews, Judd2, Kamakau, Handy, PE, Kent

(continued)

---

[5] Pukui et al., *Nānā i ke Kumu*, 34: " *ʻŌpūlauoho* did not seem to harm the person who had it. Instead, later on, it would affect the child's offspring. If a girl baby had *ʻōpūlauoho*, she would later bear dead babies or sickly ones that usually died before they were five years old. A boy who had it would grow up to be sterile, or else sire babies that would die in infancy."

Term	Alternates	Condition/translation	Source
		rottenness"; *pala kio* = "rotten protuberance," bubo?)	
pihi		a species of venereal disease; scab or scar; itch	Andrews, Handy, PE, Kent
pūhā	ma'i pūhā	gonorrhea; broken or burst open, as an abscess or lesion	Andrews, BOL, Handy, PE, Kent
puhi kaokao		active venereal sore (*lit.*, "burning syphilis")	Andrews, Kamakau, Handy, PE
waikī		gonorrhea, of males?; painful urination, perhaps due to cystitis (*fig.*, one whose father was a chief but whose mother was not, a term of contempt)	BOL, HEN, Handy, PE, Kent
waikūlono-'ako'ako'a		old name for syphilis	PE, Kent
wili	ma'i wili	gonorrhea; venereal disease (*lit.*, "to writhe, writhing sickness")	Andrews, Handy, PE, Kent

SOURCES IN CHRONOLOGICAL ORDER (SEE BIBLIOGRAPHY)

BLL	Chun, trans., *Hawaiian Medicine Book: He Buke Laau Lapaau* (1837?)
KPH	*Ka Palapala Hemolele a Iehova ko Kakou Akua* (Hebrew Bible [1838]); see *Ex.* 28:14–25, *Lev.* 15:2–15, *Num.* 25, and *Ps.* 38:1–7
Judd₁	Judd, *Anatomia* (1838)
Andrews	Andrews, *Dictionary* (1865)
Judd₂	Judd, Hawaiian-language medical book, HMCS (1867?)
Kamakau	Kamakau, *Ka Po'e Kahiko* (1869–70)
BOL	Spencer, ed., *Buke 'Oihana Lapa'au* (1895)
HEN	Hawaiian Ethnographic Notes, BM
Handy	Handy et al., *Outline of Hawaiian Physical Therapeutics*
PE	Pukui and Elbert, *Hawaiian Dictionary*
Nānā	Pukui et al., *Nānā i ke Kumu*
Kent	Kent, *Treasury of Hawaiian Words*

APPENDIX B

Population of the Hawaiian Islands

Date	Hawaiians	Part-Hawaiians (hapa haole)	Foreigners* (haole)	Hawai'i Island total pop.	Maui total pop.	O'ahu total pop.	Kaua'i total pop.	Moloka'i total pop.	Lāna'i total pop.	Ni'ihau total pop.	Kaho'olawe total pop.	Notes (see Bibliography)
1778	500,000+(a)	0	0	80,000–404,000	45,000–125,000	35,000–122,000	20,000–83,000	8,000–44,000	3,000–14,000	500–3,650	...	King, in Beaglehole, Journals, and Kirch (2012) for total; Schmitt (1971) for individual islands low estimate; Stannard (1989) for individual islands high estimate
1796	270,000?	<20?	<10(b)	...	...	...	...	...	...	...	...	Adams (1925) and Schmitt (1971) for total
1805	152,000–264,000(c)	<40?	<20?(b)	100,000(c)	48,000(c)	40,000(c)	40,000(c)(g)	25,000(c)	7,000(c)	4,000(c)	160(c)	Freycinet (1978) and Patterson (1817) for

(continued)

Date	Hawaiians	Part-Hawaiians (hapa haole)	Foreigners* (haole)	Hawai'i Island total pop.	Maui total pop.	O'ahu total pop.	Kaua'i total pop.	Moloka'i total pop.	Lāna'i total pop.	Ni'ihau total pop.	Kaho'olawe total pop.	Notes (see Bibliography)
												high estimate; Schmitt (1971) for low estimate; Freycinet (1978) for individual islands
1819	145,000(d)	...	150	...	...	...	...	...	...	...	...	Adams (1925) for total; Golovnin, in Barratt (1987), for *haole*
1823	135,000–142,000(d)	...	125–230	85,000	20,000	20,000	10,000	3,5000	2,500	1,000	50	W. Ellis to G. Burden (Oct. 5, 1823), CWM/LMS box 4 folder 3, for high estimate; Schmitt

| 1831–32(e) | 124,000–130,000(d) | ... | 400 | 46,000 | 35,000 | 30,000 | 11,000 | 6,000 | 1,600 | 1,000 | 80 | Mission census for high estimate and for individual islands; Adams (1925) for low estimate; Adams (1937) for haole |
| 1835–36 | 108,000(d) | ... | 600 | 39,000 | 24,000 | 28,000 | 9,000 | 6,000 | 1,200 | 993 | 80 | Mission census for total and for individual islands; Adams (1937) for haole |

(1971) for low estimate; Ellis (1827) and Jarves (1843) for individual islands; Stewart (1828) for haole

(continued)

Date	Hawaiians	Part-Hawaiians (*hapa haole*)	Foreigners* (*haole*)	Hawaiʻi Island total pop.	Maui total pop.	Oʻahu total pop.	Kauaʻi total pop.	Molokaʻi total pop.	Lānaʻi total pop.	Niʻihau total pop.	Kahoʻolawe total pop.	Notes (see Bibliography)
1850	84,165(d)	558(h)	1,572	25,864	21,047	25,440	6,956	3,540	604	714	...	Schmitt (1968, 1977) for total and for individual islands; mission census (1850), reproduced in E. Clark to R. Anderson, ABCFM Papers, for *hapa haole*; Adams (1937) for *haole*
1853(f)	70,036	983	2,119	24,450	17,574	19,126	6,991	3,607	600	790	...	Census data; see Schmitt 1968, 1977
1860	65,647	1,337	2,716	21,481	16,400	21,275	6,487	2,864	646	647	...	Census data; see Schmitt 1968, 1977

| 1866 | 57,125 | 1,640 | 4,194 | 19,808 | 14,035 | 19,799 | 6,299 | 2,299 | 394 | 325 | ⋯ | | Census data; see Schmitt 1968, 1977 |
| 1872 | 49,044 | 2,487(h) | 4,517 | 16,001 | 12,334 | 20,671 | 4,961 | 2,349 | 348 | 233 | ⋯ | | Census data; see Schmitt 1968, 1977 |

* All nationalities exclusive of Hawaiian; includes individuals born in Hawai'i to non-Hawaiian parents. (See Note on Language and Terminology.)

(a) Earlier estimates are by Schmitt and colleagues (1967–1978, 1989), 200,000 to 300,000; Stannard (1989), 800,000 to one million "or more"; A. F. Bushnell (1993), 400,000 "or more"; Dye (1994), 110,000 to 150,000; and Swanson (2015), 683,200.

(b) Minimum two months in residence.

(c) These figures came from an English carpenter in 1819 who seemed to Freycinet to "offer only rather arbitrary approximations" (*Hawaii in 1819*, p. 66). For lower estimates in 1800, see Schmitt (1971).

(d) Estimate is total population (includes all ethnicities and nationalities).

(e) Starting in 1831, census-takers broke the population down by sex, age, district/city, rural/urban, etc.

(f) The kingdom's first "official" census was taken in 1853. At this point, enumeration by race and national origin began; see Schmitt (1968).

(g) Lisiansky understood Kaumuali'i to be stating the population of Kaua'i as 30,000 in 1804, when the latter claimed he could raise 30,000 soldiers to defend against Kamehameha (Barratt, *Russian Discovery of Hawai'i*, 37).

(h) Swanson (2015) arrived at higher estimates using a demographic model of "backcasting" from 1910s to 1930s US census data (pp. 5, 17).

APPENDIX C

Glossary

'ahu 'ula	royal cloak made of **kapa** and bird feathers.
ahulau	pestilence, epidemic; *lit.*, "heaped-up bodies."
'ahupua'a	pie-shaped district stretching from the coast to uplands; *lit.*, "pig altar."
aikāne	male confidant, advisor, and sexual servant to a chief; *lit.*, "coitus man."
'ai kapu	segregated eating. *See* **kapu.**
'āina	land, including waterways, bays, and marine resources.
'ai noa	free eating.
akua	deity, god, spirit.
ali'i	chief (either sex).
ali'i 'au moku	district chief; *lit.*, "chief who eats the district."
ali'i nui	high chief.
aloha	love, affection, regard, greetings.
'anā'anā	sorcery, divination.
'aumakua	spirits of ancestors, personal/family gods.
aupuni	rule, order, organization (as of society).
'awa	kava (*Piper methysticum*).
hānai	adoption by a family member.
hale	hut, house, dwelling. *See* **kauhale.**
hapa haole	part-Hawaiian; *lit.*, "part foreign."
haole	foreign, foreigner(s).
Haumea	fertility deity; wife of **Kāne.**
haumia	uncleanliness, filth, defilement, contaminated.
heiau	temple, altar.
hewa	harmful. *After 1820,* sinful.
hiapo	first-born child.
Hina	female deity of medicine, associated with moon; observed by women.
ho'okupu	tribute, tax; *lit.*, "to cause to grow."

ho'omana	religious practice; observance of **akua** or **'aumakua.**
ho'onoa	to free from taboo. *See* **noa, kapu.**
Hulumanu	friends of Kauikeaouli; *lit.,* "bird feathers."
'iwi	bone(s).
Kahiki	islands of origin to the south; Tahiti.
kahuna, *pl.* kāhuna	expert, specialist, priest.
kahuna 'anā'anā	sorcerer.
kahuna hāhā	physician who diagnoses by palpation.
kahuna ho'ohapai keiki	specialist in inducing pregnancy.
kahuna lā'au lapa'au	physician specializing in (herbal) medicine.
kahuna lapa'au	medical expert; physician.
kahuna nui	high/chief priest. *Not be confused with* **kuhina nui.**
kahuna 'ō'ō	surgeon; physician specializing in lancing, and in keeping open the fontanel of infants.
kahuna pule	missionary; *lit.,* "prayer chief."
kālaimoku	chief minister, second in charge to **mō'ī**; *lit.,* "island carver."
kalo	taro (*Colocasia esculenta*).
kāma'i	brothel, place of prostitution; to prostitute.
kama'āina	long-time resident, native; *lit.,* "children of the land."
Kanaloa	deity of underworld, symbolized by the squid or octopus; complementary god to **Kāne.**
kanaka	person, human; laborer, servant, commoner. *See also* **maka'āinana.**
Kāne	male deity of the sun and flowing waters, creator; husband of **Haumea.**
kaona	hidden or double meaning.
kapa	Hawaiian cloth for garments and sleeping mats, made from bark of paper mulberry tree (*Broussonetia papyrifer*). *See* **wauke.**
kapu	prohibition, embargo; law; to mark as sacred. *See* **noa, ho'onoa.**
kapu moe	prostration taboo.
kapu pule	prayer taboo.
kauā (kauwā)	slave, outcast, pariah, untouchable.
kauhale	household; group of **hale** serving discrete functions.
kaukau ali'i	low-ranking chief, servant to chief.
ki'i	sacred image, representation of deity.
kino	human body, person, individual, self.
kōkua	help, care, aid (as for an ill or frail person).
konohiki	district chief, manager of **ahupua'a.**
Kū	male war deity, also associated with healing and medicine.
kuhina	counselor, advisor to **ali'i.**
kuhina nui	royal office created in 1819; principal advisor, along with **kālaimoku**, to the monarch; *lit.,* "great counselor."

kupuna	grandparent, elder, ancestor, forebearer.
lā'au lapa'au	medicine.
lāhui	nation, people; to unite.
lani	lofty, royal, elevated, majesty; *lit.*, sky; commonly used in ali'i names, e.g. *Kalani–*.
Lono	male deity of agriculture, fertility, rain, and medicine.
ma'i	sick(ness), illness, disease.
ma'i malihini	introduced (foreign) disease, typically infectious.
makahiki	new year festival; twelfth month of Hawaiian calendar; season of **Lono**.
maka'āinana	commoner(s); *lit.*, "people who tend the land." *See also* **kanaka**.
mālama	to care for, protect.
malo	loincloth.
mana:	spiritual power.
mana'o	thought, idea.
mō'ī	ruler, king, monarch.
moku (mokupuni)	island; district.
mo'olelo	account, history, story, narrative.
mo'okū'auhau	genealogy.
naha	coupling of a chief with his or her half-sibling; *lit.*, "bent, curved, bowlegged."
nī'aupi'o	offspring of sibling or half-sibling coupling; *lit.*, "bent coconut midrib" (that is, of the same stalk).
noa	free, unrestricted. *See* **ho'onoa, kapu**.
'oihana lapa'au	medical profession.
'ōkolehao	spirit distilled from the ti (*kī*) plant.
'ōku'u	gastrointestinal epidemic of 1804; *lit.*, "squatting sickness."
'ōlelo	language, speech, word, statement.
palapala	reading and writing; book learning; missionary instruction.
Papa	sacred male ancestor of the Hawaiian people, with **Wākea**; fertility deity.
Pele	female volcano deity, patron of hula; cult was particularly strong on the Big Island.
piko	navel; umbilical cord/stump; also, genitals and crown of the head, the body's three "organs" of power and procreation.
pi'o	coupling of full siblings; *lit.*, "arched, bent, curved."
poi	taro mashed with water, sometimes fermented; principal foodstuff of Islanders.
pono	beneficial; proper; harmonious; state of balance.
pule	prayer, appeal, petition, supplication
punalua	plural marriage; *lit.*, "two springs."
wahine	woman; female; wife.
Wākea	sacred female ancestor, with **Papa**, of the Hawaiian people.
wauke	paper mulberry (*Broussonetia papyrifer*). *See* **kapa**.

APPENDIX D

Selected Persons Appearing in Text

Keoni Ana (John Kalaipaihala Young II) — Noble, Minister of the Interior, fourth *kuhina nui*, 1845–55.

Auna — Tahitian missionary; personal teacher to **Ka'ahumanu**.

Boki — Maui high chief, brother of **William Pitt Kalanimoku**.

Ulumāheihei Hoapili — close advisor to **Kamehameha**, royal governor of Maui, father of Liliha.

(Thomas/Toma) Hopu — Protestant convert educated in Connecticut; introduced New England missionaries to *ali'i* in 1820.

(George Prince) Humehume — prince of Kaua'i, traveled to New England; rebelled against kingdom in 1820s.

John Papa 'Ī'ī — *kaukau ali'i* attendant to **Liholiho** and **Kauikeaouli**; Noble; Privy Councilor; writer; ardent Christian.

Ka'ahumanu — queen mother, later co-regent and first *kuhina nui*.

Kā'eo (Kā'eokūlani) — Maui chief; later, high chief of Kaua'i.

Kalākua Kaheiheimālie — queen consort/dowager, governor of Maui, Noble.

Kahekeli II — *mō 'ī* of Maui, 1790s.

Kahikona — Tahitian missionary, personal teacher to **Kekau'ōnohi**.

Ka'iana — with **Winee**, sailed the Pacific, visiting Macao and the Northwest Coast of North America; returned as advisor to **Kamehameha**; killed at Battle of Nu'uanu, 1795.

Kaikio'ewa — royal governor of Kaua'i (1825–39), guardian of **Kauikeaouli**.

David Kalākaua — king of Hawai'i, 1874–91.

Kalama — (Hakaleleponi Kapakuhaili) queen consort/dowager, wife of **Kauikeaouli**.

"William Pitt"
Kalanimoku
brother of **Boki**; chief minister (*kālaimoku*) to **Kamehameha**; co-regent with his cousin **Ka'ahumanu** and, later, with **Kauikeaouli**.

Kalani'ōpu'u
mō 'ī of Hawai'i Island, 1770s.

Samuel
Manaiakalani
Kamakau
O'ahu-born judge, Representative, historian.

Kamāmalu
daughter of **Kamehameha**, queen consort to **Liholiho** (her brother); died in London of measles.

Kamehameha
first *mō 'ī* of the unified Islands.

Kaomi
influential Tahitian-Hawaiian advisor to **Kauikeaouli**; also a *kahuna hāhā*.

Caesar Kapa'akea
Privy Councilor and Noble; founder of House of Kalākaua with his cousin **Analea Keohokālole**.

Kapi'olani
Big Island chiefess who defied Pele in 1824.

Lot (Lota)
Kapuāiwa
Kamehameha V, son of **Kīna'u** and **Mataio Kekūanāo'a**.

Kauikeaouli
Kamehameha III, son of **Kamehameha** and **Keōpūolani**.

Kaumuali'i
mō 'ī of Kaua'i, 1790s–1824, husband of **Ka'ahumanu** in 1824.

"George Cox"
Ke'eaumoku
(Kahekili Ke'eaumoku II) royal governor of Maui, Moloka'i, Lāna'i, and Kaho'olawe (1804–24); admiral of the king's fleet.

Deborah Kapule
(Miriam)
Kekāuluohi
wife of **Kaumuali'i**, *mō 'ī* of Kaua'i.
third *kuhina nui*, queen consort/dowager.

Kekau'ōnohi
youngest wife of **Liholiho**, also his niece; later, royal governor of Kaua'i and Noble.

Mataio
Kekūanāo'ā
kaukau ali'i royal treasurer, royal governor of O'ahu, father of two monarchs (**Lot Kapuāiwa, Alexander Liholiho**).

Kekuaokalani
Big Island chief entrusted by Kamehameha with the war god Kū; led rebel faction against **William Pitt Kalanimoku** and **Ka'ahumanu** after fall of kapu system.

Analea
Keohokālole
Noble, Privy Councilor; founder of House of Kalākaua with her cousin **Caesar Kapa'akea**.

Keōpūolani
queen mother; *nī'aupi'o*- and *naha*-ranking chiefess.

Kīna'u
second *kuhina nui*, important ally of Sandwich Islands Mission, mother of two monarchs (**Lot Kapuāiwa, Alexander Liholiho**).

"John Adams"
Kuakini
advisor to **Kamehameha**; royal governor of Big Island and later of O'ahu.

Kualelo
Moloka'i youth who sailed with Colnett in 1788, returned with Vancouver in 1792, settled on Big Island.

William Pitt
Leleiohoku I
son of **William Pitt Kalanimoku**, husband of **Nāhi'ena'ena**; royal governor of Big Island, 1844–46.

Likelike
high chiefess and first wife of **William Pitt Kalanimoku**.

Liholiho	Kamehameha II, son of **Kamehameha** and **Keōpūolani**.
Alexander Liholiho	Kamehameha IV, son of **Kīna'u** and **Mataio Kekūanāo'a**.
Liliha	wife of **Boki** and royal governor of O'ahu, 1829–c.31.
Makoa	London Missionary Society tour guide, 1823–24.
Davida Malo	court genealogist, teacher, preacher, scholar.
Nāhi'ena'ena	princess; daughter of **Kamehameha** and **Keōpūolani**; sister and lover of Kauikeaouli.
Oani	priestess of Pele on the Big Island, 1823.
'Ōpūnui	Kauai ali'i, 1790s.
(Lydia) Nāmāhāna Pi'ia	queen dowager, royal governor of O'ahu, 1825–c.29.
Pua'aiki	("Blind Bartimaeus") court performer for **Liholiho**, later a devoted member of Sandwich Islands Mission.
Tau'ā	Tahitian missionary in 1820s, along with **Auna**.
Toketa	Tahitian missionary-teacher to **John Adams Kuakini**.
Wahinepio	(also known as Kahakuha'akoi, Kamo'onohu) royal governor of Maui, 1824–c.26.
Winee	with **Ka'iana**, sailed the Pacific, visiting Macao and Northwest Coast of North America; died aboard *Iphigenia* off Philippines.

Bibliography

ABBREVIATIONS

ABCFM	American Board of Commissioners for Foreign Missions
BL	British Library, London
BM	Bishop Museum, Honolulu
CWM/LMS	Council for World Mission/London Missionary Society
HBLL	Harold B. Lee Library L. Tom Perry Special Collections, Brigham Young University, Salt Lake City
HJH	*Hawaiian Journal of History*
HL	Huntington Library, San Marino, California
HMCS	Hawaiian Mission Children's Society Library, Honolulu
HSA	Hawai'i State Archives, Honolulu
JPH	*Journal of Pacific History*
JPS	*Journal of the Polynesian Society*
NLA	National Library of Australia, Canberra
PHR	*Pacific Historical Review*
SLNSW	State Library of New South Wales, Sydney
SOAS	University of London School of Oriental and Asian Studies Archives and Special Collections
TNA	The National Archives, Kew, Surrey

ARCHIVAL MATERIAL

Bancroft Library, University of California, Berkeley

William Little Lee papers

Beinecke Library, Yale University

Thomas W. Walker, supercargo's log for the brig *Lydia*, 1805–7

Bishop Museum, Honolulu (BM)

E. S. Craighill Handy, "Hawaiian Medical Notes," Box 7
Hawaiian Ethnographic Notes, compiled and translated by Mary Kawena Pukui

British Library, London (BL)

[A collection of charts and plates, mostly of the Pacific, intended for the text volumes and atlas to *A Voyage to the Pacific Ocean ... In the Years 1776, 1777, 1778, 1779, and 1780*, by Captain James Cook and Captain James King], [London]: [W. & A. Strahan], [1781–85], Maps 185.j.1
Archibald Menzies journal, Dec. 1790–Feb. 1794, MS 32641

Hamilton Library Hawaiian and Pacific Collections, University of Hawai'i at Mānoa

Charles Barff, ed., "A Memoir of Auna Translated from a Memoir of Him Printed in Tahitian 1837" (handwritten)
Stephen Reynolds journals, 1823–55 (typescript), H00043, Boxes 1–2

Hawai'i State Archives, Honolulu (HSA)

Gerrit P. Judd 1839 report to the Sandwich Islands Mission (typescript), U178
James King manuscript log on the *Resolution*, PRO Admiralty 55/116 (photostat)
Kingdom of Hawai'i Board of Health records and reports, series 334, box 1
Kingdom of Hawai'i Interior Department Box 140
Laws of the Hawaiian Kingdom, series 418, box 1
Privy Council Records, vol. 9 (1854–55)
Stephen Reynolds journal, 1829–43 (typescript of selections)
John Young journal, compiled by Dorothy Barrère

Hawaiian Mission Children's Society, Honolulu (HMCS)

Anonymous from Waipio (O'ahu or Hawai'i Island) to Lorrin Andrews, Aug. 31, 1836
Richard Armstrong journal, 1831–58 (typescript)
Dwight Baldwin letters, 1834–48
Dwight Baldwin journal, 1831–32
Dwight Baldwin medical journal, 1836–43 (original manuscript at Lahaina Restoration Foundation)
Sybil Moseley Bingham journal, 1819–22 (typescript)
Abraham Blatchley, letters sent 1824–28
Levi Chamberlain journals, 1822–49 (typescript)
Gerrit P. Judd papers
Gerrit P. Judd, Hawaiian-language medical book (1867?), anonymous translation

Elisha Loomis journal (typescript)
Report of the Committee on Medical Instruction, no date (ca. 1829–50)
Samuel and Nancy Ruggles journal, Oct. 23, 1819, to Aug. 4, 1820 (typescript)

Huntington Library, San Marino, California (HL)

Delia Bishop diary, 1829–30 (Hawaii-Bishop Collection)
Sereno Edwards Bishop Collection, Box 1
George Anson Byron, ship's log for the HMS *Blonde*, 1824–25
Nathaniel Bright Emerson papers
William B. Rice letterbook, 1852–56

Harold B. Lee Library L. Tom Perry Special Collections, Salt Lake City, Brigham Young University (HBLL)

William Farrer journal
Ephraim Green journal
Mary Jane Dilworth Hammond journal

Library of Congress

American Board of Commissioners for Foreign Missions (ABCFM) Pacific Islands Missions Records, ABC 19.1–19.3 (microfilm)

The National Archives, Kew, Surrey (TNA)

William Charlton journal, PRO Admiralty 51/4557
James King manuscript log on the *Resolution*, PRO Admiralty 55/122

National Library of Australia, Canberra (NLA)

Archibald Menzies journal, Feb. 1794–March 1795, MS 155

Peabody Essex Museum, Salem, Massachusetts

Log book of the *Acushnet*, 1845–47
Stephen W. Reynolds, journal, 1823–55

State Library of New South Wales, Sydney (SLNSW)

Joseph Banks, *Endeavor* journal, 1768–71, two vols. (typescript)
James Burney, journal on HMS *Discovery*, 1776–79
Andrew Bracey Taylor papers, 1781–99

University of London School of Oriental and Asian Studies Archives and Special Collections (SOAS)

Council for World Mission/London Missionary Society (CWM/LMS) South Seas Incoming Correspondence (1822–25), Boxes 3B, 4, and 5A

SELECTED NEWSPAPERS AND PERIODICALS

The Friend, Honolulu, from 1845
Hawaiian Spectator, Honolulu, 1838–39
Ka Hae Hawaii, Honolulu, 1856–61
Ka Nonanona, Honolulu, 1841–45
Ka Nupepa Kuokoa, Honolulu, 1861–64
Ke Au Okoa, Honolulu, 1865–73 (renamed continuation of *Ka Nupepa Kuokoa*)
Ke Kumu Hawaii, Honolulu, 1834–39
Missionary Herald, Boston, from 1821
Pacific Commercial Advertiser, Honolulu, from 1856
Polynesian, Honolulu, 1840–41, 1844–64

PUBLISHED PRIMARY SOURCES

[ABCFM], *Instructions of the Prudential Committee of the American Board of Commissioners for Foreign Missions to the Sandwich Islands Mission.* Lahainaluna, HI: Missionary Seminary, 1838.
[ABCFM], *A Narrative of Five Youth from the Sandwich Islands, Now Receiving an Education in This Country.* New York, NY: J. Seymour, 1816.
Alexander, W[illiam] D[eWitt]. *A Brief History of the Hawaiian People.* New York, NY: American Book, 1891.
"Overthrow of the Ancient Tabu System in the Hawaiian Islands." *The Hawaiian Monthly* 1 (1884): 82–84.
Anderson, Rufus. *History of the Mission of the American Board of Commissioners for Foreign Missions to the Sandwich Islands.* Third edition. Boston, MA: Congregational Publishing Board, 1872.
Andreev, A[leksandr] I[gnat'evich], ed. *Russkie otkrytiia v Tikhom okeane i Severnoi Amerike v XVIII–XIX vekakh.* Moscow: Academy of Sciences of the USSR, 1944.
Andrews, Lorrin. *A Dictionary of the Hawaiian Language.* Honolulu, HI: Henry M. Whitney, 1865.
Arago, J[acques Etienne Victor]. *Narrative of a Voyage around the World, in the Uranie and Physicienne Corvettes* ... London: Treutell & Wurtz, 1823.
Armstrong, R[ichard], et al. *Answers to Questions Proposed by His Excellency, R. C. Wyllie* ... *to All the Missionaries in the Hawaiian Islands, May, 1846.* Honolulu, HI: n.p., 1848.
Barratt, Glynn, ed. and trans. *The Russian Discovery of Hawai'i: The Ethnographic and Historical Record.* Honolulu, HI: University of Hawai'i Press, 1987.

The Russian View of Honolulu, 1809–26. Ottawa, ON: Carleton University Press, 1988.

Bassett, Marnie. *Realms and Islands: The World Voyage of Rose de Freycinet in the Corvette Uranie, 1817–1820*. London: Oxford University Press, 1962.

Beaglehole, J[ohn] C[awte], ed. *The Journals of Captain James Cook on His Voyages of Discovery*. 4 vols. Cambridge: Cambridge University Press for the Hakluyt Society, 1967.

Beechey, F[rederick] W[illiam]. *Narrative of a Voyage to the Pacific and Beerings Strait, to Cooperate with the Polar Expeditions*. First London Quarto edition. 2 vols. London: Henry Colburn & Richard Bentley, 1831.

Bell, Edward. "Log of the *Chatham*." *Honolulu Mercury* 1 (Sept. 1929): 7–26; (Oct. 1929): 55–69; (Nov. 1929): 76–90.

[Beresford, William]. *A Voyage round the World; But More Particularly to the North-West Coast of America . . .*, by George Dixon. London: Geo. Goulding, 1789.

Birkett, Mary Ellen. "Hawai'i in 1819: An Account by Camille de Roquefeuil." *HJH* 34 (2000): 69–92.

Bingham, Hiram. *A Residence of Twenty-One Years in the Sandwich Islands*. Hartford, CT: Hezekiah Huntington, 1847.

Bishop, Artemas. "An Inquiry into the Causes of Decrease in the Population of the Sandwich Islands." *Hawaiian Spectator* 1 (1838): 52–66.

[Bishop, Elizabeth Edwards]. "A Journal of Early Hawaiian Days." *The Friend* (Sept. 1900): 72–74; (Oct. 1900): 82–83.

Bishop, Sereno Edwards. *Reminiscences of Old Hawaii*. Honolulu, HI: Hawaiian Gazette, 1916.

Bligh, William. *A Voyage to the South Sea, Undertaken by Command of His Majesty . . .* London: George Nicol, 1792.

Bloxam, Andrew. *Diary of Andrew Bloxam: Naturalist of the "Blonde" on Her Trip from England to the Hawaiian Islands, 1824–25*. Edited by Stella M. Jones. Honolulu, HI: Bishop Museum, 1925.

Boelen, Jacobus. *A Merchant's Perspective: Captain Jacobus Boelen's Narrative of His Visit to Hawai'i in 1828*. Translated by Frank J. A. Broeze. Honolulu, HI: Hawaiian Historical Society, 1988.

Broughton, William Robert. *A Voyage of Discovery to the North Pacific Ocean*. London: T. Cadell & W. Davies, 1804.

Byron, [George Anson]. *Voyage of H. M. S. Blonde to the Sandwich Islands, in the Years 1824–1825*. Edited by Maria Callcott. London: John Murray, 1826.

Campbell, Archibald. *A Voyage around the World, from 1806 to 1812*. New York, NY: Van Winkle, Wiley, 1817.

Chamisso, Adelbert. *A Voyage around the World with the Romanzov Exploring Expedition in the Years 1815–1818, in the Brig Rurik, Captain Otto von Kotzebue*. Edited and translated by Henry Kratz. Honolulu, HI: University of Hawai'i Press, 1986.

Chapin, Alonzo. "Remarks on the Sandwich Islands; Their Situation, Climate, Diseases, and Their Suitableness as a Resort for Individuals Affected with or Predisposed to Pulmonary Diseases." *American Journal of the Medical Sciences* 20 (1837): 43–60.

"Remarks on the Venereal Disease at the Sandwich Islands." *Boston Medical and Surgical Journal* 42 (1850): 89–93.

Chun, Malcom Nāea, trans. *Hawaiian Medicine Book: He Buke Laau Lapaau* [1837?]. Honolulu, HI: Bess, 1986.

Colnett, James. *The Journal of Captain James Colnett Aboard the Argonaut from April 26, 1789 to Nov. 3, 1791.* Edited by F. W. Howay. Toronto: Champlain Society, 1940. Reprint, New York, NY: Greenwood, 1968.

Cook, James. *The Three Voyages of Captain James Cook around the World.* 7 vols. London: Longman, 1821.

Cook, James, and James King. *A Voyage to the Pacific Ocean.* 3 vols. London: W. & A. Strahan for G. Nicol & T. Cadell, 1784.

Corney, Peter. *Voyages in the Northern Pacific.* Edited by W. D. Alexander. Honolulu, HI: Thomas G. Thrum, 1896.

Cox, Ross. *Adventures on the Columbia River.* New York, NY: J. & J. Harper, 1832.

Delano, Amasa. *A Narrative of Voyages and Travels, in the Northern and Southern Hemispheres ...* Boston, MA: E. G. House, 1817.

Dibble, Sheldon. *History and General Views of the Sandwich Islands' Mission.* New York, NY: Taylor & Dodd, 1839.

History of the Sandwich Islands. Lahainaluna, HI: Mission Press, 1843.

[Dwight, Edwin Welles]. *Memoirs of Henry Obookiah, a Native of Owyhee ...* New Haven, CT: n.p., 1819.

Edwards, B[ela] B[ates]. *The Missionary Gazetteer.* Boston, MA: William Hyde, 1832.

Ellis, William. *A Journal of a Tour around Hawaii, the Largest of the Sandwich Islands.* Boston, MA: Crocker & Brewster, 1825.

Narrative of a Tour through Hawaii, or Owhyhee. Second enlarged edition. London: H. Fisher, Son, & P. Jackson, 1827.

Polynesian Researches, during a Residence of Nearly Eight Years in the Society and Sandwich Islands. 4 vols. Second enlarged edition. London: Fisher, Son, & Jackson, 1831.

A Vindication of the South Sea Missions ... London: Frederick Westley & A. H. Davis, 1831.

Emerson, Oliver Pomeroy. *Pioneer Days in Hawaii.* Garden City, NY: Doubleday, Doran, 1928.

[Etches, John]. *An Authentic Statement of All the Facts Relative to Nootka Sound.* London: Debrett, 1790.

Falck, N[ikolai] D[etlef]. *The Seamen's Medical Instructor ...* London: Edward & Charles Dilly, 1774.

Fleurieu, C[harles] P[ierre] Claret [de]. *A Voyage round the World, Performed during the Years 1790, 1791, and 1792, by Étienne Marchand.* 2 vols. London: T. N. Longman & O. Rees, 1801.

Fornander, Abraham. *An Account of the Polynesian Race.* 2 vols. London: Trübner, 1880.

Fornander Collection of Hawaiian Antiquities and Folk-lore. 6 vols. Edited by Thomas G. Thrum. Honolulu, HI: Bishop Museum, 1916–1920.

Thirteen Letters to Erik Ljungstedt. Edited by Christian Callmer. Lund, Sweden: C. W. K. Gleerup, 1973.

Freycinet, Louis Claude de Saulses de. *Hawaii in 1819: A Narrative Account.* Edited by Marion Kelly. Translated by Ella L. Wiswell. Honolulu, HI: Bishop Museum, 1978.

Voyage Autour du Monde, Entrepris par Ordre du Roi, vol. 2, *Historique.* Paris: Chez Pillet Ainé, 1839.

Galois, Robert M., ed. *A Voyage to the North West Side of America: The Journals of James Colnett, 1786–89.* Vancouver, BC: University of British Columbia Press, 2004.

Gast, Ross H., and Agnes C. Conrad, eds. *Don Francisco de Paula Marin: The Letters and Journal of Don Francisco de Paul Marin.* Honolulu, HI: University Press of Hawaii, 1973.

Golovnin, V[asily] M[ikhailovich]. *Around the World on the* Kamchatka, *1817–1819.* Translated by Ella Lury Wiswell. Honolulu, HI: Hawaiian Historical Society, 1979.

Green, J[onathan] S[mith]. *Notices of the Life, Character, and Labors of the Late Bartimeus L. Puaaiki . . .* Lahainaluna, HI: Mission Seminary, 1844.

Gulick, Luther H. "On the Climate, Diseases and Materia Medica of the Sandwich (Hawaiian) Islands." *New-York Journal of Medicine* 14 (1855): 169–211.

Heffinger, Arthur C. "Elephantiasis Arabum in the Samoan Islands." *Boston Medical and Surgical Journal* (1882): 154–56.

Hempel, Charles J., trans. *Dr. Franz Hartmann's Diseases of Children and Their Homeopathic Treatment.* New York, NY: William Radde, 1853.

Hill, S[amuel] S. *Travels in the Sandwich and Society Islands.* London: Chapman & Hall, 1856.

Hillebrand, William. *Flora of the Hawaiian Islands.* London: Williams & Norgate, 1888.

Hopkins, Manley. *Hawaii: The Past, Present, and Future of Its Island-Kingdom.* Second edition. London: Longmans, Green, 1866.

Hopoo. "Memoirs of Thomas Hopoo." *HJH* 2 (1968): 42–54.

Howay, Frederic W., ed. *Voyages of the "Columbia" to the Northwest Coast, 1787–90 and 1790–93.* Cambridge, MA: Massachusetts Historical Society, 1941.

'I'i, John Papa. *Fragments of Hawaiian History.* Translated by Mary Kawena Pukui. Edited by Dorothy B. Barrère. Honolulu, HI: Bishop Museum, 1959.

Iselin, Isaac. *Journal of a Trading Voyage around the World, 1805–1808.* Cortland, NY: McIlroy & Emmet, n.d.

Jackman, S. W., ed. *The Journal of William Sturgis.* Victoria, BC: Sono Nis, 1978.

Jarves, James Jackson. *History of the Hawaiian or Sandwich Islands.* Boston, MA: Tappan & Dennet, 1843.

Kiana: A Tradition of Hawaii. Boston, MA: James Munrow, 1857.

Judd, Gerrit P. *Anatomia, 1838.* Translated by Esther T. Mookini. Honolulu, HI: University of Hawai'i Press, 2003.

Anatomia: He Palapala ia e Hoike Ai i ke Ano o ko ke Kanaka Kino. O'ahu, HI: Mission Press, 1838.

Judd, Laura Fish. *Honolulu: Sketches of Life Social, Political, and Religious, in the Hawaiians Islands from 1828 to 1861.* Edited by Albert Francis Judd. New York, NY: Anson D. F. Randolph, 1880.

Kaaiakamanu, D. M., and J. K. Akina. *Hawaiian Herbs of Medicinal Value (1922)*. Translated by Akaiko Akana. Honolulu, HI: Pacific Book House, 1968.

Kahananui, Dorothy M., ed. and trans. *Ka Mooolelo* [sic] *Hawaii*. Honolulu, HI: Committee for the Preservation of Hawaiian Language, Art and Culture, 1984.

Kalākaua, David. *The Legends and Myths of Hawaii: The Fables and Folk-Lore of a Strange People*. Edited by R. M. Daggett. New York, NY: Charles L. Webster, 1888.

Kamakau, Samuel Manaiakalani. *Ka Poʻe Kahiko: The People of Old*. Translated by Mary Kawena Pukui. Edited by Dorothy B. Barrère. Honolulu, HI: Bishop Museum, 1964.

Ruling Chiefs of Hawaii. Rev. ed. Translated by Mary Kawena Pukui et al. Honolulu, HI: Kamehameha Schools, 1992.

Ka Manao o na Alii [Thoughts of the Chiefs]. Utica, NY: W. Williams, 1827 (originally published Oʻahu, 1825).

Kamehameha IV. *Speeches of His Majesty Kamehameha IV. to the Hawaiian Legislature* ... Honolulu, HI: Government Press, 1861.

Ka Palapala Hemolele a Iehova ko Kakou Akua [The Bible]. 2 vols. Oʻahu, HI: Mission Press, 1838.

Kepelino. *Kepelino's Traditions of Hawaii*. Edited by Martha Warren Beckwith. Honolulu, HI: Bishop Museum, 1932.

Kotzebue, Otto von. *A New Voyage round the World in the Years 1823, 24, 25, and 26*. 2 vols. London: Henry Colburn & Richard Bentley, 1830.

A Voyage of Discovery into the South Sea and Beering's Straits ... 3 vols. London: Longman, 1821.

Krusenstern, A[dam] J[ohann] von. *Voyage round the World in the Years 1803, 1804, 1805, & 1806* ... 2 vols. Translated by Richard Belgrave Hoppner. London: John Murray, 1813.

Lamb, W. Kaye, ed. *A Voyage of Discovery to the North Pacific Ocean and round the World, 1791–1795, by George Vancouver*. 4 vols. London: Haklyut Society, 1984.

Langlas, Charles, and Jeffrey Lyon. "Davida Malo's Unpublished Account of Keōpūolani." *HJH* 42 (2008): 27–48.

Langsdorff, Georg Heinrich von. *Remarks and Observations on a Voyage around the World from 1803 to 1807*. Translated by Victoria Joan Moessner. Edited by Richard A. Pierce. Kingston, ON: Limestone, 1993.

Voyages and Travels in Various Parts of the World, during the Years 1803, 1804, 1805, 1806, and 1807. Carlisle, PA: George Philips, 1817.

La Pérouse, J[ean]-F[rançois de] G[alaup de]. *A Voyage round the World, in the Years 1785, 1786, 1787, and 1788*. 3 vols. Edited by M. L. A. Millet-Mureau. Second edition. London: J. Johnson, 1799.

Ledyard, John. *Journal of Captain Cook's Last Voyage*. Edited by James Kenneth Munford. Corvallis, OR: Oregon State University Press, 1964.

Liliʻuokalani. *Hawaii's Story by Hawaii's Queen*. Boston, MA: Lothrop, Lee & Shepard, 1898.

Linden, Diederick Wessel. *A Treatise on the Three Medicinal Mineral Waters at Llandrindod, in Radnorshire, South Wales*. London: J. Everingham & T. Reynolds, 1756.

Lisiansky, Urey. *A Voyage round the World, in the Years 1803, 4, 5, & 6.* London: John Booth, 1814.

Macrae, James. *With Lord Byron at the Sandwich Islands in 1825.* Edited by William F. Wilson. Honolulu, HI: n.p., 1922.

Malo, David(a). *Hawaiian Antiquities (Moolelo Hawaii).* Translated by Nathaniel B. Emerson [1898]. Honolulu, HI: Bishop Museum, 1951.

Ka Moʻolelo Hawaiʻi: Hawaiian Traditions. Translated by Malcolm Nāea Chun. Honolulu, HI: First People's, 1996.

The Moʻolelo Hawaiʻi of Davida Malo. Vol. 2. Edited and translated by Charles Langlas and Jeffrey Lyon. Unpublished manuscript (forthcoming, University of Hawaiʻi Press).

"On the Decrease of Population on the Hawaiian Islands." Translated by L[orrin] Andrews. *Hawaiian Spectator* 2 (1839): 121–31.

Manby, Thomas. "Journal of Vancouver's Voyage to the Pacific Ocean, 1791–1793." *Honolulu Mercury* 1 (June 1929): 11–25; (July 1929): 33–45; (Aug. 1929): 39–55.

Mann, Horace. *Enumeration of Hawaiian Plants.* Cambridge, MA: Welch, Bigelow, 1867.

Martin, Margaret Greer, ed. *The Lymans of Hilo.* Hilo, HI: Lyman House Memorial Museum, 1979.

Mathison, Gilbert Farquhar. *Narrative of a Visit to Brazil, Chile, Peru, and the Sandwich Islands, during the Years 1821 and 1822.* London: Charles Knight, 1825.

Meares, John. *Voyages Made in the Years 1788 and 1789, from China to the North West Coast of America . . .* London: Logographic Press, 1790.

Moessner, Victoria Joan, trans. *The First Russian Voyage around the World: The Journal of Hermann Ludwig von Löwenstern, 1803–1806.* Fairbanks, AK: University of Alaska Press, 2003.

Montgomery, James, ed. *Journal of Voyages and Travels by the Rev. Daniel Tyerman and George Bennet, Esq. . . .* 3 vols. Boston, MA: Crocker & Brewster, 1832.

Nicol, John. *The Life and Adventures of John Nicol, Mariner.* Edinburgh: William Blackwood, 1822.

Papa Ola Lōhaki (Native Hawaiian Health Board). *Ka ʻUhane Lōkahi: 1998 Native Hawaiian Health & Wellness Summit and Island ʻAha; Issues, Trends, and General Recommendations.* Honolulu, HI: n.p., 1998.

Patterson, Samuel. *Narrative of the Adventures and Sufferings of Samuel Patterson . . .* Palmer, MA: The Press in Palmer, 1817.

Portlock, Nathaniel. *A Voyage round the World; But More Particularly to the North-West Coast of America . . .* London: J. Stockdale & G. Goulding, 1789.

Reynolds, Stephen. *Journal of Stephen Reynolds, 1823–1829.* Edited by Pauline N. King. Honolulu, HI: Ku Paʻa Inc.; and Salem, MA: Peabody Museum, 1989.

Richards, Mary Atherton. *The Chiefs' Children's School: A Record Compiled from the Diary and Letters of Amos Starr Cooke and Juliette Montague Cooke.* Honolulu, HI: Star-Bulletin, 1937.

Rickman, John. *Journal of Captain Cook's Last Voyage to the Pacific Ocean, on Discovery* ... London: E. Newbery, 1781. Reprint, New York, NY: Da Capo, 1967.

Rivière, Marc Serge. *A Woman of Courage: The Journal of Rose de Freycinet on Her Voyage around the World, 1817–1820.* Canberra: National Library of Australia, 2003.

Rock, Joseph F. *The Indigenous Trees of the Hawaiian Islands.* Honolulu, HI: E. Herrick Brown, 1913.

Rudkin, Charles N., trans. and ed. *The First French Expedition to California: Lapérouse in 1786.* Los Angeles, CA: G. Dawson, 1959.

Samwell, David. "Observations, Respecting the Introduction of the Venereal Disease into the Sandwich Islands." In *A Narrative of the Death of Captain James Cook,* 29–34. London: G. G. & J. Robinson, 1786.

Shaler, William. "Journal of a Voyage between China and the North-Western Coast of America, Made in 1804." *American Register* 3 (1808): 137–75.

Simpson, Alexander. *The Sandwich Islands: Progress of Events since Their Discovery by Captain Cook* ... London: Smith, Elder, 1843.

Snow, Jade. "Pihana: A Hula Dancer's Return to Self on Her Journey to Becoming Miss Aloha Hula 2013." *MANA: The Hawaiian Magazine* (May 2014): 24–31.

Spencer, Thomas P. (Kamaki), ed. *Buke ʻOihana Lapaʻau me nā ʻApu Lāʻau Hawaiʻi* (Book of Medical Practices and Hawaiian Prescriptions) (1895). Honolulu, HI: Bishop Museum, 2003.

Spilsbury, F[rancis]. *A Treatise on the Method of Curing the Gout ... and Other Cutaneous Eruptions.* London: n.p., 1775.

Stewart, C[harles] S[amuel]. *Journal of a Residence in the Sandwich Islands ...* Second edition. New York, NY: John P. Haven, 1828.

Private Journal of a Voyage to the Pacific Ocean, and Residence at the Sandwich Islands ... New York, NY: John P. Haven, 1828.

A Visit to the South Seas, in the U.S. Ship Vincennes, during the Years 1829 and 1830. 2 vols. New York, NY: John P. Haven, 1831.

Townsend, Ebenezer. "Extract from the Diary of Ebenezer Townsend, Jr." (1798). *Hawaiian Historical Reprints,* no. 4 (1924): 1–33.

Turnbull, John. *A Voyage round the World, in the Years 1800, 1801, 1802, 1803, and 1804 ...* London: Richard Phillips, 1805.

"The Turrill Collection, 1845–1860." In *Sixty-Sixth Annual Report of the Hawaiian Historical Society for the Year 1957,* 27–92. Honolulu, HI: Advertiser, 1958.

Vancouver, George. *A Voyage of Discovery to the North Pacific Ocean, and round the World.* 3 vols. London: G. G. & J. Robinson, 1798.

Wharton, W. J. L., ed. *Captain Cook's Journal during His First Voyage round the World Made in H. M. Bark "Endeavour" 1768–71.* London: Elliot Stock, 1893.

Whitman, John B. *An Account of the Sandwich Islands.* Edited by John Dominis Holt. Honolulu, HI: Topgallant, 1979.

Wilkes, Charles. *Narrative of the United States Exploring Expedition.* 5 vols. New York, NY: G. P. Putnam, 1856.

SECONDARY SOURCES

Abbott, Isabella Aiona. *Lā'au Hawai'i: Traditional Hawaiian Uses of Plants.* Honolulu, HI: Island Heritage, 1992.

Adams, Romanzo. *Interracial Marriage in Hawaii: A Study of the Mutually Conditioned Processes of Acculturation and Amalgamation.* New York, NY: Macmillan, 1937.

Adams, Romanzo, T. M. Livesay, and E. H. Van Winkle. *The Peoples of Hawaii: A Statistical Study.* Honolulu, HI: Institute of Pacific Relations, 1925.

Alexander, Mary Charlotte. *Dr. Baldwin of Lahaina.* Berkeley, CA: n.p., 1953.

Anderson, Benedict. *Imagined Communities: Reflections on the Origin and Spread of Nationalism.* London: Verso, 1983.

Andrade, Carlos. *Hā'ena: Through the Eyes of the Ancestors.* Honolulu, HI: University of Hawai'i Press, 2008.

Archer, Seth. "Colonialism and Other Afflictions: Rethinking Native American Health History." *History Compass* 14 (2016): 511–21.

Arista, Noelani. "Captive Women in Paradise 1796–1826: The *Kapu* on Prostitution in Hawaiian Historical Legal Context." *American Indian Culture and Research Journal* 35 (2011): 39–55.

"Histories of Unequal Measure: Euro-American Encounters with Hawaiian Governance and Law, 1793–1827." PhD diss., Brandeis University, 2009.

"Listening to Leoiki: Engaging Sources in Hawaiian History." *Biography* 32 (2009): 66–73.

Armstrong, R. Warwick, and James Allen Bier, eds. *Atlas of Hawaii.* Honolulu, HI: University of Hawai'i Press, 1983.

Armus, Diego. *The Ailing City: Health, Tuberculosis, and Culture in Buenos Aires, 1870–1950.* Durham, NC: Duke University Press, 2011.

Ballantyne, Tony. *Entanglements of Empire: Missionaries, Māori, and the Question of the Body.* Durham, NC: Duke University Press, 2014.

Ballou, Howard M., and George R. Carter. "The History of the Hawaiian Mission Press, with a Bibliography of the Earlier Publications." *Papers of the Hawaiian Historical Society* 14 (1908): 9–44.

Banner, Stuart. *Possessing the Pacific: Land, Settlers, and Indigenous People from Australia to Alaska.* Cambridge, MA: Harvard University Press, 2007.

Barman, Jean, and Bruce McIntyre Watson, *Leaving Paradise: Indigenous Hawaiians in the Pacific Northwest, 1787–1898.* Honolulu, HI: University of Hawai'i Press, 2006.

Barr, Juliana, and Edward Countryman, eds. *Contested Spaces of Early America.* Philadelphia, PA: University of Pennsylvania Press, 2014.

Barrère, Dorothy, Mary Kawena Pukui, and Marion Kelly. *Hula: Historical Perspectives.* Honolulu, HI: Bishop Museum, 1980.

Barrère, Dorothy, and Marshall Sahlins. "Tahitians in the Early History of Hawaiian Christianity: The Journal of Toketa." *HJH* 13 (1979): 19–35.

Beamer, Kamanamaikalani. *No Mākou ka Mana: Liberating the Nation.* Honolulu, HI: Kamehameha Publishing, 2014.

Beckwith, Martha Warren. *Hawaiian Mythology.* Honolulu, HI: University of Hawai'i Press, 1970.

Bender, Thomas. *A Nation among Nations: America's Place in World History.* New York: Hill & Wang, 2006.

Berkhofer, Robert F. *The White Man's Indian: Images of the American Indian from Columbus to the Present.* New York, NY: Knopf, 1978.

Blackhawk, Ned. *Violence over the Land: Indians and Empires in the Early American West.* Cambridge, MA: Harvard University Press, 2006.

Blaisdell, Richard Kekuni Akana. "'Hawaiian' vs. 'Kanaka Maoli' as Metaphors." *Hawaii Review* 13 (1989): 77–79.

"The Health Status of Kanaka Maoli (Indigenous Hawaiians)." *Asian American and Pacific Islander Journal of Health* 1 (1993): 117–160.

"Historical and Philosophical Aspects of Lapaʻau: Traditional Kanaka Maoli Healing Practices." *In Motion Magazine*, April 28, 1996.

Bolkhovitinov, N. N. "The Adventures of Doctor Schäffer in Hawaii, 1815–1819." Translated by Igor V. Vorobyoff. *HJH* 7 (1973): 55–78.

Boyd, Robert. *The Coming of the Spirit of Pestilence: Introduced Infectious Diseases and Population Decline among Northwest Coast Indians, 1774–1874.* Seattle, WA: University of Washington Press, 1999.

Bradley, Harold Whitman. *The American Frontier in Hawaii: The Pioneers, 1789–1843.* Stanford, CA: Stanford University Press, 1942.

Brantlinger, Patrick. *Dark Vanishings: Discourse on the Extinction of Primitive Races, 1800–1930.* Ithaca, NY: Cornell University Press, 2003.

Brown, Marie Alohalani. *Facing the Spears of Change: The Life and Legacy of John Papa ʻĪʻī.* Honolulu, HI: University of Hawaiʻi Press, 2016.

Bushnell, Andrew F. "'The Horror' Reconsidered: An Evaluation of the Historical Evidence for Population Decline in Hawaiʻi, 1779–1803." *Pacific Studies* 16 (1993): 115–61.

Bushnell, O. A. *The Gifts of Civilization: Germs and Genocide in Hawaiʻi.* Honolulu, HI: University of Hawaiʻi Press, 1993.

"Hygiene and Sanitation among the Ancient Hawaiians." *Hawaii Historical Review* 2 (1966): 316–36.

Byrne, Joseph P. *Encyclopedia of Pestilence, Pandemics, and Plagues.* 2 vols. Westport, CT: Greenwood, 2008.

Cameron, Catherine M., Paul Kelton, and Alan C. Swedlund, eds. *Beyond Germs: Native Depopulation in North America.* Tucson, AZ: University of Arizona Press, 2015.

Campbell, I. C. *Island Kingdom: Tonga Ancient and Modern.* Christchurch: Canterbury University Press, 1992.

Carlson, Keith Thor. *The Power of Place, the Problem of Time: Aboriginal Identity and Historical Consciousness in the Cauldron of Colonialism.* Toronto: University of Toronto Press, 2010.

Chang, David A. *The World and All the Things upon It: Native Hawaiian Geographies of Exploration.* Minneapolis, MN: University of Minnesota Press, 2016.

Chappell, David A. "Active Agents versus Passive Victims: Decolonized Historiography or Problematic Paradigm?" *The Contemporary Pacific* 7 (1995): 303–26.

Double Ghosts: Oceanian Voyagers on Euroamerican Ships. Armonk, NY: M. E. Sharpe, 1997.

"Shipboard Relations between Pacific Island Women and Euroamerican Men 1767–1887." *JPH* 27 (1992): 131–49.

Char, Tin-Yuke, and Wai Jane Char. "The First Chinese Contract Laborers in Hawaii, 1852." *HJH* 9 (1976): 128–35.

Chun, Malcom Nāea. *No Nā Mamo: Traditional and Contemporary Hawaiian Beliefs and Practices.* Honolulu, HI: University of Hawai'i Press, 2011.

Clayton, Daniel W. *Islands of Truth: The Imperial Fashioning of Vancouver Island.* Vancouver, BC: University of British Columbia Press, 1999.

Clifford, James. "Indigenous Articulations." *The Contemporary Pacific* 13 (2001): 468–90.

Conroy-Krutz, Emily. *Christian Imperialism: Converting the World in the Early American Republic.* Ithaca, NY: Cornell University Press, 2015.

Cook, Sherburne F., and Woodrow Borah. *Essays in Population History: Mexico and California.* Berkeley, CA: University of California Press, 1979.

Cooter, Roger. "The End? History-Writing in the Age of Biomedicine." In *Writing History in the Age of Biomedicine*, edited by Roger Cooter and Claudia Stein, 1–40. New Haven, CT: Yale University Press, 2013.

Cordy, Ross. "Reconstructing Hawaiian Population at European Contact: Three Regional Case Studies." In *The Growth and Collapse of Pacific Island Societies: Archaeological and Demographic Perspectives*, edited by Patrick V. Kirch and Jean-Louis Rallu, 108–28. Honolulu, HI: University of Hawai'i Press, 2007.

Corley, J. Susan, and M. Puakea Nogelmeier. "Kalanimoku's Lost Letter." *HJH* 44 (2010): 91–100.

Cottrell, Christopher A. "Splinters of Sandalwood, Islands of 'Iliahi: Rethinking Deforestation in Hawai'i, 1811–1843." MA thesis, University of Hawai'i at Mānoa, 2002.

Crosby, Alfred W. *Ecological Imperialism: The Biological Expansion of Europe, 900–1900.* New York, NY: Cambridge University Press, 1986.

"Hawaiian Depopulation as a Model for the Amerindian Experience." In *Epidemics and Ideas: Essays on the Historical Perception of Pestilence*, edited by Terence Ranger and Paul Slack, 175–202. Cambridge: Cambridge University Press, 1992.

"Virgin Soil Epidemics as a Factor in the Aboriginal Depopulation in America." *William and Mary Quarterly* 33 (1976): 289–99.

Culliney, John L. *Islands in a Far Sea: Nature and Man in Hawaii.* San Francisco, CA: Sierra Club, 1988.

D'Arcy, Paul. *The People of the Sea: Environment, Identity, and History in Oceania.* Honolulu, HI: University of Hawai'i Press, 2006.

"Warfare and State Formation in Hawaii." *JPH* 38 (2003): 29–52.

Davenport, William. "The 'Hawaiian Cultural Revolution': Some Political and Economic Considerations." *American Anthropologist* 71 (1969): 1–20.

Daws, Gavan. *Shoal of Time: A History of the Hawaiian Islands.* Honolulu, HI: University Press of Hawaii, 1968.

Del Piano, Barbara. "Kalanimoku: Iron Cable of the Hawaiian Kingdom, 1769–1827." *HJH* 43 (2009): 1–28.

Dening, Greg. *Islands and Beaches: Discourse on a Silent Land; Marquesas, 1774–1880.* Honolulu, HI: University Press of Hawaii, 1980.

Performances. Melbourne: Melbourne University Press, 1996.

Denoon, Donald, ed. *The Cambridge History of Pacific Islanders.* Cambridge: Cambridge University Press, 1997.

Diamond, Jared. *Guns, Germs, and Steel: The Fates of Human Societies.* New York, NY: Norton, 1998.

Dippie, Brian W. *The Vanishing American: White Attitudes and U.S. Indian Policy.* Lawrence, KS: University Press of Kansas, 1982.

Douglas, Bronwen. "Pre-European Societies in the Pacific Islands." In *Culture Contact in the Pacific: Essays on Contact, Encounter and Response*, edited by Max Quanchi and Ron Adams, 15–30. Cambridge: Cambridge University Press, 1993.

"Religion." In *Pacific Histories: Ocean, Land, People*, edited by David Armitage and Alison Bashford, 193–215. Basingstoke: Palgrave Macmillan, 2014.

Science, Voyages, and Encounters in Oceania, 1511–1850. Basingstoke: Palgrave Macmillan, 2014.

Dow, Derek A. *Maori Health and Government Policy, 1840–1940.* Wellington: Victoria University Press, 1999.

DuVal, Kathleen. *The Native Ground: Indians and Colonists in the Heart of the Continent.* Philadelphia, PA: University of Pennsylvania Press, 2007.

Dye, Tom. "Population Trends in Hawai'i before 1778." *HJH* 28 (1994): 1–20.

Edmunds, R. David. "Native Americans, New Voices: American Indian History, 1895–1995." *American Historical Review* 100 (1995): 717–40.

Eiseman, Alberta. "On the Neptune, Three Years under Sail." *New York Times*, March 2, 1997.

Elbert, Samuel H. "The Chief in Hawaiian Mythology." *Journal of American Folklore* 69 (1956): 99–113, 341–55; 70 (1957): 264–76, 306–22.

Else, 'Iwalani R. N. "The Breakdown of the *Kapu* System and Its Effect on Native Hawaiian Health and Diet." *Hūlili: Multidisciplinary Research on Hawaiian Well-Being* 1 (2004): 241–55.

Emerson, Joseph S. "The Bow and Arrow in Hawaii" [1906]. In *Twenty-Fourth Annual Report of the Hawaiian Historical Society for the Year 1915*, 52–55. Honolulu, HI: Paradise of the Pacific, 1916.

Emory, Kenneth P. *Archaeology of Nihoa and Necker Islands.* Honolulu, HI: Bishop Museum, 1928.

Evison, Harry C. *Te Wai Pounamu: The Greenstone Island; A History of the Southern Maori during the European Colonization of New Zealand.* Wellington: Aoraki Press, 1993.

Fischer, John Ryan. "Cattle in Hawai'i: Biological and Cultural Exchange." *PHR* 76 (2007): 347–72.

Forbes, David W. *Hawaiian National Bibliography, 1780–1900.* 3 vols. Honolulu, HI: University of Hawai'i Press, 1999.

Fowles, Severin M. *An Archaeology of Doings: Secularism and the Study of Pueblo Religion.* Santa Fe, NM: School for Advanced Research Press, 2013.

Fujikane, Candace, and Jonathan Y. Okamura, eds. *Asian Settler Colonialism: From Local Governance to the Habits of Everyday Life in Hawai'i.* Honolulu, HI: University of Hawai'i Press, 2008.

Fur, Gunlög. *A Nation of Women: Gender and Colonial Encounters among the Delaware Indians.* Philadelphia, PA: University of Pennsylvania Press, 2009.

Gardner, Robert W., and Robert C. Schmitt. "Ninety-Seven Years of Mortality in Hawaii." *Hawaii Medical Journal* 37 (1978): 297–302.

Gascoigne, John. *Encountering the Pacific in the Age of the Enlightenment.* Cambridge: Cambridge University Press, 2014.

Gilson, Richard. *The Cook Islands, 1820–1950.* Wellington: Victoria University Press, 1980.

Gone, Joseph P. "Redressing First Nations Historical Trauma: Theorizing Mechanisms for Indigenous Culture as Mental Health Treatment." *Transcultural Psychiatry* 50 (2013): 683–706.

Gracey, Michael, and Malcolm King. "Indigenous Health Part 1: Determinants and Disease Patterns." *The Lancet* 374 (2009): 65–75.

Green, Laura C., and Martha W. Beckwith. "Hawaiian Customs and Beliefs Relating to Sickness and Death." *American Anthropologist* 28 (1926): 176–208.

Greenberg, Amy S. *Manifest Manhood and the Antebellum American Empire.* Cambridge: Cambridge University Press, 2005.

Greer, Richard A. "Honolulu in 1847." *HJH* 4 (1970): 59–95.

"In the Shadow of Death." *Hawaii Historical Review* 2 (1966): 311–25.

"Oahu's Ordeal: The Smallpox Epidemic of 1853." *Hawaii Historical Review* 1–2 (1965): 221–42, 248–66.

Grimshaw, Patricia. *Paths of Duty: American Missionary Wives in Nineteenth-Century Hawaii.* Honolulu, HI: University Press of Hawaii, 1989.

Gutmanis, June. *Kahuna La'au Lapa'au: The Practice of Hawaiian Herbal Medicine.* Aiea, HI: Island Heritage, 1976.

Haake, Claudia B. "'In the Same Predicament as Heretofore': Proremoval Arguments in Seneca Letters from the Buffalo Creek Reservation in the 1830s and 1840s." *Ethnohistory* 61 (2014): 57–77.

Haas, Glenn E., et al. "The Flea in Early Hawaii." *HJH* 5 (1971): 59–74.

Hackel, Steven W. *Children of Coyote, Missionaries of Saint Francis: Indian-Spanish Relations in Colonial California, 1769–1850.* Chapel Hill, NC: University of North Carolina Press, 2005.

Halford, Francis John. *9 Doctors & God.* Honolulu, HI: University of Hawai'i Press, 1954.

Handy, E. S. Craighill. *The Hawaiian Planter: His Plants, Methods and Areas of Cultivation.* Honolulu, HI: Bishop Museum, 1940.

Handy, E. S. Craighill, and Mary Kawena Pukui. *The Polynesian Family System in Ka-'u, Hawai'i.* Wellington: Polynesian Society, 1958.

Handy, E. S. Craighill, Mary Kawena Pukui, and Katherine Livermore. *Outline of Hawaiian Physical Therapeutics.* Honolulu, HI: Bishop Museum, 1934.

Handy, E. S. Craighill, Elizabeth Green Handy, and Mary Kawena Pukui. *Native Planters in Old Hawaii: Their Life, Lore, and Environment.* Honolulu, HI: Bishop Museum, 1972.

Hauʻofa, Epeli. "Our Sea of Islands." In *A New Oceania: Rediscovering Our Sea of Islands*, edited by Epeli Hauʻofa et al., 2–16. Suva, Fiji: School of Social and Economic Development, 1993.

Hays, J. N. *The Burdens of Disease: Epidemics and Human Response in Western History*. New Brunswick, NJ: Rutgers University Press, 1998.

Henige, David. *Numbers from Nowhere: The American Indian Contact Population Debate*. Norman, OK: University of Oklahoma Press, 1998.

Herman, R. D. K. "Out of Sight, Out of Mind, Out of Power: Leprosy, Race and Colonization in Hawaiʻi." *Journal of Historical Geography* 27 (2001): 319–47.

Hilgenkamp, Kathryn, and Colleen Pescaia. "Traditional Hawaiian Healing and Western Influence." *Californian Journal of Health Promotion* 1 (2003): 34–39.

Hixson, Walter L. *American Settler Colonialism: A History*. New York, NY: Palgrave Macmillan, 2013.

Hommon, Robert J. *The Ancient Hawaiian State: Origins of a Political Society*. New York, NY: Oxford University Press, 2013.

"The Formation of Primitive States in Pre-Contact Hawaiʻi." PhD diss., University of Arizona, 1976.

Hyde, Anne F. *Empires, Nations, and Families: A New History of the North American West, 1800–1860*. New York, NY: HarperCollins, 2012.

Igler, David. "Diseased Goods: Global Exchanges in the Pacific Basin, 1770–1850." *American Historical Review* 109 (2004): 699–716.

The Great Ocean: Pacific Worlds from Captain Cook to the Gold Rush. New York, NY: Oxford University Press, 2013.

Inglis, Kerri A. *Maʻi Lepera: Disease and Displacement in Nineteenth-Century Hawaiʻi*. Honolulu, HI: University of Hawaiʻi Press, 2013.

Joesting, Edward. *Kauai: The Separate Kingdom*. Honolulu, HI: University of Hawaiʻi Press, 1984.

Johnson, David B., et al. "Papa Ola Lohaki Hawaiian Health Update: Mortality, Morbidity, and Behavioral Risks." *Pacific Health Dialog* 5 (1998): 297–314.

Jones, David S. *Rationalizing Epidemics: Meanings and Uses of American Indian Mortality since 1600*. Cambridge, MA: Harvard University Press, 2004.

"Virgin Soils Revisited." *William and Mary Quarterly* 60 (2003): 703–42.

Josephson, Jason Ānanda. *The Invention of Religion in Japan*. Chicago, IL: University of Chicago Press, 2012.

Judd, Charles S. "Depopulation in Polynesia." *Bulletin of the History of Medicine* 51 (1977): 585–93.

Judd, Gerrit P., IV. *Dr. Judd, Hawaii's Friend: A Biography of Gerrit Parmele Judd, 1803–1873*. Honolulu, HI: University of Hawaiʻi Press, 1960.

Kameʻeleihiwa, Lilikalā. "Malama LGBT," part 1. *Equally Speaking*. Aired Nov. 13, 2011. ʻŌlelo Community Media.

Native Land and Foreign Desires: How Shall We Live in Harmony? Honolulu, HI: Bishop Museum, 1992.

"A Synopsis of Traditional Hawaiian Culture, the Events Leading to the 1887 Bayonet Constitution and the Overthrow of the Hawaiian Government (0 AD–1898)," unpublished manuscript (May 23, 1995).

Kamehiro, Stacy L. *The Arts of Kingship: Hawaiian Art and National Culture of the Kalākaua Era.* Honolulu, HI: University of Hawai'i Press, 2009.

Kapā'anaokalāokeola Nākoa Oliveria, Katrina-Ann R. *Ancestral Places: Understanding Kanaka Geographies.* Corvallis, OR: Oregon State University Press, 2014.

Kapiikauinamoku (Samuel Apolo Kapiikauinamokuonalani Amalu). "The Story of Maui Royalty." *Honolulu Advertiser*, April 18–June 29, 1956.

Karskens, Grace. *The Colony: A History of Early Sydney.* St Leonards, NSW: Allen & Unwin, 2010.

Kashay, Jennifer Fish. "Agents of Imperialism: Missionaries and Merchants in Early-Nineteenth-Century Hawai'i." *New England Quarterly* 80 (2007): 280–98.

Kauanui, J. Kēhaulani. *Hawaiian Blood: Colonialism and the Politics of Sovereignty and Indigeniety.* Durham, NC: Duke University Press, 2008.

Kelton, Paul. *Epidemics and Enslavement: Biological Catastrophe in the Native Southeast, 1492–1715.* Lincoln, NE: University of Nebraska Press, 2007.

Kenney, Scott G. "Mormons and the Smallpox Epidemic of 1853." *HJH* 31 (1997): 1–26.

Kent, Harold Winfield. *Treasury of Hawaiian Words in One Hundred and One Categories.* Honolulu, HI: Masonic Public Library of Hawai'i, 1986.

Kessler, Lawrence H. "A Plantation upon a Hill; Or, Sugar without Rum: Hawai'i's Missionaries and the Founding of the Sugarcane Plantation System." *PHR* 84 (2015): 129–62.

King, Malcolm, Alexandra Smith, and Michael Gracey. "Indigenous Health Part 2: The Underlying Causes of the Health Gap." *The Lancet* 374 (2009): 76–85.

Kiple, Kenneth F., ed. *The Cambridge World History of Human Disease.* Cambridge: Cambridge University Press, 1993.

Kirch, Patrick Vinton. *Feathered Gods and Fishhooks: An Introduction to Hawaiian Archaeology and Prehistory.* Honolulu, HI: University of Hawai'i Press, 1985.

How Chiefs Became Kings: Divine Kingship and the Rise of Archaic States in Ancient Hawai'i. Berkeley, CA: University of California Press, 2010.

Kua'āina Kahiko: Life and Land in Ancient Kahikinui, Maui. Honolulu, HI: University of Hawai'i Press, 2014.

"'Like Shoals of Fish': Archaeology and Population in Pre-Contact Hawai'i." In *The Growth and Collapse of Pacific Island Societies: Archaeological and Demographic Perspectives*, edited by Patrick V. Kirch and Jean-Louis Rallu, 52–69. Honolulu, HI: University of Hawai'i Press, 2007.

A Shark Going Inland Is My Chief: The Island Civilization of Ancient Hawai'i. Berkeley, CA: University of California Press, 2012.

Kirmayer, Laurence J., et al. "Rethinking Resilience from Indigenous Perspectives." *Canadian Journal of Psychiatry* 56 (2011): 84–91.

Kōmike Hua'ōlelo (Hawaiian Lexicon Committee) et al. *Māmaka Kaiao: A Modern Hawaiian Vocabulary.* Honolulu, HI: University of Hawai'i Press, 2003.

Kramer, Raymond J. *Hawaiian Land Mammals.* Rutland, VT: C. E. Tuttle, 1971.

Krauss, Beatrice H. *Ethnobotany of Hawaii*. University of Hawai'i Department of Botany, n.d.

Krech, Shepard, III. *The Ecological Indian: Myth and History*. New York, NY: Norton, 1999.

Kroeber, A[lfred] L. *Anthropology: Race, Language, Culture, Psychology, Prehistory*. New York, NY: Harcourt Brace, 1948.

Kunitz, Stephen. "Globalization, States, and the Health of Indigenous Peoples." *American Journal of Public Health* 90 (2000): 1531–39.

Kuykendall, Ralph S. *The Hawaiian Kingdom*, vol. 1, *1778–1854: Foundation and Transformation*. Honolulu, HI: University of Hawai'i Press, 1938.

 The Hawaiian Kingdom, vol. 2, *1854–1874: Twenty Critical Years*. Honolulu, HI: University of Hawai'i Press, 1953.

Langdon-Davies, John. *Carlos: The King Who Would Not Die*. Englewood Cliffs, NJ: Prentice-Hall, 1963.

Lange, Raeburn. *May the People Live: A History of Maori Health Development, 1900–1920*. Auckland: Auckland University Press, 1999.

Larsen, Nils P. "Medical Art in Ancient Hawaii." In *Fifty-Third Annual Report of the Hawaiian Historical Society for the Year 1944*, 27–44. Honolulu, HI: n.p., 1946.

Law, Anwei Skinsnes. *Kalaupapa: A Collective Memory*. Honolulu, HI: University of Hawai'i Press, 2012.

Lévi-Strauss, Claude. *Tristes Tropiques*. Translated by John and Doreen Weightman. New York, NY: Penguin, 2012.

Levin, Stephanie Seto. "The Overthrow of the *Kapu* System in Hawaii." *JPS* 77 (1968): 402–30.

Linnekin, Jocelyn. *Sacred Queens and Women of Consequence: Rank, Gender, and Colonialism in the Hawaiian Islands*. Ann Arbor, MI: University of Michigan Press, 1990.

Lukere [Luker], Victoria. "Mothers of the Taukei: Fijian Women and 'the Decrease of the Race.'" PhD diss., Australian National University, 1997.

Lyons, Paul. *American Pacificism: Oceania in the U.S. Imagination*. New York, NY: Routledge, 2006.

Mailer, Gideon, and Nicola Hale. "Decolonizing the Diet: Synthesizing Native-American History, Immunology, and Nutritional Science." *Journal of Evolution and Health* 1, no. 1 (2015), article 7.

Maly, Kepā, and Onaona Maly. *He Mo'olelo 'Āina No Ka'eo me Kāhi 'Āina e A'e ma Honua'ula o Maui: A Cultural-Historical Study of Ka'eo and Other Lands in Honua'ula, Island of Maui*. Hilo, HI: Kumu Pono, 2005.

Marshall, Wende Elizabeth. *Potent Mana: Lessons in Power and Healing*. Albany, NY: State University of New York Press, 2011.

Martin, Craig. *A Critical Introduction to the Study of Religion*. Sheffield: Equinox, 2012.

Matsuda, Matt K. *Pacific Worlds: A History of Seas, Peoples, and Cultures*. New York, NY: Cambridge University Press, 2013.

McMullin, Juliet. *The Healthy Ancestor: Embodied Inequality and the Revitalization of Native Hawaiian Health*. Walnut Tree, CA: Left Coast, 2010.

Menton, Linda K. "A Christian and 'Civilized' Education: The Hawaiian Chiefs' Children's School." *History of Education Quarterly* 32 (1992): 213–42.

Merry, Sally Engle. *Colonizing Hawai'i: The Cultural Power of Law.* Princeton, NJ: Princeton University Press, 2000.

Mihesuah, Devon A. "Decolonizing Our Diets by Recovering Our Ancestors' Gardens." *American Indian Quarterly* 27 (2003): 807–39.

Miller, Susan A., and James Riding In, eds. *Native Historians Write Back: Decolonizing American Indian History.* Lubbock, TX: Texas Tech University Press, 2011.

Molle, Guillame, and Eric Conte. "Nuancing the Marquesan Post-Contact Demographic Decline: An Archaeological and Historical Case Study on Ua Huka Island." *JPH* 50 (2015): 253–74.

Moorehead, Alan. *The Fatal Impact: An Account of the Invasion of the South Pacific, 1767–1840.* New York, NY: Harper & Row, 1966.

Moran, Michelle T. *Colonizing Leprosy: Imperialism and the Politics of Public Health in the United States.* Chapel Hill, NC: University of North Carolina Press, 2007.

Morris, Robert J. "*Aikāne*: Accounts of Hawaiian Same-Sex Relationships in the Journals of Captain Cook's Third Voyage (1776–80)." *Journal of Homosexuality* 19 (1990): 21–54.

Mouritz, A[rthur] A[lbert] St. M[aur]. *Our Western Outpost, Hawaii, in the Eye of the Sun …* Honolulu, HI: n.p., 1935.

"The Path of the Destroyer": A History of Leprosy in the Hawaiian Islands … Honolulu, HI: Star-Bulletin, 1916.

Musick, John R. *Hawaii: Our New Possessions.* New York, NY: Funk & Wagnalls, 1898.

Mykkänen, Juri. *Inventing Politics: A New Political Anthropology of the Hawaiian Kingdom.* Honolulu, HI: University of Hawai'i Press, 2003.

Nash, Linda. "Beyond Virgin Soils: Disease as Environmental History." In *The Oxford Handbook of Environmental History*, edited by Andrew C. Isenberg, 76–107. Oxford: Oxford University Press, 2014.

Newbury, Colin. *Tahiti Nui: Change and Survival in French Polynesia, 1767–1945.* Honolulu, HI: University Press of Hawaii, 1980.

Newell, Jennifer. *Trading Nature: Tahitians, Europeans, and Ecological Exchange.* Honolulu, HI: University of Hawai'i Press, 2010.

Newson, Linda A. *Conquest and Pestilence in the Early Spanish Philippines.* Honolulu, HI: University of Hawai'i Press, 2009.

Nogelmeier, M. Puakea. *Mai Pa'a i ka Leo: Historical Voice in Hawaiian Primary Materials; Looking Forward and Listening Back.* Honolulu, HI: Bishop Museum, 2010.

Nongbri, Brent. *Before Religion: A History of a Modern Concept.* New Haven, CT: Yale University Press, 2013.

Obeysekere, Gananath. *The Apotheosis of Captain Cook: European Mythmaking in the Pacific.* Princeton, NJ: Princeton University Press, 1992.

O'Brien, Jean M. *Firsting and Lasting: Writing Indians Out of Existence in New England.* Minneapolis, MN: University of Minnesota Press, 2010.

O'Brien, Patty. *The Pacific Muse: Exotic Femininity and the Colonial Pacific.* Seattle, WA: University of Washington Press, 2006.

"Think of Me as a Woman: Queen Pomare of Tahiti and Anglo-French Imperial Contest in the 1840s Pacific." *Gender & History* 18 (2006): 108–29.

Okihiro, Gary Y. *Island World: A History of Hawai'i and the United States.* Berkeley, CA: University of California Press, 2008.

O'Malley, Vincent. *The Meeting Place: Māori and Pākehā Encounters, 1642–1840.* Auckland: Auckland University Press, 2012.

Osorio, Jonathan Kay Kamakawiwo'ole. *Dismembering Lāhui: A History of the Hawaiian Nation to 1887.* Honolulu, HI: University of Hawai'i Press, 2002.

Osterhammel, Jürgen. *Colonialism: A Theoretical Overview.* Translated by Shelley L. Frisch. Princeton, NJ: Princeton University Press, 1997.

The Transformation of the World: A Global History of the Nineteenth Century. Translated by Patrick Camiller. Princeton, NJ: Princeton University Press, 2014.

Packard, Randall M. *White Plague, Black Labor: Tuberculosis and the Political Economy of Health and Disease in South Africa.* Berkeley, CA: University of California Press, 1989.

Pirie, Peter. "The Effects of Treponematosis and Gonorrhea on the Populations of the Pacific Islands." *Human Biology in Oceania* 1 (1972): 187–206.

Plews, John H. R. "Charles Darwin and Hawaiian Sex Ratios, or, Genius Is a Capacity for Making Compensating Errors." *HJH* 14 (1980): 26–49.

Pool, Ian. *Te Iwi Maori: A New Zealand Population Past, Present & Projected.* Auckland: Auckland University Press, 1991.

Powell, Mary Lucas, and Della Collins Cook. "Treponematosis: Inquiries into the Nature of a Protean Disease." In *The Myth of Syphilis: The Natural History of Treponematosis in North America*, edited by M. L. Powell and D. C. Cook, 9–62. Gainesville, FL: University Press of Florida, 2005.

Pukui, Mary Kawena. "Hawaiian Beliefs and Customs during Birth, Infancy, and Childhood." *Occasional Papers of Bernice P. Bishop Museum* 16 (1942): 357–81.

'Ōlelo No'eau: Hawaiian Proverbs and Poetical Sayings. Honolulu, HI: Bishop Museum, 1983.

Pukui, Mary Kawena, and Samuel H. Elbert. *Hawaiian Dictionary.* Honolulu, HI: University of Hawai'i Press, 1986.

Pukui, Mary Kawena, Samuel H. Elbert, and Esther T. Mookini. *Place Names of Hawaii.* Revised edition. Honolulu, HI: University of Hawai'i Press, 1974.

Pukui, Mary Kawena, E. W. Haertig, and Catherine A. Lee. *Nānā i ke Kumu (Look to the Source).* 2 vols. Honolulu, HI: Hui Hānai, 1972.

Ralston, Caroline. "Changes in the Lives of Ordinary Women in Early Post-Contact Hawai'i." In *Family and Gender in the Pacific: Domestic Contradictions and the Colonial Impact*, edited by Margaret Jolly and Martha Macintyre, 45–64. Cambridge: Cambridge University Press, 1989.

"Early Nineteenth Century Polynesian Millennial Cults and the Case of Hawai'i." *JPS* 94 (1985): 307–32.

"Hawaii 1778–1854: Some Aspects of Maka'ainana [*sic*] Response to Rapid Cultural Change." *JPH* 19 (1984): 21–40.

Richter, Daniel K. "Whose Indian History?" *William and Mary Quarterly* 50 (1993): 379–93.

Rifkin, Mark. "Debt and the Transnationalization of Hawai'i." *American Quarterly* 60 (2008): 43–66.

Roberts, Stephen H. *Population Problems of the Pacific*. London: G. Routledge & Sons, 1927.

Robinson, Michael P. *Sea Otter Chiefs*. Calgary, AB: Bayeux Arts, 1996.

Rodman, Julius Scammon. *The Kahuna Sorcerers of Hawaii, Past and Present*. Hicksville, NY: Exposition, 1979.

Rohrer, Judy. *Staking Claim: Settler Colonialism and Racialization in Hawai'i*. Tucson, AZ: University of Arizona Press, 2016.

Rosenthal, Gregory. "Hawaiians Who Left Hawai'i: Work, Body, and Environment in the Pacific World, 1786–1876." PhD diss., Stony Brook University, 2015.

Sahlins, Marshall. *Anahulu: The Anthropology of History in the Kingdom of Hawai'i*, vol. 1, *Historical Ethnography*. With the assistance of Dorothy B. Barrère. Chicago, IL: University of Chicago Press, 1992.

"Cosmologies of Capitalism: The Trans-Pacific Sector of 'The World System'." In *Culture/Power/History: A Reader in Contemporary Social Theory*, edited by Nicholas B. Dirks et al., 412–55. Princeton, NJ: Princeton University Press, 1994.

"Goodbye to *Tristes Tropes*: Ethnography in the Context of Modern World History." *Journal of Modern History* 65 (1993): 1–25.

Historical Metaphors and Mythical Realities: Structure in the Early History of the Sandwich Islands Kingdom. Ann Arbor, MI: University of Michigan Press, 1981.

Islands of History. Chicago, IL: University of Chicago Press, 1985.

Salmond, Anne. *Aphrodite's Island: The European Discovery of Tahiti*. Berkeley, CA: University of California Press, 2009.

Between Worlds: Early Exchanges between Maori and Europeans, 1773–1815. Honolulu, HI: University of Hawai'i Press, 1997.

Schmitt, Robert C. "Catastrophic Mortality in Hawaii." *HJH* 3 (1969): 66–86.

"Catastrophic Mortality in Hawai'i: An Update." *HJH* 23 (1989): 217–27.

Demographic Statistics of Hawaii, 1778–1965. Honolulu, HI: University of Hawai'i Press, 1968.

"Differential Mortality in Honolulu before 1900." *Hawaii Medical Journal* 26 (1967): 537–41.

"Famine Mortality in Hawaii." *JPH* 5 (1970): 109–15.

Historical Statistics of Hawaii. Honolulu, HI: University of Hawai'i Press, 1977.

"New Estimates of the Pre-Censal Population of Hawaii." *JPS* 80 (1971): 237–43.

"The Okuu: Hawaii's Greatest Epidemic." *Hawaii Medical Journal* 29 (1970): 359–64.

Schmitt, Robert C., and Eleanor C. Nordyke. "Death in Hawai'i: The Epidemics of 1848–1849." *HJH* 35 (2001): 1–13.

Scott, James C. *Weapons of the Weak: Everyday Forms of Peasant Resistance*. New Haven, CT: Yale University Press, 1985.

Seaton, S. Lee. "The Hawaiian *Kapu* Abolition of 1819." *American Ethnologist* 1 (1974): 193–206.

Shoemaker, Nancy, ed. *Clearing a Path: Theorizing the Past in Native American Studies.* New York, NY: Routledge, 2002.

"A Typology of Colonialism." *Perspectives on History: The Newsmagazine of the American Historical Association* 53 (Oct. 2015): 29–30.

Silva, Kalena, et al. "Princess Ruth Keʻelikōlani, Hawaiian Aliʻi." In *Biography Hawaiʻi: Five Lives; A Series of Public Remembrances.* Honolulu, HI: University of Hawaiʻi at Mānoa Center for Biographical Research, 2003.

Silva, Noenoe K. *Aloha Betrayed: Native Hawaiian Resistance to American Colonialism.* Durham, NC: Duke University Press, 2004.

Silverman, David J. *Red Brethren: The Brothertown and Stockbridge Indians and the Problem of Race in Early America.* Ithaca, NY: Cornell University Press, 2010.

Silverman, Jane L. *Kaahumanu: Molder of Change.* Honolulu, HI: Friends of the Judiciary History Center, 1987.

Sinclair, Marjorie. *Nāhiʻenaʻena, Sacred Daughter of Hawaiʻi.* Honolulu, HI: University Press of Hawaii, 1976.

Sissons, Jeffrey. *The Polynesian Iconoclasm: Religious Revolution and the Seasonality of Power.* New York, NY: Berghahn, 2014.

Sivasundaram, Sujit. *Nature and the Godly Empire: Science and Evangelical Mission in the Pacific, 1795–1850.* Cambridge: Cambridge University Press, 2005.

Snow, Charles E. *Early Hawaiians: An Initial Study of Skeletal Remains from Mokapu, Oahu.* Lexington, KY: University Press of Kentucky, 1974.

Stannard, David E. *Before the Horror: The Population of Hawaiʻi on the Eve of Western Contact.* Honolulu, HI: University of Hawaiʻi Social Science Research Institute, 1989.

"Disease and Infertility: A New Look at the Demographic Collapse of Native Populations in the Wake of Western Contact." *Journal of American Studies* 24 (1990): 325–50.

"Recounting the Fables of Savagery: Native Infanticide and the Functions of Political Myth." *Journal of American Studies* 25 (1991): 381–418.

Stannard, David E., et al. "Book Review Forum." *Pacific Studies* 13 (1990): 269–301.

Swanson, David A. "The Number of Native Hawaiians and Part-Hawaiians in Hawaiʻi, 1778–1900: Demographic Estimates by Age, with Discussion," unpublished manuscript (2015).

Taylor, Alan. *American Colonies: The Settling of North America.* New York, NY: Penguin, 2001.

Taylor, Albert Pierce. *Under Hawaiian Skies: A Narrative of the Romance, Adventure and History of the Hawaiian Islands.* Honolulu, HI: Advertiser, 1922.

Tcherkézoff, Serge. *"First Contacts" in Polynesia: The Samoan Case (1722–1848); Western Misunderstandings about Sexuality and Divinity.* Canberra: Australian National University E-Press, 2008.

Thigpen, Jennifer. *Island Queens and Mission Wives: How Gender Remade Hawaiʻi's Pacific World.* Chapel Hill, NC: University of North Carolina Press, 2014.

Thomas, Nicholas. *Discoveries: The Voyages of Captain Cook*. London: Allen Lane, 2003.
Islanders: *The Pacific in the Age of Empire*. New Haven, CT: Yale University Press, 2010.
Titcomb, Margaret. "Kava in Hawaii." *JPS* 57 (1948): 105–71.
Valeri, Valerio. *Kingship and Sacrifice: Ritual and Society in Ancient Hawaii*. Translated by Paula Wissing. Chicago, IL: University of Chicago Press, 1985.
Wallace, Lee. *Sexual Encounters: Pacific Texts, Modern Sexualities*. Ithaca, NY: Cornell University Press, 2003.
Webb, M[alcolm] C. "The Abolition of the Taboo System in Hawaii." *JPS* 74 (1965): 21–39.
Wharton, Glenn. *The Painted King: Art, Activism, and Authenticity in Hawai'i*. Honolulu, HI: University of Hawai'i Press, 2012.
Whistler, W. Arthur. *Polynesian Herbal Medicine*. Lawai, HI: National Tropical Botanical Garden, 1992.
White, Ashli. *Encountering Revolution: Haiti and the Making of the Early Republic*. Baltimore, MD: Johns Hopkins University Press, 2010.
White, Richard. *The Middle Ground: Indians, Empires, and Republics in the Great Lakes Region, 1650–1815*. Twentieth anniversary ed. New York, NY: Cambridge University Press, 2011.
Wolfe, Patrick. *Settler Colonialism and the Transformation of Anthropology: The Politics and Poetics of an Ethnographic Event*. London: Cassell, 1999.
Wood, Houston. *Displacing Natives: The Rhetorical Production of Hawai'i*. Lanham, MD: Rowman & Littlefield, 1999.
Young, Kanalu G. Terry. "An Interdisciplinary Study of the Term 'Hawaiian.'" *Hawaiian Journal of Law and Politics* 1 (2004): 23–45.
Rethinking the Native Hawaiian Past. New York, NY: Garland, 1998.
Yzendoorn, Reginald. *History of the Catholic Mission in the Hawaiian Islands*. Honolulu, HI: Star-Bulletin, 1927.

Index